Developing Expert
Leadership for
Future Schools

Developing Expert Leadership for Future Schools

Kenneth Leithwood, Paul T. Begley and J. Bradley Cousins

Routledge
Taylor & Francis Group

LONDON AND NEW YORK

First published in this edition 1994
By Falmer Press.

Published 2004
by Routledge
2 Park Square, Milton Park, Abingdon, Oxfordshire OX14 4RN
711 Third Avenue, New York, NY 10017

First issued in hardback 2016

Routledge is an imprint of the Taylor and Francis Group, an informa business

© 1994 Kenneth Leithwood, Paul T. Begley and J. Bradley Cousins

A catalogue record for this book is available from the British Library

Library of Congress Cataloging-in-Publication Data are available on request

Jacket design by Caroline Archer
Typeset in 9½/11pt Bembo
by Graphicraft Typesetters Ltd, Hong Kong

ISBN 13: 978-1-138-15782-8 (hbk)
ISBN 13: 978-0-7507-0327-7 (pbk)

Contents

Contents

List of Figures

List of Tables

Acknowledgments

Several of our colleagues have made quite direct contributions to this book, although their names do not appear on the cover. Doris Jantzi was responsible for much of the data collection and analysis reflected in Chapter 9 and participated extensively in the development of some of the ideas presented in Chapter 3. Rosanne Steinbach carried out much of the data collection and analysis reflected in Chapters 6, 7, 10, and 12. Both Doris and Rosanne offered extremely helpful suggestions about the text as a whole.

All of the word processing for the text was accomplished by Irene Switankowsky. Her speed and accuracy contributed much to meeting our deadlines and kept editorial chores to a minimum.

Finally, significant portions of the research reported in the book were funded by the Social Sciences and Humanities Research Council of Canada. Funding was also received from the Ontario Ministry of Education through its block transfer grant to OISE. We are extremely grateful for their continued support.

Foreword

In reading *Developing Expert Leadership for Future Schools* I was stimulated to reflect on my experience of the past decade as a researcher and practitioner. As a graduate student at Stanford University in the late 1970s and early 1980s I recall reading numerous reviews of research on school leadership. Surprisingly, the tone of these reviews contrasted markedly with the optimism engendered by studies of effective schooling. While professional journals were replete with confident, 'research-based recommendations for effective practice', respected researchers were considerably less sanguine about the depth and breadth of the knowledge base in school leadership.

For example, in 1982 Edwin Bridges published a critical review of research in educational administration. He was unequivocally negative in his conclusions.

> The state of the art is scarcely different from what seemed in place nearly 15 years ago ... [Researchers] ... continue their excessive reliance on survey research designs, questionnaires of dubious reliability and validity, and relatively simplistic types of statistical analyses. Moreover, these researchers persist in treating research problems in an *ad hoc* rather than a programmatic fashion. Equally disturbing is the nature of the knowledge accumulated during this period. Despite the rather loose definition of theory that was used in classifying the research ..., most [studies] proved to be atheoretical. Likewise, the research seemed to have little practical utility.[1]

For a practitioner and fledgling researcher interested in administrator development and school improvement, conclusions such as these were disheartening. Researchers were not, however, alone in expressing their dismay with the state of leadership research and development. Several years later Roland Barth wrote an insightful critique, in which he lamented the misuse of research in the name of school improvement. His voice was that of a highly respected former principal.

> Our public schools have come to be dominated and driven by a conception of educational improvement that might be called 'list logic' ... the intention of one state legislature is to 'identify competencies of effective

principals through research and develop training, certification, selection, and compensation procedures that recognize and support these competencies' . . .

School improvement, then, is an attempt to identify what school people should know and be able to do, and to devise ways to get them to know and do it . . . The list logic of educational change seems simple, straightforward and compelling. Its only flaw is that it doesn't seem to work very well.[2]

Barth refers here to the tendency of policymakers during the 1980s to reify research findings and to employ them in ways unsupported by the research itself. Research results were disseminated in ways that ignored the craft knowledge accumulated by school-leaders and that failed to account for the varying contextual forces faced by leaders in real schools.

A decade later, *Developing Expert Leadership for Future Schools* seems to justify the cautious optimism of practitioners that principals can make a difference in schools while satisfying researchers' concerns about the validity of at least a portion of our knowledge base. The research, as well as the perspective, that Leithwood, Begley and Cousins bring to bear on school leadership respond to longstanding criticisms lodged by practitioners and researchers. As suggested by my comments, this is no small feat. I will elaborate briefly.

First, unlike most research in our field, the studies on which this book is based have a clear theoretical orientation. Conceptions of learning, information processing, thinking and problem-solving developed by cognitive psychologists have informed the direction of the authors' research and the interpretation of their findings. This theoretical orientation is interwoven in discussions of leadership and problem-solving throughout the book.

While the authors' research on expert leadership is theoretically informed, it does not attempt to ape the social sciences for the sake of academic prestige. This book and its research base are explicitly grounded in 'problems of practice'. That is, while their selection of research problems has been influenced by cognitive theory, both the form and substance of their work remains rooted in problems faced by live administrators in real schools. The book is primarily concerned with what we now know about the problem-solving of school leaders and how this might be applied to the improvement of schools.

The authors' respect for the craft knowledge of administrators is evident in the nature of their research designs and in the role practicing administrators played in generating and verifying their results. This is particularly apparent in Chapters 6, 7 and 8 in which they discuss how administrators address 'swampy' problems, the ones our training programs seldom consider. Only direct interaction between researchers and practicing administrators could produce the results they present. Readers will be heartened to know that the knowledge base for this book has benefitted from the numerous critiques and reality checks of practitioners and other researchers.[3]

This leads to another notable feature of the book. It is based on 'programmatic research' on the behavior and thinking of school-leaders. Ken Leithwood and his colleagues were not the only scholars to review others' research on school leadership during the early 1980s. However, to my knowledge, they are the only researchers in the United States and Canada who persist in systematically follow-ing through with a program of original research that explicitly addresses the criticisms identified in the published reviews. Their research program parallels developments in the field from the early 1980s, when the emphasis was on identifying the behaviors of effective principals, to the early 1990s when the focus shifted to understanding the thinking that underlies those behaviors. Thus, the arguments presented by the authors about the nature of expert school leadership are based upon carefully developed propositions that have, for the most part, been tested in their own research. While Leithwood and his colleagues at OISE would be the first to acknowledge the boundaries of this knowledge base, the effects of their programmatic efforts to understand administrative problem-solving are undeniable.

One last facet of the book strikes me as especially worthy of mention: the authors' grounding of expert leadership in an explicit vision of the future. Their assumptions about the nature of leadership and the future context of schooling are clearly stated for the reader to accept or reject. Their distinctions among different approaches to school leadership and the associated linkages to the needs of schools in the future seem compelling.

In conclusion, the ideas contained in this book have the potential to deepen the reader's conception of school leadership, whether you are a veteran principal, an aspiring teacher or administrative leader, or a researcher. The concepts pre-sented by the authors will be particularly useful to those charged with assisting others in developing the craft of school leadership. This belief is based upon my own experience. I have already begun to incorporate concepts presented in this volume into my research, as well as into the training and development programs Vanderbilt University offers to school-leaders. I have found the body of work represented in *Developing Expert Leadership for Future Schools* useful and trust that other readers will as well.

Philip Hallinger
Sapphire Bay, St. Thomas
1991

Notes

1 E. Bridges (1982) 'Research on the school administrator: The state of the art, 1967–1980', *Educational Administration Quarterly*, **18**, *3*, p. 25.
2 R. Barth, (1986) 'On sheep and goats and school reform', *Phi Delta Kappan*, December, p. 294.
3 Readers will note that an article describing the program of research described in this volume was recognized as the pre-eminent piece of research published in the *Educational Administration Quarterly* during 1990.

Introduction

This is a book about change, change in the nature of school leadership as required by the nature of future schools. As with any change, the problem is one of gap reduction. In this case, the gap is between the nature of school leadership which will contribute productively to future schools and the nature of current school leadership. Accordingly, these are the issues addressed by the two chapters included in the first of the three parts making up the book. Chapter 1 develops the perspective on leadership for future schools explored in detail in Part 2 of the book: this perspective is based on currently emerging ideas about expert leadership now and in the future. Chapter 2 describes what is known about the present state of school leadership, a description grounded in a systematic review of research on school leadership carried out over the past fifteen years. Taken together, these two chapters clarify the extent of the change required in developing expert leaders for future schools.

The second part of the book consists of seven chapters. They describe the nature of leadership we claim would be productive for future schools. A shared vision of the future school, we suggest in Chapter 1, is a key to the potency of future leaders. Chapter 3 raises several important issues involved in developing such a vision and, for purposes of illustration, develops one such vision.

Chapters 4, 5 and 6 offer a research-based model of leadership as a problem-solving process: Chapter 4 clarifies the value and consequences of distinguishing between the solution of routine ('high ground') and non-routine ('swampy') problems; Chapter 5 describes effective school leadership on the high ground; and Chapter 6 describes expertise in the swamp.

The remaining three chapters in Part 2 are devoted to selected aspects of problem-solving on both the high ground and in the swamp. Chapter 7 examines the nature and role of values in the problem-solving of school-leaders. Contributing to the growth of others in the school, as we argue in Chapter 1, is a major component of the leadership problem. Chapter 8 offers one conception of teacher development which may assist future school-leaders and outlines several strategies that seem promising in fostering such development. Creating a collaborative school culture is one of the most powerful of these strategies: Chapter 9 describes, in some detail how school-leaders might develop such a culture.

The six chapters comprising Part 3 address issues concerning the development of expert leadership. Chapter 10 identifies a broad array of formal and informal experiences potentially contributing to such development and estimates their relative value. Characteristics of formal preparation programs effective in developing expertise on the high ground and in the swamp are outlined in Chapters 11 and 12 respectively. Chapters 13 and 14, using a common framework, examine how administrator ppraisal and selection processes might be designed and implemented in order to contribute more than is typical to the development of expert leadership. Finally, Chapter 15 proposes five broad strategies which district leaders might use in their efforts to foster the development of leaders for future schools.

We have tried to take up the issues addressed in this book in a serious but readable way. The book is a product of the past four years of a research program carried out at OISE's Centre for Leadership Development. With few exceptions, each chapter is based on our own original research within that program and/or a careful review of the research of others. In each case, research methods are briefly described but no effort is made to provide the amount of detail and justification one would expect in an academic journal. Readers of the book, we assume, are interested primarily in our results, after some assurance that those results are the product of careful inquiry. Additional sources are noted for those with more extensive, methodological interests.

Throughout the book we use, more or less interchangeably, the terms principal, vice-principal and school-leader. Conceptually, we agree that leadership may be exercised by virtually anyone in the school, although hard evidence suggests serious limitations and obstacles for those not in formal leadership roles. However, our treatment of school leadership is research-based and most such research (ours and others) has been carried out with principals and vice-principals. In reality, then, most of our claims about school leadership are claims about leadership exercised by those in principal or vice-principal roles. Furthermore, throughout the book the term 'school-leader' is applied to those who might aspire to the actual exercise of leadership, whether or not they realize that aspiration.

Part 1

A Perspective on Developing Expert Leadership for Future Schools

Chapter 1

A Conception of Expert Leadership for Future Schools

Of all the hazy and confounding areas in social psychology, leadership theory undoubtedly contends for top nomination. Probably more has been written and less is known about leadership than any other topic in the behavioral sciences. (Bennis, 1959, p. 259)

Adding a future's twist to the leadership story, as we do in this book, would hardly make Bennis more confident about what we write. But we are fearless. We possess the kind of self-confidence that Klemp and McClelland (1986) labeled a 'generic' leadership skill – which seems fitting (the Greeks called it *'hubris'*[1] – but no matter).

Schools of the past, present and future needed, and will continue to need, competent management. They need people who can establish and maintain the daily routines that make individual people in the organization dispensable – that allow the basic purposes of the school to be achieved even though members of the school inevitably change. Schools also need to change. And for change to result in improvement, schools require expert leadership. This book is primarily about leadership, but it is also about how to carry out managerial work in a way that contributes to leadership.

This chapter is intended to clarify the purposes of the book. It is also an opportunity to share with you some of the assumptions and perspectives we hold, insofar as they have shaped our thinking about future schools and leadership. Five assertions provide a framework for doing this:

- schools are durable institutions
- schools are instruments of social change
- school-leaders are key artisans
- the leadership problem has three parts
- the leadership process is usefully viewed as problem-solving

Schools are Durable Institutions

Potential readers, we suspect, will quickly judge us to be either hopelessly trapped in a mind-set shaped by current institutions or conservatively optimistic.

4

And the judgment may well be rendered even while reading the title of this book. If you believe that schools are brittle, bureaucratic anachronisms incapable of meaningful adaptation to the brave new world of the twenty-first century, this book is not for you. After all, we use the term 'future schools' in our title, whereas for you, the term (like 'airplane) food' or 'pleasant nightmare') is an oxymoron. Give your old Ivan Illich (Illich, 1971) another read instead.

Conservatively optimistic is our own self-concept. We believe schools are imperfect but enduring and improvable institutions that society will not be prepared to do without, for longer than any of us are likely to be around. After all, schools in western societies have borne the brunt of a more or less bad press, in cycles, throughout at least this century. In the face of a constant barrage of both constructive criticism and hopelessly uninformed carping, many schools have responded with continuous, adaptive changes while still preserving their essential form and function. That is a formula for successful evolution whether the organism be biological or social. Our general purpose in this book is to make a modest and indirect contribution toward the subsequent evolution of schools by influencing the development of those who will be their leaders.

Schools are Instruments of Social Change

Concerns about what the future holds for schools are everywhere; they may be found, for example, in the successive 'waves of reform' initiated by states in the United States (e.g., Bacharach, 1988), in the dramatic efforts to refocus the locus of control over schools in Australia (e.g., Marsh, 1988) and the United Kingdom (e.g., Walford, 1990), and in the comprehensive curricular reforms now being introduced in some parts of Canada (e.g., Province of British Columbia, 1989). The strength of these concerns and their undeniable impact on schools is largely explained by a renewed belief in the link between education and the achievement of fundamentally important social goals for the future. Some view this link as economic salvation through educational excellence. As Drucker (1989) asserts: 'in a world where knowledge has become the true capital and the premier wealth-producing resource, the process of education is the ultimate supplier of power'. While rejecting the values of perpetual growth and materialism on which the economy–education link is forged, others also look to education as a key to their preferred image of the future. One such image, developed by Ornstein and Ehrlich (1989), concerns itself with the long-term, collective well-being of the species, a well-being dependent upon appreciating the fragile nature of the planet and upon a set of values and lifestyles in harmony with its fragile nature. And, in Ornstein and Ehrlich's view, with such an image in mind, 'refashioning how people are educated could have enormous import for the future of the species' (cited in Mitchell, 1990, p. 29).

School-Leaders are Key Artisans

If education, in general, and schools, in particular, are seen as tools for social change, educational leaders are assumed to be among the most critical artisans. This assumption is widely held by the public-at-large, as well as by education professionals (e.g., Schlecty, 1990). It is also an assumption warranted by relevant evidence (e.g., Immegart, 1988). Indeed the 'leadership effect' becomes increasingly prominent the more one focuses attention on schools as opposed to other types of organizations. Research on effective schools (e.g., Wilson and Corcoran, 1988) is especially clear on this point. Developing school-leaders, therefore, is one of the most promising avenues available for successfully addressing the changes which will challenge future schools. A more specific purpose of this book is providing insights from research about the development of leaders capable of facilitating the changes which will be required of schools in the future.

The Leadership Problem Has Three Parts

> There are many people who are able to get out in front of the band who have nothing to do with what song the band is playing. (Corbett, Wilson and Aducci, 1990, p. 1)

Having a vision of what they would like their schools to be in the future is critical for school-leaders; it may even put them in front of the band. But it is (among other things) the creation of a shared vision among those playing the instruments that determines what song is being played, and whether it is one or many. With this as a critical task, it is reasonable to ask whether the front of the band is the best place for the leader to be. Our conception of the leadership required for future schools suggests that the rear of the band and the midst of the band will offer opportunities that are at least equally as important as opportunities available at the front.

George Terry (1960) defined the leadership problem as 'how to influence people to strive willingly for group goals', which pretty much sums up the message contained in our band metaphor. Two components of the leadership problem are evident in this definition: one focuses on how to influence people (the process of leadership); the other focuses on determining the goals toward which influence is exercised (the intended product of leadership). Leaders need to be able to assist individuals, often working in groups, to identify agreed-upon goals, the framework for which ought to be a vision of a future school. Leaders also need to be able to influence the same individuals and groups to strive willingly for the achievement of these goals. This is what Sergiovanni (1987, p. 121) refers to as 'leadership by purpose'. As he points out:

> Purposing is a powerful force because of our needs for some sense of what is important and some signal of what is of value.... The object of purposing is the stirring of human consciousness, the enhancement of meaning, the spelling out of key cultural strands that provide both excitement and significance to our work.

Exercising influence, the process component of leadership, involves the exercise of power. It is useful, for present purposes, to distinguish among four sources of power. Two of these include: (a) the power that comes from the authority vested in the position (jurisdictional powers) held by the leader (e.g., principal, superintendent), and (b) the power from support provided by those who are pursuing their own interests (e.g., political power). Leaders relying on these sources of power usually spend most of their time at the front of the band. However, these two sources of power are less and less available, at least for school-leaders now and in the future. Not many principals, for example, attribute much vested authority to their position for a variety of reasons: for example, the growing strength of teacher unions, and the trend toward decentralizing educational decisions (school-based management, school-based curriculum development), which seems to have as its primary goal the empowerment of teachers, not school-leaders. These obvious, pragmatic reasons for school-leaders to reduce their reliance on traditional sources of power are consistent in their effect with efforts to build teacher leadership into a more powerful force in future schools (Smylie and Brownlee-Conyers, 1990). These reasons are also consistent with efforts to reconceptualize leadership from a feminist perspective. Reflecting on her own intellectual voyage as a school-leader, Regan (1990, p. 568) for example, speaks of the need to give much greater attention to those aspects of leadership which involve 'caring and nurturing relationship, and community building' or the 'soft' side of leadership. Similarly, studies of district leadership are beginning to suggest that:

> a strong superintendent in future years is less likely to be a 'take charge' boss than an 'unheroic' and more consultative leader ... working with others ... facilitating, finding common ground, listening and persuading. (Crowson and Morris, 1990, p. 41)

These are what Crowson and Morris refer to as 'considerative qualities of culture and choice'.

Such views of leadership in the future will be based on two other sources of power for influencing people. One of these is the power that is awarded by virtue of one's content or technical expertise (e.g., knowledge about schooling and skill in performing valued functions). To be used effectively, this source of power is best exercised in the midst of the band, in concert with those considerative qualities alluded to above. The purpose for exercising such power is to assist directly members of the school community to overcome the obstacles they face in striving for their vision of the school. In Leiberman and Miller's (1990) terms, this is what it means to be a leader of leaders, a person whose power of expertise is used to achieve ends rather than control people. Management and leadership are intertwined in the midst of the band. Given a vision of what it means to do the right things, content or technical expertise focuses on doing those things right.

A final source of power comes through the ability to empower others, something often best accomplished from the rear of the band. Leadership based on this source of power is often referred to as 'transformational' (e.g., Burns, 1978, Bass, 1985, Sergiovanni, 1990) or developmental (Schlecty, 1990). The term 'transform' implies major changes in the form, nature, function and/or potential of some phenomenon; applied to leadership, it specifies general ends to be pursued although it is largely mute with respect to means. From this beginning, we consider the central purpose of transformational leadership to be the enhancement of individual and collective problem-solving capacities of organizational members; such capacities are exercised in the identification of goals to be

7

achieved and practices to be used in their achievement. As Bennis and Nanus (1985, p. 217) clarify, leaders are transformative when they are able to 'shape and elevate the motives and goals of followers'. Such leadership:

> is collective, there is a symbolic relationship between leaders and follow-ers and what makes it collective is the subtle interplay between the followers' needs and wants and the leader's capacity to understand ... these collective aspirations.

Transformational leadership, thus, is culture changing (Coleman and LaRocque, 1989). Specific ways in which school-leaders effectively solve this part of the leadership problem are explored in Chapter 9.

Technical expertise exercised in a 'considerative' context and the ability to empower others are the two sources of power through which future school-leaders are most likely to influence others, and which they must be prepared to use. These are also the most defensible sources of power for leaders of organiza-tions, dedicated to such fundamental values as respect for individual persons, representative democracy, and professionalism with its emphasis on client welfare.

The leadership problem, in sum, has three parts: developing a widely shared, defensible vision; in the short run, directly assisting members of the school community to overcome obstacles they encounter in striving for the vision; and, in the long run, increasing the capacity of members of the school community to overcome subsequent obstacles more successfully and with greater ease. Schools operate in a dynamic environment which exerts constant, often contradictory pressures for change: future schools are likely to experience even greater press-ures of this sort. For this reason, future school-leaders will have to respond to these problems in what Vail (1989) refers to as 'permanent white water'. Turbu-lence will be the norm not the exception.

The Leadership Process is Usefully Viewed as Problem-Solving

A recent review of studies of leadership and leader behavior in education, by Immegart (1988), concluded that research on educational leadership has actually declined over the past decade. This has been the case in spite of the increased challenges which have confronted schools during the 1980s and will continue and likely escalate throughout the 1990s. Furthermore, much greater attention needs to be given to the conceptualization of educational leadership, according to Immegart (1988), attention that acknowledges the multidimensional nature of leadership. Our response to this current state is to offer an initial conception of leadership as problem-solving, and to elaborate on the dimensions of that con-ception throughout the chapters of Part 2 of this book.

Problem-solving is a productive conception of leadership for two reasons. First, problem-solving is a generic human function, and as a result, capable of helping unearth the roots of otherwise puzzling human activity. As a conception of leadership, problem-solving competes with a host of more superficial concep-tions as identified, for example, by Bass (1981): leadership as a focus of group processes, personality and its effects, a form of persuasion, a power relationship, the exercise of influence, and the initiation of structure (and some five others).

Problem-solving is also a productive conception of leadership because it represents a plausible next step along the path that has been trod by those actively engaged in leadership research and theory. According to Immegart (1988), this path began with efforts to uncover personal traits of leaders (e.g., intelligence, dominance, self-confidence, high energy level). Subsequent steps down the path focused on leader styles, and then, through efforts to operationalize styles, on specific leader behaviors (a step on which studies of leadership, emanating from the effective schools' research, stalled). Current conceptions include efforts to understand the situational or contingent nature of leadership: that is, the extent to which a particular leader act and styles or behaviors depend for their effects on the context in which leadership is to be exercised. The central skill of situational leaders is to decide – to choose, from their repertoires, responses that are called for by the circumstances: 'Given what I know of this teacher's ability and disposition, and given the placement request being made by this parent, I am going to turn down the parent's request without further consultation with anyone'. Decision-making, however, is only one form of problem-solving and among the simplest forms, at that. Faced with relatively simple and routine problems, what school-leaders do is captured reasonably well by the notion of decision-making. But a more comprehensive understanding of the full range of intellectual and emotional activity which constitutes problem-solving is required to appreciate the responses of leaders to complex and non-routine problems.

In education, the dominant conception of school leadership with which our problem-solving conception competes at present, is 'instructional leadership'. This term symbolizes the importance, to school leadership, of an emphasis on student growth, and on much of the direct service provided by schools in fostering student growth. Such an emphasis was wholly appropriate and timely to bring to school leadership during the early 1980s, when the term gained a widespread following. But 'instructional leadership' conveys a meaning which encompasses only a portion of those activities now associated with effective school leadership. This is quite apparent, even in texts which explicitly adopt 'instructional leadership' as their thematic orientation: for example, Duke's (1987) *School Leadership and Instructional Improvement*, and Smith and Andrew's (1989) *Instructional Leadership*. These texts explore many issues of importance to school leadership (including visions of effective schools, for example) that fall outside the bounds of 'instruction' as it is normally conceived. Instructional leadership, as well, seems not to adequately encompass what has now been learned about the need for school-leaders to redesign professional work cultures to support teacher growth (e.g., Rosenholtz, 1989), as a context for instructional improvement, for example. Nor does this term (instructional leadership) acknowledge the contribution of non-instructional features of schools (e.g., informal, non-instructional relations between teacher and individual student) to their attractiveness to students typically considered at risk of dropping out (Rumberger, 1987, Lawton and Leithwood, 1988). Furthermore, schools of the future may well provide a significant portion of their services through means not readily associated with instruction as presently conceived (an image of the teacher as resource, rather than instructor, might be appropriate for future schools).

Summary and Conclusion

We began this chapter by affirming our assumptions about the durability of schools as future institutions, about their instrumental role in social change, and about the significant contribution of leadership to the functioning of schools, now and in the future. We then argued that the problem for leadership in the future had three parts: developing a shared, defensible vision of a future school considered desirable by those with a stake in it; directly assisting members of the school in addressing the challenges encountered in their efforts to achieve the vision; and increasing the capacity of school members to address those and future challenges themselves, more successfully. Problem-solving, we suggested, is an appropriately generic and comprehensive conception of what will be demanded of future leaders, more appropriate, for example, than 'instructional leadership'.

Our view of leadership, as problem-solving, encompasses dispositions and orientations toward leadership, now being given special attention in the leadership literature. It encompasses, for example, both transactional[2] and transformational leadership processes; it reinforces the continued importance of the content expertise of school-leaders, usefully highlighted in the term 'instructional leadership'. But it extends the scope of the school-leader's role to thinking like an organizational designer. Such thinking expands the array of problems given explicit attention by school-leaders to include the underlying structural and cultural conditions of work in the school and how they influence the nature of service provided to students.

Notes

1   The approximate translation of *'hubris'* is overweening self-confidence.
2   Transactional leadership is based on exchange theory. It assumes that the leader motivates followers by exchanging various kinds of incentives, for the cooperation of followers in working toward organizational goals.

Chapter 2

What Research Tells Us about the Present State of School Leadership

Assuming the principalship of a school – becoming the formal school-leader – appears to involve taking on certain requisite duties and challenges. Everything we know about the role suggests that it is hectic and fast-paced, involving significant amounts of interpersonal contact, of which more is unplanned than planned. And this seems to be the case for virtually all school principals. Indeed, at the close of many days, most principals would express considerable support for the applicability of 'chaos theory' (Gleick, 1987) as an explanation for their work: the metaphorical butterflies, flapping their wings in the Far East, seem to have created unique and unpredictable 'weather patterns' in Joan Fitzgerald's school in Newfoundland. But this is as close as we come to identifying natural laws of school leadership.

Beyond what might be called this ecology of the role (and we don't wish to minimize its importance), everything else is up for grabs. Which is to say that formal school leadership is a socially constructed role, the expectations for which have changed dramatically since its inception. Recently, expectations have changed at a sufficiently rapid rate to create incompetence among some of those with long tenure in the role. That is, at some earlier point in their careers, the performance of these people matched the socially determined expectations for exemplary school leadership. But the social ground shifted from under them and they did not shift with it. When planned change is defined as a process of reducing the gap between current and desired states, sometimes you have to run hard to stay in the same place. This happens when the desired state changes faster than you do. Under such circumstances, if you only amble forward, you actually lose ground!

'What is the purpose', you ask, 'in acknowledging the problem of change and the socially constructed nature of expectations for school leadership?' Developing leaders for future schools, in our view, ought to be considered a problem of planned change at two levels: at the level of how school leadership for future schools is conceptualized (e.g., what qualities are associated with such leadeship) and at the level of how individual people can be assisted in acquiring those capacities or qualities needed to exercise leadership in future schools. While most of this book addresses change at the individual level, such change depends on being clear about change at the conceptual level. At both levels, clarity about the changes which need to be made depends on defining the ends of the planned

Figure 2.1: An orientation to understanding current school leadership

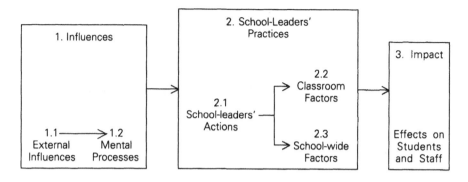

change gap. Chapter 1 provided an overview of what we conceptualize to be desirable leadership for future schools. This chapter[1] clarifies what can be learned about the current state of school leadership from existing research. This research has focused almost exclusively on principals and vice-principals, and so, these roles are the exclusive focus of this chapter.

Understanding Current School Leadership

An adequate understanding of current school leadership depends on much more than what is provided, for example, by descriptions of overt leadership behaviors. Figure 2.1 identifies one important set of variables and relationships that are central to such an understanding: it concerns the nature, causes and consequences of what current school-leaders do. An earlier version of this framework was proposed as a consequence of Leithwood and Montgomery's (1986) review of research. The framework is also similar to one proposed by Dwyer *et al.* (1984). The Figure is intended to suggest that what school-leaders do – their 'practices' (component 2) – is most directly a consequence of what they think – their mental processes (component 1.2). Such mental processes are a function of certain characteristic ways of understanding, applied to the environment in which they work. Elements in this environment (component 1.1) may be interpreted by school-leaders in many ways and certain elements turn out to have much greater impact on their thinking than other elements. School-leaders have been observed to engage in quite distinct patterns of practice (component 2.1), shaped by how they think about their work. Three or four such patterns are particularly evident among North American principals and these patterns have demonstrated widely varying impacts on classroom practices or factors (component 2.2) and factors within the school but outside the classroom (component 2.3). It is primarily through such influence that school-leaders affect pupils and others (component 3), although some aspects of their practices are more direct than others in their impact.

As suggested by the orientation to current school leadership represented in Figure 2.1, this chapter addresses three sets of questions: questions about the impact, practices, and influences on the practices of current school-leaders. These sets of questions are addressed through a relatively comprehensive review of empirical research reported between 1974 and 1988. The review was conducted in two parts. For research reported between 1974 and 1984, three literature reviews (examining a total of seventy-five original empirical studies) (Leithwood and Montgomery, 1982, Leithwood, 1982, Leithwood and Montgomery, 1986) were relied on. For the 1985 to 1988 period, sixty original studies were identified through systematic search techniques described in detail in Leithwood, Begley and Cousins (1990).

We turn now to a report of what the results of these studies of elementary and secondary school principals (135 in total) contribute to the three questions of concern in this chapter. Results of the more recent studies (1985–1988) are described in more detail than results of the 1974–1984 studies. Consistent with our practice in all chapters of the book, we make quite explicit the evidence used, in order to address each question. In addition, we also identify directions for subsequent research which would expand the knowledge-base relevant to the task of developing leaders for future schools.

What is Known About the Impact of Current School-Leaders?

The three reviews of pre-1985 research identified forty empirical studies of elementary principals' impact on some aspect of students and teachers. With respect to students, the impact included: positive attitudes toward school (two studies), achievement in basic reading and math skills (fifteen studies), and reduced vandalism and absenteeism (two studies). Principals impacted on teachers' job satisfaction (seven studies), use of innovative practices in the class-room (eleven studies), and teachers' perception of the principal's leadership (five studies). Seven studies conducted between 1985 and 1988 provided additional evidence concerning principals' impact on students' basic skills, teachers' job satisfaction, and their use of innovative teaching practices. Four additional types of impact on teachers were explored in these studies.

Andrews *et al.* (1986) used the gain scores of students on standardized achievement tests to explore the effects of principals rated by their teachers as strong, average, or weak leaders. Significant correlations were found between achievement and strength of leadership for both math and reading gain scores. In this study, strength of leadership was a function of (a) the extent to which the principal mobilized personnel and other types of resources to achieve the school's goals, (b) the clarity of communication concerning the school's goals, (c) the extent of active involvement in the school's instructional program, and (d) the extent to which the principal was a visible presence in different parts of the school (teachers were given these criteria).

Blase, Dedrick and Strathe (1986) used teachers' responses to questions about their principal's behavior, stress caused by their principal, and the principal's impact on their classroom performance, to explore correlations with teacher job satisfaction. A moderately strong association was found between teacher satisfaction and the degree to which principals' initiation of structure (the extent to which a leader initiates, organizes and defines work to be done and the manner in which it will be done) and consideration behaviors (behaviors related to enhancing teachers' self-esteem) were perceived to help teacher performance. Brady

(1985) found 'principal supportiveness' or consideration, in particular, to be the most consistently significant predictor of staff perceptions concerning the prevalence of group, as opposed to individual, decision-making in the school. Such supportiveness, in the teachers' view, was also related to: principals' involvement in curriculum decisions, the use of an interactive (rather than an objectives-driven) curriculum-planning model, intimacy (e.g., good social and interpersonal relations) among staff, and satisfaction with the school curriculum.

Sharman (1987) explored the relationship between the degree of teachers' implementation of a new math program, and principals' evaluation, supervision and staff development initiatives. Results suggested that the more directly such initiatives were seen to support implementation, the greater the level of use of the innovation by teachers.

Loyalty, the extent to which teachers are committed to the principal and have an unquestioning faith and trust in the principal, was the nature of the impact of interest in Johnson and Venable's (1986) study. Different types of principals' 'rule administration behavior' (e.g., democratic vs. authoritarian) and principals' influence in the school-system hierarchy were types of school-leader practices related to such impact. Results suggested differences among elementary and secondary teachers in their reaction to different types of rule administration. Greater loyalty among elementary teachers was most closely related to less 'punishment-centered' rule administration (less conflict, less tension, and less explicit enforcement of rules) by principals. More representative rule administration (joint rule, initiation, and acceptance) was most closely related to secondary teachers' loyalty to the principal. The loyalty of both groups of teachers was associated with their perception of the principals' ability and willingness to exert influence upwards in the school-system hierarchy and to do things for the teacher.

Hoy and Brown (1986), like Blase *et al.* (1986) and Brady (1985) examined the effects of principals' consideration (e.g., attention to interpersonal relations) and initiation of structure (e.g., attention to the task and how to get it done). Both aspects of leadership were found to be related to the teachers' 'zone of acceptance' (their readiness to accept decisions made for them by the principal). Together, these two sets of behaviors accounted for 38 percent of the variance in teachers' zone of acceptance. As with Johnson and Venable (1986), differences between elementary and secondary teachers were found: secondary teachers attributed overriding importance to the principals' initiation of structure.

What do these studies have to contribute, in sum, to the question of current school-leaders' impact on schools? And what new research would be helpful to support leaders of future schools? First, we must acknowledge significant limitations in the research-based knowledge about the nature of current school-leaders' impact. But based on the number of studies alone, one can reasonably conclude that current school-leaders are capable of having a significant influence on the basic skills' achievement of students. A recent review of school effects in the Third World also attributes such impact to school-leaders (Fuller, 1987). As well, current principals seem capable of influencing teachers' adoption and use of innovative classroom practices, and teachers' job satisfaction. Evidence concerning other types of impact is extremely thin, however.

Several suggestions for subsequent research which would support leaders of future schools are worth mentioning. First, research to date has been concerned with the principals' impact on an important but highly restricted set of student outcomes (attitudes toward school, basic skills, vandalism and absenteeism). Such outcomes reflect neither the scope nor the emphasis of the full range of student outcomes to which many schools aspire now and, certainly not, in the future (see Chapter 3 for more on this). Such schools, for example, now often view basic math and reading skills as instrumental in fostering growth in higher order thinking skills and in the acquisition of complex, discipline-based concepts and theories. Many schools, now and in the future, assume responsibility for assisting students in the development of social and attitudinal outcomes (e.g., self-concept, esteem for the culture and customs of others) of special importance, in light of changing family and community contexts. The research-knowledge base required to assist leaders of future schools will need to inquire into how such leaders can impact on outcomes of this sort, outcomes which better reflect the likely mission of future schools.

A second suggestion for research concerns the nature of principals' impact on teachers. There is no underlying, comprehensive theory dictating the choice by researchers of what types of impact on teachers to examine. Further, with the notable exception of teachers' use of innovative practices, all of the research to date has focused on attitudes and dispositions only loosely linked to teachers' performances. Of more value to leaders of future schools would be a choice of teacher outcomes, driven by a theory or theories of teacher growth in classroom effectiveness, such as the one described in Chapter 8. As we argue in that chapter, contributions to teacher development are central aspects of the job of leaders for future schools.

Third, perhaps the school characteristic currently of most interest in efforts to understand effective schools is school culture, or ethos (the norms, values, beliefs, and associated behaviors shared by those in the school). This characteristic is not independent of students and teachers. It is, however, a more composite feature of schools that cannot be understood by looking only and separately at students and teachers. While schools which vary in effectiveness also appear to vary in the nature of their culture, it is not clear whether principals can significantly influence school culture. This makes culture a promising focus for attention in subsequent research on principals' impact. Chapter 9 explores, in more detail, some quite recent research which gives warrant for optimism about the role of school-leaders in respect to school culture. This chapter is relatively specific about what school-leaders should also do to foster the development of more productive school cultures.

What is the Nature of Current School-Leader Practices and How Do They Vary?

Seventy-five pre-1985 studies provided information about principals' practices. Of the thirty 1985–8 studies with such a focus, four inquired into roles, five described principals' overall patterns or styles, seven focused on the practices of 'typical principals', and fourteen studies examined the practices of highly effective principals.

Roles

Prior to 1985, research on the principalship included efforts to clarify principals' roles, beginning from two quite different premises. One premise was that the role could be viewed as predominantly unidimensional and the research objective was to discover the dimension which best captured the role. Principals, for example, were claimed to play a largely 'manager' role or a largely 'leadership' role: they were concerned mostly with administration or with instructional leadership. Results of this research usually found typical practice consumed by managerial or administrative tasks, but desired practice best captured in leadership roles focused on such substantive educational decisions in the school as instruction.

Other research on principals' roles, however, was based on the premise that the role was multidimensional. Sergiovanni's (1984) five 'leadership forces' illustrate reasonably well the range of dimensions the principal's role was found to encompass in this research. These dimensions included: technical management activities, provision of interpersonal support and encouragement to staff, instructional intervention, modeling important goals and behaviors, signaling to others what is important (symbolic leadership), and developing an appropriate and unique school culture.

All four of the 1985–8 studies of principals' roles assumed a multidimensional view of the role. Brubaker and Simon (1987) inquired about the actual and preferred roles of principals from among five possibilities: principal teacher, general manager, professional and scientific manager, administrator and instructional leader, and curriculum leader. Each of these roles was described in paragraph length and included at least several dimensions of practice. Most principals viewed their current roles as administrator and their preferred role as instructional leader. General manager was rated a distant second, as current role, and curriculum leader and professional scientific manager tied for second choice, as preferred role. Gender differences emerged in this study, with women giving much higher ratings for actual and preferred roles to administrator, instructional leader and curriculum leader. Men, in contrast, rated the general manager role much higher than women, as both an actual and preferred role.

Gousha's (1986) survey also found highest ratings given to instructional leadership as a description of actual and preferred roles. Other roles rated highly were school manager, personnel leader and disciplinarian. These role ratings were not consistent with principals' estimates of the time spent on five key tasks associated with their role. School management and teacher/student concerns (personnel leadership) consumed 40.8 percent and 34.1 percent respectively. School improvement (instructional leadership), on the other hand, consumed only 15 percent of their time.

The disciplinarian role was the special focus of attention in Montgomerie, McIntosh and Mattson's (1987) study. Opinions were solicited from teachers, superintendents, principals, and board chairs, concerning the relative importance of roles played by principals. The framework for this study was a modified version of Sergiovanni's leadership forces: the disciplinary role was added, and cultural and symbolic forces were collapsed. Results of this study, combining the opinions of the four groups of respondents, gave strongest weight to the symbolic, disciplinarian and humanistic roles, and least weight to the instructional and technical roles. Teachers, however, showed a strong preference for the disciplinarian role of the principal.

A fourth study of roles by Bradeson (1986) identified three metaphors for the role adopted by principals and others with whom they interacted. The role appeared to be dominated by a metaphor of maintenance: principal, as the person who sees and understands the total process and is responsible for keeping the process going. About three-quarters of the time of principals was devoted to maintenance tasks, and about 5 or 6 percent of this time was devoted to tasks associated with each of two additional role metaphors: survival and vision. Survival tasks were those focused on meeting such immediate needs as short-range planning. The ability of the principal to holistically view the present, to reinterpret to all its constituents the school's mission, and to speculate about future directions was Bradeson's meaning of vision.

Patterns or Styles

Research aimed at describing patterns or styles of principal practice has examined such practice in more depth than the roles' perspective has: it has attempted either to identify dominant orientations to the role, without concern for differences in impact, or to define progressively more effective styles or patterns of practice. Results of four pre-1985 studies using this approach can be summed up in four leadership styles which we refer to as A, B, C and D.

Leadership style A is characterized by a focus on interpersonal relationships, on establishing a cooperative and congenial 'climate' in the school, and effective, collaborative relationships with various community and central office groups. Principals adopting this style seem to believe that such relationships are critical to their overall success and provide a necessary springboard for more task-oriented activities in their schools.

Student achievement and well-being is the central focus of leadership style B. Descriptions of this class of practices suggest that while such achievement and well-being is the goal, principals use a variety of means to accomplish it. These include many of the interpersonal, administrative, and managerial behaviors that provide the central focus of other styles.

Compared with styles A and B, there is less consistency, across the four studies reviewed, in the practices classified as style C (program focus). Principals adopting this style, nevertheless, share a concern for ensuring effective programs, improving the overall competence of their staff, and developing procedures for carrying out tasks central to program success. Compared with style A, the orientation is to the task, and developing good interpersonal relations is viewed as a means to better task achievement. Compared with style B, there is a greater tendency to view as a goal the adoption and implementation of apparently effective procedures for improving student outcomes, rather than the student outcomes themselves.

Leadership style D is characterized by almost exclusive attention to what is often labeled 'administrivia': the nuts and bolts of daily school organization and maintenance. Principals adopting this style, according to all four studies, are preoccupied with budgets, timetables, personnel administration, and requests for information from others. They appear to have little time for instructional and curriculum decision-making in their schools and tend to become involved only in response to a crisis or a request.

Hall *et al.* (1986) argue that their three styles (responder, manager, initiator) have different effects on the process of school improvement. Initiators are more successful in their school-improvement efforts, responders are least successful. Paragraph-length descriptions are provided for each of these styles.

In order to better understand the specific practices associated with each of the Hall *et al.* styles, Stevens and Marsh (1987) inquired about principals' vision and strategies for achieving their vision. Results suggested that more effective styles were associated with better integrated visions more directly focused on program-related matters and with a greater number of them. More effective styles also were associated with a greater range of strategies and more effort in their strategies to focus on a combination of daily, small-scale, and comprehensive large-scale changes.

Research by Leithwood and Montgomery resulted in a much more detailed (chapter length) description of four multidimensional patterns of practice, ordered from least to most effective in accomplishing a complex array of student outcomes. The patterns are labeled: administrator (least effective), humanitarian, program manager, and systematic problem solver (most effective). In Chapter 4, these patterns are described in much greater detail, as are increasingly effective approaches to solving predictable, routine school-leadership problems.

Three additional studies since 1985 have focused on principals' styles more or less directly based on a conception of leadership, provided by the Ohio State Leadership Studies in the 1960s. Consideration and initiation of structure are the two dimensions defining this conception. Hoy and Brown's (1986) survey suggested that high degrees of both principals' consideration and (especially) initiation of structure influenced teachers' readiness to accept decisions made for them by principals (their 'zone of acceptance'). Blase *et al.* (1986) reported similar results in relation to teacher satisfaction and classroom performance. Teachers and principals responding to Brady's (1985) survey attributed substantial importance to the supportiveness (or consideration) of principals in fostering a variety of desirable attitudes among staff.

Typical Practice

Judged by the quantity of research available, interest in describing multiple patterns or styles of practice has been quite restricted. In contrast, there has been a relatively large number of studies designed to describe and understand both 'typical' and 'highly effective' forms of practice. Of the seventy-five empirical studies conducted between 1974 and 1984, fifty-two (69 percent) were concerned wholly, or in part, with the nature of typical practice.

Studies of typical practice usually differ from studies of principal roles and patterns of practice in terms of the detail of information they provide. Leithwood and Montgomery's 'dimensions' of principals' practices or behavior are a useful tool for bringing some conceptual coherence to such detailed descriptions. These dimensions include (a) *goals* principals attempt to achieve in their schools (nature, source, and use of such goals), (b) *factors* in classrooms and the school which principals believe they must influence to accomplish their goals (choice of factors, nature of expectations held for factors, source of these expectations), (c) *strategies* used to influence such factors (criteria for choosing strategies, emphasis among strategies, characteristics of strategies), and (d) the nature of *decision-making* processes.

Descriptions of 'typical' practice, while sometimes quite detailed, are consistent with the pattern of practice described above as leadership style D, with some elements of A. All but one of the seven recent studies provided information about at least one of the four dimensions: goals, factors, strategies, and decision-making. Kingdon (1985) compared expectations for the role of the full-time teaching principal, on the part of such principals, with expectations normally held for the role; other aspects of their activity were also examined. Few differences in expectations were found but teaching principals did give first priority to their teaching assignments and did most of their administrative work outside regular school hours.

Bradeson's (1986) was the only study to provide information about the goals of the typical principal. Such information was available in his analysis of the purposes served by carefully recorded daily communications. These purposes and the percentage of communications devoted to them by principals were (a) maintenance messages, concerned with policies and procedures (49.8 percent), (b) human messages, concerning peoples' attitudes, morale and satisfaction (25.6 percent), (c) task messages, concerned with the quality and quantity of educational services (23.7 percent), and (d) innovation messages, concerned with school improvement (1 percent) These four sets of purposes correspond closely to the focuses of major concern in each of the four leadership styles that have been described. 'Running a smooth ship', both organizationally and interpersonally, appeared to preoccupy the typical principal.

The single study (Chater, 1985) of principals' decision-making, among the seven reviewed, was conducted in seven secondary schools in Great Britain. No effort was made to identify relative levels of effectiveness of the principals (heads). Results suggested that while most principals sought relatively low involvement from staff on financial matters there was some variation among schools in other decision areas. Many staff were satisfied to have low levels of involvement in school decisions because it reduced their uncertainty. Only one school used highly participatory forms of decision-making.

Three studies provided information about principals' strategies. Focusing on communication patterns, Bradeson (1986) found considerable variation in the location of principals' communication. Almost three-quarters of principals' activities were interpersonal and took place with only one other person, over half involving face-to-face contact. The main thrust of these results was replicated by Davies (1987) in Great Britain and by Gally (1986) in Israel. In fact, typical principals' activities in most countries, where data are available (e.g., US, Canada, Australia, Great Britain, Israel), appear to be characterized by brevity, fragmentation and variety.

Four studies touching on factors principals' influence provided minimal information about practices within this component. Williams (1986) inquired into principals' influence on fourteen components (factors) of teachers' instruction. Classroom composition, teaching materials and resources, and instructional methods were factors principals perceived themselves to influence. Instructional methods, including student grouping, facilities, and the community were do-mains (factors) used by Gally (1986) to explore the location of administrative activities. The extent to which principals influenced these factors was not ex-plored in this study. A similarly designed study (Taylor, 1986) in Great Britain, although not directly investigating specific factors influenced by principals, sug-gested that heads spent nearly half their time dealing with classroom factors. This is not typical practice in most countries and may be a function of the traditional 'head-teacher' role of the school-leader in Great Britain. Ehiametalor (1985) examined the actual and expected levels of performance of principals in Nigeria, in influencing factors classified as curriculum and instruction, staff and students, the community, school organization and structure, and budget. Principals were classified by age, experience, and training. For the most part, all categories of principals performed below expected levels; performance was substantially high-er, however, for principals with twelve to nineteen years experience.

Effective Practice

A relatively large amount of research activity between 1974 and 1984 (fifty-one studies) was devoted to studies of effective practice. Results of this research provide a detailed account of what has been described above as leadership style B (a student-achievement focus) with elements of style C (program focus). Thirteen studies of effective practice conducted between 1985 and 1988 were included in this analysis. These of these studies explicitly compared typical and effective practice. By far the largest proportion of attention (twelve studies) was devoted, in these studies, to strategies used by principals: four studies spoke to the goals of effective principals, two compared factors, and three described aspects of decision-making. With respect to goals, highly effective principals were found to demonstrate high levels of commitment to goals for the schools, especially instructional goals. They ensure that school instructional goals are congruent with district policies. Such principals articulate an overall vision for the school which is multifaceted. This vision emerges from a belief that all children can learn what the school has to offer. Effective principals set relatively high profes-sional and school standards for goal achievement and actively work toward the development of widespread agreement concerning such standards (Taylor, 1986, Dwyer *et al.*, 1984, Andrews *et al.*, 1986, Larsen, 1987).

Two studies provided information about effective principals' approaches to classroom and school factors. Larsen's (1987) data suggested substantial efforts to influence the classroom curriculum, teachers' instructional behaviors, material resources for instruction, and the general environment of the school (climate or culture). Dwyer's (1984) study identified seven such targets for principals: work structure, staff relations, student relations, the environment, plant and equip-ment, community relations, and institutional relations.

The relatively large number of studies identifying strategies used by effective principals generated twenty-two such strategies. Ten of these strategies were identified in just one study and are not reported here. Those strategies identified in three or more studies included: monitoring student progress; teacher evalua-tion and supervision; establishing and communicating clear, high expectations for students and staff; establishing and enforcing an equitable discipline code; and maintaining a positive school climate. Strategies associated with effective principals in two studies included: goal setting; planning and program development; mobilizing and allocating resources; modeling; being actively involved in staff development for teachers and self; and developing good working relationships with staff, community, and central office staff.

Two of the three studies touching on effective decision-making processes of principals provide additional support for already well-established claims concerning the benefits of participatory decision-making. Stanard's (1986) case study of a single principal attributed a portion of the principal's success in solving discipline problems to her involvement of parents and staff in both curriculum and discipline decisions. Johnson and Venable (1986) found that participatory forms of decision-making ('representative rule administration') were associated with greater teacher loyalty to the principal among at least secondary teachers; the data were less conclusive with respect to elementary teachers.

High and Achilles's (1986) data were partly at odds with the general support found for participatory forms of decision-making. Their study inquired into principals' and teachers' preferences, for the use of seven different bases of social power by the principal. Teachers ranked highest bases of power labeled: expert power, legitimate authority, and norm-setting power. Principals awarded more potential to involvement and less to legitimate authority bases than did teachers. These results prompted High and Achilles to comment in their conclusions:

> Principals in general have apparently been reading too much of the 1960s
> literature (togetherness) and believing it. (1986, p. 15)

Given the image of desirable, future school leadership, loosely framed in Chapter 1, results in this section appear to offer useful insights for developing future school-leaders. There are holes in these results which, if filled, would also be of value.

The significance of research to date, on roles, appears to be threefold. First, the school-leader's role, now and in the future, is clearly multidimensional and further efforts to identify the 'most important' dimension would be misdirected (Pitner and Hovecar, 1987). Second, among the many role categories used as frameworks for research, Sergiovanni's (1984) five 'leadership forces' supplemented by a disciplinary category, seem to represent available data as well as any. Finally, in light of the more detailed knowledge about principals' practices generated from other perspectives, a role perspective no longer offers a useful framework for subsequent research aimed at helping develop future school-leaders.

Available research on patterns or styles of practice supports the claim that school-leaders carry out the job in distinctly different ways. Most of these differences are well represented by four focuses: a student achievement focus, a program focus, an interpersonal focus, and a focus on routine maintenance activities. Furthermore, these focuses appear to constitute levels of effectiveness in which the main concerns defining lower levels (e.g., a focus on routine maintenance) are incorporated into, and subsumed by, the concerns defining higher levels (e.g., a student achievement focus). Additional empirical tests of the claim that the four patterns of practice represent a hierarchy of effectiveness are needed, as is a more detailed description of how school-leaders come to adopt certain patterns of practice. Such description is basic to the task of developing future school-leaders and the results of our own, just completed research on this matter are outlined in Chapter 10.

The extensively researched dimensions of leadership labeled consideration and initiating structure are important dimensions within each of these four levels or styles, consideration being the main concern of principals with an interpersonal focus. But further research within the limitations of theoretical and methodological frameworks traditionally used to explore these dimensions cannot be justified: the importance of the two dimensions is no longer in question and you will recall the special emphasis we attributed to consideration in Chapter 1. Detailed knowledge of practice within each dimension is what is still lacking and would be of value for developing future school-leaders.

Recent studies of typical practices reinforce but do not extend prior knowledge about such practices. Such studies paint a surprisingly uniform picture of such practive across many national contexts. Heads in Great Britain were somewhat unique in their orientation to classroom factors. With empowerment and school improvement as goals, more research simply describing typical practice does not seem likely to be of much use in the development of future leaders.

Results of research on effective current practice appear to be quite useful in describing in more detail the qualities valued in future school-leaders. This research confirms the central role that principals' goals play in understanding the source of effective practice. These goals form a central part of the vision principals use to bring consistency to an otherwise unmanageably diverse set of demands. Developing a widely shared, defensible vision is central to future school leadership, as we discussed in Chapter 1. Effective principals act to influence a broad array of school factors with an extensive repertoire of strategies. This is using technical expertise in the midst of the band, as also discussed in Chapter 1. Their priorities are expressed in their day-to-day actions; they are better attuned, than are typical principals, to behaviors that actually influence teachers. Effective principals use participatory decision-making, selectively but frequently, depending on their assessment of the context. Nevertheless, as Pfeifer (1986) has noted, much of the data on effective practice has been generated in the context of turbulent, urban schools. Further studies of effective practice in diverse contexts are essential if results are to be used with confidence as guides to practice, in a broad array of settings, in the future.

What Influences the Practices of Current School-Leaders?

Results of research concerning influences on current principals' practices are useful in beginning to think about what sorts of experiences will contribute most usefully to future school-leader development (or growth). Influences on current principals' practices were examined using two sets of research. The first set included eighteen empirical studies previously analyzed by Leithwood and Montgomery in their 1982 literature review: results of these studies are only briefly summarized in this section. The second set, receiving more attention, included studies reported from 1982 through 1987, with greatest emphasis on the 1985 to 1987 period. These studies were organized according to their conceptualization of independent, mediating, and dependent variables, as follows:

Set A: Studies which examine the relationship between external influences and principals' practices (Previous reviews of literature spoke only to this set of relationships)

Set B: Studies which examined the relationship between external influences and principals' internal mental states or processes

Set C: Studies which inquired about relationships between internal mental states or processes, and principals' practices

Set D: Studies which examined relationships among all of external influences, internal mental states or processes and principals' practices.

Set A: External Influences and Principals' Practices

Leithwood and Montgomery's review of eighteen relevant studies identified five classes of 'obstacles' standing in the way of principals providing instructional leadership (the dependent variable); four of these were external to the principal.

Obstacles presented to principals by teachers included: lack of knowledge and skill about new practices; uneven professional training; and lack of motivation to change, to participate in in-service training, and to collaborate in planning. Obstacles also identified were teacher autonomy and constraints on program decision-making resulting from collective bargaining and union contracts. Several features of the principals' role were viewed as obstacles: ambiguity (unclear expectations, conflict about responsibilities) and complexity (number of people to consider, number of tasks). Hierarchical structures and problems they created in making changes were characteristics of school systems, identified as obstacles to principals. So too were excessively rigid and time consuming policies and procedures; provision of inadequate resources; and conservative stance of central administrators toward school-initiated change. We address influences such as these and their consequences for district leadership in more detail in Chapter 15. Finally, aspects of the community were also viewed as a source of obstacles to principals in their efforts to be more effective. These included: the interests of parents (too much or too little), pressure of special interest groups in the community, and excessively conservative views about the nature of appropriate school programs.

Four 1985–8 studies provided support for the general thrust of the results reviewed by Leithwood and Montgomery. In a follow-up study by Leithwood and Montgomery (1984), principals reported having only moderate concerns about the four sets of obstacles (above) as a whole. Obstacles associated with school districts appeared to present the greatest difficulties, a finding also reported by Goldman and Kempner (1990), but no strong relationships were found between classes of obstacles and principals' effectiveness. Obstacles associated with the district also dominated evidence presented by Crowson and Morris, and Louis. Crowson and Morris (1985) suggested that in one large urban school district, between a half and a third of principals' time was consumed in responding to formal, hierarchical controls largely having to do with budget, personnel, and pupil behavior. Informal reward systems provided by the system (e.g., getting a better school, promotion) attracted considerable additional time of principals. Louis (1989) also reported a strong but indirect influence by super-intendents and other district office staff on the planning and design of school-improvement efforts in a large sample of US secondary schools. While the district was not the dominant source of problems in school-improvement efforts, conflicts with district office staff, staff turnovers, competing priorities for change, and eroded school autonomy were viewed by a large proportion of principals as serious challenges to their school-improvement initiatives. The main thrust of these findings was supported by Gousha (1986).

Leithwood and Stager's (1986) study of problem-solving processes suggested that highly effective principals, with administrative experience, become more reflective about their own processes and refine these processes with time. Although similar to moderately effective principals in general moral values and in personal values, effective principals are more influenced by their beliefs concerning principals' roles and responsibilities, and are more able to specify day-to-day consequences of such beliefs; they are also more aware of school-system needs and requirements, and try harder to take them into account in school-level problem-solving. Effective principals derive more personal enjoyment from problem-solving, and partly as a consequence of this, are more proactive in dealing with school problems. Chapter 6 expands on, and adds to, these results in reference to future school-leaders.

Finally, Tracy (1985), and Brubaker and Simon (1987) linked differences in the socialization experiences of men and women with differences in career aspirations and view of the principal's role. Such experiences appear to cause more men to seek the principalship earlier in their careers (before the age of 30) and to aspire to the superintendency as a career move. Gender-related socialization experiences also seemed to contribute to a relatively large proportion of women viewing themselves, as already noted, more as curriculum and instructional leaders. Relatively larger proportions of men, in contrast, viewed themselves as general managers. Greater amounts of formal education were also associated with a tendency for principals to view themselves as curriculum and instructional leaders. These matters are explored in detail in Chapter 10 as they bear on developing future school-leaders.

Set B: External Influences and Internal Mental States or Processes

Eight studies (1985–8) provided data on the relationship between external influences and internal mental processes. Two of the eight studies concerned perceived job stress or feelings of 'burnout' (Sarros and Friesen, 1987, Kotkamp and Travlos, 1986). Volume of work, poor interpersonal relations with staff and others, pressures from higher authorities and role conflict were external factors appearing to contribute to feelings of burnout.

Three studies examined a variety of external influences on principals' job satisfaction (Caldwell and Paul, 1984, Sparkes, 1986, Gunn and Holdaway, 1986). External influences identified in these studies, contributing to positive attitudes toward the job, included larger schools and communities, length of experience in the role, and more qualification/training. Such influences also included high levels of teacher ability, cooperative teacher attitudes, recognition by others of one's work, and relatively lower levels of conflict and workload.

Set C: Internal Mental States or Processes and Principals' Practices

Five studies conducted since 1985 which focus on this area of the principalship were located. The independent variables in these studies were principals' beliefs, values, and problem-solving processes.

Taylor (1986) reported a strong association between the effectiveness of principals, and their belief that all students can learn. Principals' use of student-achievement data in decision-making was associated, by Glasman, with three sets of beliefs by principals concerning their control over the use of such data, and its value in program and teacher evaluation.

Using a hierarchy of values proposed by Hodgkinson (1978), Begley (1988) inquired into the role of such values in principals' decisions to adopt micro-computer technology in their schools (discussed more fully in Chapter 6). Principals with greater knowledge of the innovation and those with an instructional orientation to their roles were more likely to make their adoption decison using the value 'consequences for students'. Other principals more often based their decisions on their personal preferences, a desire for consensus (e.g., among staff), or some broad moral principle. Values of consequence increased as the basis for choice with increased knowledge among all types of principals. Subsequent research suggests a particularly crucial role for values in the work of future school-leaders. As a consequence, Chapter 7 is devoted to a more detailed examination of that role.

Leithwood and Stager compared problem-solving processes used by 'highly effective' principals with those used by more 'typical' principals. Results of these studies, we believe, are central to our expectations for future school-leaders. Hence, further discussion is saved for the detailed treatment contained in Chapter 6.

Set D: External Influences, Internal Mental States or Processes and Principals' Practices

The five studies in this set address three problems. The first problem, addressed by Daresh (1987), and Marshall and Greenfield (1987) concerns effectiveness in the early years of the principalship. These studies suggest that reduced effective-ness during these years as a principal and one's unwillingness to take risks is a direct function of inadequate skills (internal states) in: (a) carrying out routine administrative procedures, (b) conflict management, and (c) determining system-wide decision-making processes. It is also a function of feelings of dissonance with one's values and reduced excitement about school improvement. Such feelings and skill deficiencies are, in turn, attributed to external influences, such as: restricted administrative experiences as a vice-principal, inadequate formal training for the role, and socialization processes prior to assuming the principal-ship.

Effective principals differ from their less effective peers, in part, in terms of the extent and quality of information used in their decision-making. McColskey, Altschuld and Lawton (1985) inquired into the reasons for variation among principals in this component of their practice. Training in social-science research methods appeared to be an important external influence on such practice. Open-mindedness and beliefs concerning the principal's role and the autonomy and power available to effect change in the school were internal influences identified.

Cousins (1988) studied principals' use for professional development of appraisal data concerning their own performance. He found that principals' attitudes toward the appraisal processes were predictive of the extent to which they learned about their performance. Attitudes were found to be associated with high levels of motivation for professional growth and inversely related to principals' experience and working knowledge. Use of appraisal data for decision-making was found to be linked to external variables (e.g., nature of decision to be made, communicative aspects of the appraisal process). In Chapter 13, we extend the insights available in this and other research to an exploration of selection and appraisal procedures appropriate for leaders of future schools.

Finally, in the context of implementing policies initiated outside their schools, Trider and Leithwood (1988), and Leithwood (1986) found significant differences in influences on principals' practices depending on: (a) principals' orientation to the role, (b) stage in the implementation process, and (c) principals' training and/or policy-relevant knowledge. More instructionally oriented principals were less influenced by district factors and more guided by their own beliefs. As implementation proceeded, organizational context factors (e.g., staff input to decisions) within the school took on greater significance for all principals, to the extent that such factors had the potential for solving emerging problems of implementation in the school; so, too, did the support available from various groups outside the school. This was consistent with evidence reported by Fullan, Anderson and Newton (1986) in relation to secondary-school principals' efforts to implement a major instructional innovation in their school. Finally, school administrators with specialized knowledge in the policy area being implemented made decisions in a relatively autonomous fashion, guided largely by their own beliefs. These findings suggest the possibility, in fact, that principals' special knowledge (often the result of training) is one of the central determinants of the pattern of policy-implementation behavior in which they engage. Principals without special knowledge seemed to rely extensively on the guidance provided by central office staff and the existing skills of staff. Perhaps their concern for working relationships can be attributed to their dependence on knowledge possessed by others, and their desire to gain cooperation from such people to apply that knowledge in their school.

By way of summary, current school-leaders' practices are influenced by four types of external factors: the principals' role (e.g., expectations, complexity), a large cluster of influences concerning the attitudes, abilities and behaviors of others (e.g., teachers' willingness to innovate), characteristics of the school system (e.g., district policies and procedures), and the principals' own 'background' (e.g., training, socialization experiences). These external factors interact with principals' internal mental processes and states: personal traits (e.g., openmindedness), knowledge and beliefs (e.g., about what is best for students), values (e.g., consequences for students), attitudes and feelings (e.g., job satisfaction), and skills (e.g., problem-solving, conflict management). Through such interactions the specific nature and effectiveness of principals' practices are shaped.

As we reviewed these influences above, we pointed to results of special consequence for future school-leader development and identified subsequent chapters in the book where such matters are taken up in depth. There are some obvious holes in the research results, however, with the development of future school-leaders as a goal. First and most generally, this body of research evidence currently available is extremely limited in quantity. It is also uneven in quality both conceptually and methodologically: for instance, there are no experimental studies exploring cause-and-effect relationships, and little of the research is guided by a coherent theory to explain or suggest relationships among the variables of interest, if choices must be made. There is, arguably, a greater need for research exploring these relationships than there is more descriptive research on effective practice, for example. Such research would help us understand how effective practice develops, a crucial matter about which current research has little to say. What factors lead a school-leader to adopt a particular one of the four dominant orientations to the role (A, B, C, D)? Can school-leader's dominant orientation change? If so, how does this happen? How can the experiences of future school-leaders be constructed so as to contribute best to the development of effective orientations to the role? Productive answers to these questions, we suspect, are rooted in a better understanding of principals' internal mental processes and states: the rational aspects of these processes, such as the content and organization of knowledge structures, as well as such non-rational elements as beliefs, attitudes and values.

Further research, addressing issues discussed here, also seems likely to clarify some of the fundamental reasons underlying differences in practices observed among male and female principals. There is some urgency about developing a better understanding of this matter, since much larger numbers of women are now actively preparing themselves for leadership in future schools.

Conclusion

The purpose of this chapter was to sum up what is presently known from research about current school leadership. Comparing the results of this research with the conception of leadership for future schools, described in Chapter 1, provides a clearer sense of the nature and size of the change required to move from current leadership practices to those suitable for future schools. Such a comparison leads us to several broad conclusions. First, typical current school-leadership practices are woefully inadequate, given present expectations for schools and leaders – never mind the considerably more ambitious expectations anticipated for schools of the future. Redesigning the experiences that produce such patterns of practice is a crucial developmental strategy. Such redesign involves not only individuals' socialization experiences directly (see Chapter 10) but also the wider organizational structures which account, to a significant degree, for those experiences (see Chapter 15). Second, practices currently viewed as effective have much to offer to leaders of future schools. But the sources of such practices are not well understood. Because these sources unavoidably involve what has been termed, in this chapter, 'internal processes', efforts to develop future school-leaders will need to focus much more directly on such processes. Chapters 4–7 describe what is presently known about these processes. Chapters 11 and 12 describe formal programs for developing such processes.

Finally, knowledge about school leadership at present reveals little or nothing about those transformational aspects of the role, identified in Chapter 1, as so important for leaders of future schools. While this may be due to inadequacies in the research base, there is little doubt, as well, that transformational leadership is poorly understood and rarely practiced. Developing the individual and organizational capacity for exercising transformational leadership is one of the most significant challenges in developing leaders for future schools.

Note

1　This chapter is based on a comprehensive review of literature by Leithwood, Begley and Cousins (1990).

Part 2

The Nature of Expert Leadership for Future Schools

Chapter 3

Envisioning Future Schools

The source of the authority of the practical intelligence ... is derived from some kind of overall vision of society. Every person with any function in society at all will have some kind of ideal vision of that society in the light of which he operates. One can hardly imagine a social worker going out to do case work without thinking of her as having, somewhere in her mind, a vision of a better, cleaner, healthier, more emotionally balanced city, as a kind of mental model inspiring the work she does. (Frye, 1988, p. 70)

While Northrop Frye is undoubtedly correct, not all mental images of an ideal tomorrow are created equal. What this means is nicely illustrated in Steven's (1986) study of the visions held by elementary principals who differed in their basic patterns or styles of practice, and their resulting effectiveness as described in Chapter 2. This study found that principals with more effective patterns or styles of practice had more extensive, detailed, and integrated visions than did principals with less effective styles. Furthermore, those with the most effective style (e.g., student-oriented, referred to as Style B in Chapter 2) had the strongest program-related visions and worked hardest and most persistently to change their schools in the direction of their visions. It is reasonable to infer from such results that the nature of principals' visions, as well as their efforts to implement those visions, help account for their impact on schools.

The Virtues of Vision

Predicting the future is a hazardous business, as our daily surprises about oil crises, political events in eastern Europe, holes in the ozone layer, and the like, attest. But so long as we aspire to some control over our own destiny, we have to continuously give it our best shot. Some aspects of our lives, in any event, can be shaped significantly by our aspirations, and the nature of schools is among them, to a point. No matter the type of organization (e.g., Morgan, 1989, Vail, 1989) or the conception of leadership (e.g., Bass, 1981, Chapter 1), a vision or picture of what the organization ought to be seems to be vital to success, especially during turbulent times. As one of the executives in Morgan's study noted:

> The world is such a changeable place that you need to have a well articulated long-term sense of where you're going, which gives you the base, the confidence to take on whatever adaptability issues come along without losing your sense of direction. You've got to respond to the issues of the moment without losing that long-term sense. (1989, p. 46)

Useful visions provide relatively precise guides to action and allow reasonably subtle discrepancies in need of attention to be detected in one's school. How, for example, can school-leaders interpret those aspects of a situation encountered in the schools which deserve their attention without a standard for comparison? The nature and size of the discrepancy between one's vision of 'what ought to be' and one's perception of 'what is' constitutes problem interpretation. Without a defensible standard for comparison one has to rely on others to tell them what issues are worth attention. Educational leaders use their vision of the healthy school much as a physician uses an understanding of the healthy, well-functioning body. With the vision or silhouette of excellence in mind, the school-leader assesses the organization. A defensible vision makes for responsible autonomy in a leader. It is also the basis for proactivity, for determining priorities about how to spend time now, for setting clear goals, and for other aspects of planning. Useful, defensible visions are the product of careful thought, systematic effort and continuous evaluation and refinement. They are not the fluffy products of armchair daydreaming which the term itself suggests and many current administrators seem to believe.

To be of greatest value in informing the work of school-leaders and their colleagues, a vision must be widely shared. Such sharing will usually be the product of much collective thought and discussion. That vision will also reflect unique aspects of the school and the community which it serves. This is not to say, however, that a vision is entirely context-bound or informed only by sources within the school's environment. As one among several other sources, research has an important role to play in identifying elements of a vision which warrant adoption across many schools. Results of research can also provide stimulating points of departure as school-leaders begin to work with their communities and professional colleagues to build a sense of direction. Broad but predictable social and professional trends are other sources useful in informing one's vision.

Developing a useful, defensible, shared vision in these terms, while critical to do, is not a simple business. It is a do-able business, nevertheless, although you may be doubtful about this point. Anticipating such doubt, the remainder of this section illustrates what we mean by broad social and professional trends and how they may be used in shaping a vision. We also demonstrate the uses that might be made of relevant research and what we mean by detail and precision in reference to a leader's vision. The product of our effort is one vision of future schools in which the horizon is about ten years from now. Other visions are possible, of course. Duke (1987) for example offers an alternative with aspects which are both similar to, and different from, what is described in this chapter.

Most of the differences are traceable to the use of different information, not surprisingly.

Illustrative Social Trends and How They Might Be Reflected in a Vision of Future Schools

Among the many social trends which may influence the nature of schools during the 1990s, five seem especially powerful and their effects predictable. One of these is a trend for the economies of most developed nations to continue to move rapidly from an agricultural and industrial base toward an information technology base (Hay and Roberts, 1989). This trend seems likely to increase the value attached by the public to education since specialized skills, especially amenable to schooling, are required in such economies. It also seems likely to create a need for schools to give much more serious efforts than in the past, for accomplishing a more ambitious and complex set of goals (e.g., higher order thinking skills) along with more flexible and efficient curricula and instruction for their achievement. The availability of information technology provides, as well, opportunities for greater organizational diversity in schools: for example, a division of instructional labour between teachers and computers; more site-based decision-making, made possible through ready access to information previously accessible only to those in the central office.

A second social trend of consequence for schools is a gradually aging population, a population with little vested interest in the education of youth but with quite direct interests in life-long learning opportunities for themselves. Schools wishing to respond to such interests will need to address a broader range of goals, a quite different set of goals than those appropriate for pre-adult clients. Also required will be more flexible, client-centered forms of instruction, and a willingness to collaborate with other education agencies in providing meaningful services.

Increasing cultural, religious, and ethnic diversity within communities is a third, well established trend likely to continue through the 1990s and to have profound effects on schools. Such diversity creates a more ambiguous context in which to decide on school goals and priorities. A broadened range of intellectual and non-intellectual goals will have to be considered by the school in response to a broader range of values and aspirations in the community. Changes in forms of education also seem warranted not only by such broadening of goals but also as a response to cultural norms which do not condone some of the behaviors associated with 'tried-and-true' forms of instruction in western society (e.g., public displays of knowledge, competition among individuals). Ethnic diversity also places pressure on personnel-selection criteria: the need for the ethnic composition of the teaching force to reflect that diversity, at least in some measure.

Increasing respect for the rights of individuals independent of income, class, ability, religion, age, race or sex is a fourth trend of consequence for future schools. This trend is being given considerable force not only through the courts but also through the efforts of many advocacy groups, and even through the changes to the constitution of some nations, Canada among them. This trend reinforces the legitimacy of equity as an educational goal, especially regarding equal access to knowledge, not just educational resources. Perhaps the main force of this trend is, and will continue to be, felt on instructional practices: teachers will need to master a larger, more flexible repertoire of strategies, and such practices as ability grouping, will come under irresistible criticism as discriminatory, however attached education professionals might be to such practices for their own reasons. Greater respect for individual rights is changing and will continue to change the ethnic and gender balance in positions of responsibility in schools; many more members of minority groups and women will assume such positions, shortly.

Finally, the gradual but dramatic shift underway for the past twenty years in the nature of families and their role in the education of youth will continue to create sometimes subtle but nevertheless quite compelling demands on schools. For example, James Coleman's (1983) concept of 'social capital' helps point out that what schools do best – provide students with intellectually demanding tasks, participation in which makes growth possible – depends on a stable, supportive family environment. Such an environment gives students the self-esteem and self-confidence to respond to such challenges, as they are intended. Yet, there has been a clear trend, likely to continue for some time, toward the destabilization of traditional family forms and the increase in proportion of new family structures. Many of these new structures do not provide the social capital for children that schools assume, as they attempt to carry out their role. A successful response by future schools to this change will include even greater attention to the socio-emotional needs of students and the provision of nurturance in a form not uncommon in many elementary schools, at present, but quite rare in most secondary schools.

Many more trends than the five discussed here will influence schools over the next ten years. But from just this small selection of trends, it is plausible to envision future schools, in sum: addressing a broader, more complex set of goals; using forms of instruction not much in evidence at present and possessing a larger repertoire of such strategies; and possibly serving a group of clients other than their traditional youthful clients. It also seems plausible to envision future schools with the technical resources to make a larger portion of their own decisions, in collaboration with other education agencies and with a professional staff more closely matching the gender and ethnic composition of the student population.

Illustrative Professional Trends and How They Might Be Reflected in the Vision

Schools, of course, have been immersed in efforts to change over the past decade in response to aspects of the social trends discussed above, as well as others. These efforts have kicked into play a number of movements, within the profession, which have sufficient momentum to be viewed as independent sources of influence on schools throughout this decade: school-leaders will need to at least consider what part, if any, these movements will play in the vision developed for their schools. McDonnell (1989) provides a useful, fourfold classification of these movements as they have been experienced in the United States. They include greater decentralization of authority and empowerment of teachers (a movement toward site-based management, also strongly advocated in the UK and Australia) and increased public accountability (experienced almost everywhere as evidenced by increased attention given to student testing and the establishment of 'benchmarks'). Additionally, there are substantial efforts being made to alter the content and process of classroom instruction and to strengthen the links between schools and their communities.

Unlike broad social trends, the implications for schools of these professional trends are obvious and quite direct. Depending on one's school setting, some of these trends already may have the weight of policy. For example, versions of site-based management are legislated in the UK and Australia, and a potentially empowering form of shared decision-making (staff collegial councils) is a requirement for all schools in the Canadian province of British Columbia. For most schools, however, significant portions of these professional trends remain optional, and school-leaders and their colleagues must consider whether or not to include them in their vision of the future school.

Incorporating Research Results into the Vision

Most research describes some aspect of the present or the past. One might well ask: 'How is that useful in formulating a vision for the future?' The most practical answer we have to this question (there are others: see Morgan, 1989, for example) depends on the acceptance of an intermediate term definition of the future, such as the ten-year horizon we have adopted. With such an horizon, it is reasonable to claim that research describing especially effective current practice is useful. By definition, such practices are found rarely and in those cases, usually only piecemeal. Implementing such practices, more or less comprehensively, in our future school would be an ambitious task to undertake in a ten-year time frame, especially as those practices are modified to reflect the broad social and professional trends referred to earlier. This line of reasoning assumes a gradual evolution of aspirations for schools (not the imposition of a radically new set) and an incremental approach to educational change.

In order to illustrate what the outcome would be of using a relevant body of research in formulating a vision of future schools, we reviewed twenty original studies of effective secondary schools. These studies were supplemented by several research reviews of effective elementary schools in order to identify possible differences between effective secondary and elementary schools. The twenty original studies were identified through a process of ERIC searches and bibliographic follow-up, and on prior knowledge of the authors, selected by using predetermined criteria.

In addition to school leadership, six categories of characteristics or dimensions within which secondary schools appear to vary in effectiveness were evident in the studies reviewed. They include the goals given priority by the school, the attributes and practices of teachers and school-leaders (omitted from discussion in this section, but discussed in subsequent chapters), the nature of school programs and classroom instruction, school policies and organizational features, school culture, and the nature of school-community relations. These categories of characteristics appear to have either direct and/or indirect influences on students' school experiences; their experiences, in turn, determine such outcomes of in-

Envisioning Future Schools

terest for students as academic achievement, types of attitudes and behaviors, such as vandalism, attendance, drop-out and the like.

Goals

Four studies[1] explicitly identified some aspect of the school's goals as an explanation of differences in secondary-school effectiveness. Such goals included both short and long-term outcomes considered important for students to achieve; they also included the conditions in the school that would be necessary to accomplish such outcomes. Exemplary secondary schools were characterized as having an unusually high degree of clarity about the purposes of schooling and the outcomes to be accomplished by students. These schools also emphasized cognitive learning goals as especially important, within the larger purpose of providing a basic high-school education to all students. Effective schools make their goals effective tools for decision-making: this was done by having written goal statements, using goals as the basis for communicating to others, insisting that priorities fit goals, and using data to monitor progress toward goals and to refine and redefine goals. Finally, such schools used their goals as a shared ideology to provide a web of identification and affiliation which inspired loyalty to the school among staff and students.

As helpful as these results might be in helping shape a school-leader's vision of the form and use of goals, they provide limited guidance in respect of the substance of such goals. The broad social and professional trends discussed above are helpful in this respect. In a nutshell, as Corbett, *et al.* (1990) suggest, schools of the future will need to be both excellent and equitable. And whereas such schools seem justified in continuing to emphasize cognitive learning goals, these will not be narrowly defined by the conventional content of academic disciplines or the basic intellectual skills measured by many current standardized tests. A helpful illustration of the substance of goals for future schools is provided in a selection of results from a series of working conferences we have held with cross sections of the public and profession over the past two years (Leithwood and Jantzi, 1989). Several broad goals, among many, emerging from these conferences about which there is much consensus were, for example:

- being able to reflect on one's actions and learn from such reflection
- being curious and actively attempting to make personal sense out of as much of one's world as possible
- being able to manage information; to locate, sort, organize and assimilate large bodies of information for the purpose of solving one's problems
- assisting in the clarification of core family values and acting in a manner consistent with such values (reinforces moral and ethical standards)
- being able to cope with stress in a healthful manner

One of the most noteworthy features of these examples is the press they create for future schools to consider how they might respond to the comprehensive, developmental needs of the student viewed in the several contexts of authentic life challenges; these include not only school and work but also family, community, and leisure contexts. One might well argue that future schools which were successful in addressing such a broad, complex array of goals would provide much more meaningful experiences for a larger proportion of their student–clients (perhaps especially the non-university bound student served particularly poorly by today's secondary schools).

Teachers

Nine studies[2] in our review of effective schools research identified qualities of teachers found in exemplary secondary schools. These qualities addressed four aspects of the teacher (several of which overlap with aspects addressed in a subsequent category labeled 'Programs and Instruction'): relevant personal qualities, view of a teacher's role, disposition toward students and disposition toward collaboration with other teachers.

With respect to relevant personal qualities, teachers in exemplary schools experienced high levels of job satisfaction and believed that they had employment status. These teachers also demonstrated highly developed verbal skills and had high attendance rates at school. Teachers in exemplary schools were dedicated to the profession of teaching and expressed an ongoing interest in professional self-improvement through taking courses, and the like. They accepted responsibility for a focus on student achievement, generally, fostering individual student growth, adapting school practices to meet individual student needs and for creating additional learning opportunities for students. Such teachers were willing to meet with students informally outside school hours and took initiative in developing new teaching programs. They also modeled what Rutter *et al.* (1979) refer to as 'mental and moral probity' (for example, being prepared for class, being punctual, not wasting time in class and rarely ending classes early). In exemplary secondary schools, teachers held high academic and behavioral expectations for students which they transmitted to students in a positive way. They were sensitive to the age of the students, the peer pressures, and social interests associated with adolescence (this was especially important for teachers in intermediate and junior high schools).

Teachers in exemplary schools were disposed toward collaboration with their colleagues and others. This collaboration was evident in shared efforts to design and prepare curricula, and participation in instructional improvement efforts, where they could learn from their colleagues. Collaborative attitudes were also demonstrated by these teachers, through a willingness in their own classrooms to adhere to the school curriculum agreed upon by the school staff. Mutual observation and critique of instructional practices was standard practice in these effective schools, as was participation with other teachers in setting and monitoring well defined standards for teaching. Teachers in these schools established good relationships with parents and they actively encouraged interaction between parents and themselves.

The results of the research concerning teachers in exemplary secondary schools is summed up well in Lightfoot's comment (1983, p. 342) that 'Good schools collect mostly good teachers and treat them like chosen people'. To these research-derived qualities of teachers for inclusion in a school-leader's vision, the five social trends argue, as well, for a larger repertoire of instructional skills, an issue explored in more depth in Chapter 7.

School Organizational Characteristics and Policies

Seven studies[3] identified school policies, affecting students and teachers as well as several other organizational features, as among the attributes of exemplary secondary schools.

With respect to students, exemplary secondary schools emphasized academic achievement through policies which reinforced high academic standards: they also enforced competency requirements. These schools minimized disruptive student behavior through the provision of simple, clear standards and rules for students, often established with student and parent participation, and by valuing and rewarding exemplary student behavior. Students' sense of affiliation with the school was increased through policies which ensured students' access to counselors, provided students with a pleasant, comfortable environment, and ample opportunities for students to take responsibility and participate in running the school. This is related to the need, suggested by changes in families, for schools to take on a more nurturing role with students.

Policies of exemplary secondary schools focused on acquiring experienced teachers (e.g., more than five years) and those with higher levels of attainment in their discipline, often with advanced degrees. Such policies also include a system for monitoring teacher performance, usually through regular reviews of such performance by a school administrator, and discussions with the teacher concerning the results of such reviews. Exemplary schools, this research suggests, have ways of explicitly recognizing teacher accomplishments. Staff stability is encouraged and resources are provided for ongoing staff development. Such activity tends to be more locally defined (as distinct from board or district defined) and more group-based (as distinct from whole staff based). Teachers are assisted in finding the kind of staff development which they think they need. Given the press toward greater instructional flexibility likely to be created by several of the social trends we have discussed (as well as one of the professional trends), staff development will take on ever increased importance through the decade. Policies in effective schools often provide teachers with access to discretionary funds to support their own improvement initiatives, a feature consistent with the initiative to further empower teachers. These policies also involve teachers in school-level policy decisions, often including, for example, the assignment of students to classes. Duke and Gansneder (1990) provide useful data on the complexities of implementing this policy in a way viewed as satisfactory by teachers.

Outside of policies focused specifically on students and teachers, exemplary secondary schools tend to be relatively small in terms of student enrollment. They are organized to make the best use of available time, including maximizing the use of hours in the school year, the design of a carefully structured school day, and flexibility for classroom-level decision-making within the day. Such schools have considerable school-level discretion for determining the means to be used in addressing problems of increasing academic performance. This is consistent with the professional trend toward decentralization. As McNeil's (1986) study points out, effective secondary schools are not primarily organized and managed to keep them running smoothly (although they do tend to run smoothly). Such schools are organized and managed to support the purposes of the curriculum and the requirements for instruction implied by the school's philosophy of education. Effective secondary schools have the support of their school boards or districts for their improvement initiatives.

Programs and Instruction

Thirteen[4] of the twenty studies in our review identified some aspect of programs and instruction responsible for the exceptional impact of effective secondary schools. For these purposes, the term 'program' included the curriculum content presented to students, the degree of choice among courses available to students, and the extent of 'articulation' among program components. As compared with typical or ineffective schools, the programs of exceptionally effective schools had a strong academic curriculum, requiring more advanced coursework and more effort from students. A rigorous core curriculum, with limited elective choices involving assigned homework, was also evident. These were core requirements within a 'rich' curriculum. The curriculum was carefully coordinated and organized, the result of a preoccupation with coherence and integrity.

The term 'instruction' encompassed the teachers' general orientations to classroom activity, the quality of specific teacher-student interaction, the use of time for instruction, and the approach to collecting and providing information about student progress. Exceptionally effective secondary schools were associated with carefully planned instruction: this included a limited focus within a single lesson, actively structured and directed classroom activities, establishment of a clear framework for pursuing sub-themes and small group or individual activities; emphasizing opportunities for competence and achievement; and provision of diverse experiences for students. Specific teacher-student interactions reflected defensible principles of learning. These included: clear communication of instructional goals to students, promotion of extensive interaction in class, and use of factual questions to establish a foundation followed by higher order questions requiring more interpretation, for example. Efforts in exemplary schools studied were also made to keep classroom discussion very concrete and to demonstrate the relevance of curriculum material to the everyday world of students.

In these effective schools, efficient use was made of instructional time in moving toward goals. This included: maintaining a fairly rapid pace often through teacher-directed forms of instruction, and minimizing time loss due to absenteeism, lateness and inattention. A more rigorous, disciplinary climate was established, as was frequent communication with students, either individually or on a whole-class basis. Systematic monitoring of student progress was common in these schools. This included: assessments of performance keyed to instructional objectives, emphasizing students' being on task, keeping written records, providing feedback to students, and rewarding students for significant achievement.

These results reflect a set of goals much narrower than one is likely to aspire to for future schools. Less conventional forms of instruction need to be incorporated in a school-leader's vision, forms of instruction which make greater use of other students and adults other than the teacher, as resources for learning.

School Culture, Ethos or Climate

Rossman, Corbett and Firestone (1985, p. 5) define culture as a 'unique set of core [norms], values and beliefs that are widely shared throughout the organization'. Rutter, *et al.* (1979, pp. 55–6) use the term 'ethos' in reference to 'a climate of expectations or modes of behaving' suggesting that, in many cases, individual actions are less important in their own right than in the accumulated impact they have on what it feels like to be a member of the school organization. Although an abstract dimension of schools, effective schools' research has given culture, ethos or climate prominence as an explanation for differences among schools. School culture is also an object for 'restructuring' in the profession on the grounds that teacher empowerment and more decentralized decision-making is not likely in the traditionally isolated culture of most schools (Feiman-Nemser and Flodden, 1986).

Results of our review of eleven studies[5] suggest that exemplary secondary schools are safe and orderly. Neither staff nor students are concerned about physical harm; the school is free of discipline and vandalism problems; and teachers understand and are not threatened by adolescents. The school refuses to condone or conceal indiscipline, and staff have what Lightfoot (1983, p. 342) refers to as a 'fearless, empathetic regard for students'. Cultures in exemplary schools are positive: there is less emphasis on punishment and critical control, and more attention to praise and student reward, especially with regards to their industry and exemplary behavior. Student self-control is encouraged, and both students and teachers take school seriously.

Teachers engage in precise, concrete talk about teaching practice and its improvement in exemplary schools, and specific support is provided for discussion of classroom practice. As already suggested, the shared technical cultures of exemplary schools are built on norms of collegiality, collaborative planning, and continuous improvement. The staff are cohesive and have a strong sense of community. Norms are established which contribute to the integration and cohesiveness of the student body; they may be done through collective events of various types that are directed so as to reinforce the purposes of the school (e.g., scholastic competition). There is reciprocity between and among staff and students. These cultures are also student centered. This is evident in much of what has been said about the school culture already. School-wide recognition of academic success is promoted.

School-Community Relationships

School-community relationships were identified, in three studies,[6] as an important discriminator among schools which varied in effectiveness. Unlike the case in elementary schools, such relationships were not with parents directly but were instead with non-parents who had a direct contribution to make to the school, and with the community at large. Effective secondary schools, it was reported, made effective use of such community resources as volunteers and student tutors. Solid working relationships were developed with local business and industry for career training, for example. Similar types of relationships were also evident with colleges and universities for assistance to academically talented students. These schools were responsive to their particular social and political milieux, and generated high levels of community support. These characteristics reflect quite literally the professional trends, discussed earlier, regarding school-community relations: they also reflect a concern for public accountability. We might add to what these schools are doing, the establishment of closer links with social service agencies in order better to provide the social capital that some changing family structures are not providing.

Elementary–Secondary School Differences

It has been suggested that effective secondary schools are likely to differ from effective elementary schools for a variety of reasons (Farrar, Neufeld and Miles, 1984, Firestone and Herriott, 1982). As compared with elementary schools, secondary schools are usually larger, have greater role differentiation, and pursue more diverse outcomes. This makes communication more difficult, complicates the process of arriving at a consensus about instructional goals, and reduces the possibility of principals exercising direct instructional leadership. Murphy and Hallinger (1985), however, argue that these differences are more apparent than real in terms of their consequences for effective schooling. As a way of inquiring about elementary-secondary school differences, the twenty secondary school studies were compared with five reviews of research on effective elementary schools (Cohen, 1982, Duckett, 1980), Edmonds, 1979, Mackenzie, 1983, Weil, *et al.*, 1984). This was a 'convenience' sample of reviews, for which no special justification is offered. Our analysis suggests that, as compared with effective elementary schools, effective secondary schools may:

- pursue a broader range of goals (providing a basic high-school education vs. basic skills, for example)
- be more concerned about developing a sense of community and affiliation within the school, and use goals, in part for that purpose
- attribute more importance to the job satisfaction, employment status, verbal skills, and attendance rates of teachers
- attribute more importance to such basic beliefs of school-leaders as viewing teachers as professionals
- require school-leaders to consider a broader array of factors in the school in order to exercise influence
- have to address problems related to size of staff and student body more explicitly
- require more school-level decision-making discretion
- expend more effort on the design of a program which is useful for all students and provides enough variety to address a more diverse set of needs
- have to promote and support more precise, concrete talk among teachers, concerning their classroom practices
- have less need for close parent involvement

In spite of such real or apparent differences, the comparative analysis lends support to at least some aspects of twenty-three of the thirty-four characteristics of effective secondary schools identified in the review of the twenty original empirical studies.

Conclusion

This review of research concerning six dimensions of effective schools illustrates how such evidence might be used to envision a future school. In the case of most dimensions, the research alone had to be supplemented with inferences drawn from one or more of our broad social trends. What is remarkable, however, is the extent to which the features of today's exemplary schools, reported in the research, incorporated features which anticipated many of the consequences for schools of those broad social trends which were considered. They also appear to have implemented a number of the professional trends being advocated for schools just now. These results, then, support our initial contention that research about exemplary practice in the present is a useful resource for envisioning future schools, assuming a not too distant horizon.

In sum, the chapter was designed to assist school-leaders in developing a defensible vision of future schools. At first blush, the attempt to offer this assistance (especially in such limited space) seems naively ambitious. There is, after all, a wealth of information, relevant to such a vision, to which we did not refer. What we hoped to accomplish was not a definitive vision for school-leaders. That is neither possible nor desirable. Rather, we wanted to demonstrate that there are specific sources of information to be used in developing a defensible vision. We also wanted to demonstrate that developing a defensible vision entails careful, systematic effort; some aspects of what makes a good school are sufficiently clear (from research evidence, for example) that they ought to be carefully considered in any vision; and in order to provide real guidance in future problem-solving, a vision must be quite detailed. A blurred vision offers little guidance for school-leaders and their colleagues.

Notes

1 Included were Huddle (1986), Lightfoot (1983), Ford Foundation (1984) and Lipsitz (1984).
2 See Huddle (1986), Murphy and Hallinger (1985), Roueche and Baker (1986), Lipsitz (1984), Rutter, *et al.* (1979), Ford Foundation (1984), Goodlad (1984), Madaus, Kellaghan and Rakow (1976), Lightfoot (1983).
3 Studies providing data concerning these issues included Harnisch (1987), Huddle (1986), Ford Foundation (1984), Lipsitz (1984), McNeil (1986), Goodlad (1984) and Rutter *et al.* (1979).
4 These studies included Lipsitz (1984), Roueche and Baker (1986), Huddle (1986), Lightfoot (1983), Coleman and Hoffer (1987), Keith and Page (1985), Arehart (1979), Goodlad (1984), Walberg and Shanahan (1983), Harnisch (1987), Murphy and Hallinger (1985), Morgan (1979), Frederick, *et al.* (1979).
5 See Lipsitz (1984), Roueche and Baker (1986), Huddle (1986), Murphy and Hallinger (1985), Goodlad (1984), Rossman, Corbett and Firestone (1985), Rutter, *et al.* (1979), Coleman and Hoffer (1987), Lightfoot (1983), Ford Foundation (1984), Gunn and Holdaway (1986).
6 See Huddle (1986), Ford Foundation (1984), Lipsitz (1984).

Chapter 4

Expert School Leadership on the High Ground and in the Swamp

> In the varied topography of professional practice, there is a high hard ground overlooking a swamp. On the high ground, manageable problems lend themselves to solution through the application of research-based theory and technique. In the swampy lowland, messy confusing problems defy technical solution. (Schön, 1987, p. 3)

In Chapter 1, we made a case for thinking about the leadership process as problem-solving. A problem, as Baird (1983) and others define it, has three ingredients: givens – the current fact or situation (e.g., this parent standing in my office complaining about his son's teacher); goals – different, more valued fact or situation (e.g., this same parent satisfied with his son's teacher and not standing in my office); and obstacles or constraints that must be overcome before the given state can change (e.g., the parent's perception of the unfairness of the teacher's grading practices). Research on problem-solving (e.g., Fredericksen, 1984, Shulman and Carey, 1984) has identified two sources of variation in the difficulty experienced by people in solving problems. One of these sources of variation is the clarity or extent of knowledge a person has about those three ingredients of a problem; the other is the specificity of the steps the person is able to identify in order to successfully overcome obstacles or constraints, and thereby transform the complaining parent into the satisfied parent.

When school-leaders are well informed about the givens in a problematic situation, clear about what goals, if accomplished, would solve the problem, and (perhaps through previous experiences with similar problems) have reliable procedures for overcoming obstacles, they are on what Schön (1983) refers to as the 'hard high ground'. But the ground on which school-leaders base their practices becomes increasingly swampy, as fewer and fewer of these conditions are met: the swamp is especially deep when one only vaguely understands the present situation, has no clear way of knowing what would be better, and lacks procedures for addressing the obstacles or constraints in the situation. The most predictable aspect of the future for school-leaders will be the continuing need to solve swampy problems.

This is our understanding of at least part of what Vail (1989) means in his reference to leaders of future organizations being 'in permanent white water' (a swamp with whitecaps!!). No matter how complex a problem might be, in an objective sense (e.g., technically difficult or fraught with interpersonal conflict), its 'swampiness' is a purely subjective matter. So, the more a person knows about how to solve any problem, the less swampy it becomes for that person. At first blush, then, it seems that given enough time and effort, we ought to be able to dramatically reduce the number of problems, faced by school-leaders, that are truly swampy. More research, better education of those entering the role, growing experience in the role, and ongoing professional development seem like obvious strategies to such an end. But this picture of a gradually draining swamp assumes both a static context, within which future school-leadership will be exercised, and an unchanging set of expectations for those exercising such leadership. No one in their right mind would bet on that assumption. Indeed, the nature and rate of change that can be anticipated in the future means that some of the problems, now on the high ground, will become largely irrelevant for tomorrow's school-leaders. This will be the case, for example, because of growing availability of 'user friendly' technical solutions (like, for example, constructing school timetables), because altered professional norms will support practices which, at present, remain tough problems to deal with in many schools (e.g., helping some teachers appreciate the value of genuine peer collaboration), as well as for many other reasons. Indeed, if predictions about exponential rates of change in the future prove to be true, then even a substantial increase in efforts to 'dehydrate' future school-leaders' problems may be accompanied by higher water levels in the swamp.

All of this is to say that expert school leadership will depend in the future, as it does now, on dealing effectively with both high ground and swampy problems. Chapters 5 and 6 describe the nature of such expertise. The next two sections of this chapter address three sets of questions, each with a concern about the implications for future school leadership:

- What basic characteristics of problems cause them to be considered, by current school-leaders, as high ground or swampy?
- What specific types of problems do school-leaders presently classify as high ground and swampy?
- How do school-leaders decide on the importance of a problem?

The primary data used to address the three sets of questions in the remainder of this chapter are drawn from five studies. Three of the studies were about how groups of expert and non-expert elementary principals (Study One: Leithwood and Stager, 1986), secondary principals (Study Two: Leithwood and Steinbach, 1990) and, for comparison purposes, superintendents/chief education officers (Study Three: Leithwood, 1988) classified and managed their problems. Two studies inquired about the nature of both elementary and secondary principals' problems, and the ratio of high ground to swampy problems (Study Four: Leithwood, Cousins and Smith, 1989/90, Study Five: Leithwood, 1990); these studies also examined the frequency of occurrence of problems over a school year.

What Makes a Problem Swampy for School-Leaders?

To this point, a swampy problem has been defined as one about which the solver possesses very little knowledge, regarding how to accomplish some valued goal.

We have also said that this is a highly subjective matter. One school-leader's quagmire may be another's dance floor. It depends on their existing knowledge, skills and dispositions – presumably a function of such things as previous experience with similar problems, relevant education and support. This is limited clarification, at best, of the meaning of a swampy problem, however. The question to be addressed in this section is: Given the unique demands and expectations of school-leaders, what causes them to classify a problem as difficult or swampy?

In Study Two (Leithwood and Steinbach, 1990), secondary principals, as a group, were readily able to indicate their criteria for classifying problems, but there was not much consensus among them. Impact on staff (the extent to which a problem affects individual staff) was the criteria identified by the largest number of principals. At least two principals, out of the eleven in this study, identified the remaining as: availability of clear procedures; number of people involved in a solution; the possibility of value conflicts arising; whether the solution would be acceptable to all (a 'win-win' solution); and whether those affected by the solution would accept it (be 'reasonable', even if the solution did not favor them). The extent to which the problem could be solved within the school, and therefore, be 'controlled' was also a basis for estimating problem difficulty. As one principal said:

> [easy problems] are in-house – we have control of the resources and the people being involved. It becomes more difficult as you move out [of the school].

Data from elementary principals in Study One was similar, in respect to three of the seven criteria: availability of clear procedures; impact on staff (essentially, problems affecting people directly and likely to have significant emotional content); and number of people required to solve the problem. On the other hand, CEOs in Study Three used all of the same criteria as secondary principals, in their estimates of problem difficulty. The extent of a problem's impact across the school or school system was a criterion associated with problem difficulty, by elementary principals and CEOs, but not secondary principals.

What are we to make of these data? Problems tend to be considered swampy by expert school-leaders, the more that they are primarily 'people problems', a result also evident in Goldman *et al.*'s (1990) study. Problems have this character, not only when they are directly about a person, as in the case, for example, of the performance of a teacher. They also have this character, as more people are required for a solution, as the particular people involved are viewed as inflexible – perhaps a function of significant value differences relevant to the problem, and as the problem or its solution impacts on increasing numbers of people. In contrast, problems are not seen to be swampy when there is a clear procedure available for solving it. Most of the time, such problems are relatively technical in nature and have been encountered routinely in the past. For example:

> [easy problems are] things like budget allocation in as much as I have done it for a long time. I know how to negotiate with the people who are responsible for the various accounts.

Such problems can also be solved by those within the organization, often those over whom the principal has some vested authority.

While the designation of a problem as swampy is, theoretically, a purely subjective matter, the common features of school-leaders' work (e.g., state, district and school contexts; see Goldman *et al.*, 1990) mean that many identify the same problems as swampy or not swampy. In our research, for example, a problem almost always designated as swampy by school-leaders, from among an array given to them, was the Principal-Entry problem:

> You have been assigned to a new position. The present principal, who is very highly regarded by staff, community, and students is being moved to a larger school after only two years in this present assignment. The school community (staff and parents) are very displeased that a new principal has been assigned. They feel that the board has not considered their wishes. How would you enter this situation?

But our setting-school-objectives problem was almost always considered to be a high ground problem:

> Your new school is one in which staff have never been involved in the setting of school objectives and are not apparently very interested in doing so. You have come to believe that it is a very important thing for staff to set school objectives and to evaluate them at the end of the year.

A comparison of these two problems illustrates, a bit further, the meaning of the results described to this point. The Principal-Entry Problem involves many people; there is the potential for value conflicts; emotions are intense; and the entering principal's reputation is on the line. Furthermore, one of the most prominent groups of people in the problem, parents, owe no bureaucratic allegiance to the school organization. Setting school objectives also involves the participation of many people, but it is the school staff who are involved. Most expert principals are also able to identify an array of well-developed procedures for solving this problem and have had experience in using one or more of these procedures at least several times.

In sum, then, the more that a problem involves people, and requires the cooperation and participation of increasing numbers of diverse people, the swampier it is likely to be for school-leaders. This, of course, places a high premium on the quality of one's interpersonal skills as a prerequisite for solving swampy problems in schools (the 'considerative' aspect of future school-leaders' practices discussed in Chapters 1 and 2).

What Specification Kinds of Problems Do School-Leaders Find Swampy and How Prevalent are They?

Even though swampy problems are, by definition, challenging to solve, much of their significance in the work of school-leaders depends on how often they are encountered. If swampy problems are infrequently experienced, one might argue that it is not especially crucial to devote much time or effort to further developing school-leaders' capacities for solving them as effectively as possible. Muddling through will do. But swampy problems are expensive to deal with: they require a lot of thought. And school-leaders do not have time to give a lot of ineffective and inefficient thought to many problems. So, what is the case? Are swampy problems a common occurrence or not, and, specifically, what are they?

Studies Four and Five (Leithwood, Cousins and Smith, 1989/90; Leithwood, 1990), including a total of twenty-six elementary and twenty-six secondary school-leaders, provide the only evidence that we are aware of concerning this question. So the answer must be considered tentative. Relevant parts of these studies documented the full array of problems reported by principals over an eight-month period, including the principals' designation of each problem, as either relatively routine or non-routine (swampy). These problems were organized into sixteen categories, frequencies of occurrence calculated and comparisons made between elementary and secondary schools, and routine and non-routine problems (Study Five results replicated those of Study Four almost exactly).

Four problem categories were reported much more frequently than the rest (these frequencies are drawn from Leithwood, Cousins and Smith (1989/90)

1. *Teachers (247 Problems)*

    1. Assignment of Teaching Duties
    2. Conflicts Among Teachers
    3. Conflicts Between Teachers/Students/Administration
    4. Curriculum Review, Development, Implementation
    5. Dereliction of Duty (reporting, deadlines, supervision)
    6. Dress Code
    7. Extra-Curricular
    8. Judgment of Teacher-Proposed Ideas
    9. Level of Competency
    10. New Teachers
    11. Personal Problems
    12. Professional Development
    13. Staff/Department Meetings
    14. Teacher Coverage
    15. Teacher Evaluation
    16. Teacher Exchange

2. *School Routines (138 Problems)*

    1. Assemblies
    2. Attendance
    3. Budget
    4. Commencement Planning
    5. Dances
    6. Drills and Routine For Students
    7. Feeder-School Visit
    8. Field Trips
    9. Fire Drills

10. Fund Raisers
11. Graduation Awards
12. Home Room Visits
13. IPRC (Individualized Program and Review Committee) and Special Education Meetings
14. Public Address Announcements Meeting
15. Re-timetabling of Classes
16. Registering Students
17. Report Cards
18. September Report
19. Student Council Meetings
20. Teacher Routines/Plans
21. Timetabling
22. University Night

3. Students (113 Problems)

1. Abuse
2. Adult Students
3. Attendance
4. Cafeteria
5. Commendation
6. Complaints
7. Discipline
8. Evaluation
9. Injuries
10. Placement
11. Special Requests
12. Student Council
13. Student Problems
14. Vandalism

·4. Parents (105 Problems)

1. Communication
2. Complaints
3. Parent Councils/Groups
4. Parents' Night
5. Parental Involvement in the School or lack thereof ...

As the specific problem labels within each of the four categories indicate fully, two-thirds of principals' problems (402) revolve around the internal workings of the school, its staff and clients. These are problems over which the principal has a fairly high degree of control. The remaining problems arise from aspects of the internal workings of the school which appear to require very infrequent attention by the principal (e.g., non-teaching staff, plant, special events). Requiring relatively infrequent attention by principals are problems arising from sources also external to the school. Consistent with evidence about external influences on principals, reported in Chapter 2, senior administrators (72) are the most frequently cited of these sources. They place accountability demands on principals, visit their schools, provide approval or non-approval of principals' initiatives, request attendance by principals at board meetings for a variety of purposes, and insist on adherence to system procedures. Trustees, the Ministry of Education, and outside agencies of several types (e.g., social-service groups, community-health groups) appear to impinge very little on principals' problem space.

Boyd and Crowson's (1981) review of research concluded that principals typically have an 'insider' focus, and spend the bulk of their time on organizational maintenance tasks and pupil-control tasks. Our evidence concerning the types of problems encountered by principals is consistent with only a part of this conclusion. Three of the four most frequently encountered categories of problems were found inside the school: teachers, school routines, and students. The fourth, parents, could also be viewed as an 'inside' problem category. If parents are so considered, 'outside' problems encountered by principals amounted to only about 19 percent of the total.

It is not difficult to understand the need for school principals (indeed middle managers in other organizations, as well) to have an 'insider focus'. This is why they were hired, one may argue. But is the focus of their work actually just maintenance and control? This question is best answered by examining specific subcategories of problems. Such problems do not suggest a necessary preoccupation with maintenance and pupil control. For example, the subcategory of 'teacher' problems entitled 'assignment of teaching duties' contained fifteen cited problems in Study Four (not shown in text). Several of these problems clearly were of a maintenance nature (e.g., plan for lunchroom supervision, finding supply teachers). But most could be plausibly linked to the school's instructional program (e.g., setting goals with teachers, reorganizing the grade 7 class, arranging more planning time for teachers). Over the total of 247 specific references in Study Four to 'teacher' problems, at least a majority had the potential for a direct impact on instruction. Further, 'student' problems were by no means limited to the control of students. The majority had some direct link to the likelihood of student growth: for example, incidences of child abuse, counseling adult students on diploma requirements, 'behavioral' student running away from school. A large minority of this category of problems did involve control: discipline, attendance, and the maintenance of order were examples. Our data suggesting that an 'insider' focus by school-leaders is likely, but that such a focus may well concern school improvement, not simply maintenance matters, is consistent with evidence from the work of effective principals, reported by Smith and Andrews (1989) and by Pavan and Reid (1990).

In terms of categories of problems experienced, there appeared to be few differences between elementary and secondary principals, with respect to non-routine problems. 'Student' problems were the sole exception to this result: elementary principals encountered over 50 percent more of such problems. Substantial differences were evident with respect to four categories of routine problems and in each case, elementary principals facing a greater number: approximately three times as many 'parent' problems, eight times more 'plant' problems, fourteen times more problems associated with other principals, and twice as many school-routine problems.

In line with earlier discussions of the criteria school-leaders use in determining problem difficulty, the incidence of non-routine problems is much higher in three of the four categories in which principals encounter most problems overall:

students (43 percent), teachers (17 percent), and parents (19 percent) – all 'people' problems. While problems related to school routines are frequently encountered by principals, their responses appear to be well rehearsed, requiring little conscious attention. Only three non-routine problems were reported in this category (these results conflict, to some extent, with data reported in Chapter 10, indicating that school-leaders do not feel well prepared to solve such problems).

Studies Four and Five (Leithwood, Cousins and Smith, 1989/90; Leithwood, 1990) also reported ratios of routine to non-routine problems in each of six problem categories. These ratios are a much better estimate of just how 'swampy' the problems, are in each category, for principals. At least this is the case where the data provided a sufficient sample of problems, for such estimates to be meaningful. 'Student' problems are clearly the most non-routine, in the minds of principals. Problems related to the school plant are the next most non-routine, but very few such problems were reported. Categories of problems including the community at large, the Ministry of Education, parents, teachers and vice-principals/department heads were similar in their ratio of routine to non-routine problems. There was about a five to one ratio of routine to non-routine problems encountered in these five categories, as well as in all sixteen problem categories combined.

Descriptions of the day-to-day activities of principals have pictured their jobs as hectic, fast-paced, characterized by brief encounters, and spontaneous face-to-face interactions (Willower and Kmetz, 1982, Martin and Willower, 1981, Wolcott, 1978, Morris, *et al.*, 1984). Such characterizations of what principals do, often leave the impression that their problems, while numerous, are largely routine. In contrast, our data suggest that experienced principals perceive a much higher proportion of their problems to have, at least, significant components which are non-routine (about one in five and considerably higher in the case of 'student' problems). Principals do not see themselves simply applying a well-rehearsed repertoire of solutions, over and over again, to the same problems – a technical view of their role. Rather, adaptation of old solutions to new contexts and circumstances, as well as fresh thinking about largely novel problems seem to describe better a significant proportion of the demands faced by principals.

This characterization is consistent with Schön's (1983) depiction of expert practice in other professional fields. It is also consistent with what we know about the number of reforms, new expectations, and shifting environments schools now face. Furthermore, the willingness and ability of principals to see novelty in problems which have a familiar cast appear to be important features of expert school-leader problem-solving. For example, in comparing a sample of non-expert and expert principals, Leithwood and Stager (1989) found that non-expert principals were much more likely to become hostages to their existing knowledge and experience; they were unable, as a result, to recognize new features of a problem that required special attention if the problem was to be adequately resolved. Expert principals were quick to see and to act on such features.

Studies reviewed in Chapter 2 suggested that principals perceive senior administrators not only as a significant source of problems, but as an impediment to, rather than a resource for, their school-improvement efforts. For example, Crowson and Morris (1985) found that from a third to a half of Chicago principals' school-site activity was governed by what they called 'hierarchical controls'. Principals, in Leithwood and Montgomery's (1984) study, reported that the major hurdles they faced in improving their schools were: hierarchical structures which made change difficult, excessively rigid and time-consuming district policies and procedures, provision of inadequate resources, and the conservative stance of central administrators toward school-initiated change. Similarly, Duke's (1988) inquiry about why principals quit their jobs suggested five sources of job dissatisfaction, three of which were associated with the work of senior administrators.

Available evidence, although quite limited, appears to reinforce the claim that school-leaders often view the work of senior administrators as less than helpful. Senior administrators were viewed by school-leaders in Studies Four and Five as the greatest source of problems outside the school (about 13 percent of the total). Yet, less than 10 percent of the problems identified were considered to be non-routine by school-leaders, and even these included a number with a clear maintenance focus. Problems one might have expected school-leaders to view as non-routine, such as development of a professional growth plan, were not. This suggests that at least some procedures characteristically relied on by senior administrators as change strategies may turn out to be relatively benign as they are implemented.

In brief, the limited evidence which is available suggests that a surprisingly high proportion of school-leaders' problems are non-routine – a higher ratio for secondary than elementary leaders. Most of these are 'people' problems, more specifically people within the school. The most noteable exception to the 'insider' focus concerns problems related to district administrators.

How Do School-Leaders Decide on the Importance of a Problem?

Time, according to most school staffs, is the scarcest of all the resources which they need. And since (like land) no one is making any more of it these days, decisions school-leaders make about how to allocate their time centrally, affect the contribution they are able to make to their schools. No school-leader has enough time to address carefully all the problems encountered in the course of a day. Variations, among school-leaders, in their ability to pick the 'right' problems to address seriously, the 'right' problems to ignore, and the 'right' problems to pass over lightly, account for much of the variation in their effectiveness. Evidence regarding this aspect of school-leaders' problem-solving was provided by Studies One and Two (Leithwood and Stager, 1986; Leithwood and Steinbach, 1990).

Results of these studies suggest, first of all, that the most direct response to this question of prioritizing for non-expert school-leaders was that they don't. That is, moderately effective school-leaders appear not to have an explicit process for deciding which to address (except the order in which problems are encountered). As one such person said, when asked about his way of prioritizing problems:

> To be honest with you, I really don't. I don't think of things and try to put them in slots. I try to deal with a problem when it comes and I don't

believe in delaying. If somebody is really upset about something, I want to know right then and there, I don't want to leave it for half an hour, or go home and think about it.

In contrast, expert school-leaders quite consciously use an explicit strategy (other than order of encounter) for sorting, in their daily problem-solving. For example:

Yes, I do. I'm fairly conscious of that ... I have a VP in the school and she knows where I'm coming from, and I ask her to help keep me on task. Last night at the divisional meeting we were reviewing our report cards. I outlined some of the modifications we have made ... and that was strictly a 'review-tell' decision. Now I then moved into an area of evaluation ... [cites an example of problem and process used] ... That was getting into a somewhat of a 'sharing' but it was kind of mixed because I was laying on what I think is somewhat of a base from which to work.

Beyond the presence or absence of an explicit problem-sorting strategy, expert school-leaders consider a number of other criteria when assessing the priority a problem ought to get for the time available. Some of those who sort problems according to who will be involved in them do such sorting according to organizational groups (e.g., 'file it for the lead-teacher meeting', 'file it for the staff meeting'); others sorted in terms of type of decision (e.g., 'tell' vs. 'sell', vs. 'share'), role responsibilities (e.g., a 'teacher-owned' problem), or numbers involved (e.g., joint problem vs. individual problem). The main point seems to be that these school-leaders have some way of consciously discriminating among problems and that they consistently apply this to assist in their problem management. Their moderately effective counterparts do not.

Most school-leaders are concerned about student and staff needs, and feel overburdened with paperwork, identifying this as something preventing them from spending as much time as they would like on other priorities. Expert school-leaders tend to award priorities to problems impacting on the school program and on overall school directions (without ignoring the problems of individuals). When asked about problems which he prioritized, a participant in Study Two said:

ones that are going to have great impact on people, in terms of cooperation. A problem that impacts on one person versus one that impacts on the whole school, I see quite a difference in approach to that, in terms of time and the amount of communication involved because you're dealing with so many people.

Non-experts, on the relatively infrequent occasions when they establish priorities among problems, tended to do so on the basis of which group of people is involved. As an example of this, one stated:

any problem that is going to affect the kids get priority. Then, after that, if it affects staff ... and then head office gets to the bottom, unless head office is saying 'Get the report in by three days time!'

Some non-experts also set priorities in terms of deadlines, order of arrival, or amount of time required for solution. One moderately effective school-leader in Study Two said: 'No, I can't say that I have any way of deciding what gets done first.'

As compared with non-experts, experts have more deliberate strategies for managing their time and for ensuring that time is available for high-priority problems. For example:

> I have to come in about 7:15 to deal with my items and there is a chunk of the day that I can also work on my items once the programs are started.

However, these strategies of experts extend beyond daily time-management routines. One expert elementary school-leader described the importance of predicting what the problems will be and thus preventing their occurrence. He noted that many 'crises' are the result of not being prepared:

> when that happens, you can find that you are spending most of your time [during a term] dealing with it because usually if one thing has gotten out of whack, so has another ... Usually during that time, while you're kicking yourself, you're saying 'That's not going to happen again next term!' You are preparing yourself and you are predicting.

This approach to time management may also be viewed as a problem-prevention strategy. Differences between non-experts and experts in problem-prevention strategies such as these are pronounced. Much more than the non-experts, experts are explicitly concerned with preventing unwanted problems from arising in the first place, and have more strategies to do so. For example, they are out of their offices, around the school and in classrooms regularly and frequently; this allows them to detect the early signs of discipline problems, instructional problems and the like. They attempt to focus staff on program initiatives that are exciting and absorbing, thereby reducing the likelihood of 'staff morale' problems. Most of these experts, furthermore, are quite aware that developing excellent programs and instruction not only contributes to student growth, but also prevents many parental complaints from arising.

Summary and Implications

Summary

We view the generic process of school leadership as problem-solving where the notion of a 'problem' is free of the negative connotations with which it is often associated in everyday talk. For our purposes, a problem is any challenge or task or job to be done which requires thought (conscious or unconscious) and some type of action. This chapter has distinguished between two types of basic problems facing school-leaders labeled, metaphorically, 'high ground' problems and 'swampy' problems. High ground problems are those about which a school-leader possesses a considerable amount of relevant knowledge, and probably has had considerable previous experience. Because of this background, the school-leader's response may be reliably effective, relatively smooth, largely automatic, and consume very little conscious, thoughtful effort. In contrast, problems are considered to be swampy when one possesses little relevant knowledge and probably has little previous experience in resolving at least some non-trivial aspect of the problem. Problems of this sort require the invention of responses which may need to be fine tuned, in process. Above all, such problems demand considerable thought.

The distinction between high ground and swampy problems is one of degree not of kind: more like taking a humidity reading than sorting into two piles. Nevertheless, the distinction proves to be quite useful in better understanding expert school leadership. Furthermore, the distinction is entirely a subjective matter. The existing knowledge, skills, and dispositions of the individual school-leader will determine the degree of swampiness of a given problem. And it is because increases in the individual school-leader's repertoire change the humidity reading of a problem, that swampy problems are eventually allowed to dry out.

Notwithstanding the subjective nature of these problem designations, school-leaders' experiences and resulting repertoires share common features. This explains why the research reported in this chapter found similarities in the types of problems considered by school-leaders to be high ground and swampy. Problems were considered swampy when they involved many people, especially including people outside the school whose responses could not be controlled in any systematic way. Problems were thought of as high ground when they were of a more technical nature, where a well rehearsed procedure for solving was available.

The chapter also examined evidence which suggests that swampy problems are a surprisingly high proportion of the problems encountered by school-leaders; the proportion may be as high as one in five for secondary school-leaders and only slightly lower for those in elementary schools.

Implications

Evidence reviewed in this chapter has at least six implications for developing expert leadership for future schools. First, we interpret the evidence about the nature of school-leaders' problems to suggest that the 'naturally' occurring problems encountered by school-leaders provide them with ample opportunities for exercising leadership. But this leadership is not often the type that comes to mind when the term 'instructional leadership' is used; the term implies direct and pervasive interactions with teachers about their teaching strategies. Our data suggest that, normally, expert school-leaders influence instruction by establishing the conditions within which such instruction occurs. In our view, this is especially important work for future school-leaders if the teaching profession continues its current trend toward accepting more responsibility for instructional improvement. Creating conditions to enhance the instructional improvement efforts of teachers is something school-leaders in positions of formal authority are well situated for. (Chapter 9 elaborates on the importance of school culture, as one 'condition' which critically frames the instructional practices of teachers and which can be significantly shaped by school-leaders.)

Under circumstances of increased teacher responsibility for instructional improvement, there will be less and less need to assume that unless school-leaders are constantly in classrooms observing instruction, they have little effect on the quality of education in their schools. School-leaders, in the future, will be confronted, as they are now, with literally hundreds of small, spontaneously occurring leadership opportunities (problems to be solved). The key to expert leadership will be to have these opportunities accumulate in a consistent and desired direction. Many current school-leaders are unable to develop such consistency, most likely, we believe, because they do not have a set of goals, values, and vision for their staffs and schools, clearly formulated, at least in their own minds. This further reinforces the importance for future school-leaders of developing a widely shared, defensible vision, as we said in Chapter 3.

A second implication for developing future school-leaders, emerges from data concerning the proportion of non-routine to routine problems experienced by school-leaders. There is a large enough proportion of school-leaders' non-routine problems to suggest that experiences which are effective in improving the capacity to solve such problems would be very useful. There is, as yet, little attempt to focus school-leader development explicitly on such capacity, and little guidance about the nature of experiences that would be suitable. This is an important area taken up much more carefully in Chapter 12.

Third, our results also argue strongly for the development of a better understanding of how the work of district leaders can foster development of expert school leadership. The recent focus on effective schools has often created the impression that the larger organizational context in which schools function is irrelevant to their decisions. But evidence reviewed in this chapter supports reviews of recent multi-level research (Leithwood and Jantzi, 1989) suggesting an urgent need to better understand how school districts and senior administrators can best facilitate the work of schools and their leaders. This matter is addressed directly in Chapter 15.

Fourth, the secondary as compared with elementary-school administrative context that emerges from this study is one which is marginally less fast-paced, with increased opportunities, and a greater need to focus one's energies on a larger proportion of non-routine problems. At the same time, the role seems likely to demand much more systematic and sustained attention to the development of staff, such as department heads, who mediate principals' relations with teachers and students. Without such attention, it is easy to imagine the secondary principals' influence on students to be undetectable. Our own informal but substantial experience suggests, however, that a great many secondary principals feel quite uncertain about how to proceed with such staff development. The development of specific, credible advice on this matter would be very helpful. But such advice requires, as a prerequisite, a much better understanding of the secondary department-head's role than is presently available.

Two final implications for developing future school-leaders are evident in the research reviewed in this chapter. It will be important to help such leaders acquire defensible procedures for setting priorities among their problems, and to work especially well with many different types and groups of people.

Chapter 5

Expert School Leadership on the High Ground

Expert school leadership on the high ground depends upon the application of significant amounts of knowledge relevant to the problem area, through the skillful use of procedures capable of reliably accomplishing their purposes. Expertise in most fields of endeavor is typically associated with increases in the repertoire of knowledge and techniques that make smooth, effortless responses to high ground problems possible. As Bloom (1985) and others have pointed out, mastery of such responses in complex areas of human functioning (e.g., music, sport, medicine, law) typically require at least a decade of devoted effort. We assume that comparable effort is required before 'virtuoso' school-leadership performance on the high ground is likely. Of course, some of this preparation usually does, and should take place before entry into a formal school-leadership position.

The theoretical orientation that guided research on which this chapter is based (as well as Chapter 6) is approximately similar to the orientation used in many studies of problem-solving in other fields of endeavor. This is an 'information-processing' orientation which explains how the individual mind functions in response to a problem and why some peoples' responses seem more expert than others. According to this orientation, individuals initiate the sort of thinking normally called problem-solving when they are motivated to accomplish a goal which they value – like implementing a new program in their school – but have not achieved. To move toward that goal, they search their memory for a procedure or routine that informs them about what to do. From this perspective, the major resource available to problem solvers is their existing stock of knowledge, skills and dispositions. In very general terms, it is the process of searching through, selecting, reorganizing, reinterpreting, often adding to, and then applying this existing stock of knowledge, skills and dispositions that we call problem-solving.

Studies of problem-solving, comparing novices and experts from fields other than school leadership, have identified at least seven differences between them. Experts, as compared with novices:

- are better able to regulate their own problem-solving processes (Berliner, 1986): this control appears to be what Schön (1983) refers to as 'reflecting-in-action' and 'reflecting-on-action'

- possess more problem-relevant information (Berliner, 1986, Norris, 1985) and have it stored in memory in a better organized, more richly linked manner, thereby increasing its accessibility and extending its application (Bereiter and Scardamalia, 1986)
- represent problems using more abstract categories (as opposed to more superficial features of the problem) with reference to more basic principles (Berliner, 1986, Chi, Feltovich and Glaser, 1981, Voss *et al.*, 1983); they also have better and faster pattern-recognition skills (Bereiter and Scardamalia, 1986, Berliner, 1986)
- identify and possess more complex goals for problem-solving, and goals related to action plans (Bereiter and Scardamalia, 1986, Berliner, 1986)
- spend more time at the beginning of problem-solving, planning their initial overall strategies; also, they are more flexible, opportunistic planners during problem-solving, and are able to use a greater variety of approaches to a solution (Berliner, 1986, Norris, 1985)
- have developed 'automatic' responses to many recurring sequences of problem-solving activity (Norris, 1985)
- are more sensitive to the real requirements for solving the problem, and social contexts within which problems are to be solved (Berliner, 1986)

At the time the research reported in this book was undertaken, these differences between experts and novices, which had been the product of studies in many areas of activity, were of unknown relevance to school-leadership problem-solving. This deficiency gave rise to our research.

In order to describe how expert school-leaders solve problems on the high ground, we draw on a series of related studies including both systematic literature reviews[1] and original empirical inquiries.[2] The three literature reviews have been summarized and updated in Chapter 2 of this volume and need not be described in further detail here. Suffice to say that these reviews encompassed a total of 135 studies, empirical and case-studies, conducted by other researchers between 1974 and 1988, which provided evidence about aspects of school leadership. Most of these original studies provided information (from a variety of perspectives) about either non-expert (typical) or expert (highly effective) school-leadership practices in dealing with problems on the high ground. These studies, however, do not recognize the distinction we consider extremely important, in this book, between high ground and swampy problems.

Our own empirical research relevant to this chapter included a sequence of diverse data-collection procedures aimed at answering five questions. The first question was: What 'dimensions' or 'categories' would serve to organize descriptions of variations in the expertise of school-leaders' problem-solving on the high ground? Intensive interviews with a random sample of two dozen elementary-school principals provided the data for answering this question. Given such dimensions or categories (e.g., decision-making), the second question asked about the nature of expert, high ground problem-solving within each dimension. Opinion data from samples of principals, teachers, department heads and central office staff were collected to assist in answering this question. These data were integrated with relevant findings from the literature reviews by a working group of researchers and practitioners from a variety of roles.

The third question of interest concerned alternative approaches to high ground problem-solving which might vary in their degree of expertness. Methods used to answer this question were similar to those used to answer the previous question. Results were described as a 'profile of growth' (four levels) in school-leaders' expertise on the high ground. Four separate studies, each using quite different methods, were then conducted to verify the claim that these alternative approaches to high ground problem-solving (our fourth question) differed in their effectiveness, as suggested by the profile. Interview techniques were then used to collect data from sixty principals in order to answer our final question about similarities and differences in the high ground problem-solving of elementary and secondary school-leaders.

The general pattern of results from this series of studies appears to be quite robust. Other independent research efforts with similar intents have produced remarkably similar, although usually less detailed results (e.g., Hall *et al.*, 1984, Blumberg and Greenfield, 1980, Salley *et al.*, 1978, Dwyer *et al.*, 1984, Heck, Larsen and Marcoulides, 1990). Direct efforts by others to confirm claims from our research have generally been supportive (e.g., Trider, 1986).

Components of School-Leaders' Problem-Solving on the High Ground

Four components or dimensions of problem-solving appear to encompass a high proportion of differences in expertise among school-leaders on the high ground. These include:

Goals: the long term, internalized aspirations held by school-leaders which form the basis for their decisions and actions; such goals might be derived from a school-leader's vision

Factors: those aspects of the school which are experienced directly by students, that significantly influence what they learn, and that can be influenced by school-leaders

Strategies: clusters of related actions or procedures used by school-leaders to influence factors

Decision-making: processes used to identify and choose from alternative goals, factors, and strategies

These categories of high ground problem-solving processes emerged from our own research data in a 'grounded' or quite natural way. That is, in the early stages of our research we clustered apparently similar types of information about how school-leaders solved high ground problems with these categories as the result. After the fact, however, there are good reasons why these categories ought to have emerged as they did. Other research indicates that problems are increasingly high ground in nature with the increased availability of significant amounts of knowledge relevant to the 'domain' or the problem area. On these grounds, it is reasonable that the 'Factors' component would turn out to account for considerable variation in school-leaders' expertise. This component encompasses the school-leader's knowledge about curriculum, instruction, and other relevant aspects of the school's educational program, broadly conceived.

It is also evident from literature discussed previously that the availability of reliable procedures for solving problems (transforming the 'givens' in the problem situation to the 'goals') helps reduce the swampiness of a problem. For this reason, school-leaders' increasing mastery of the techniques described as 'Strategies' allows them to demonstrate increasing degrees of expertise on the high ground. Finally, the 'Decision-making' component acknowledges that high ground problem-solving demands less novelty and less 'mindfulness' than problem-solving in the swamp, as will be examined in Chapter 6. Indeed some frequently encountered high ground problems may require no conscious thought at all. Others require choices to be made from known alternatives. But as long as these known alternatives are a sufficient response, the problem remains on the high ground and decision-making captures the type of thinking required by the problem. The 'Goals' component includes processes that are relevant to both high ground and swampy problems.

Table 5.1 summarizes the results of our research describing four levels of school-leader expertise in solving high ground problems. These levels of expertise, described within the four components of our high ground problem-solving model, have been given labels. The labels (systematic problem solver, level 4; program manager, level 3; humanitarian, level 2; building manager, level 1) attempt to capture differences in the customary responses of school-leaders to high ground problems. Higher levels of expertise represent an accumulation of skills, knowledge, and attitudes from lower levels on the part of the school-leader, as well as some significant shifts in the nature of beliefs. School-leaders at higher levels continue to engage in many processes evident at lower levels but such processes are usually parts of a more extensive repertoire, rather than the whole repertoire.

Before describing the contents of what we refer to as the 'Principal Profile', several indirect but important findings should be noted. First, most school-leaders about whom data have been collected varied, to some degree, in the level of their expertise across the dimensions and subdimensions of the profile. Second, only a very small proportion of the school-leaders involved in our studies worked predominantly at the highest level described in the profile (about 10 percent, based on data from about 200 principals across six school systems). Third, most school systems studied considered the lowest level in the profile to describe minimally acceptable, rather than unacceptable, principal behavior. Finally, the profile focuses on processes that seem to be largely acquirable, given adequate school-district support of the type discussed in Chapter 15.

Subsequent sections of this chapter describe variations in high ground problem-solving expertise[3] comparing primarily the highest and lowest levels of expertise captured by our research. Much fuller descriptions are provided in Leithwood and Montgomery (1986) for elementary principals, and Leithwood (1986) for secondary principals. The relatively modest differences found between elementary and secondary school-leaders are left to the end of the chapter for description.

Goals

Virtually no conflict exists within current research, our own or others, regarding the types of goals and goal-related processes associated with high ground expertise. Variations in expertise can be described in terms of the nature, sources, and uses of goals.

Nature of goals

Highly expert (Level 4) school-leaders had an implicit or explicit philosophy of education including an image of what it means to be educated. This image was consistent with the values of the larger public served by the school and was likely to encompass student knowledge and skill, as well as attitudes and values. All categories of outcomes were considered important by these school-leaders. With this comprehensive set of student outcomes as a frame of reference, experts' goals were to provide the best education and best experiences possible for students served by the school. For example:

> For a K–6 [kindergarten to Grade 6] school, I would like to know that when children leave us they are reliable, independent, productive learners, and in terms of problems that are going to come up, they can solve problems.

Such experiences tended to extend beyond the formal instructional setting. Because definitions of the educated person evolve with time, experts were knowledgeable about changes relevant to goals for students, and receptive to changes that might have helped to achieve such goals.

In contrast to experts, non-experts (Level 1) believed that teachers teach and the principal runs the school. As one principal commented:

> I have a really good staff. They know more about their subject matter than me. So, basically, I stay out of their way and let them teach and spend my time making sure the school runs smoothly.

Maintaining a smooth-running ship was their main goal, bringing with it a dominant concern for administrative logistics. While these principals sometimes justified their focus on the grounds that students and teachers required a tranquil environment in which to work, running a smooth ship had become an end in its own right. Change was a source of annoyance to these principals since it challenged the maintenance of established rules and routines.

As the nature of school-leaders' goals grew in adequacy, their goals became increasingly based on a view of the educated person, increasingly consistent with those of the larger school community, and increasingly open to change, in the face of reasonable evidence of the need to change.

Sources of goals

School-leaders differed about the sources from which their goals were derived. As expertise increased, the sources from which their goals were selected became increasingly public in origin and greater in number. Experts systematically selected their goals from those espoused for students by agencies of the state (e.g., state education department or ministry of education), the local school board, and the perceived needs of the community and students served by the school. Because the least expert principals valued running a smooth ship

Table 5.1: *Expert school-leaders' problem-solving on the high ground: A summary of levels*

Level	Problem-Solving Components			
	Goals	Factors	Strategies	Decision-making
4 (High) Systematic Problem Solver	Selected from multiple public sources Highly ambitious for all students Transformed into short-term goals for planning Used to actively increase consistency among staff in directions they pursue	Attempts to influence all factors bearing on students Expectations within factors are specific Expectations derived from research and professional judgment	Uses a wide variety of strategies Criteria for choice include goals, factors, context, and perceived obstacles Makes extensive use of strategies to achieve	Skilled in use of multiple forms; matches forms to setting and works toward high levels of participation Decision processes oriented toward goals of education, based on information from personal, professional and research sources Anticipates, initiates, and monitors decision processes
3 Program Manager	Selected from several sources, some of which are public Particular focus on exceptional students Encourages staff to use goals for planning Conveys goals when requested or as particular need arises	Attempts to influence factors bearing on the school program Expectations within factors are specific Expectations are derived from personal and staff experiences, and occasionally from research	Relies on limited number of established, well-tested strategies Choice based on student needs (especially special students), desire to be fair and consistent, concern to manage time effectively Uses factor-specific strategies that are derived largely from personal experience and system direction	Skilled in use of several forms: selects form based on urgency and desire to involve staff Decision processes oriented toward school's program based on information from personal and professional sources Anticipates most decisions and monitors decision process

	Goals	Factors	Strategies	Decision-making
2 Humanitarian	Derived from belief in the importance of interpersonal relations to effective school = happy school Goals may be ambitious but limited in focus Goals not systematically used for planning Conveys goals to others if requested	Attempts to influence factors bearing on interpersonal relations Expectations within factors are ambitious but vague Expectations are mostly derived from personal experiences and beliefs	Chooses strategies which focus on interpersonal relationships Choice based on view of good school environment view of own responsibilities and desire to make jobs of staff easier Makes little use of systematic factor-specific strategies	Uses primarily participatory forms of decision-making based on a strong motivation to involve staff so they will be happy Tends to be proactive concerning decisions affecting school climate but largely reactive in all other areas unless required to act
1 (Low) Building Manager	Derived from personal needs Focus on school administration rather than students Pursuit of instructional goals considered to be responsibility of staff, not principal Conveys goals to others if requested	Attempts to influence bearing on school appearance and day-to-day-operations (mostly non-classroom factors) Expectations within factors are vague Expectations are derived from personal experiences	Chooses strategies based on personal need to maintain administrative control and remain un-involved in classroom Strategies mostly limited to use of vested authority and assist staff with routine tasks Attends to factor-specific strategies in a superficial way, if required to do so	Uses primarily autocratic forms of decision-making Decision processes oriented toward smooth school administration based on personal sources of information Decision processes are re-active, inconsistent and rarely monitored

(administratively), their goals were derived from a sense of the administrative tasks requiring attention in order for this to be achieved. Goals did not often spring from curricular, instructional, or interpersonal considerations.

Uses of goals

Internalized goals serve as a potential focus for school-leaders in planning their actions, and as a source of criteria for deciding what those actions will be. Research results suggested that as school-leaders increased in their expertise, there was greater congruence between their espoused goals for school improvement, and their planning and decision-making. Less expert school-leaders sometimes espoused goals very similar to those of their highly expert colleagues, but seemed to ignore them in practice.

In addition to these personal uses for goals, highly expert school-leaders sought out opportunities to clarify goals with staff, students, parents, and other relevant members of the school community. They worked toward consensus about these goals and actively encouraged their use in departmental and divisional planning. While those displaying non-expert forms of problem-solving sometimes included such clarification of goals, it was common for these school-leaders to simply assume staff knowledge and agreement. One principal said simply, 'I'm not very talky about these things'.

Factors

In order to accomplish their chosen goals, all school-leaders select for attention aspects of the school – or factors – which, they believe, contribute directly to such goals. The task for the school-leader, then, is to determine what the characteristics of that factor need to be in order to help achieve their goal(s), and work toward producing those characteristics. Our research identified eighteen factors which were attended to by school-leaders. Of these, ten appeared to bear directly on students' classroom experiences, largely through the teacher.

- which teacher teaches which students
- the objectives or outcomes teachers work toward with students, including the emphasis teachers place on different types of objectives
- teaching strategies, including the types of learning activities these strategies are designed to provide for students
- the types and amount of material and resources available, and the nature and degree of their use
- the ways in which teachers assess, record, and report student performance and experience
- the way in which time is allocated and the strategies teachers use to get (and keep) students focused on the learning task, including student discipline and control
- the subject matter, themes, or topics encountered by students in their programs
- the organization and appearance of the physical environment of the classroom

- the nature of the relationships between students, and between the teacher and students in the classroom
- the nature and degree of integration among curricular objectives within, and across, programs and grades

A second cluster of factors considered by expert school-leaders were thought to affect the experiences of students while in the school but outside the classroom:

- the functions, assignments, and roles of people in the school and classroom (including decisions about which teachers teach what grades and subjects; the role of the psychologist, the janitor, etc.)
- the form and substance of communications and relationships with the community
- the nature and degree of organized, out-of-classroom experiences for the students
- the adult-role models provided by staff as individuals, and as they interacted with one another; the form and substance of communications among staff
- the form and substance of communications and relationships with out-of-school, school-system staff
- the conduct of students while the school was responsible for them
- the nature of the relationships teachers developed with students on the playground, in the halls, and the like, and the role model provided by teachers in these relationships

Variations in principal expertise concerning factors were a function of the factors principals selected for attention, and the source and nature of expectations held for these factors.

Factors of most concern
As school-leaders increased in expertise, the factors they attempted to influence increased in number and changed in focus. To a predominant concern for factors bearing on school appearance, and the day-to-day operations of the school (Level 1, building manager), especially outside the classroom (e.g., student behavior, material and physical resources) was added a concern for interpersonal factors (Level 2, the humanitarian). These, in turn, were subsumed, but not replaced, by attention to program-related factors, such as program objectives, and use of time and its management (Level 3, the program manager). Those school-leaders with greatest expertise (Level 4, systematic problem solver) paid attention to all factors, eventually. This pattern of growth toward attention to all factors seemed to be directly related to, and perhaps explained by, school-leaders' goals. The more closely linked to school improvement such goals became, the greater the likelihood that factors selected for attention included those which would help with school improvement.

While experts tended systematically to address all factors, they did so over an extended period of time. Short-term priorities often led to placing emphasis temporarily on a small set of factors. In contrast, non-expert problem-solving behavior (Level 1) was characterized by long-term, consistent inattention to many factors, and attention to others only when provoked by a crisis (e.g., parental complaints about a curriculum topic).

Nature of expectations

As school-leaders became more expert, their expectations within factors also became more defensible and more consistent with prevailing professional judgment and the results of research. This suggests that such expectations, when met, stand a better chance of actually resulting in school improvement or goal achievement. Expectations also became increasingly detailed or concrete with increased principal effectiveness. Experts, for example, were better able to see which special characteristics of their schools needed to be accounted for in formulating expectations they held for factors and, specifically, how such characteristics might influence those expectations in practice.

Non-experts (Level 1) had vague expectations regarding the limited number of factors to which they attended. For example, concerning classroom management, one 'building manager' (Level 1) offered only:

I like to see a classroom where there are a lot of meaningful things to do.

At Level 2, expectations tended to be high but still general; for example, staff were expected to 'cooperate with one another', but what such cooperation entailed was not made clear by the principal. Program managers (Level 3), although not concerned with the full array of factors, as were the most expert school-leaders, were quite specific in their expectations for those factors of concern.

Sources of expectations

Information used in formulating expectations also varied with expertise and came from many sources. Increased expertise, however, was associated with systematic rather than incidental or whimsical attention to non-personal sources. Expectations at the least expert level varied according to what school-leaders believed to be appropriate to the immediate situation. Such expectations were highly negotiable and could be swayed by staff preferences, parental demands, administrative demands, or the school-leader's interpretation of an educational trend. With increased expertise, knowledge of respected colleagues, and eventually research-based knowledge, were actively sought out and accommodated in formulating expectations. These sources of information undoubtedly increased the sophistication or validity of principals' knowledge, hence the nature of their expectations.

Strategies

Having identified factors associated with the achievement of valued goals, school-leaders still must act or intervene to influence selected factors in directions they consider most likely to assist in goal achievement. Our research showed that school-leaders employed a repertoire of both general-purpose and factor-specific strategies to accomplish goals.

General-purpose strategies were considered by school-leaders as useful in influencing the characteristics of almost any factor, depending very much on circumstances in the school at the time action was taken. Such strategies established an appropriate background and climate within which more factor-specific action still had to be initiated to ensure goal achievement. Among the seven general-purpose strategies we identified, four focused on keeping those involved in decision-making willing to participate and well informed. These included:

- the building and maintenance of interpersonal relationships and motivating staff
- provision of staff with knowledge and skills
- facilitation of within-school communication
- facilitation of communication between school and community

Two additional strategies, a general strategies that addressed the provision of adequate organizational resources for staff work were:

- allowance for non-teaching time for staff
- establishment of procedures to handle routine matters

The final strategy, a general purpose strategy, was using vested authority; the purpose for its use varied significantly between experts and non-experts.

After the appropriate background and climate were established, factor-specific strategies could begin to exercise a direct influence on selected factors. They included:

- program monitoring
- goal setting, program planning and development
- program implementation
- staff supervision
- provision of support resources
- direct relationship with students

Criteria and emphasis
Different levels of expertise among school-leaders were evident in the criteria they used for choosing strategies. As strategic expertise increased, and goals expanded, the number and nature of strategies used over extended periods of time also increased. This increase could be traced back to the changes in types of goals, from a focus on building management concerns through interpersonal relations, to the school program, and finally to student achievement. Achieving goals increasingly linked to student achievement eventually demanded attention to all factors, as we have already mentioned. Effectively influencing all factors required the use of virtually all general-purpose and factor-specific strategies. Expertise also depended on school-leaders' ability to identify strategies that would impact on weak aspects of their schools' background or climate.

Non-experts (Level 1) on this dimension (strategy selection) of problem-solving needed to feel in control of administrative matters in their school. Such control was usually assumed through the use of vested authority. These school-leaders preferred not to be involved in decisions about curriculum or instruction, designating these as exclusively teachers' responsibilities. They also selected other general-purpose strategies on the basis of intuitive judgments about what was required to keep the school operating smoothly. For example, attention would be given to interpersonal relationships among staff when a serious problem arose in such relationships.

School-leaders at the next level of expertise (Level 2) sought out strategies that contributed to a warm, friendly climate in the school, often considering positive climate an end in its own right. They frequently gave considerable attention to such strategies, as well as being positive, cheerful and encouraging, accessible to staff, acting as a role model, and facilitating communication within the school, and between the school and community. When vested authority was used, their reasons varied from a desire to make teachers' lives easier, by freeing them from decision-making responsibility, to their convictions that some decisions were too specialized or important to be left to chance, such as school budgets and teachers' record keeping.

A dominant concern for making fair, well-informed, consistent decisions and helping staff do the same was characteristic of program managers (Level 3). This concern motivated the systematic collection and distribution of information relevant to crucial decisions to staff. Such communication with the community was also viewed as an essential ingredient in building broader support for a school's program.

The most expert school-leaders (Level 4) used a complex set of considerations in choosing their strategies, including the goals to be achieved, the factors to be influenced, and characteristics of the people involved. They also considered other activities already underway in the school, school and school-system norms, past experiences, and the nature of obstacles to be overcome. These concerns were used simultaneously and were viewed clearly as means rather than ends. Most general-purpose and task-specific strategies were used at some time by experts to attain their goals.

Quality and skill
School-leaders sometimes chose strategies well suited to factors in need of influence and still failed to exercise much influence. One cause was the quality of strategies used. The effect of principals' actions was partially a function of the specific procedures associated with their strategies. Principals increased in expertise, as their procedures became relatively more efficient in influencing factors (e.g., a single strategy influencing several factors) and as their strategies were more readily used by others (many school-leader-initiated strategies depended on other members of staff to be completed). Strategies also were most effective as they became more adaptable to changing school conditions. For example, program-planning procedures, useful across all areas of the curriculum, seemed to be generally more effective in stimulating subject-matter integration by teachers than strategies that were unique to subject areas.

Differences in the quality of strategies used is particularly evident in factor-specific strategies such as program implementation. Highly expert school-leaders had a strategy for program implementation that included well-refined, detailed steps, applicable to many programs. Less expert principals either did not deal with implementation (Level 1) or had no systematic approach to the process (Level 2).

It was still possible, however, for a school-leader to select a strategy potentially able to influence the factor(s) of concern, possess extensive knowledge about how to carry out the strategy, and still not obtain the desired effect. This was the case when school-leaders' actual skill in use of the strategy was flawed in a crucial way. For example, some school-leaders knew that establishing good relationships with the community required listening carefully to parental concerns and patiently moving from such concerns, however expressed, toward a focus on how they were addressed in the school program. Yet these people allowed themselves to be frustrated with parental inquiries and frequently became defensive in their responses. Experts, on the other hand, were skilled in most of the general-purpose and factor-specific strategies. As school-leaders became highly skilled in their performance of a strategy, less conscious effort was required of them. This reduced the time required for them to respond to matters demanding their immediate attention (e.g., a report of drug use in the boys' washroom), and allowed them to attend to other problems for which solutions were less well known (e.g., increasing collaborative curriculum planning across departments in the school).

Decision-Making

Decision-making is a process that permeates the other dimensions of principal problem-solving and helps account for the quality of those processes.

Differences in the way school-leaders chose their directions, selected aspects of the school for attention, and decided to act accounted for much of the difference in their expertise. Results of this research focused on two aspects of the decision-making process. One was the context within which specific decisions were made: the forms and procedures used in decision-making, principals' attitude and stance toward the process, and the monitoring of decision-making. The second aspect concerned components of decision-making: how decisions were defined, what criteria were considered relevant, and the use of information.

Forms and procedures for decision-making

The most expert school-leaders knew about and demonstrated use of a range of different forms of decision-making in their schools. ('What I do depends on the situation and the people involved.') Sometimes they made unilateral decisions, sometimes they delegated the responsibility to others. Frequently, there was extensive participation in the processes, with choices determined through consensus or, occasionally, by majority vote. The least expert principals made many more unilateral decisions. When staff participated in the process, choices were usually based on majority vote. The same school-leaders appeared to give little conscious thought to which form of decision-making to use. In contrast, those with most expertise appeared to arrive at a choice of form by consciously reviewing: staff preferences and abilities, existing decision-making practices in the school, the nature of the decision to be made, and experiences from past decisions.

While highly expert school-leaders were consciously eclectic in the forms of decision-making they used, they nevertheless had strong preferences toward decentralization and extensive staff participation. Unlike those who were least expert, they used many decision-making occasions as opportunities to foster conditions conducive to extensive participation (staff willingness, skill, and a climate in which the motives of those participating in decisions were widely trusted). For instance:

> In terms of my teaching staff, I would like them to feel that cooperative action is the best way to solve a problem, that no problem is insurmountable, and that basically this is a pretty good place to be. They enjoy working here, so they want to go that extra mile.

These school-leaders were knowledgeable about how decisions were made in departments or divisions in their schools and worked toward compatibility in decision-making processes at all levels in the school. Non-experts tended to be out of touch with decision-making processes in which they were not directly involved. Considerable diversity in such processes was typical within their schools.

Variation in the procedures which school-leaders established for decision-making was also evident in our research. Lack of consistency in such procedures was common among those with least expertise in decision-making. For example, sometimes their procedures allowed for different points of view to be heard, sometimes not; sometimes criteria for decision-making were made explicit, sometimes not. By comparison, the most expert established procedures to help ensure consistent attention to: alternative points of view (including competing values), all criteria relevant to the decision, clarification of the decision, and collection of relevant information. Experts also had procedures (such as the development of a calendar, listing all major decision points in the year) for anticipating decisions and ensuring that needed decisions did not 'fall through the cracks'.

Attitude and stance toward decision-making
Levels of expertise in this component of decision-making varied in the extent to which school-leaders sought out decision-making opportunities or reacted to the necessity for decisions to be made. Experts tended to seek out decisions; they viewed even minor decisions as opportunities to move incrementally toward their goals. They seemed able to anticipate a large proportion of decisions that had to be made and used them to their advantage. Non-experts seemed unable or unwilling to forecast many upcoming decisions. As a result, they found themselves continually reacting to decision-making situations within a time-frame established by others. They rarely had enough time to make decisions carefully and, not surprisingly, tended to have negative attitudes toward change. Their stance toward decision-making could be called 'crisis management'.

Monitoring decision-making. Those with least expertise in monitoring the process of decision-making and its consequences relied on their feelings (i.e., informal observations, number of problems arising) about 'how well things were going'. Reactions to problems were in a piecemeal fashion with little effort to prevent them from recurring. At Level 2, staff satisfaction with decisions was frequently assessed. At Level 3, routine checks were typically made of school decision-making; special attention was given to how well the process met the principals' standards of fairness and consistency, and to the principals' perceptions of how well school needs were being met. In monitoring, the most expert principals systematically reviewed and refined the forms and procedures used. Information was usually sought out regarding the satisfaction of most of those affected by the decision, including school staff; typically, resources or costs of the decision process (e.g., amounts of time spent by department staff in selecting a new textbook) and the contributions of decisions toward school goals (e.g., if the textbook selected seemed to be the best one to contribute to program objectives) were examined.

Defining decisions and selecting criteria. Variation in how school-leaders defined decisions and the criteria they used appeared to be closely related to variations in their goals. When running the school smoothly was the overriding concern, as in Level 1, school-leaders tended to take the path of least resistance in their decision-making: they responded swiftly to symptoms (e.g., placating a parent concerned about the amount of homework given to his child) but ignored underlying causes (e.g., absence of a school-homework policy). The transformation of primarily managerial goals into criteria for decision-making sometimes led to questionable emphases in the school. For example, some school-leaders responded to broad pressures regarding the basics, in such a way as to entirely ignore other equally important goals. In some decisions where these school-leaders' usual criteria could not be applied, choices were made intuitively with the claim that much about education was intuitive.

An overriding concern for a broad range of student outcomes, as in Level 4, was associated with efforts to uncover and clarify the fundamental causes of problems. Criteria, directly based on the goals of education, included: the need for individual programs, students' stages of development, and the need to balance emphasis among knowledge, skill, and effective objectives. Other staff were actively encouraged to use similarly oriented criteria in their decision-making.

Growth was also evident in how realistic and solvable the decisions defined by the school-leader were. Less expert school-leaders had a greater tendency to portray problem solutions as inaccessible (e.g., not enough time or money, not their problem, age of staff). The same basic problems were frequently cast in much more accessible terms by those with more expertise (e.g., weighing school priorities, staff motivation and interest).

Use of information. Those with least expertise in their use of information in decision-making collected little information within the school, except what was requested by district administrators. They tended to read report cards and were open to receiving other information but did not seek it. In contrast, experts accumulated information about most major functions of the school in a systematic way. They had procedures for routinely ensuring adequate information as a basis for major decisions. Further, they encouraged staff to do the same and expected them to be able to identify the sources of information for their decisions. Those with least expertise only pressed staff for information sources if the decision was of special interest to them.

Information used most frequently by non-experts concerned building management matters, and their responsibilities in such matters. This information was usually available in the form of memos and policies from the district or ministry of education. Level 2 forms of problem-solving were characterized by seeking out information from staff, particularly about such issues as student morale and relationships with parents. Frequent informal visits to classrooms was a typical method of collecting this information. At Level 3, information was also sought about curriculum development and implementation activities in the school, and program requirements as outlined by the board or ministry of education. School-leaders at this level gathered this information through classroom visits, analyses of test results, reading of report cards, parental surveys, teacher plans, and other formal assessments of student needs.

In their use of information, experts added to the processes described in Level 3 a general knowledge about curriculum and education, gleaned from reading recent research. This information was interwoven with school-specific information during decision-making. Experts also encouraged their staff to be familiar with, and take account of, research-based information in their own decision-making; they attempted to keep staff well informed, by, for example, developing a handbook of procedures for school routines and carefully orienting new staff to school expectations and procedures.

Elementary and Secondary School-Leaders: Differences on the High Ground

Our concern for the development of school-leaders stimulated us to inquire about possible differences that might exist in the context of high ground problem-solving for elementary, as compared with secondary, school-leaders. If there are significant differences, these should be addressed, for example, in formal preparation programs which, at present, pay very little systematic attention to school level. Furthermore, only a handful of studies could be located which explicitly compare elementary and secondary school leadership (e.g., Caldwell and Lutz, 1978, Eastabrook and Fullan, 1978, Gersten, Carnine and Green, 1982, Johnston, 1983, Licata and Hack, 1980, Martin and Willower, 1981, Morris *et al.*, 1986, Newberg and Glatthorn, n.d., Salley, McPherson and Baehr, 1978, Willower and Kmetz, 1982). The results of these studies are sufficiently tentative to make them an unreliable basis for either understanding or action.

Our study (Leithwood, 1986) of possible differences included both opinion data from a random sample of sixty elementary and secondary principals, as well as a comparative content analysis of our elementary and secondary school-leader profiles (Leithwood and Montgomery, 1986, Leithwood, 1986). Results identified eleven differences distributed across each component of our high ground problem-solving model (Table 5.2). Of these differences, six appear to be at least partly a function of school size rather than school level. Two of these school-size differences provide potential advantages to the decision-making of secondary (larger school) principals:

- Greater opportunities to delegate responsibilities because of more staff with administrative responsibilities (number 10)
- Improved opportunities for effective decision-making because of the special resources (people and other types of resources) available within the school (number 11)

Table 5.2: School-leaders' problem-solving on the high ground: Elementary vs. secondary

Problem-Solving Component	Difference	Perceived Reason for Difference
1. Goals	(1) nature of goals: the wide array of destinations for which secondary schools prepare their students make their mission more complicated	• need more diverse program • nature of links with post-secondary institutions • nature of policies to be implemented
	(2) source of goals: secondary-school principals have significantly less influence on school direction than have elementary principals	• number of secondary staff • complexity of organization • scope and multiplicity of program and interests
2. Factors	(3) program: although the secondary principals' impact on the program is similar, their relationship to the instructional program is less direct than that of the elementary principals	• role of heads • degree of specialization number of staff
	(4) nature of student relations with others: student problems are generally less severe in nature for principals in elementary schools	• age of student • smaller numbers of elementary schools allow for greater closeness to students
3. Strategies	(5) support resources: budgetary concerns occupy much less time for elementary than for secondary-school principals	• vastly smaller sums of money • elementary-school finances much less complex
	(6) routine procedures: secondary principals spend more time on paper work than do their elementary colleagues	• timetabling activities • grading responsibilities
	(7) elementary principals spend less time on record-keeping activities than their secondary-level colleagues	
	(8) school-community communications: parents are much more directly involved and far more influential in elementary school than they are in secondary schools	• at elementary age, parents are more involved in all aspects of their children's lives • elementary schools generally are closer to and more accessible to the community
	(9) within-school communication: effective communication is easier in elementary schools than it is in secondary school	• secondary principals have more 'parts' to monitor, coordinate and meld together, and their accountability for larger sums of money necessitates their keeping volumes of detailed statistical records • fewer people • smaller plant
4. Decision-making	(10) forms of decision-making: elementary principals are able to delegate fewer responsibilities than secondary principals	• may be the only on-site administrator
	(11) use of information: secondary-school principals are more likely to have support networks, and resource bases immediately at hand within school to assist in decision-making	• various specialists are on site

The remaining differences attributable to school size appear to offer potential advantages to elementary (smaller school) principals:

- It is easier to communicate effectively with and among staff members (number 9)
- One's impact on program decisions and school directions can be more direct in a smaller school where there are no other positions, such as department heads, through which one normally works (numbers 3 and 2)
- There is less time and effort required for record-keeping and other paper work; timetabling is simpler, grading responsibilities are less demanding (numbers 7 and 6)
- Budgets require less effort to develop and monitor (number 5)

Two of the eleven differences in Table 5.2 (number 4 and 8) can be traced to perceived differences in the clients of elementary and secondary schools. Many secondary school-leaders, in particular, reported spending large proportions of their time on student problems more complex and severe than those they anticipated were normally faced by their elementary-school counterparts (e.g., teenage pregnancies, higher incidence of substance abuse). These were perceived as problems often extending beyond the competence or authority of the school-leader to deal with, although they were, at least initially, confronted with them. Parents, on the other hand, were viewed as having a more pervasive role in elementary than secondary schools because of the more dependent natuure of younger children and the closer identification of elementary schools with their immediate community. This fact may add a dimension of complexity to the job of elementary principals, compared to their secondary colleagues.

Finally, there appear to be differences in the mandate of elementary and secondary schools that contribute to difference in the work of principals (number 1). Elementary schools foster the general and relatively homogeneous development of young children and prepare them for entry into secondary-school programs which can be known and controlled to a significant degree by the public school system itself. The secondary school, in contrast, is faced with the task of increasingly specializing the training it offers students, accompanied by an inevitable press toward pragmatic and organizational compartmentalization: secondary schools must offer highly diverse programs to students whose destinations include the world of work and a plethora of post-secondary education institutions.

Summary and Implications for Leaders of Future Schools

This chapter has described variations in the processes used by school-leaders at four different levels of expertise, to solve well-structured or high ground problems. Four components or elements of such problem-solving, initially derived from a series of studies (Leithwood and Montgomery, 1982, 1986, Leithwood, 1986) were used to organize the description of these processes. These components included: the nature, sources, and uses of goals; classroom and school factors directly influencing the achievement of goals; strategies used by school-leaders to influence factors; and the nature of decision-making about the other three components. Within each of the problem-solving components, four levels of problem-solving expertise were described. The labels associated with each of these levels capture the dominant orientation to problem-solving of school-leaders at that level; building manager (least expert), humanitarian, program manager, and systematic problem-solver. Differences were also identified in the context for high ground problem-solving of elementary as compared with secondary school-leaders. These differences appeared to be a function of either school size, nature of students, or the mandates for elementary and secondary schools.

What implication for leaders of future schools flow from this analysis of school leadership on the high ground? Three such implications seem to us to be especially noteworthy: the value of a clear, 'working' vision of what the school should be; the central importance of precise and defensible knowledge about the school's main business of teaching; and the critical contribution of effective communication in transacting the school's business.

Vision

While Chapter 3 was devoted entirely to the importance of a school-leader's vision, we extend several aspects of that discussion here, because the importance of vision is especially clear in the context of high ground problem-solving. As we asserted in Chapter 3, having a relatively clear, comprehensive picture of one's school in its future, ideal state is a powerful leadership tool. Indeed without such a picture in mind it is difficult to imagine what would be the basic focus of leadership in a school (or anywhere else, for that matter). Vision includes the goals one aspires to accomplish for one's students, as well as those practices (factors) engaged in by school personnel when such goals are being accomplished. A truly comprehensive vision might also include the strategies one would use and the nature of the decision-making required to bring about those practices among school staffs and to accomplish desired goals for students.

While it seems essential for school-leaders to possess visions of their schools in their preferred states, such visions contribute little to school improvement unless they are widely shared. This is the case because a leader has only a limited, direct role in moving the school toward the vision. In terms of broad strategy, one may start with a vision and then convince others to accept it, start with a vision and negotiate a version of it with others, or build a vision collaboratively with relevant others (e.g., students, staff, district personnel, and community members). Each of these broad strategies for arriving at a shared vision might be justified as most suitable in some contexts. But the collaborative strategy is to be preferred, in principle, since it offers the greatest promise for the sort of authentic, meaningful internalization of direction which actually guides people's daily decisions and actions. Because internalized visions are such powerful guides to people's decisions and actions, the time spent in their development contributes to clarifying the nature of the changes to which a school may aspire and to implementing those changes as well. In brief, it can be extremely efficient to 'waste a lot of time' building a shared vision. This is especially the case as demands likely to be placed on future schools by increasingly diverse school clients become more complex and uncertain. Or, as the president of a large successful corporation, quoted by Peters and Austin (1985, p. 285) put it: 'I think we'd all be better off if we spent more time articulating our corporate plans [vision] and less time on perfecting them'.

Technical Knowledge

The 'technical core' of schools is their curriculum and its instructional delivery. Few issues have been more persistently debated than the proper relationship between school-leaders and knowledge of the technical core. One position on this relationship is exemplified in the 'building manager' approach to high ground problem-solving. Essentially it is an unconsumated relationship; the technology for teaching language arts (or any ther curriculum area) is virgin territory for the building manager. That technology is married to the teacher and the building manager wouldn't think of coming between them (even though he or she may retain some 'carnal' knowledge from an earlier life as a teacher).

In contrast to the building manager's position, the current '*zeitgeist*' for school leadership is captured in the term 'instructional leadership' (e.g., Smith and Andrews, 1989, Duke, 1987). The term exemplifies what we believe to be the appropriate orientation of future school-leaders toward knowledge about the technical core: that is, an intimate, long term, continually evolving and deepening relationship. Why? Because, in the arcane language of cognitive scientists, 'domain-specific knowledge' is one of the main pillars of expertise on the high ground. School-leaders cannot just manage the process of problem-solving in their schools and expect to accomplish the best for their students. To resort to this approach implies an unrealistic expectation of teachers even under working conditions quite different from those that currently prevail. This approach implies that teachers have the opportunity and motivation to seek out continually the best technical knowledge and to implement it. It implies, further, that they will be able to introduce such knowledge at appropriate times during deliberations among staff members and make the case, in convincing terms, so as to be taken seriously; all without the substantive understanding and consequent intervention of the school-leader. This does not seem too likely (besides, no one earning the salary of a school principal should get away with being of such little use). We consider a willingness and ability to work continuously on mastering the technical core, to be a minimum requirement for leaders of future schools. We also consider this to be a realistic expectation because, in spite of the warehouses full of writing about the technical core, there is not that much to know! This does not mean that it would be easy to become a skilled performer in all areas of the technical core. It does mean that it is feasible to become an expert critic and coach in many areas of the technical core.

Communication

Peters and Austin have also said:

> Make no mistake about it. 'Techniques' don't produce quality products, educate children or pick up the garbage on time: people do, people who care, people who are treated as creatively contributing adults. (1985, p. 199)

Having just spent several hundred words on the importance of technical know-ledge for future school-leaders, we hasten to point out (more briefly) what seems less obvious in practice than one would expect. The 'potential' of the leader's knowledge is likely to be very disappointing in the face of poor-quality com-munication and unproductive interpersonal relations among members of the school. This is evident, for example, in the amount of attention we had to devote to interpersonal and communication strategies in our description of that compo-nent of high ground problem-solving. It is also evident in data suggesting that school-leaders spend about three-quarters of their time involved in communica-tions of some sort (Martin and Willower, 1981).

The skills of communication and of establishing productive interpersonal relations are what Miles (1988) asserts to be the basic building blocks for school improvement. These skills have to be reliably and continuously delivered or the school-improvement effort breaks down. Future school-leaders will have to interact productively with a wider array of clients and publics than is presently the case. And they will have to do so with less certainty than at present about the values, expectations, and customs of those with whom they interact. This will place a premium on the possession of effective communication and interpersonal skills as vehicles through which their technical knowledge can be put to good use.

Conclusion

Are leaders made, or are they born that way? This chapter has described what we consider to be a large proportion of school leadership: expertise in solving high ground problems. This characterization of such expertise makes our answer to the perennial question quite clear: they are 'made', at least to a significant degree. One does not come 'naturally' to a productive vision and set of goals for one's school. Nor does one have intuitive mastery of the technical knowledge of which this chapter spoke. To say that school-leaders are made, in this context, then, is to claim that there is much to be developed. One's expertise as a school-leader ought to be considered a highly elastic phenomenon. Even two school-leaders with comparable expertise will vary in the smoothness of their execution. Jack, the first systematic problem solver (Level 4) we identified in our research was only two years from retirement. He was so 'laid back' about what he was doing that you had to watch very closely, to realize just how pervasive his presence was and how much of an impact he made on his school. We have since observed many less experienced, systematic problem solvers going about their work. They do many of the things Jack did, but it requires much more overt energy on their part. Jack remains for us, the 'Wayne Gretsky of school leadership'. But it took him twenty-five years to look so slow, skating so fast.

Notes

1 See Leithwood and Montgomery (1982), Leithwood (1982), Leithwood and Montgom-ery (1986, Chapter 11) and Chapter 2 this volume.
2 See Leithwood and Montgomery (1986, Chapter 13), Leithwood and Montgomery (1985), Leithwood (1986).
3 The following description is adapted from Leithwood and Montgomery (1985).

Chapter 6

Expert School Leadership in the Swamp

Expert leadership in the swamp does not depend on the possession of an extensive stock of knowledge about the specific content of one's problems. For this reason, the 'Factors' dimension of the high ground problem-solving model described in Chapter 5 is not a promising element to include in a model describing expert problem-solving in the swamp. Nor does expert leadership, in response to ill-structured problems, spring from the more or less direct and skilled application of some set of tried and true procedures or techniques. Hence, the 'Strategies' dimension of the high ground problem-solving model is of much reduced value in explaining expertise in the swamp. It is not that what was incorporated within the 'Factors and Strategies' dimensions, described in Chapter 5, is suddenly irrelevant. It is the case, rather, that these dimensions do not capture enough of what is important to account for much of the variation in school-leaders' expertise in the swamp.

The model of problem-solving in the swamp, used as the basis for describing expert school leadership in this chapter, gives most weight to a set of general cognitive strategies or thought processes (referred to as 'fluid ability' in contemporary theories of intelligence, Lohman, 1990). Also, the model includes a general disposition toward problem-solving. School-leaders' values and principles are also critical parts of this model. Indeed, they are so pervasive that we touch on them very lightly in this chapter, choosing instead to devote all of Chapter 7 to their nature and role in solving swampy problems.

In order to describe how expert school-leaders solve swampy problems by themselves and in groups, we draw most directly on two studies. Both studies were premised on the assumption that comparing and contrasting the problem-solving processes of expert school-leaders with their more typical or non-expert peers adds precision to judgments about what is especially crucial in the experts' problem-solving processes. Accordingly, in both studies, the total sample of principals was identified in advance as being either 'expert' or 'non-expert', using a combination of techniques including nominations by senior administrators familiar with their work, and interview techniques refined through the research described in Chapter 5. As it turned out, almost all principals labelled as experts in both studies were 'systematic problem solvers', as designated in Chapter 5: 'non-expert' principals were 'humanitarian' in their orientation.

Study One, used to describe school-leaders' individual problem-solving

(Leithwood and Stager, 1989) included a total sample of twenty-two principals who responded to simulated problems which each of them identified in advance as swampy. Their responses were tape recorded, transcribed, coded and content analyzed. Study Two (Leithwood and Steinbach, 1991a) is used as the basis for illustrating how expert and typical school-leaders solve problems in groups. Using a sample of nine principals, data for this study were collected in the context of staff meetings which were tape recorded. Principals were asked to describe what they were thinking about at various points during the meeting as they listened to the tape immediately after the meeting (a technique called 'stimulated recall').

Results of these studies are described in the next two sections of this chapter organized around the components of a model of problem-solving which emerged initially from the data collected in the Leithwood and Stager (1989) study. These components include:

- **Interpretation**: principals' understanding of the specific nature of the problem, often in situations where multiple problems may be identified
- **Goals**: the relatively immediate purposes that the principals are attempting to achieve, in response to their interpretation of the problem
- **Principles/Values**: the relatively long-term purposes, operating principles, fundamental laws, doctrines, values, and assumptions guiding the principals' thinking
- **Constraints**: 'barriers or obstacles' which must be overcome, if an acceptable solution to the problem is to be found
- **Solution Processes**: what the principals do to solve a problem (in light of their interpretation of the problem, principles, goals to be achieved, and constraints to be accommodated)
- **Affect**: the feelings, mood and sense of self-confidence the principals experience when involved in problem-solving

These components ought to be considered more like categories of things school-leaders think about in solving a problem than steps in the process. Indeed, the process is quite fluid and components may be revisited several times; for example, efforts to develop a solution may reveal information that causes one to change one's initial interpretation of the problem.

Having said the process is fluid, we hasten to add that there are limits to the fluidity. For example, initial interpretations of a problem sometimes lead to solution processes from which one cannot recover. This would be the case if a problem involving a teacher was interpreted as incompetence; such an interpretation leads to goals and solution processes of a quasi-legal nature. The initiation of such processes closes off the option of subsequently interpreting the problem as one of teacher development. It is important to 'get the problem as right as possible' early in the process.

How Expert School-Leaders Solve Swampy Problems by Themselves

Interpretation

Two aspects of interpretation seemed important from our research in Study One: the ways that principals attempted to understand problems, and principals' use of anecdotes to interpret problems or to explain their understanding of problems.

Principals attempted to understand swampy problems in three ways: by relying on past experience (as with the most structured problems); by collecting new information; and/or by making assumptions. In Study One, the only assumptions made by experts concerned the hypothetical nature of the problems presented to them and the experts were very explicit about these assumptions. On the other hand, non-experts tended to make assumptions rather than collect information and were somewhat less explicit about their assumptions. This is illustrated, for example, in the analysis of one non-expert response to a problem involving a new principal taking over a school in which the existing principal was very popular and the community was upset by her departure (described in Chapter 4). The response revealed six assumptions, though they were not identified explicitly as such: the previous principal was 'doing a good job'; the established procedures in the school 'were good'; changing procedures would lead to confrontations with staff; there were cliques to be dealt with 'ruthlessly'; there would be a core of staff opposed to the principal's initiatives; and there were 'people who control the school'. As this example also indicates, many assumptions of non-experts were concerned with constraints or obstacles to problem-solving.

These assumptions, along with an observed tendency to consider a number of tangential or irrelevant issues, led to considerable 'floundering' on the principals' part in interpreting the least structured problems. For example, one non-expert, in considering the Principal-Entry problem, reported that he would spend a great deal of time and energy trying to find out why the previous principal had been moved. To him, it was an issue of substantial importance whether his predecessor had been moved to another school or promoted to a superintendency, and he mentioned the matter repeatedly.

Principals frequently used anecdotes to explain and illustrate their approaches to problems. In contrast to non-experts, experts' anecdotes tended to be directly relevant to the problems at hand. Non-experts were more likely to recount difficult experiences than highly successful ones.

In short, experts differed from non-experts in their ability to arrive at a clear, comprehensive interpretation of a problem, one that would enable them to get on with the actual solution of the problem. Experts did not appear to become involved in irrelevant issues and did not become dysfunctionally preoccupied with the feelings of others associated with the problem.

Goals

Both the nature and number of goals school-leaders attempted to achieve in dealing with a problem distinguished experts from non-experts. Principals indicated, through their responses to the three least structured problems used in Study One, that they were attempting to accomplish five types of goals. These goals concerned staff, students and program, parents and the community, perceptions of others about the principals' expertise, and finding an appropriate balance among goals.

Most principals had staff-oriented goals for problem-solving. Non-experts mentioned this type of goal more often than other types. There were certain differences between experts and non-experts in the particular staff-related goals that they expressed. For instance, non-experts were directly concerned with staff feelings; in dealing with the Principal-Entry problem, one principal's goal was to have 'good feelings about what you are doing ... and everybody happy with that'. An expert, dealing with the same problem, believed that a more important goal was to have the staff understand his philosophy of education: 'I spent two or three hours ... sharing [with staff] what I believed to be important about education so that they would gain an insight into my philosophy'.

All principals identified goals related to students and programs in response to a problem about implementing a primary language program. They wanted to improve the quality of student programs. With problems which had less obvious impact on students, however, an important difference between expert and non-expert principals was apparent; only the experts outlined how they would include the student and program categories of goals in their problem-solving. In a problem about school consolidation, an expert identified implications for the grouping of new students in terms of program, while the closest a non-expert came to a student-oriented goal was 'selling the school' to prospective students. In the Principal-Entry problem, one expert was particularly emphatic about the program and student goals that should be addressed in solving the problem:

> The whole fine reputation of the school ... and the confidence in the school and the programs that are in place are at stake ... so you are dealing with the continuation of the program with the kids ... and so you want that to be continued.

In this problem, also, goals of two experts included a concern with achieving a balance between their own and others' ideas concerning the nature of programs.

Most principals had goals for problem-solving that were related to parents or the larger school community. In this category of goals, experts were concerned with providing parents with knowledge, the better to understand the problem and its eventual solutions. Examples of such goals from the school-consolidation problem were statements such as: 'parents get to know where their kids are going to be', 'provided a vehicle for parents of new students to ask questions', and 'have parents' questions answered'. Non-experts, on the other hand, wanted parents to be happy and comfortable with the solutions, as indicated in such statements as: 'to make people feel better about the new school' and 'make them feel comfortable'.

Two other goals were mentioned much less frequently and, for the most part, in connection with the Principal-Entry problem. One of these was to be knowledgeable about educational matters and the school, and to be seen by the staff and community in this light: 'I would [want people to get the] impression very, very quickly that I knew what the situation was, that I'd done my homework, and that I knew the community and the program. I'd endeavor to be really well informed'.

The second goal was to achieve an appropriate balance, in this case between continuity (of the most desirable features of the present school) and change (of those features that could be improved); experts were very concerned about developing personal initiatives that would contribute to their new school, but they wanted to do so in an appropriate manner.

In sum, principals' goal-related thinking suggested that experts pursued a broader range of goals and were more concerned than non-experts with knowledge (their own and others) as distinct from feelings. They were also better able to see the implications, for students and for program quality, of problems not obviously or directly concerned with students or programs, and were in general more concerned about achieving a balance among various goals.

Principles and Values

This component is, in our view, an especially critical and pervasive aspect of school-leaders' problem-solving. Study One found this to be the case especially with experts. They were able to be much more explicit about the principles and values they used in their work. With such explicitness, principles and values served as substitutes for knowledge in solving swampy problems.

As mentioned earlier, we save more extensive treatment of this problem-solving component to the next chapter.

Constraints

Although the number of responses coded as constraints in Study One was rather small, the observed variation in their function was extremely important. There appeared to be little difference in the nature and operation of constraints for the most structured and least structured problems, but there were marked differences between experts and non-experts with both types of problems. Experts did not indicate any constraints that would bring them to a standstill, whereas many non-experts did. This was particularly so with least structured problems. Matters that non-experts indicated as constraints or obstacles were viewed by experts simply as matters to take into account during problem-solving; potential constraints were addressed through the solutions that they generated. Rather than viewing public opposition as a constraint in the school-consolidation problem, for example, one expert simply noted, as part of the solution process:

> I'd provide a vehicle for parents of new students to ask questions ...
> perhaps through letters and return slips of paper ... They have to have
> the opportunity to get to know where their kids are going to go ... I
> would have open-house public meetings, invite families and perhaps
> students to come and see the building, and [hold] a meet-the-teacher
> night with some kind of general assembly.

In contrast, a non-expert dealing with the same question mentioned a number of constraints, which are representative of those mentioned by others, such as: a lack of knowledge or information ('so there's all sorts of questions that are coming up that will need answers before I can really sit down and prepare'); opposition from others ('I'm going to be dumped on with a lot of this stuff', 'people in the other school are probably going to fight it and be very anti this move'); and a potential lack of resources ('it may be too much of a drain on the resources of the school, and we may not be able to handle all they think we can').

In sum, expert school-leaders assume that all swampy problems include constraints but that such constraints can be overcome as part of their problem-solving; they are not deterred or dismayed by the prospect of having to tackle such constraints.

Solution Processes

Experts indicated, in Study One, marked efforts at thinking through solution processes in considerable detail and planning how the process would be carried out. In response to the Principal-Entry problem, one expert stated:

> But the actual steps ... I guess is what wasn't really clear to me exactly
> what I would do ... I would have to sit down and I'd have to think it
> through and plan it out and look at the individual steps and where I
> could go with each one.

Non-experts showed very little evidence of attention to planning. Most principals met in some way with staff, parents and/or students, depending on the nature of the problem. All but a few non-experts stressed the importance they attached to the details of the solution process in the context of such meetings. Again, in response to the Principal-Entry problem, one expert noted, for example:

> In my first communication with parents, I would talk about a lot of the
> good things that the former principal had started and what my plans are.
> I would want to state my particular goals over the next school year.

Experts and non-experts differed substantially, however, in their orientation to such meetings – a matter explored in greater depth in the next section of this chapter. Experts provided evidence of high levels of consultation in working out a solution process. One of the most marked features of the Principal-Entry problem was that two of the three experts who solved it described explicitly (and the third expert alluded to) very extensive consultation about their new school with the best possible informant, the outgoing principal; none of the non-experts did this. Experts also stressed a broad array of features of the problem to be examined through such consultation. One expert, for example, in solving the school-consolidation problem, mentioned numbers of students at each grade level, nature of students, community support, projected enrollments, school organization, staff ratio, student groupings, budget preparations, and plans for textbooks and supplies. In general, the consultations of the experts in the least structured problems had to do with information collection. Non-experts consulted less frequently than did experts. When they did, some may have done so because they were confused as to how to proceed. For instance, two non-experts sought the support of the superintendent before they even attempted to deal with the problem, rather than going to him or her for a specific purpose after they had begun to formulate a solution.

All but one principal attached some importance to information collection as a solution activity. Experts awarded this activity greater importance and spent more effort on it than did non-experts. Non-experts never followed up the consequences of solution activities. Although it was not a marked aspect (as was, for example, information collection) of the problem-solving of experts, three of the six did include some sort of monitoring or follow-up process.

In sum, experts and non-experts differed markedly in their solution processes. Experts spent more effort planning for the solution process and identified more detailed steps to be included in the process than did non-experts. Experts also consulted others more about the solution and attempted to elicit widespread support for it. They stressed the value of careful information collection.

Affect

Finally, the mood or affective states of principals in approaching and solving problems was quite different. Experts were invariably calm and relatively confident in their own abilities. Non-experts, when responding to swampy problems, were sometimes fearful, often not confident, and occasionally somewhat belligerent and/or arrogant.

Responses of an expert and then a non-expert, collected in Study One, describing setting school objectives (a problem that both regarded as easy) illustrate several of these differences.

From the expert:

> This did not present a difficulty for me at all, because, first of all, I believe in having staff give their input in terms of providing directions for the school. So I had no difficulty with that, and I've done that as a principal from day one. I don't feel, just because I'm the principal, that I set the entire goals of where the school is going. There are certainly many, many directions that come from staff, and always have, in my experience. And, as a teacher, I wanted input. And so that was just a simple situation for me, not even a problem.

And in contrast:

> Setting school objectives, that's a process that's built in, it's a process that I've done for a number of years. I can show you the outcomes, and I can show how ... You know, it's there, it's a book. I could give it to you, it's done ... If I were coming to a new school, I believe as the principal, you say, 'Here's what I stand for. Here are my expectations'. And you say all that stuff up front at the opening staff meeting. Anybody who waffles and says, 'I'm going to spend six months looking around' is either lying or stupid.

Table 6.1 summarizes experts' processes, as they have been described in this section.

How Expert School-Leaders Solve Swampy Problems in Collaboration with Others

Corporate entrepreneurs – single minded individuals that they are – still get their projects done by crafting coalitions and building teams of devoted employees who feel a heightened sense of joint involvement and contribution to decisions. ... Masters of change are also masters of the use of participation. (Kanter, 1983, p. 241)

The results presented in the previous section, describing principals solving problems by themselves, showed that completely autonomous problem-solving is relatively rare among expert school-leaders. While some components of the process are carried out by the school-leader alone, this is not often the case for the solution-process component, in particular. Indeed, our research suggests that novice school-leaders often believed that they were hired because they knew the answers and tended to solve problems without much involvement of others because they thought that was what was expected of them. Increased experience, expertise, and leadership responsibilities, however, tend to be associated with a decrease in isolated problem-solving, at least for non-routine, non-technical problems (Leithwood and Stager, 1986, Leithwood and Steinbach, 1991a, Leithwood and Steinbach, in press, b). As an expert secondary principal said to us:

There are very large decisions, and I'm trying to think of one – there are almost none that would not be made by a group of people. And normally that group of people would be the group that's interested in making a decision.

Some degree of collaboration with others, then, is the norm as expert school-leaders solve swampy problems. But there is a significant difference in the demands placed on the problem-solving of school-leaders by modest degrees of collaboration (e.g., asking teachers for information about a specific element of a problem) as compared with fully participative processes (e.g., involving teachers in interpreting the problem through to finding a solution). This is evident in the results reported by Duke and Gansneder (1990) showing significant variations across individual teachers in their preferences for extent of participation and type of problem they consider appropriate to participate in solving. How expert school-leaders solve problems in this fully participative manner is the focus of this section.

Using components of the problem-solving model introduced in the previous section, we describe how four expert and five non-expert principals in Study Two solved swampy problems (a real problem they were working on in their school at the time of the research, and different in each case) in collaboration with others.

Table 6.1: Expert school-leaders' problem-solving processes: Without collaboration

Components	Indicators of Effectiveness
Interpretation	• Classifies problems (in terms of urgency, personal time priority, and who should be involved) • Indicates awareness of possibility of more than one perspective (e.g., educational, political, legal, financial) on the nature of the problem and, where appropriate, shifts among perspectives • Indicates awareness of goals and values of other individuals and organizations who are involved in the problem • Accurately detects similar and different (from past situations) features of problem situation • Is responsive to particular opportunities and constraints in a situation
Goals	• Identifies goals from various sources that are appropriate to the problem • Balances a number of goals, including those of others, in finding solutions
Principles / values	• Refers to principles or values in considering problem • Refers to personal and professional principles or values in considering problem • Indicates, in complex situations, which goals and principles are inviolable and which are flexible and negotiable
Constraints	• Indicates only those constraints which do in fact exist in the situation (e.g., does not make erroneous assumptions regarding constraints) • Accurately identifies constraints in situation • Either converts these constraints into subproblems for solution, or interprets problem differently in order to avoid constraints
Solution Processes	• Collects appropriate amount of information from optimal sources • Develops and/or monitors a deliberate solution plan • Uses and, in some circumstances, shares a framework for tackling problems • Involves others in problem-solving where appropriate • Indicates in group problem-solving situations a concern for insuring shared understanding of problem situation and goals of all involved
Affect	• Appears confident, calm, and 'centered' • Enjoys problem-solving as providing opportunities

Interpretation

Expert and non-expert principals differed significantly in their approach to problem interpretation. For the most part, these are differences in degree. Evidence from the non-expert principals revealed no signs of conscious reflection on their own problem-interpretation processes. While such reflection was not extensive on the part of expert principals either, one explicitly talked about the importance of having a clear interpretation of the problem.

> To me the critical part is identifying what the problem is ... and the problem is different for different people.

Expert and non-expert principals did vary substantially on the extent to which they took into account the interpretation others had of the problem they were addressing. Two of the four experts explicitly checked their own assumptions and actively sought out the interpretations of their staff members as well. In contrast, none of the non-expert principals did this and three of the five assumed that their staff had the same interpretation of the problems as they had.

Another difference in problem interpretation between expert and non-expert principals concerned the context in which problem interpretation took place. Most expert principals viewed the immediate problem they were addressing in the context of the larger mission and problems of their schools. For example, one effective principal noted in his introduction to the topic:

> Discipline is a school thrust [and] the PA day [we had on it] was too brief. We need to equip ourselves with more strategies, refine our skills, because of the greater challenges we [now] face in the classroom, for example, the integration of special kids.

Finally, a particularly striking difference between expert and non-expert principals was the much greater degree of clarity experts had about their interpretation of the problem, and their ability to both describe their interpretation to their staffs and to indicate the reasons they had for such an interpretation. An expert principal said, for example:

> Earlier in the fall we had a discussion about a house system and some of the ideas were of some concern to one division more than another. I don't think you were really able to come to a decision that it should be school-wide and yet there was a feeling that it might very well work out that way ... We took it to a lead teacher meeting ... with some guidelines I had. We've done some revising of those guidelines and what I will give you is an outline of that and some of the ideas behind it. Hopefully, then the meeting will come to you as a house system that could really work for [this school]. I favour for that to happen if it can – under the whole philosophy we have here of lots of participation and low key amount of competition.

> This does not really deal with school teams ... We're talking about in-school activities and its not just sports teams and I think that's part of what S is after too. Each of you will get a sheet with a revised set of guidelines and thoughts and S will carry forth from here.

Non-expert principals frequently were unclear about their interpretations and had difficulty in explaining the reasons for the interpretations they held.

Goals

Expert and non-expert school-leaders shared many similarities in this component of their problem-solving. Both had multiple goals for problem-solving: usually five or six goals in relation to any given problem. For example, in response to a problem regarding results of a survey conducted about the school one principal voiced these goals:

- share the findings [of the survey conducted]
- identify one, two, or three areas that we see as targets
- relate these target areas to overall school goals that will be formulated shortly
- invite staff input
- 'I'm not looking for solutions' – looking for agreement among the group

Furthermore, both groups of school-leaders made a point of sharing their own goals with others involved in problem-solving. Eight of the nine principals also set goals not only for the problem to be solved but also for the meeting in which collaborative problem-solving was to occur. One non-expert principal established goals only for the problem and gave little or no attention to the process for problem-solving.

However, there were two differences between expert and non-expert principals with respect to goals. One of these differences concerned the relationship between the principals' goals for problem-solving and the goals that other staff members held. Expert principals indicated a strong concern for the development of goals that could be agreed on by both themselves and their staff. For example:

> I want this to go, quite frankly I do, but I want it to be something that they have set up the way they can make it work. It's not something I intend as principal to give out great big awards for; it's something that I want the teachers to feel comfortable that they are able to build a program.

Non-expert principals, in contrast, were concerned only with achieving their own goals and with persuading their staffs to agree with them about what those goals should be. As one principal said: 'I think I got them [the teachers] to identify the several key areas that are relevant from my point of view.'

The second difference between expert and non-expert principals was the stake held by the principals in a preconceived solution. Non-expert principals were often strongly committed to such a solution prior to entering the 'collaborative' problem-solving process and constantly manipulated the process in an effort to gain support for that solution. Expert principals, on the other hand, had much less stake in any preconceived solution. They wanted the best possible solution the group could produce and took steps to ensure that such a solution was found. For example, one principal said:

> I can either see it happen or let it wash through and say it was a good try, maybe another time. I'm willing to go with it either way.

Values

As already noted, we leave a detailed treatment of this component to Chapter 7. Suffice to say at this point that experts made more use of their values than did non-experts and relied on different values in some of their problem-solving than did non-expert principals.

Constraints

Expert as compared with non-expert principals were better able to anticipate the obstacles likely to arise during group problem-solving. Non-expert principals either did not anticipate obstacles or they identified relatively superficial obstacles. Even when they did anticipate obstacles, non-expert principals rarely considered, in advance, how they might respond to those obstacles should they arise. This is in contrast to expert principals who planned carefully in advance for how they would address anticipated obstacles, should they arise. In addition, expert principals adapted and responded in a flexible way to unanticipated obstacles which arose. For instance, during the 'stimulated recall' sessions involved in Study Two, one principal said:

> The point he is making which I hadn't taken into account ... I'm bringing up discipline, so obviously it's interpreted that I'm not happy with discipline in the school.

The principal went on to say during the meeting:

> I am glad that point has been raised. By doing this, I'm not saying that things are falling apart. People are on top of things and I appreciate that. At the same time, it's something we must continually be at.

He then provided a personal example of a difficulty he had in handling a discipline problem.

Expert principals tended not to view obstacles as major impediments to problem-solving in the same way that our previous evidence has suggested non-experts do. Furthermore, whereas experts were concerned to learn and build on the perception of their teachers, non-experts viewed differences in their perceptions and those of their teachers as frustrating constraints. This is not surprising given their preconceived ideas about what goals were to be achieved at the meeting.

Solution Processes

The greatest differences between expert and non-expert principals were found within this component of their problem-solving. Non-expert principals rarely planned for collaborative problem-solving. In contrast, experts developed careful plans, as is evident in these remarks:

> [First] I'll share with them what the problem is for me ... [Then] I'll have them working in small groups to identify the problem or what they see as the problem – brainstorm some ideas of what they think the problem is ... After we have a look at what the problems are we can look at some potential solutions.

During the process of collaborative problem-solving, in the context of a staff meeting, experts ensured that the stage for effective collaborative problem-solving was set by providing a clear, detailed introduction to the problem and its background. This was not a matter given much attention by non-experts, one of whom provided no background at all to his staff. Although one non-expert did develop a clear plan for problem-solving at the meeting, he did not share that plan with his staff. Most of the experts shared not only the background to the problem but the process that they were suggesting for its solution – how the meeting would be conducted, for example.

Part of the process for conducting the meeting, on the part of experts, was the careful checking with staffs regarding their interpretation of the problem, and the extent to which their assumptions were shared by staffs. Non-experts invariably assumed that others had the same interpretation of the problem which they held and did not check to see whether or not that was the case. Non-experts, because of their prior commitment to a set of goals and a problem solution, tended to either argue overtly for their own view of what the solution should be during the meeting with their staffs, or manipulated the meeting subtly so that it supported such a view. For example:

> I did cut off one person in the group who spoke only once, and tried to solicit more time to pursue all the data but that was not part of my agenda.

This principal also deflected the need that teachers had to vent feelings of disappointment or outrage over prior results in a survey, even though he had the opportunity and need to do just that.

> I went through that stage and now look at it as a reality ... Let's not stay with the raw numbers here; let's get past that.

Other non-experts changed topics or called on teachers who used the strategies the principal wanted accepted.

Expert school-leaders were able to make clear their own view of the problem without intimidating or restraining their teacher colleagues. In addition, they were open to new information and, if such information warranted it, were prepared to change their views of what the solution should be. Experts, in contrast with non-experts, facilitated collaborative problem-solving by synthesizing the views of others, summarizing progress in the meeting from time to time, providing clarification as needed, and gently prodding the group to keep on task.

None of the non-experts considered how to follow up on decisions made during the meeting, whereas this was done by almost all experts.

Affect

Both experts and non-experts usually appeared to be calm and confident during the problem-solving process with their staffs. One non-expert's frustration was visible on one occasion. There were substantial differences, however, in the amount of anxiety or frustration actually experienced (but not demonstrated) by principals. This was evident in their discussion following the staff meeting. In that context, the majority of non-experts expressed some frustration over the meeting. Their source of frustration was the unwillingness of the staff to agree on what the problem should be:

> Inside me I say, your question is not relevant. It has nothing to do with what we're doing. Damn it, I don't need that ... Outside I hope I didn't show it.

One non-expert also showed some signs of insecurity about his own ability to solve problems collaboratively.

> I guess the problem that I had in the first place was to find a problem for you to see. So I guess the kind of thing I want is some feedback [about] how I conduct meetings on all problems.

There were few signs of such frustration on the part of experts, although one expressed a mild form of frustration with her own seeming inability to help the staff to arrive at a suitable solution. Experts and non-experts made use of humor to diffuse tension and to clarify information during collaborative problem-solving.

Table 6.2 summarizes the processes used by expert and typical school-leaders as they solved swampy problems in collaboration with their teacher colleagues.

Summary and Implications for Leaders of Future Schools

This chapter has described the processes used by expert school-leaders to solve ill-structured or swampy problems. Six components or elements of such problem-solving, initially derived from Leithwood and Stager's study (1989), were used to organize the description of these processes. These elements included problem interpretation, the setting of goals, the nature and use of principles and values, constraints, solution processes, and mood. Processes used by samples of expert school-leaders were contrasted with the processes used by their non-expert peers, in order to highlight the most significant aspects of expertise. In this section, we revisit four features associated with what has been learned about expertise in the swamp that are especially noteworthy for leaders of future schools.

Cognitive Flexibility

One noteworthy feature, evident in how experts solved problems both individually and in groups, is cognitive flexibility. By cognitive flexibility we mean,

Table 6.2: School-Leaders' problem-solving processes: With collaboration

Components	Expert School-Leaders	Typical School-Leaders
Interpretation	• understands importance of having a clear interpretation of problem • seeks out and takes into account the interpretation others have of the problem • immediate problem usually viewed in its relation to the larger mission, and problems, of school • has a clear interpretation which they can describe to others and rationalize	• no conscious reflection on this matter • assumes others share same interpretation • tendency for problems to be viewed in isolation • less clarity about their interpretation, difficulty in explaining it to others
Goals	• has multiple goals for problem-solving • shares own goals with others involved in problem-solving • has goals for both the problem and the meeting in which collaborative problem-solving occurs • strong concern for the development of goals both the principal and staff can agree to • less of a personal stake in any pre-conceived solution, wants the best possible solution the group can produce	• has multiple goals for problem-solving • shares own goals with others involved in problem-solving • has goals for both the problem and the meeting in which collaborative problem-solving occurs concerned with achieving only own goals and getting staff to agree to those goals • often strongly committed to a pre-conceived solution and attempts to manipulate group problem-solving so as to result in support for the pre-conceived solution
Principles/ Values	• see Chapter 7	• see Chapter 7
Constraints	• accurately anticipates obstacles likely to arise during group problem-solving • plans in advance for how to address anticipated obstacles should they arise • adapts and responds flexibly to unanticipated obstacles which arise • does not view obstacles as major impediments to problem-solving	• does not anticipate obstacles or identifies relatively superficial obstacles • rarely considers in advance how to respond to those obstacles that are predicted

Solution Processes

- has well developed plan for collaborative problem-solving (meeting)
- provides clear, detailed introduction to problem and its background to collaborators
- outlines clearly the process for problem-solving (e.g., how meeting will be conducted)
- carefully checks collaborators' interpretations of problem, and own assumptions
- without intimidating or restraining others, clearly indicates own view of the problem and relationship with larger problems
- remains open to new information and changes views, if warranted
- assists collaborative problem-solving by synthesizing, summarizing and clarifying as needed, and by keeping group (gently) on track
- ensures that follow-up is planned

- rarely plans for collaborative process and may value 'spontaneity'
- does not provide clear introduction to problem which occasionally is missing altogether
- is not likely to share plan for meeting with collaborators if plan exists
- assumes others have same interpretations of problem: does not check
- argues stubbornly for own view or 'orchestrates' meeting so that it supports such a view
- adheres to own view in the face of competing views
- shows limited action to assist collaboration and may seriously underestimate time required for collaborators to explore problem
- rarely considers plans of follow-up

Affect

- always appears to be calm and confident
- has hidden anxieties, usually the result of inability to find a workable solution
- invariably treats others politely
- uses humor to diffuse tension and to clarify information

- usually appears calm but frustration may occasionally become visible
- frequently feels frustrated, especially by unwillingness of staff to agree with principal's views
- occasional signs of insecurity about own ability to solve problems
- uses humor to diffuse tension and to clarify information

for example, the ability to exercise control over one's own thought processes and feelings, the ability to detect that one has gone down a blind alley and the willingness to back up and consider other alternatives. Cognitive flexibility also means being open to the views of others, not being held hostage by one's own previous experience (e.g., not seeing every new problem as just a version of an old problem) and being able to change one's interpretation of a problem when confronted with new information. Cognitive flexibility is also a function of one's attitude toward problem-solving; one displays flexibility when 'problems' are considered interesting 'challenges' and 'opportunities' to accomplish one's goals. Many of these aspects of cognitive flexibility were observed among experts in the two studies reviewed in this chapter. All were evident in another of our studies inquiring about the meaning of cognitive flexibility in the context of school leadership (Leithwood and Stager, 1989). These aspects are consistent with the findings of research on social cognition in other fields of activity (Showers and Cantor, 1985).

Stager and Leithwood (1989) also found evidence among typical principals of the kind of cognitive 'errors' associated with inflexible thinking in other fields of activity, as reported by Nisbett and Ross (1980) and others. Such principals, for example, were prone to set priorities for problem-solving based solely on how emotionally vivid or immediately pressing the problems seemed to be ('I keep prioritizing. When there are no problems in the in-basket or walking into my office, I go and play with the kindergarten's ...'). They also tended to generalize from small or biased samples (e.g., involve only like-minded staff in setting school objectives), and failed to determine the actual cause of problems, or that some problems had important elements that were unique ('No brand-new problems come to mind. I sometimes say "I was doing this exact same thing twenty years ago".'). These are examples of inflexible thinking, of which there were others, not evident in the problem-solving of expert school-leaders.

By way of summary, then, our studies of problem-solving in the swamp point to the fundamental importance of cognitive flexibility, as one basis for expert school leadership, now and in the future. Such flexibility involves a total avoidance of cognitive errors and an ability, noted by many authors (e.g., Morine-Dershimer, 1986, Nisbett and Ross, 1980, Schön, 1983) to make very fine discriminations among details of particular situations. Second, cognitive flexibility involves controlling one's negative moods and approaching problem situations with an air of calm confidence. Klemp and McClelland (1986), in studying characteristics of intelligent functioning among managers, found that the 'competency' of self-confidence was absolutely essential and served to drive the other intellectual competencies. Third, cognitive flexibility involves being responsive to the possibilities in the situation, affording a clear illustration of what Sternberg and Wagner (1986) would regard as 'practical intelligence'. These authors use Neisser's (1976) definition of 'intelligent performance in natural settings ... as responding appropriately in terms of one's long-range and short-range goals, given the actual facts of the situation as one discovers them' (p. 137).

It should be noted that cognitive flexibility never involves what Bolman and Deal (1984) refer to as 'overresponsiveness' or 'spinelessness'. Expert school-leaders have core values, beliefs, and goals (or vision) that are inviolable. That is, they display extreme cognitive flexibility, but they are always guided by vision and a coherent set of values.

Using the Capacity of the School Staff to Invent Powerful Solutions

The ability to make the most of the talent of those within the school itself in identifying powerful solutions to swampy problems was evident in our research on expert group problem-solving. 'Bounded rationality' offers a powerful theoretical perspective from which to appreciate how collaborative problem-solving can lead to better solutions. The phrase, initially coined by Simon (1957) was intended to draw attention to the limitations in a person's capacity to process information in the face of the complex demands placed on that processing by frequently encountered problems. The limited capacity of short-term memory was of particular interest to Simon (1957) and others who elaborated the idea. As Shulman and Carey (1984) explain, however, bounded rationality focused exclusively on individual thinking and did not adequately recognize how individuals 'participate in jointly produced social and cultural systems of meaning that transcend individuals' (p. 503). Because human rationality 'whether bounded or not, is practiced in the context of social exchange and human interaction' (p. 515), a view of people as collectively rational is offered as a better conception of problem-solving in many life circumstances. From such a view, problem solvers use others to compensate for their own limitations. They do this by transforming, redefining, and distributing parts of the problem task to others in the working group, in an opportunistic way according to each individual's unique abilities. More specifically, under ideal collaborative problem-solving conditions, better solutions seem likely to be the result of, for example:

- A broader range of perspectives from which to interpret the problem (Expert school-leaders do this when they actively seek out staff interpretations, are explicit about their own interpretation, and place problems in a larger perspective)
- An expanded array of potential solutions from which to choose (Expert school-leaders foster this by assisting group discussions of alternatives, by ensuring open discussion, and avoiding commitment to preconceived solutions)
- A richer, more concrete body of information about the context in which the problem must be solved (In our research, experts did this by actively listening to staff views, clarifying, and summarizing information during meetings)
- The reduced likelihood of individually biased perspectives operating in the solution process (Experts assisted with this by keeping groups on task, not imposing their own perspective, changing their own views when warranted, checking out their own and others' assumptions and remaining calm and confident)

When such conditions prevail:

Humans liberate rationality from its bonds through the collective work of civility. (Shulman and Carey, 1984, p. 518)

Empirical evidence in support of the value of collaborative problem-solving can be found in the now extensive body of research on peer interaction (see

Webb, 1989, for a review of this research). This research unpacks, in more detail, forms of group interaction most helpful in reaching productive outcomes. Schoenfeld (1989) provides a useful, personal case study of how a collaborative research setting fostered achievements not possible for him to accomplish working alone.

Contributing to the Long-Term Growth of Staff

Another important set of abilities for future leaders to possess, evident in the group problem-solving of experts, is contributing to the long-term growth of staff. Vygotsky's concept of a 'zone of proximal development' has been used in research on peer interaction, to help explain how such interaction may stimulate individual development in a collaborative setting (e.g., Damon and Phelps, 1989). This concept also seems valuable in helping to understand why and under what conditions group problem-solving by school-leaders and teachers may contribute to their long-term growth. According to Vygotsky, an individual's independent problem-solving is a function of processes in which they have participated in the past – for the most part, processes involving interaction (or collaboration) with others. In this sense, an individual's independent problem-solving capacity, at a given point in time, is an internalization of previously experienced, collaborative problem-solving processes; it is their actual developmental level. The zone of proximal development:

> is the distance between the actual development level as determined by independent problem solving and the level of potential development as determined through problem solving ... in collaboration with more capable peers. (Vygotsky, 1978, p. 86)

In the context of school-leader/staff collaborative problem-solving, the long-term growth of staff seems likely when, for example:

- The process used by the group is actually superior to an individual's independent problem-solving and the individual participants recognize that superiority. (Experts in our study seemed to be achieving this, by planning carefully in advance for how group problem-solving would occur, by actively facilitating the group's problem-solving, and by anticipating constraints)
- There are opportunities for the group to reflect consciously on the process in which they are involved, to evaluate it, and to participate in its refinement. (Experts provided for this by explicitly outlining to teachers the process they planned, by planning for follow-up, and by gently keeping the group on task)
- Individual members of the group compare their own independent problem-solving with the group's processes and identify ways of increasing the robustness of their own independent processes. (This was a condition experts in our research appeared not to address, but one that is important, nevertheless)

Joseph Schwab's (1983) conception of curriculum deliberation is based on a set of premises very similar to those captured in this discussion of collegial rationality. He also argues that teacher involvement, in the kinds of deliberations which he advocates, leads to a form of long-term growth, critical to his conception of teaching as a complex and demanding art. Teachers, from this view, are required to decide hundreds of times a day and, as Shulman (1984) notes, their options arise differently every day with every group of students. No theoretical principles or abstract guidelines are sufficient to the task faced by teachers under these circumstances. What is required, rather, is a deep understanding of their purposes and how such purposes may be accomplished flexibly and often opportunistically (what we have been referring to as 'vision'). Such understanding arises through thoughtful and extensive deliberations about the nature of instruction, the school curriculum, and other problem areas that teachers are expected to address at higher stages in their development (Fullan and Connelly, 1987, see also Chapter 8).

Developing Staff Commitment to, and through, Shared Goals

Future schools seem likely to provide opportunities for teachers to play a more professional role. Trends, for example, toward school-based management and teacher empowerment, as discussed in Chapter 3, can be viewed as having that result. As many argue, however, (e.g., Little, 1982, Rosenholtz, 1989, Fullan, 1990) for this role change to result in better experiences for students, this professionalism will have to be pursued in a collegial way. School-leaders will need to be able to develop among staff a strong commitment to shared goals, and a widely shared, defensible vision.

There is much evidence in support of the claim that at least some forms of involvement or collaboration in problem-solving lead to greater commitment by participants to implement solutions arising from such problem-solving (e.g., Ettling and Jago, 1988). Under what conditions of involvement does commitment arise and why? Conventional wisdom has it that it is simply the participation in the solution process that leads to greater commitment to the solution itself. Though this is no doubt true, we see that the reason for the increased commitment is due to the concept of shared goals. Increased commitment as a result of shared goals occurs because: (a) an individual's goals are a prime motivator of their behavior; (b) an individual's goals are arrived at, in part, through social interaction; (c) certain characteristics of goals are more motivating than others; and (d) some forms of social interaction produce goal characteristics better than others, in particular, forms of social interaction which lead to shared goals.

> When individuals commit themselves to explicit goals, perceived negative discrepancies between what they do and what they seek to achieve create dissatisfactions that serve as motivational inducements for change ... Once individuals have made self-satisfaction contingent upon goal attainment, they tend to persist in their efforts until their performances match what they are seeking to achieve. (Bandura, 1977, p. 161)

In our research on expert problem-solving in groups, school-leaders helped make goals more explicit by sharing their own goals for problem-solving and interpreting problems in relation to the larger mission of the school.

Certain characteristics of goals contribute to their role in motivating behavior. Relatively explicit goals provide a clearer basis for self-evaluation than do ambiguous goals. Moderately difficult goals are more motivating than those which seem trivial because of their simplicity, or those which seem unrealistic because of their excessive difficulty. Experts, in our research, seemed to assist with this by encouraging staff discussion of goals and, as already noted, interpreting problems in relation to the larger vision and mission of the school. In addition, relatively immediate or proximal goals (or subgoals) serve as greater stimulants to action than do remote goals, especially when there are competing demands on one's attention.

Goals are actively constructed by the individual through social interaction. The nature of such interaction is substantially influenced by the context (or culture) in which people find themselves. Rosenholtz's (1989) research provides evidence of this influence on teachers. Her study showed that in school contexts which she described as 'static' (dominated by norms of self-reliance and isolation), teacher's goals were, for example, idiosyncratic, focusing on maintenance activities and interaction with others about social issues or discipline problems. School contexts described as 'moving', in contrast, appeared to foster shared goals focused on student learning and interaction with others about instructional improvement. In 'moving contexts':

> principals interacted with teachers to shape their school reality, to construct school traditions ... goals about the importance of students' basic skills came to be commonly shared. (Rosenholtz, 1989, p. 39)

Shared goals, in Rosenholtz's formulation, constitute the initial foundation on which to build teacher commitment, certainly about instructional practices, and for the confidence to participate in further collaboration. Experts in our research manifested a strong concern for arriving at goal consensus.

Collaboration with one's colleagues seems likely to generate not only shared goals but also goals which have highly motivating properties. Interaction requires one to put one's purposes in words and to be clear enough to explain one's purposes to others. Furthermore, the public nature of such interaction creates pressure to set goals which seem worthwhile to others and therefore not likely trivial. Continuous interaction about shared goals supplements, through the evaluation of others, one's own evaluation of discrepancies between performance and desired achievement. Finally, because they are worked out in a deliberative manner (with the aid of others), such goals are less likely to be remote or unrealistic.

Conclusion

Fewer things are more predictable in the life of leaders of future schools than the consistent presence of swampy problems. Many of the swampy problems facing current school-leaders will be on the high ground for future school-leaders. So, knowing what they are is not of much help. But the processes used by today's experts are of significant assistance to future school-leaders. Learning from and about these processes is a useful way of reducing the time and effort required for developing expertise. It also seems clear from the research reviewed in this chapter that expert group problem-solving processes serve double duty. On the one hand, they solve the immediate swampy problem. And on the other, they contribute to the long-term capacity of the school to solve future problems. This is 'transformational leadership' – the empowerment of others – which we identified as one of the three components of the leadership problem, in Chapter 1, of special consequence for future school leaders.

Chapter 7

The Special Role of Values in School Leadership

About the nature and role of values in solving school-leader problems, there is considerably more heat than light. Values, somehow, ought to be important. Social psychology, for example, has long offered impressive empirical support for their role in peoples' thinking and problem-solving (e.g., Rokeach, 1975). Furthermore, students of educational leadership and administration acknowledge such importance in their theoretical reflections. 'Values are central to educational administration', notes Willower (1987, p. 17) in the sense that administrators make choices among competing values and consider the desirability of alternative courses of action on a daily basis. But as Greenfield has persistently pointed out, the empirical study of administration has traditionally 'ignore[d] value and sentiment as springs of human action' (1986, p. 59).

The research on which this chapter is based was stimulated indirectly by such evidence, unrelated to school leadership, as Rokeach's (1975). It was also encouraged by theoretical arguments of the sort offered by students of educational administration like Willower and Greenfield. Research describing expert problem-solving in the swamp, summarized in Chapter 6, created a much more direct stimulus for this work, however. Whether solving problems alone or in groups, this research points to substantial differences between expert and non-expert school-leaders in the role played by their values. Such values also appeared to be pervasive and critical: as we noted, for example, in the discussion of cognitive flexibility in Chapter 6, expert school-leaders 'display extreme cognitive flexibility, but they are always guided by a coherent set of values'. Given these starting points for examining the nature and role of values more carefully, this chapter addresses four sets of questions. The first question is whether empirical evidence from school-leaders supports implications regarding the significance of values in their problem-solving and, if so, what role do such values play? A second set of questions is aimed at more specifically mapping the terrain of school-leaders' values: Which values are used (or come to the surface) during the process of problem-solving and do some appear more frequently than others?

If, as Greenfield (1986) suggests, values are 'springs of human action', different levels of school-leaders' expertise (e.g., as in Chapter 5) may be explained, in part, by adherence to different values. Indeed, such differences may be as important in accounting for variations in school-leaders' problem-solving as is knowledge and skill, the most popular source of explanation. Our third set of questions is about the relationship between values and different levels of problem-solving expertise. Finally, we ask how school-leaders resolve value conflicts – this, in recognition of the competing values typically encountered, especially in solving the kind of swampy, 'people problems' evident in the research reported in Chapter 4 and by others (e.g., Strike, Soltis and Haller, 1989).

Three of the studies used to answer these questions were designed and conducted in parallel and largely independent of one another. They were guided by different frameworks and used different methods of data collection. The fourth study was specifically designed with the results of the first three in mind. Its purpose was to develop a conception of the nature and role of values that could account for the results of the previous studies and to further test the claims resulting from those studies.

The next section of the chapter briefly summarizes the theoretical frameworks and data-collection methods used in each of the four studies: more details are provided on these matters in this chapter than is our practice in other chapters because we believe it to be more crucial to an appreciation of the results. This is followed by a section in which the combined results of all studies are brought to bear on each of the four sets of questions of interest in the chapter. A subsequent section explores the implications of the studies for the leadership of future schools.

Frameworks and Methods: Four Studies

Overview

Each study conceived of a value as: 'a conception, explicit or implicit, distinctive of an individual or characteristic of a group, of the desirable which influences the selection from available modes, means and ends of action' (Hodgkinson, 1978, p. 121). Embedded in this definition are attributes of values also evident in the work of Rokeach (1975), Kluckhon (1951), Smith (1963) and Williams (1968). That is, a value:

- is an enduring belief about the desirability of some means; and
- once internalized, a value also becomes a standard or criterion for guiding one's own actions and thought, for influencing the actions and thought of others, and for morally judging oneself and others

A person's value system, Rokeach (1975) suggests, is a learned system of rules for making choices and for resolving conflicts. While based on this common definition of a value, the four studies thought about value types and relationships differently. Studies One and Two were guided by previously developed values frameworks: those of Christopher Hodgkinson (1978) and Clive Beck (1984a) respectively. Study Three 'discovered' values among a set of data, thought to be primarily concerned with purely rational aspects of principals' problem-solving. These data were largely useful in clarifying the role that values play in such problem-solving. The final study was guided by an original values' framework consistent with results of the previous three studies.

Methods used to collect data about school-leaders' values involved, in one way or another, having school-leaders talk out loud about how they would solve a problem. Sometimes this was a problem they had solved in the past, sometimes a simulated problem given to them. Sometimes they were asked to listen to a tape recording of themselves and their staffs, engaged in group problem-solving and tell the researcher what they were thinking about at the time. In combination, these different methods serve to control for most of the sources of invalidity usually attributed to verbal reports (Ericcson and Simon, 1984, Nisbett and Wilson, 1977) including the distorted reporting of cognitive processes, incompleteness of description, and failure of respondents to rely on memory or to rely only on what can be retrieved from long-term memory.

Study One: Begley (1988)

School-leaders' decisions to adopt and promote the use of computers in their schools provided the context for this study. Its purpose was to learn more about the nature of values related to such decisions, the relative influence of values in comparison with other factors on these decisions, and the relationship between school-leaders' orientation to their role and the values which they used in decision-making.

Hodgkinson's (1978) conception of value types and relationships served as a framework for collecting data about school-leaders' values (Evers, 1985, offers a critical analysis of the framework). Three categories of values are included in Hodgkinson's framework:

1.   **Transrational values** grounded in principle.
2a. **Rational values** based on an individual's assessment of consequences, the attainment of what is perceived as right.
2b. **Rational values** based on an individual's assessment of consensus, again, the attainment of which is perceived as right.
3.   **Subrational values** related to personal preferences or what is perceived as good.

Type 3 values represent an individual's conception of what is 'good'. Such values are grounded in affect or emotion and constitute the individual's preference structure. They are self-justifying and primitive. Each of the two remaining categories of values describes a 'rightness' that, according to Hodgkinson, is higher than the one below it. Type 3 values, unlike the others, represent what is 'good' as opposed to 'right'.

Type 2 values are subclassified: Type 2b values attribute 'rightness' to consensus or the will of the majority in a given collectivity. Type 2a values define 'rightness' in relation to a desirable future state of affairs or analysis of the consequences entailed by the value judgment. Type 2 values, as a whole, are rational; Type 3 values subrational; and Type 1 values are transrational.

Hodgkinson argues that Type 1 values are superior, more authentic, better justified or more defensible than the other two types. Indeed, use of these 'sacred' values in decision-making, according to Hodgkinson, is the hallmark of the ethical educational leader. Such a leader: 'seeks to increase his own degrees of freedom (a Type 1 value) and the degrees of freedom of those who function under his aegis' (1986, p. 8). However, Hodgkinson (1978) also claims that values tend to lose their level of grounding with time, thereby reducing their authenticity or their force of moral insight. He is critical, for example, of what he sees as the widespread use of Type 2 rational values in administration and attributes it to a positivistic, impersonal view of organizations and a natural desire to avoid the messiness and unpredictability associated with use of other types of values. This tendency toward rational values is greatly reinforced by the characteristics of contemporary culture, according to Hodgkinson.

Interviews conducted with fifteen elementary school principals (about two-thirds of the principals in one central Ontario school system) provided data for Study One. Each interview lasted from one and a half to three hours and was tape recorded and transcribed.

Study Two: Campbell-Evans (1988)

In addition to the purposes for Study One, Campbell inquired about how principals responded to problematic situations in which courses of action proposed by others (e.g., senior administrators) conflicted with their values. The values' framework used in this study was developed by Beck (1984a,b,c). It is based on the premise that a fairly common set of universal values exists. Priorities and emphases may shift over time and with respect to specific circumstances. Nevertheless, a set of 'Basic Human Values' can be identified, since values arise from need and many individuals have similar needs. These values are 'part of human nature and the human condition' (Beck, 1984b, p. 3) and include for example: survival, health, happiness, friendship, helping others (to an extent), respect for others, knowledge, fulfillment, freedom, and a sense of meaning in life. Some of these values are means to others but this cluster of basic human values, according to Beck, is mainly ends-oriented. Furthermore, these values are interconnected and are continuously being balanced (or traded off) with others. A sense of fluidity, openness and flexibility exists within this formulation.

In addition to basic human values, Beck (1984a, p. 3) identifies four other categories of values: moral values (e.g., carefulness, courage, responsibility); social and political values (e.g., tolerance, participation, loyalty); intermediate-range values (e.g., shelter, entertainment, fitness); and specific values (such as a car, a telephone and a high school diploma). According to Beck's conception there are no absolute values. He emphasizes the importance of regarding values within their own system rather than in isolation. Values are both means and ends. Viewing a value as merely a means is to deny its intrinsic worth. Viewing it merely as an end is to make it into an absolute. Even the 'Basic Human Values' category forms a set 'each of which has considerable importance in itself but must also be weighed against other values' (Beck, 1984c, p. 4).

All eight elementary and junior high school principals in a small urban school district in Alberta provided data for Study Two. These data were collected in three phases. Phase One included retrospective, audio-taped interviews with principals, concerning two or three prior but recent decisions considered 'important' by the principals; these data were analyzed before the second phase of data collection was initiated.

Phase Two required principals to think aloud as they responded to five simulated decision problems presented by the researcher; these responses were also audiotaped and transcribed. At the completion of think-aloud responses, principals were asked to react to the 'accuracy' of an analysis of their responses in Phase One. Each principal was given a written report of the identification and prioritization of values revealed in their Phase One interviews and their reaction was requested.

Phase Three consisted of an interview designed to identify the level of expertise on the high ground of each principal.

Study Three: Leithwood and Stager (1989)

Study Three, other parts of which were described in Chapter 6, did not begin with an interest in school-leaders' values. Rather, as described in Chapter 6, its explicit objectives were to identify the components of school-leaders' problem-solving processes and to explore similarities and differences between expert and non-experts in the swamp with respect to such components. As we reported earlier, however, values emerged from the results as an important component of problem-solving and one within which expert and non-expert school-leaders differed markedly. This study was most helpful in clarifying the role of values in their problem-solving.

Study Four: Leithwood and Steinbach (1991) (reported here for the first time)

This study was intended to test the extent to which some of the results of the previous three studies could be generalized. It inquired about the nature and role of values with an additional set of data. The six components of problem-solving identified in Study Three provided the overall framework for the study. But to guide questions specifically about the nature of values, Beck's (1984) framework (Study Two) was modified on the basis of what had been learned in the previous studies, specifically about administrators' values (see Table 7.1). The modified framework also incorporated those categories of values in Hodgkinson's (1978) framework shown to be relevant to administrators in Study One.

The first category 'Basic Human Values' incorporates values at the apex of Hodgkinson's hierarchy which he calls principles. These are primarily terminal values: they refer to 'end states of existence' (Rokeach, 1975, p. 160). The remaining categories of values worth striving for are more instrumental in nature. They represent preferable modes of conduct although, as Beck (1984a) warns, the distinction between means and ends is difficult to maintain. Peoples' values act as interdependent systems to influence their problem-solving. Categories entitled 'Gereral Moral Values' and 'Professional Values' include norms of conduct or guidelines for judging the ethics of an individual's actions. 'Professional Values', an addition to Beck's framework, includes values uniquely relevant to guiding decisions in one's work life; Hodgkinson's (1978) values of consequence are included here. As Bayles (1981) suggests, in order for 'Professional Values' to be guides to ethical conduct they must be consistent with and subordinate to 'Basic Human Values'.

Table 7.1:   A classification of values and illustrative statements

Categories of Values	Illustrative Statement
Set 1. Basic Human Values	
• Freedom	Staff is not forced to supervise dances by the Education Act ... I would not force people to do this
• Happiness	Most people felt pretty good about those goals
• Knowledge	I would collect as much information about the probable suspects as possible
• Respect for others	In a blanket approach you could offend many fine teachers
• Survival	I don't think you can let an issue like this dominate a lot of time
Set 2. General Moral Values	
• Carefulness	[Check] to indeed see if whether or not we have a problem
• Fairness (or justice)	Make sure that some people who are a little unsure of themselves also have an opportunity to speak
• Courage	Their responsibility is to speak out when vandalism occurs
Set 3. Professional Values	
• General Responsibility as Educator	Your value system is interfering with the mandate that we have in education
• Specific Role Responsibility	Staff have to feel they are supported by the office
• Consequences ...	Kids deserve a certain number of social events
• Consequences (other)	There's an impression that ... students aren't under control
Set 4. Social and Political Values	
• Participation	Involve groups such as Heads' Council, Special Education, Student Services
• Sharing	Allow people to get things off their chests – talk about the problems they perceive
• Loyalty, Solidarity and Commitment	We [admin. team] have to be seen as being philosophically in tune
• Helping others	Let's help each other [school and parent] deal with that child

'Social and Political Values', incorporating Hodgkinson's (1978) values of consensus, recognize the essentially social nature of human action and the need for individuals to define themselves in relation to others to make their lives meaningful. There is also a close link between the specific values in this category and the 'Basic Human Value' of respect for others.[4]

The categories of values included in Table 7.1 do not include Beck's short or intermediate range values. Such values did not emerge in Studies One, Two or Three as of much relevance for principals.

Data for Study Four resulted from a replication of methods used in Study Three (think-aloud responses to a set of simulated problems), with a group of eleven expert secondary principals; in this case, they were selected as experts in the manner also described in Study Three (see Chapter 6).

The next four sections of the paper use these studies as a whole to answer the questions of interest in this chapter. In each section we also point out the similarities and differences between results of these studies and relevant studies carried out with managers of non-school organizations.

The Role and Significance of Values in School-Leaders' Problem-Solving

Three studies helped clarify the role that values play in school-leaders' problem-solving. Study One inquired about the role of values in their decisions about the adoption and implementation of computer technology in their schools. Results demonstrated a pre-eminent role for values in the adoption decision but a much less important role in the subsequent process of solving the implementation problem. For that problem, factors identified in school-improvement research (e.g., fit, building user commitment) appeared to be more influential. These results appear to reflect one of two relationships between values and actions proposed by Hambrick and Brandon (1988): a direct relationship – that is, dominant or very strong managerial values are thought to be capable of dictating behavior without any (or much) regard for facts. Indeed, Study One provides especially relevant support for this role of values since a number of school-leaders in the study decided to adopt computers without knowing what the consequences would be for students or others. This role for values has been termed 'behavior channeling' (England, 1967).

Study Two examined the role of both internal influences (i.e., beliefs and values) and external influences (e.g., time, money) on school-leaders' problem-solving. Results argue for a more pervasive role for values than did Study One by suggesting that values give meaning to potential external influences and act as filters in determining whether potential external influences will be allowed to be actual influences. So, for example, factual information in a report available to school-leaders, relevant to some aspect of their work, is more likely to influence that work if they strongly value 'knowledge' (a 'Basic Human Value') than if they do not. These results illustrate the second type of relationship between values and action suggested by Hambrick and Brandon (1988): this is an indirect relationship, termed by England (1967) 'perceptual screening'. Values influence school-leaders' perceptions of events causing them to attend closely to some and ignore others altogether. These highly subjective perceptions then lead to action.

Finally, Study Three which compared the problem-solving of expert and non-expert school-leaders, especially in response to ill-structured problems, found that, for experts, explicit values acted as substitutes for knowledge. An ill-structured problem, by definition, is one about which the solver possesses little problem-relevant knowledge. Unlike non-expert school-leaders, experts were relatively clear about their principles and values, and so were able to make use of them as guidelines for problem-solving (e.g., 'I may not know exactly how to solve this problem but whatever we do, we are going to be open and honest with everyone'). This role played by values when there is little problem-relevant knowledge appears to be the same role proposed by Barnard (cited in Hambrick and Brandon, 1988) when managers face the opposite: excessive knowledge about a problem. Values, he suggests, provide a moral code for sorting a bewildering load of information and options that may confront the manager. In the absence of such a code, the manager bogs down.

In sum, then, dominant values appear to play an especially explicit and important role (behavior channeling) at key points in the problem-solving process. But throughout, they also act, more subtly, as perceptual screens for determining what aspects of the wider environment will be considered. And they are substitutes for knowledge (or moral rules of thumb) in the face of novel problems.

These studies provide considerable support for the theoretical claims that have been made by Hodgkinson (1978, 1986), Greenfield (1986) and others about the importance of values in school-leaders' problem-solving.

Types of Values and Their Relative Importance

Only Study Three did not inquire about the nature of values used by school-leaders in their problem-solving and the relative importance of such values. Results from Study Four represent the findings of Studies One and Two reasonably well and are reported first. These results speak to not only types of values used by school-leaders and their relative weight but they also explore possible differences that might arise, depending on whether a problem is viewed by the school-leader as a high ground or swampy problem.

Results from Study Four indicated that 'Professional Values' was the most frequently cited category of values; the least frequently cited was 'General Moral Values', and 'Basic Human Values' and 'Social-Political Values' ranked second and third.

Within categories, there was consistency in the specific values cited whether most or least clear problems were being addressed. 'specific role responsibility', 'consequences for one's immediate clients' (e.g., students) and 'knowledge' appear to be the dominant specific values cited by school-leaders in their problem-solving. Also cited frequently in relation to most and least clear problems were 'general responsibilities as an educator', 'participation' and 'respect for others'.

Consistent with findings in Study Three, values emerged more frequently in principals' responses to least clear (total frequency = seventy-four) as compared with most clear (total frequency = forty-nine) problems. This contrast is, in fact, greater than it appeared in our data because results were unavailable for one principal's response to the least clear problems. Adjusting for these missing data suggests that values were mentioned about 65 percent more frequently in response to least clear as compared with most clear problems.

Most of the differences between the results of Study Four and the results of Studies One and Two were due to differences in the frameworks used for coding. Study One, guided by Hodgkinson's framework, found values of consequence and consensus to be used most frequently by principals. Study Two attributed greatest weight to Beck's 'Social and Political' category of values and found the specific value 'Responsibility' to be used quite frequently. 'Responsibility' and 'consequences' values are part of the most frequently used category of 'Professional Values' in Study Four; 'consensus' is part of the category 'Social and Political' values common to Study Two and Four frameworks – ranked first in Study Two and third in Study Four (although only marginally less frequently mentioned than the second ranked category). 'Respect for others' and 'knowledge' appear to receive comparable frequencies of mention in Studies Two and Four; they were not a part of the Study One framework.

In sum, results from the three studies concerned with types of values and their relevant importance were highly consistent. This consistency appeared in spite of the use of somewhat different data-collection procedures, school-leaders drawn from different geographical regions and school levels (elementary and secondary), and school systems varying widely in size and expectations for their principals. Even though the size of the combined sample of principals studied was small (thirty-four), such consistency adds to the confidence one can have in the robustness of the results.

Based on their review, Hambrick and Brandon (1988) concluded that six sets of values encompass the results of efforts, to date, to identify managerial values. At least some aspects of four of these six sets appear in our values framework (see Table 7.1):

- **Collectivism**: includes at least 'Respect for Others' (in set 1) and probably 'Fairness' (in set 2)
- **Duty**: includes 'General Responsibility as Educator' and 'Specific, Role Responsibility' (in set 3) 'Loyalty and Solidarity' and 'Sharing' (in set 4)
- **Rationality**: includes 'Knowledge' (in set 1)
- **Materialism**: may be aspects of 'Happiness' and 'Freedom' (in set 1) for some people

Our classification scheme does not directly reflect Hambrick and Brandon's (1988) 'novelty' (to value change, the new, the different) category although Hodgkinson's personal preferences seem to be this. Nor is their evidence among school-leaders in our four studies of the Hambrick and Brandon's category 'power' (to value control of situations and people). Parenthetically, Leithwood and Steinbach (1991) did find evidence of a power/control value among chief education officers whose roles more closely approximated the executive roles included in much of the research reviewed by Hambrick and Brandon. Perhaps position in the hierarchy has some relationship to leaders' values.

Comparing the Hambrick and Brandon (1988) results with those from Studies One, Two and Four suggests that a large core of values are shared not only among school-leaders but across managers in many different types of organizations. This comparison also suggests some differences, with school-leaders showing greater evidence of such social values as 'participation' and less evidence of valuing 'novelty' (or personal preferences). This combination of differences supports a relatively conservative orientation to change by present school-leaders: conservative, because opportunities for radical change are blunted by others through participation, and the value 'novelty' is more weakly held.

Relationships Between School-Leaders' Values and Expertise

Studies Two and Three examined the relationship between school-leaders' values and their levels of problem-solving expertise (see Chapters 5 and 6).

School-leaders included in Study Two (using Beck's framework of values) divided themselves evenly between two levels of expertise on the high ground. Half the principals appeared to be humanitarians (Level 2) and half were program managers (Level 3) (Fig. 5.1). Evidence from this study suggested that, while both sets of school-leaders shared a common core of values, a strong relationship existed between levels of high ground expertise and some specific values, most notably within the category 'Basic Human Values', mentioned most frequently. 'Respect for others' was the most frequently mentioned 'Basic Human Value' by school-leaders labelled humanitarians. For the more expert program managers 'knowledge' was the most frequently mentioned 'Basic Human Value'. Within the category of 'Social and Political Values', both sets of school-leaders frequently mentioned 'participation', but humanitarians made greater mention also of 'sharing'. 'Responsibility' was the moral value mentioned most by both sets of school-leaders. Humanitarians also identified 'carefulness' as a value in this category.

School-leaders in Study Three were divided into an expert group and a non-expert group. For the most part, the expert group engaged in Level 4 high ground problem-solving (see Fig. 5.1). Most non-experts were humanitarians. Comparing the responses of these two groups to high ground problems revealed few differences with respect to principles and values. Three differences were evident, however, in responses to swampy problems. As compared with the non-expert group, experts more frequently drew upon principles and values in their problem-solving. Given current expectations for the role, the principles on which the experts drew also seemed more defensible: for example, greater attention was given to consequences for students. Finally, the expert group more frequently relied on 'Specific Role Responsibility' as a value in approaching swampy problems: this finding is consistent with evidence collected from chief education officers (Leithwood and Steinbach, 1991) and expert secondary principals (Leithwood and Steinbach, in press b).

Our research suggests, in sum, that school-leaders rely on a common core of values in their problem-solving, independent of their levels of expertise. This is the case, in particular, with 'General Moral Values' and 'Social and Political Values'. Since education is indeed a 'moral' enterprise and therefore likely to attract people with similar 'Basic Moral Values', this is not surprising. Furthermore, as a 'boundary spanner', principals are regularly in communication with many different groups of people and spend as much as three-quarters of their time in personal communication (Martin and Willower, 1981). It would be difficult to avoid seriously acknowledging the influence of 'Social and Political Values' in such an environment.

But there does appear to be evidence of relationships between patterns of practice and both 'Basic Human' and 'Professional' values. For example, the humanitarians' preoccupations with school climate and interpersonal relationships seems consistent with the frequency of mention of the value of 'sharing'. Similarly, program managers' concerns for the quality of the classroom learning environment seems consistent with the stress they give to 'knowledge'. These relationships provide tentative support for school-leaders' values as a partial explanation for or a variable interacting with their levels of expertise.

More specifically, results concerning the dominant values of effective school-leaders are intriguing in light of Hambrick and Brandon (1988). Their review stimulated the suggestion that the more managers value rationality (what we have called 'knowledge') the more their other values will operate through percep-tual screening: this also appears to be the case as managers increasingly value duty (our 'responsibility' values). Since our evidence depicts the most expert school-leaders adhering strongly to both sets of values, a substantial direct influence of values on action seems likely. This assertion assumes considerable discretion for school-leaders to act in concert with their values since organizational constraints on school administrators' actions will blunt the influence of values on action. Indeed, as school-based management creates more discretion for school-leaders, their values are likely to become an increasingly productive focus of attention, especially for purposes of school-leader selection.

Resolving Value Conflicts

This issue was addressed by Studies Two and Four. As part of Study Four, school-leaders were asked to: (a) describe a problem in which they had been involved which had a great deal of value conflict, (b) indicate what were the competing values, and (c) outline how they had dealt with the conflict.

Our understanding of responses to this question indicates that school-leaders encountered two types of value-related conflicts. One type involved competition between two or more values for recognition in the formulation of a solution. Such competition took three different forms:

- Value conflicts between two or more people other than the principal with the principal acting as mediator (e.g., enrichment teachers and regular classroom teachers disagreeing about the meaning of treating students fairly in the context of an 'honor week');
- Value conflicts between the principal and other staff members (e.g., general moral value of principal with respect to adultery in conflict with the values of two married staff members having an affair with one another; the principal was also quite concerned about the consequences for students);
- Value conflicts concerning the principal alone (e.g., principal 'caught' between the need to act quickly to remove from the classroom a teacher accused of inappropriate behavior with an older student, and the value of fair treatment and due process for the value of fair treatment and due process for the teacher)

A second source of conflict for school-leaders was between a set of values strongly held by them, and their actions. This conflict was usually experienced as an inability to act in a manner consistent with values held. One school-leader, for example, held a strongly nurturant attitude toward his teachers and experienced considerable conflict in being unable to effectively counsel one teacher toward a consistent and productive career plan:

It's a value conflict for me because I think she's making all the wrong decisions and it breaks my heart and I cannot do anything about it.

Principals also used two distinct processes for attempting to resolve value conflicts. The first type we called 'deep and strong' because it appeared to be analogous to the solution processes of expert school-leaders in response to other sorts of swampy problems. This process, used by about half of the school-leaders to resolve conflicts between competing values, included: taking considerable care and effort in the early stages to clarify the nature of the conflict; satisfying themselves that the problem could not be usefully interpreted as involving anything but serious value conflicts (i.e., avoiding such an interpretation where possible); and clarifying for themselves their own priority among the competing values. As part of the process, school-leaders relied on formal, organizational procedures, where appropriate, for resolving value conflicts (e.g., teacher-dismissal procedures) once the conflicts were clarified. Other less formal but systematic procedures such as information collection, collaboration with others, and consensus-reaching techniques were also used. When these procedures failed, as they sometimes did, school-leaders capitalized on unanticipated opportunities (e.g., a parental complaint about a teacher).

The second type of conflict-resolution process used by school-leaders, we labelled 'surface and weak'. Only one school-leader used a version of this process to resolve a conflict between two values. Three school-leaders, however, used it in an effort to find a course of action consistent with their values. In no case did this process result in a solution satisfactory to the school-leader. The process was one in which school-leaders often sought out others' interpretations of the conflict and consulted with others about solutions. Nevertheless, the cause of the conflict usually remained unclear (e.g., a teachers' erratic behavior, a teacher's lack of interpersonal skill) and possible courses of action were considered and tried sequentially (and, in one case, only half-heartedly). School-leaders using this process seemed less clear about their own relevant values and had fewer existing procedures to call on as supports for their own actions.

Study Two approached principals' resolution of value conflicts from a different perspective than Study Four. As a result, the two sets of research results are best viewed as combining to reveal a larger proportion of a still incomplete picture, rather than two separate snapshots of the same complete picture. Whereas Study Four included school-leaders' responses to value conflicts arising from problems within the school, Study Two examined conflicts created through the imposition of policy from outside the school. School-leaders were presented with a simulated demand from their districts to implement a policy which conflicted with some of their central values. This type of value conflict constrains alternatives for acting more severely than does the value-conflict situations of interest in Study Four. It required school-leaders to weigh one specific value 'respect for authority' (Hambrick and Brandon's 'duty') against a range of personally held values which varied across school-leaders in the study.

Seven out of eight school-leaders in the study clearly indicated that it was their duty to implement the policy as written. Comments such as 'you still follow the policy because it's policy', 'you are bounded by Board policy', and 'as an administrator, I must administer the policy', reflect the degree to which they felt committed to the implementation of official policy. Their individual preferences took second place to their 'respect for authority' principle which compelled them to follow the policy as an initial action. In this study, 'respect for authority' is difficult to separate from 'specific role responsibility' in Study Four. One school-leader recalled a conflict which was the result of staff having no role in policy development. For another, a situation was perceived as unfair because of the demands placed on staff. Conflict, in a third example, arose from what the school-leader perceived as insufficient time available to meet the requirements of new policy.

In spite of whatever differences school-leaders had with the policy, however, they initiated its implementation. Then they began to deal with the conflict. A common, first step of implementation initiated a series of events. While acting within the policy, all eight principals indicated that they would 'do something', that is, some action would be taken. Action was first an expression of concern to significant others about the policy's content which subsequently involved these individuals or groups in the conflict situation. In most cases this expression of concern involved the immediate school staff initially and then expanded to include the broader community of other school-leaders and/or the superintendent, or the elected trustees. The opinion of other school-leaders was sought in five of eight cases through the forum of the school-leaders' meeting. A desire to increase the understanding of staff was expressed by three principals. This expression of concern took shape through formation of school committees, working from within the policy toward change, working with the policy, working with staff, preparing a presentation for the Board, and letters to the superintendent. In sum, they dealt with the conflict by working with colleagues to change it. These actions reflect other important values which came into play for each school-leader. Their value structures readjusted and the values of participation and sharing, for example, became apparent.

As a whole, these studies suggest that when school-leaders encounter value conflicts their responses are more productive when the conflict itself is treated as a problem and subjected to the same (deep and strong) processes that would be used with other types of swampy problems. It also appears that even when conflicts arise between two unequal values (e.g., where one of the two values clearly carries more weight in the school-leader's value system) school-leaders do not simply choose one and reject the other. Rather, they search for compromises.

Such processes for resolving value conflicts are similar to conclusions drawn by Toffler (1986) in her study of twenty-one non-school-based managers. Her results attribute importance to managers defining the elements of the conflict, assessing their own 'specific role responsibility' and using their imagination to identify a key factor on which the dilemma hinges or developing a mechanism to turn that key factor. When a key factor cannot be found, managers give greater weight to one value but also respond to the other as fully as possible.

Summary and Implications for Developing Leaders for Future Schools

Four studies reported in this chapter have been used to answer questions about the special role that values play in solving swampy school-leadership problems.

Concerning their role and significance, first, these studies depicted values as pervasive in the problem-solving of school-leaders through their direct stimulation of action and their roles as perceptual screens and moral codes or substitutes for knowledge in response to ill-structured problems. Second, with respect to the type of values held by school-leaders and their relative weight, the studies supported the comprehensiveness of a four-fold classification of values including 'Basic Human', 'General Moral', 'Professional' and 'Social and Political' Values. Within these categories, school-leaders cited most frequently the specific values of 'role responsibility', 'consequences' for students and 'knowledge'.

The four studies also pointed to a plausible set of relationships between values and school-leaders' levels of expertise, although principals did share a common core of values. Greater emphasis was placed on social values (e.g., 'sharing') by those engaged in moderately expert (humanitarian) problem-solving. 'Knowledge' and 'role responsibilities' were dominant values for experts.

Finally, conflict-resolution strategies used by school-leaders in the face of competing values were of two types. The most successful strategies, 'deep and strong', conceptualized value conflicts as problems in their own right and employed a set of deliberate problem-solving processes to resolve them. Less successful were 'surface and weak' strategies which gave short shrift to problem interpretation or clarifying the source and nature of the conflict, and used a sequential, trial-and-error procedure for determining the consequences of alternative solutions.

A number of implications for developing leaders of future schools are inherent in the results of the four studies.

Use Values as Criteria during the Selection of School-Leaders

Although school-leaders' values may change, it is not likely that they will change quickly or easily (Hambrick and Brandon, 1988). Beliefs and attitudes will need to change in order to stimulate and reinforce value change. The challenge of change in school-leaders' values, to serve better the interests of the school, is best avoided, where possible, by school-leader selection processes which collect evidence about: the nature of applicant values, the degree to which applicants are clear about their values, and how well they are able to resolve value conflicts. This possibility is examined more fully in Chapter 14.

Redesign School-Leader Socialization Processes

Values develop more through the usually lengthy periods of informal socialization than through formal programs. But the socialization of administrators in most school districts is largely left to chance. More planful efforts to redesign socialization experience which will reinforce values important to future schools are called for. Chapter 10 provides information useful when pursuing this implication further.

Provide the Discretion Needed to Act on One's Values

When satisfactory steps have been taken to hire and/or develop school-leaders whose values are consistent with the needs of future schools, it will be important to give them the discretion to act on the basis of those values. This may turn out to be an argument for more school-based management in one form or another. It is, at minimum, a call to design school districts in a way that support and enhance the work of expert school-leaders. What this might entail is explored further in Chapter 15.

Conclusion

These three implications for developing leaders of future schools seem warranted, given the limited research on which this chapter was based. Nevertheless, much more research is clearly called for. It already seems clear that several of the questions raised in this chapter will be relatively easy to answer and others much more complex. For example, values clearly play a significant role in problem-solving. But the nature of that role is by no means fully captured by our data. In order to build on our data in subsequent research, an explicit theory about the role of values in managerial thinking and action, such as Hambrick and Brandon's (1988), would be useful: their hypotheses offer productive starting points for subsequent inquiry.

Perhaps the most theoretically interesting and practically useful focus for subsequent study concerns the resolution of conflicting values. Such conflicts are a part of the everyday work world of school-leaders and likely to remain so. Yet the few current texts intending to offer disciplined advice to leaders (e.g., Strike, Soltis and Haller, 1989, Toffler, 1986) fall short of accomplishing that goal. Research describing an array of strategies used by expert school-leaders for resolving value conflicts would be helpful for leaders of future schools.

Pursuit of these implications for practice and research is likely to be a challenging but worthwhile business. As Hambrick and Brandon note:

> to study executive values is to delve into the murkiest of organizational phenomena. Yet the role of values in influencing organizational processes, membership and outcomes is enormous. (1988, p. 30)

Chapter 8

Teacher Development:
A Central Problem for Leaders
of Future Schools[1]

Transformational leadership, as it was described in Chapter 1, involves developing the capacity of organizational members: the capacity to meet both the immediate and long-term challenges involved in moving toward a vision of the future widely shared by members of the school. As Schlecty notes:

> the key result is the growth and development of others; for the [transformational] leader, the goal is to help others succeed. (1990, p. 105)

The most promising focus for the developmental effort of school-leaders is the teaching staff. To the extent that school-leaders solve the problem of contributing to teachers' growth, they can be viewed as exercising transformational leadership. Having devoted most of the previous four chapters to the processes used by school-leaders to solve problems, in general, we now turn to one of the most important specific problems facing leaders of future schools.

The chapter is intended to accomplish two purposes. First, by providing one brief synthesis of existing knowledge about the nature of teacher development, we make the problem, at least for the reader, less swampy. This seems worth doing in the face of the continuing debate about the feasibility of an 'instructional leadership' role for the principal (e.g., Rallis and Highsmith, 1986, Gersten *et al.*, 1982). Using Baird's (1983) definition of a problem, as explained in Chapter 4, our description of teacher development simplifies problem-solving for the school-leader by adding clarity to the 'givens' and 'goals' of the problem. It is difficult to contribute to teacher development in the absence of a clear image of what such development looks like. Such an image ought to be part of the school-leader's overall vision for the school.

The second purpose for the chapter is in response to those school-leaders who, while acknowledging their responsibility for teacher development, do not feel that it is a problem they are capable of addressing adequately. It is, in their view, excessively swampy because of a perception of their jobs as fast-paced, hectic, unpredictable, interpersonally intense, and sometimes consumed by seemingly trivial but pressing 'administrivia'. In such a context, many school-leaders believe they do not have the opportunity to contribute to teacher development. The second part of the chapter identifies a small number of guidelines for fostering teacher development accepting this perception of the job. Indeed, we make the case that the job is ideally suited for assisting in teacher development, although commonly held misconceptions about productive forms of such assistance belie this claim. Again, with reference to Baird (1983), our identification of guidelines for fostering teacher development makes problem-solving for school-leaders less complex. It does this by contributing specificity to steps or actions school-leaders can use to overcome constraints to teacher development. This helps transform the given or current state (lower levels of teacher development) into the goals or desired state (higher levels of teacher development).

The Nature of Teacher Development

This section of the chapter synthesizes evidence from three distinct areas of research to build a multi-dimensional description of teacher development. It is offered to school-leaders as an aid in reflecting upon and possibly making more robust their own views of such development. Table 8.1 describes three dimensions of teacher development with which school-leaders have an opportunity to assist: development of professional expertise, psychological development, and career-cycle development. Each of these dimensions reflect quite different lines of inquiry about teacher development.

Development of Professional Expertise

The dimension of teacher development with the most obvious consequences for classroom, school, and district improvement is identified in Table 8.1 as 'Development of Professional Expertise'. It is through such expertise that teachers contribute directly to the growth of students (amount learned, range of outcomes achieved and ranges of students who benefit from instruction). Six stages of development are included in this dimension. Stages One through Four are concerned with teachers' classroom responsibilities; Stages Five and Six explicitly address the out-of-classroom and out-of-school roles of the 'mature' teacher. Each of the stages (beyond the first) includes expertise acquired in previous stages. Furthermore, it seems likely that the seeds of expertise in higher stages will begin to develop quite early, given appropriate, formative experiences. Hence, this conception of growth does not imply restricting teacher experiences only to those that will prepare them for the next stage of development. Some preparation for Stage Six practices might well begin during a teacher's initial entry into the role. Table 8.2 illustrates in more detail those aspects of professional expertise likely to be a part of each of the six stages. While others might describe the aspects of expertise in each of these stages differently, there is at least good warrant for the substance of Table 8.2. Stages One to Four are based on an image of effective classroom instruction as requiring a large repertoire of instructional techniques. Such a repertoire is reflected, for example, in Joyce and Weil's (1980) twenty-three models of teaching, organized into four 'families' or categories. Expertise, in these terms, increases as teachers acquire greater skill in application of a given model and as an increasing number of such models are mastered. Teaching, however, involves more than the unthinking application of such models, although 'automaticity' is an important characteristic of expertise in most

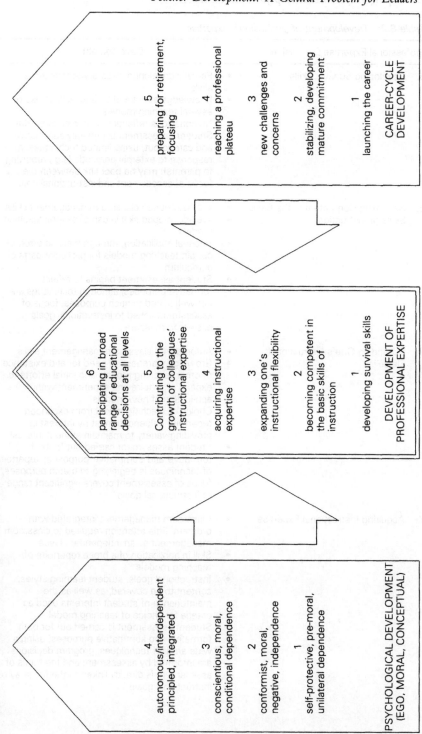

Table 8.1: Interrelated dimensions of teacher development

CAREER-CYCLE DEVELOPMENT

5 preparing for retirement, focusing

4 reaching a professional plateau

3 new challenges and concerns

2 stabilizing, developing mature commitment

1 launching the career

DEVELOPMENT OF PROFESSIONAL EXPERTISE

6 participating in broad range of educational decisions at all levels

5 Contributing to the growth of colleagues' instructional expertise

4 acquiring instructional expertise

3 expanding one's instructional flexibility

2 becoming competent in the basic skills of instruction

1 developing survival skills

PSYCHOLOGICAL DEVELOPMENT (EGO, MORAL, CONCEPTUAL)

4 autonomous/interdependent principled, integrated

3 conscientious, moral, conditional dependence

2 conformist, moral, negative, independence

1 self-protective, pre-moral, unilateral dependence

Table 8.2: *Development of professional expertise*

Professional Expertise Dimension	Development
1. Developing Survival Skills	• Partially developed classroom-management skills • Knowledge about and limited skills in use of several teaching models • No conscious reflection on choice of model • Student assessment is primarily summative and carried out, using limited techniques in response to external demands (e.g., reporting to parents); may be poor link between the focus of assessment and instructional goal
2. Becoming Competent in the Basic Skills of Instruction	• Well-developed classroom-management skills • Well-developed skill in use of several teaching models • Habitual application, through trial and error, of certain teaching models for particular parts of curriculum • Student assessment begins to reflect formative purposes, although techniques are not well suited to such purposes; focus of assessment linked to instructional goals easiest to measure
3. Expanding One's Instructional Flexibility	• Automatized classroom-management skills • Growing awareness of need for and existence of other teaching models and initial efforts to expand repertoire and experiment with application of new models • Choice of teaching model from expanded repertoire influenced most by interest in providing variety to maintain student interest • Student assessment carried out for both formative and summative purposes; repertoire of techniques is beginning to match purposes; focus of assessment covers significant range of instructional goals
4. Acquiring Instructional Expertise	• Classroom management integrated with program: little attention required to classroom management as an independent issue • Skill in application of a broad repertoire of teaching models • Instructional goals, student learning styles, content to be covered, as well as the maintenance of student interests used as criteria for choice of teaching model • Student assessment is carried out for both formative and summative purposes, using a wide array of techniques; program decisions are informed by assessment and the focus of assessment is directly linked to the full array of instructional goals

Table 8.2 (cont.)

Professional Expertise Dimension	Development
5. Contributing to the Growth of Colleagues' Instructional Expertise	• Has high levels of expertise in classroom instructional performance • Reflective about own competences and choices and the fundamental beliefs and values on which they are based • Able to assist other teachers in acquiring instructional expertise through either planning, learned experiences such as mentoring or more formal experiences such as in-service education and coaching programs
6. Participating in a Broad Array of Educational Decisions at all levels of the Education System	• Is committed to the goal of school improvement • Accepts responsibility for fostering that goal through any legitimate opportunity • Able to exercise leadership, both formal and informal, with groups of adults inside and outside the school • Has a broad framework from which to understand the relationships among decisions at many different levels in the education system • Is well informed about policies at many different levels in the education system.

areas of human endeavor. Along with Joyce and Weil (1980), Darling-Hammond *et al.* (1983), Bacharach *et al.* (1987) and Shavelson (1973, 1976) and others point out that deciding which model or technique to apply in a particular situation is central to instructional expertise. As teachers develop, their choice of models is based on increasingly defensible criteria (e.g., instructional objectives vs. need for variety) and diagnosis of the instructional needs of students.

While the notion of teacher-as-decision-maker appropriately recognizes the contingent nature of the classroom tasks routinely faced by teachers, it is not sufficiently comprehensive to encompass those unanticipated, non-routine 'swampy' problems encountered in the classroom from time to time. Schön (1983) depicts the way in which experienced professionals in many domains think about and eventually resolve such problems. This involves a process of 'reflecting-in-action' as well as a process of 'reflecting-on-action' in which the unique attributes of the setting are carefully weighed and the professional's repertoire is adapted in response to such uniqueness. These processes are the same as described for expert school-leaders.

Stages Five and Six acknowledge the roles of teachers in school improvement and educational decisions beyond the classroom and school. While such roles are by no means new, they have received much greater attention recently. Peer coaching (Brandt, 1987, Garmston, 1987) and mentoring (Gray and Gray, 1985, Wagner, 1985) strategies, for example, assume those aspects of expertise identified in Stage Five, as do many of the recent career-ladder programs which place teachers in the role of evaluators (e.g., Peterson and Mitchell, 1985). Stage

Six conceptualizes the mature teacher as one who plays a leadership role, formal or informal, in a variety of contexts both inside and outside the classroom and school. Teachers, according to this view, share in the responsibility for most decisions that directly or indirectly touch on students' experiences. Such a view is consistent with recent proposals for reshaping teacher education (e.g., Fullan and Connelly, 1987) and for 'empowering' teachers (e.g., Maeroff, 1988) in the process.

Psychological Development

As outlined in Table 8.1 'Psychological Development' is a synthesis of three distinct and independently substantial strands of psychological stage theory: Loevinger's (1966) seven-stage theory of ego development, Kohlberg's (1970) six-stage theory of moral development and Hunt's (1966) four-stage theory of conceptual development. These three strands of psychological development are both conceptually and empirically related (Sullivan, McCullough and Stager, 1970). The synthesis provided by Table 8.1 is for heuristic purposes and gives a rough approximation of how the three strands might intersect in real time. Generally, ego development occurs as a person strives to master, to integrate and otherwise to make sense of experience. Greater ego maturity is associated with a more complex and better differentiated understanding of oneself in relation to others. Moral development occurs when the bases on which one's views of rightness and goodness shift from a basis of personal preference toward a basis of universal ethical principles. Finally, conceptual development occurs as one moves toward greater differentiation and integration of concepts, which means a growth from concrete toward more abstract thought processes.

Viewing the three strands of psychological development together, as in Table 8.1, provides descriptions of teachers in various stages of growth. A 'Stage One 'teacher has an overly simplistic view of the world and a tendency to see choices as black or white. Such a teacher believes strongly in rules and roles, views authority as the highest good and most questions as having one answer. Stage One teachers discourage divergent thinking and reward conformity and rote-learning (Oja, 1979). Their classrooms are highly teacher directed.

Stage Two teachers (conformists) are especially susceptible to the expectations of others; their wish is to be like their peers and they may hold stereotyped, distrustful views of those outside their immediate group. The classrooms of conformist teachers are what we think of as 'conventional'. Rules are quite explicit and student behavior is expected to adhere to such rules without much regard for individual differences or contingencies which might justify exceptions to the rules.

At the third stage of psychological development (conscientious), teachers have become much more self-aware and have developed an appreciation for multiple possibilities in situations (e.g., multiple explanations for student behavior). Rules are internalized and applied with an appreciation for the need for exceptions to the rules given the circumstances. Teachers at this stage are future-oriented, and achievement-oriented; their classrooms are the product of rational planning and a concern for good interpersonal communication.

At the highest stages of psychological development, teachers are inner-directed but appreciate the interdependent nature of relationships in a social setting such as a classroom. In addition, according to Oja (1981), these teachers have achieved more of a synthesis in their classrooms between an emphasis on achievement and an interpersonal orientation. They are not only able to view a situation from multiple perspectives but are also able to synthesize such perspectives. Teachers at the highest stage understand the reasons behind rules and so can be wiser in their application; they maintain a broad perspective and are able to cope with inner conflicts as well as conflicting needs and duties. The classrooms of these teachers are controlled in collaboration with students and the emphasis is on meaningful learning, creativity, and flexibility. Being more cognitively complex themselves, teachers at this stage encourage more complex functioning in their students (Oja, 1979, Hunt, 1966).

Career-Cycle Development

The dimension called 'Career-Cycle Development' in Table 8.1 views teachers' careers from a life-cycle perspective. Five stages of development have been derived primarily from recent research by Huberman (1988) and Sikes, Measor and Woods (1985). The latter work adopted Levinson *et al.*'s (1978) conceptualization of life development as a framework. Huberman (1988) and Sikes, Measor and Woods (1985) carried out their research with secondary school teachers in Switzerland and Great Britain, respectively. Nevertheless, their results appear to be sufficiently similar and consistent with other research (e.g., Ball and Goodson, 1985) to warrant tentative generalization to other contexts and teaching assignments in the modified form described in Table 8.1. Our main interest in teachers' career-cycle development is how it interacts with the development of professional expertise. More particularly, we want to know what career experiences, at each stage, seem likely to foster or detract from the development of professional expertise.

Stage One, 'launching the career', encompasses up to the first several years of the teacher's classroom responsibilities. Sikes *et al.* (1985) suggest that most teachers at this stage experience a 'reality shock in coming to grips with problems of disciplining and motivating students' (p. 17), as well as some degree of culture shock, the amount of shock depending on the values and perspectives of staff in the school in which they find themselves. Nevertheless, Huberman's (1988) data suggest that experiences at this stage are perceived by some teachers as 'easy' and by others as 'painful'. Conditions giving rise to perceptions of easy beginnings include: positive relationships with students, 'manageable' students, and a sense of instructional mastery and initial enthusiasm. Painful beginnings are associated with: role overload, anxiety, difficult pupils, heavy time investment, close monitoring, and feelings of isolation in the school. For those who experience such pain, there may be a protracted period of trial and error in an effort to cope with such problems.

'Stabilizing', the second career-cycle stage, often coincides with receiving a permanent contract and making a deliberate commitment to the profession. This stage is characterized by: feeling at ease in the classroom, mastery of a basic repertoire of instructional techniques, and being able to select appropriate methods and materials in light of student abilities and interests. Furthermore, at this stage teachers act more independently, are less intimidated by supervisors, and feel reasonably well integrated into a group of peers. Some teachers at this stage begin to seek greater responsibility through promotion and/or participation in change efforts.

The stage following stabilization may take several forms. In the main, teachers at this stage tend to be between the ages of 30 and 40 years. As Sikes *et al.* (1985) point out, their experience is substantial by this point as is their physical and intellectual energy. For some teachers such energy is channeled into intense professional effort. Huberman's (1988) study identified a category of teachers at this stage who actively diversify their classroom methods, seek out novel practices and often look outside their own classrooms for professional stimulation. Another group of teachers at this stage focused their efforts on seeking promotion to administrative roles or appointment to key district or state-wide projects. Yet a third group of teachers, also identified by Sikes *et al.* (1985), reduced their professional commitments. Members of this group sometimes experienced difficult classes and achieved poor results with their students. Building an alternative career was an option pursued by many teachers in this group.

Sikes *et al.* (1985) estimate the fourth stage, 'reaching a professional plateau', to occur between the ages of approximately 40 and 50 to 55 years. It is a traumatic period for many; teachers at this stage are reappraising their successes in all facets of their lives. Their own sense of mortality is accentuated by continually being surrounded by young students and by having, as colleagues, young teachers who may be the same age as their own children. Responses to this stage appear to be of two sorts. One group of teachers stop striving for promotion and simply enjoy teaching. These teachers may become the backbone of the school, guardians of its traditions, and enjoy a renewed commitment to school improvement. A second group, however, stagnates; they become bitter, cynical and unlikely to be interested in further professional growth.

Depending to a large extent on which of the two responses (discussed above) is adopted at Stage Four, teachers in the final stage, 'preparing for retirement', may behave in quite different ways. Huberman's (1988) study identified three different patterns of behavior, each of which involved some type of contraction of professional activity and interest. One pattern of behavior, 'positive focusing', involved an interest in specializing in what one does best. Such specialization might target a grade level, a subject or a group of students, for example. Teachers adopting this pattern, as Sikes *et al.* (1985) also found, are concerned centrally with pupil learning, their most compatible peers, and an increasing pursuit of outside interests. A second pattern of behavior, 'defensive focusing', has similar features to the first but a less optimistic and generous attitude toward their past experiences with change, their students, and their colleagues. Finally, Huberman (1988) labels a third pattern of practice 'disenchantment'. People adopting this pattern are quite bitter about past experiences with change and the administrators associated with them; they are tired and may become a source of frustration for younger staff.

Implications: Guidelines for School-Leaders in Fostering Teacher Development

An explicit, defensible conception of teacher development provides a foundation upon which school-leaders can formulate their own approach to teacher development. In this section, four broad guidelines for building this approach are suggested. These guidelines stress the importance of attending, in parallel, to all three dimensions of teacher development and creating school cultures and structures hospitable to such development (a matter pursued in more depth in Chapter 9). Based on assumptions about teachers, as adult learners actively involved in bringing meaning to their work, the guidelines stress the importance of understanding teachers' own views of their world. Finally, the guidelines argue that the most helpful teacher-development strategies available to principals are to be found among their normal responses to their work environment.

Guideline One: Treat the Teacher as a Whole Person

As Table 8.2 indicates, growth in professional expertise consists of teachers expanding their instructional repertoires, responding more flexibly to classroom circumstances, and taking responsibility for the welfare and growth of not only students but also their professional colleagues. While the acquisition of knowledge and skill concerning instruction, as well as other educational matters, is an obviously necessary condition for such growth, it is not sufficient. That is, the practice of instructional flexibility depends on at least being able to weigh a variety of instructional alternatives. Many instructional strategies also require the teacher to relinquish exclusive control over classroom activities and to trust students to be task-oriented on their own or in groups. This suggests that prerequisite to acquiring instructional expertise (Stage Four of the professional expertise dimension) is growth to at least the middle stages of the psychological development dimension, as depicted in Table 8.1. Similarly, practices associated with professional expertise at Stages Five and Six appear to depend on: the ability to synthesize alternatives, mutuality in interpersonal relations, the ability to cope with conflicting needs and duties, and other attributes of functioning at the highest level of psychological development. Indeed, failure to attend to the interdependence of professional expertise and stages of psychological development offers an additional explanation for lack of application, in the classroom, of skills acquired through training. To this point, the most compelling explanation for this 'transfer' problem has been limited to the unique and often overwhelming demands placed on teachers' application of newly acquired skills by their particular classroom contexts (Joyce and Showers, 1980).

Typically, staff-development efforts (whether by principals or others) do not acknowledge the interdependence of psychological and professional development. While this may be due to ignorance or oversight, in some cases, it may also be due to the commonly held view that psychological development is completed by adulthood. That such a view is unwarranted is clear, however, from the evidence reported by Harvey (1970) that a large proportion of teachers in his sample were at the lowest level of conceptual development; Oja's (1981) review of similar evidence suggests that teachers typically stabilize in the middle stages of psychological development.

So far, our attention has been limited to the relationship between psychological development and the development of expertise. What of career-cycle development? The development of professional expertise seems to have an important relationship with such development. There is, for example, an obvious link between the challenges facing a teacher in the first three stages of his or her career cycle and the expertise to be acquired in the first four stages of development of professional expertise. Indeed, interventions designed to promote the development of such professional expertise seem likely to ensure positive career-cycle development. School-leaders have an opportunity to prevent painful beginnings; they are preventable through such interventions as realistic classroom assignment in combination with ongoing assistance in the development of classroom-management skills, provision of a supportive mentor close at hand and the avoidance of heavy-handed supervision practices. On the other hand, failure to provide opportunities for the development of professional expertise may well lead to professional disaffection when teachers are seeking new challenges and have new concerns. Providing opportunities to master an expanded, flexible repertoire of instruction techniques seems an effective way of ensuring that teachers experience a sense of professional self-fulfillment during this third stage in their career cycle.

A direct relationship appears also to exist between the career-cycle stage 'reaching a professional plateau' and Stages Five and Six in the development of professional expertise. A significant part of the explanation for teachers perceiving themselves to be at a plateau is the failure, in many schools and school systems, to permit teachers greater scope to know and relate to multiple classrooms, to see and work with other teachers and their classrooms. Such challenges respond to the teacher's readiness to accept more responsibility and allow the school and school system to benefit from their accumulated expertise. Teachers who have experienced such challenges seem likely to enter their final career-cycle stage either still in an expansionary frame of mind or at least as 'positive focusers', to use Huberman's (1988) term.

In brief, then, school-leaders should be sensitive to all three development dimensions and seek to help teachers develop these dimensions in a parallel, interdependent fashion.

Guideline Two: Establish a School Culture Based on Norms of Technical Collaboration and Professional Inquiry

While teachers often appear to stabilize in the middle stages of psychological development, the reason is inadequate stimulation not some innate shortcoming of teachers (Sprinthall and Theis-Sprinthall, 1983). Such is the case with professional expertise, as well. Evidence suggests that the typical school culture and its organizational structures may be responsible, in part, for stifling teacher development (for this discussion, culture includes the underlying assumption, norms, beliefs, and values that guide behavior among professionals in the school'.

Typical school cultures are characterized by informal norms of autonomy and isolation for teachers (Lortie, 1973), as well as entrenched routines and regularities (Sarason, 1971, Leiberman and Miller, 1986). Indeed, some aspects of these cultures have been dubbed sacred (Corbett, Firestone and Rossman, 1987) and, as a result, highly resistant to change. Teachers' individual, personal beliefs about the needs of students are far stronger influences on their classroom practices than other potential influences such as the views of their peers or principals or prescriptions contained in curriculum policies (Leithwood, Ross and Montgomery, 1982). Such autonomy and isolation limit the stimulation for further development to what is possible through private and unguided reflections on what one reads and experiences outside the classroom, and one's own informal classroom experiments. It is unlikely that such stimulation will create the sort of dissonance or challenge to one's ways of thinking that appears necessary to foster movement from one stage of psychological development to another. Nor would such stimulation provide the conditions outlined, for example, by Joyce and Showers (1980) for the successful application of new instructional skills to one's classroom. Little (1982, 1985), on the other hand, found that staff-development efforts were most successful where a norm of collegiality and experimentation existed.

School-leaders' efforts to foster teacher development seem most likely to be successful within a school culture in which teachers are encouraged to consciously reflect on their own practices (Oberg and Field, 1986), to share ideas about their instruction, and try out new techniques in the classroom. School-leaders need to develop norms of reflection through the substance of their own communication with teachers and the examples of their own teaching; they also need to take specific actions to foster norms of collaboration. As Rosenholtz (1989) points out, 'Norms of collaboration don't simply just happen. They do not spring spontaneously out of teachers' mutual respect and concern for each other'. Rosenholtz identifies four conditions which influence the extent to which teachers are likely to engage technical collaboration: teachers' certainty about their own instructional competence and hence self-esteem; shared teaching goals; involvement in the school's technical decisions; and team teaching opportunities which create the need to plan and carry out instruction with colleagues.

This guideline suggests, in sum, that school-leaders look below the surface features of their schools – at how teachers are treated, what beliefs, norms and values they share – and redesign their schools as learning environments for teachers as well as for students. Chapter 9 provides more detailed advice on how this might be done.

Guideline Three: Carefully Diagnose the Starting Points for Teacher Development

Teachers are not passive recipients of school-leaders' strategies 'to develop them'. Adopting the view of contemporary cognitive psychology (e.g., Schuell, 1986, Calfee, 1981), particularly as it has been applied to research on teacher thinking (e.g., Clark and Peterson, 1986), teachers actively strive to accomplish implicit or explicit goals they hold to be personally important in their work. For example, when teachers judge a new form of instruction, of which they become aware, as potentially helpful in accomplishing such goals, they make active attempts to understand and assess that new form of instruction. The primary resources used by teachers to develop such understanding are what they already know (as contained in their long-term memory). Understanding develops: as matches are made between the new form of instruction and what they already know (e.g., 'Oh! "Direct Instruction" means the traditional instruction I was taught in teachers' college.'); and existing knowledge structures are modified to accommodate novel aspects of the new form of instruction (e.g., 'Ah! "Cooperative

Learning" just means grouping with different rules that I have used.'); and/or as links are established among previously unconnected pieces of information in the teacher's memory (e.g., 'I think "mastery learning" is a combination of what I call behavioral objectives, criterion-referenced testing and remedial teaching.'). These brief examples make clear that successful ways of fostering development build on a careful diagnosis of the relevant knowledge already possessed by teachers. Such strategies will assist teachers to identify such aspects of what they already know and to use that knowledge as an instrument for giving meaning to new practices which they may wish to understand better and use.

The formal mechanism most obviously available to school-leaders for carrying out this diagnosis is teacher evaluation. Virtually all formal school-leaders (principals) spend considerable time doing it. Nevertheless, such evaluation, as it is normally practiced, rarely results in useful diagnostic information and generally appears to have little influence on teacher development (Lawton *et al.*, 1986). Recent research has provided some useful clues for how principals can redesign their approaches to teacher evaluation, so as to be a more effective 'needs-assessment front end' for teacher development (e.g., Stiggins and Duke, 1988). For example, such evaluation needs to be based on criteria or goals that both principals and teachers agree are relevant to teacher development. Multiple forms of data should be collected as a more powerful means of accurately reflecting teachers' practices and needs; regular observation of classroom practice with considerable time in the classroom is an important part of such data collection. The formality, frequency, and length of evaluation should be adapted to individual teachers' characteristics and needs. Rosenholtz (1989) found that teacher evaluation with features such as these was one of four organizational factors contributing directly to teacher-learning opportunities in the school (the other factors were school goal setting, shared values, and collaboration).

In sum, this guideline reminds school-leaders that development is an incremental process which builds on teachers' existing stock of attitudes, knowledge, and skill; they are at the same time the objects of, and instruments for, development.

Guideline Four: Recast Routine Administrative Activities into Powerful Teacher-Development Strategies

Many school-leaders, in principal or vice-principal roles, remain skeptical about the contribution which they can make to teacher development. Their skepticism is rooted in the belief that useful development strategies would include, for example, detailed planning of in-service programs, creation of large amounts of teacher release time for participation in such programs, and perhaps acting themselves as in-service instructors. It is not usually the lack of know-how that causes school-leaders the most despair in the face of such strategies. Rather, the despair is caused most directly by the lack of congruence between the demands such formal strategies place on school-leaders' work and the real demands of that work. The point of this guideline is to argue that such a view of how teacher development can be fostered is essentially misguided. As Pfieffer suggests: 'Teachers don't need Superman – Clark Kent or Lois Lane will do just fine' (1986, p. 4). Indeed, the more informal strategies available to school-leaders in their normal responses to the demands of the job can be much more effective in fostering teacher development than such formal, hard-to-implement strategies. Expert school-leaders have learned this lesson well.

What are the 'real' demands faced by school-leaders in their work? As pointed out several times in the book already, we know that principals' activities are typically characterized by brevity, fragmentation, and variety (Bradeson, 1986, Davies, 1987, Gally, 1986, Martin and Willower, 1981, Willower and Kmetz, 1982). Rarely, it seems, do principals spend more than ten minutes at a time on a single task; and they make about 150 different decisions in the course of an average day. Communication of one sort or other is the primary nature of most principals' activities; almost three-quarters of such activities are interpersonal and take place with only one other person, over half involving face-to-face contact. Formal school-leaders' work environments also require high levels of spontaneity; the largest single expenditure of a formal school-leaders' time is reported to be unanticipated meetings.

While most formal leaders experience the demands just described, recent research suggests at least one compelling source of difference in the responses of expert as compared with non-expert school-leaders (Leithwood and Montgomery, 1986). What is different is the amount of consistency that principals are able to bring to their activities and decisions. Non-experts approach these activities and decisions in a relatively piecemeal fashion: for example, decisions about budget, discipline, timetabling, reporting, and staffing all may be based on different criteria. As a consequence, the overall effects of these decisions may work at cross purposes.

In contrast, experts base their decisions and actions on a relatively consistent set of criteria: they 'can articulate direct and remote links between their actions and the instructional system' (Bossert, 1988, p. 348). As a result, the effects of the many, seemingly trivial, unrelated, and often unanticipated decisions made by these experts eventually add up to something; their impact accumulates in a way that consistently fosters school improvement. And what is the glue that holds together the myriad decisions of expert school-leaders? It is the goals which they and their staffs have developed for their schools and a sense of what their schools need to look like and to do in order to accomplish those goals. Such a clear, detailed vision (incorporating a conception of teacher development) and its systematic use on a day-to-day basis appears to be absent among non-expert school-leaders (Stevens, 1986).

This opportunistic but clearly directed approach by expert school-leaders to their work as a whole manifests itself in the strategies they use for teacher development. Such school-leaders do not attempt to deny the fragmented, interpersonal, and spontaneous demands of the job (as would be required by a formal, in-service training approach to teacher development); on the contrary, they adapt and build on strategies that are part of their normal responses to their work demands. McEvoy's (1987) results illustrate, more specifically, the types of subtle, sometimes opportunistic teacher-development strategies used by experts. In this study, twelve elementary and intermediate principals were observed using six strategies: informing teachers of professional opportunities; disseminating professional and curriculum materials to teachers with personal follow-up and discussion; focusing teachers' attention, through meetings and informal contacts, on a specific theme in order to expand the concepts and practices teachers considered; soliciting teachers' opinions about their own classroom activities, as well as school and classroom issues, thereby contributing to a sense of collegiality among staff; encouraging teachers' experimenting with innovative practices and supporting their efforts; and recognizing, sometimes publicly, the achievements of individual teachers.

Examples of other ways of fostering teacher development used by experts are provided in Leithwood and Montgomery's literature reviews (1982, 1986). These strategies include: working alongside individual teachers in their classes to resolve problems or implement changes; helping staff gain access to outside resources; and helping teachers arrange to observe other teachers in other schools. Even relatively 'impersonal' strategies normally available to school-leaders may be designed in such a way as to foster teacher development. Hannay and Chism (1988), for example, found that teacher transfers could become an effective means for fostering such development when the transfer prompted teachers to re-examine their practices.

Wilson and Firestone (1987, p. 20) refer to most of the strategies that have been mentioned as 'linkage strategies' and show how school-leaders' fostering of both bureaucratic and cultural linkages can lead to teacher development. Bureaucratic linkages (such as creating more free time for teachers) can affect how teachers interact with each other. Cultural linkages (such as introducing more consistency into school communications) work on the consciousness of teachers 'by clarifying what they do and defining their commitment to the task'.

Effective school-leaders, in sum, use the energy and momentum created naturally by the demands of their work for purposes of teacher development. They have redefined the problem as the solution.

Conclusion

Gideonese (1988, p. 65) has suggested that the teaching profession is 'undergoing revolutionary transformation', although many of us are too close to see it, as such. Such change appears to begin from a perception of teaching as a routine job conducted with craft-like knowledge, in isolation from other adults, in a hier-archical status structure. The new perception of teaching, in contrast, views it as a non-routine activity drawing on a reliable body of technical knowledge and conducted in collaboration with other professional colleagues. Awareness of this shift has been fostered by recent, effective schools' research and proposals included among second-wave reforms in the US (Bacharach, 1988).

Nevertheless, we need to devote much more attention to how this newly perceived image of the teacher can be realized. This chapter has outlined plausible stages through which teachers are likely to grow as they acquire the attributes associated with a collaborative, professional image of the role. Some general guidelines school-leaders might follow in fostering such teacher growth, have also been proposed. These guidelines only touch the surface of a problem which requires much further thought, however – the implications, for the role of the formal school-leader of an image of teaching as a collaborative, professional enterprise. Only when we have clearly conceptualized coherent images of both teacher and school-leader roles and how they develop, will we realize the com-bined contribution toward student learning of those in both roles. Much of the knowledge required for this task is already in hand. While more knowledge will be useful, using what we already know is a crucial and immediate challenge. One of the most promising contexts for using what we know is in the preparation of leaders for future schools. Such preparation, among other things, would provide them with the capacity to follow the four guidelines for teacher development discussed in this chapter.

Note

1   This chapter is adapted from Leithwood (1990).

Chapter 9

Collaborative School Cultures: A Key Part of the Solution

Teacher development, we argued in Chapter 8, is a key problem to be addressed by leaders of future schools. When they are successful in fostering such development they have provided transformational leadership to their schools. In addition to providing a description of what such development might look like, Chapter 8 also offered several guidelines useful to school-leaders in fostering teacher development. One of these guidelines was to help create a more collaborative culture among the teaching staff in the school. We offered little concrete advice in Chapter 8, however, about how school-leaders might do this.

This chapter explores in greater depth what developing a more collaborative culture means and why it is a key part of the solution to the teacher-development problem. And, of greatest practical consequence, this chapter identifies specific strategies school-leaders might use to encourage greater staff collaboration.

Interest in school culture is widespread at present, and for good reason. Current reform initiatives in Canada, the US, Australia, and a number of other developed countries are calling for the restructuring of schools. One central dimension of such restructuring is the empowerment of teachers within a school culture that is both shared and technical (Gideonese, 1988). Such cultures not only foster the types of outcomes for students that are valued by educational reformers but stimulate continuous professional growth among teachers, as well (Rosenholtz, 1989, Little, 1982).

While evidence about the positive effects of shared, technical, school cultures is growing rapidly, very little is known about how they develop (Joyce, Bennet and Rolheiser-Bennet, 1990, Fullan, 1990). Furthermore, there has been very little empirical research inquiring directly into what school-leaders might do to assist such development, although much evidence has accumulated in support of the school-leader as a crucial agent in realizing a number of other important reform objectives (see Chapter 2). To fill this void, we initiated the study on which this chapter is based.

Framework and Methods

Extending the definition of school culture begun in Chapter 8, it is usefully defined as:

> a system of ordinary, taken-for-granted meanings and symbols with
> both explicit and implicit content that is, deliberately and non-
> deliberately, learned and shared among members of a naturally bounded
> social group. (Erickson, 1987, p. 12)

A school's culture consists of meanings shared by those inhabiting the school.
Schools may include several subcultures as well: for example, a student subculture and a professional staff subculture, the focus of this study.

Attention to school culture, as part of school reform, is driven by evidence
that traditional school cultures, based on norms of autonomy and isolation, create
a work context in which realizing the central aspirations of school reform is
highly unlikely. Such norms begin to develop early in a teacher's career, perhaps
during teacher training (Su, 1990). Isolated cultures have been described by
Feiman-Nemser and Floden (1986) in terms of norms of interaction with students, teachers, administrators, and parents. Norms of authority and discipline
along with a competing need for close personal bonds characterize teachers'
interactions with students. Typical norms act to isolate teachers from asking their
peers for, or offering to their peers, professional advice. Teachers, it has been
said, have peers but no colleagues. School administrators are valued by teachers
when they act as buffers from outside pressures and maintain school discipline,
but not if they interfere in daily routines or instructional decisions. Parents are
valued as supports for the teacher's plans and practices but are not expected to
'interfere' in those plans. As a whole, these traditional norms of interaction create
a highly autonomous professional culture, one that is clearly adaptive under some
conditions, such as: traditional expectations for student outcomes in some types
of schools; school-leaders unable to provide instructional leadership; little public
interest in accountability and modest expectations for the contribution of schools
to society with few external pressures for change; prevailing images of teaching
as craft (or art) based on limited technical know-how; and traditional contributions by the family to the development of students.

Since most of these conditions no longer prevail in many schools, it is not
surprising to find evidence of a different teaching culture emerging (e.g., Little,
1982, 1990, Nias, Southwork and Yeomans, 1982, Rosenholtz, 1989, Schneider
and Hochschild, 1988). This culture is student-centered and based on norms of
interaction with students that are supportive and positive; while discipline is
maintained, it is obviously to serve the interests of learning reather than an end
in its own right. Teachers have a shared, technical culture built on norms of
collegiality, collaborative planning, and continuous improvement. Staff and the
student body are cohesive and have a strong sense of community. There is
reciprocity between, and among, staff and students. Administrators are expected
to offer instructional leadership and parents are considered co-partners in the
education of students wherever possible. Such a culture appears to be adaptive to
increasingly prevalent conditions associated with calls for reform such as: new
and more complex expectations for student outcomes; school-leaders able to
provide instructional leadership; high expectations by the public for its schools
and many associated, external pressures for change; a rapidly expanding body of
technical know-how concerning instruction; and changing family environments.
This culture is central to the 'second wave' of reform in the United States
(e.g., Bacharach, 1988). Gideonese (1988) characterizes it as a 'revolutionary

transformation' in the teaching profession, as was noted in Chapter 8, and Fullan and Connelly (1987) use it as the basis for their recommendations for reforming teacher education in Ontario.

Recently, Andy Hargreaves (1990) has identified two forms of teaching cultures in addition to those we have referred to as isolated and (truly) collaborative. 'Balkanized' cultures, common in secondary schools with department structures, feature substantial collaboration within teaching subgroups but little or no significant collaboration across such groups. 'Contrived' collaboration exists where professional interaction is mandated (perhaps by a school administrator) but where the norms of the participants would not support such interaction if the mandate were removed.

Hargreaves and Wignall (1989) have also provided compelling reasons why, even within the context of school cultures which strongly support collaboration, there are legitimate reasons for continuing to value teachers' individuality. An ethic of care, posit Hargreaves and Wignall, drives many teachers to spend as much time as possible in contact with their students. Further, while the benefits of collegiality may include spurs to creativity and effective professional problem-solving, solitude may sometimes offer the same advantages for some people. Among the goals for cultural change, then, would seem to be: the removal of 'administrative or other situational constraints' (Hargreaves and Wignall, 1989, p. 15) to collegial work; the creation of norms of collegiality which nevertheless acknowledge the value of individual, autonomous work on some matters; and the development of forms of collegial work which maximize the potential of shared problem-solving.

The study on which this chapter is based (Leithwood and Jantzi, 1991) addressed three questions. The first question concerned the reasons for variation in degrees to which schools achieved collaborative cultures when they set out with that goal. Because changes in culture seem likely to occur in the course of pursuing other goals, as well, this study was part of a more comprehensive analysis of school-improvement processes. Therefore, the second research question inquired about the significance of the larger set of improvement processes in which people engaged for the purpose of developing collaborative cultures. Finally, we asked about the strategies used by school administrators to develop more collaborative school cultures. The design of the study involved focusing on schools which were known, in advance, to have achieved collaborative cultures; data were collected in an effort to determine how such cultures developed and what role was played by school-leaders. Twelve schools (nine elementary, three secondary) were selected for the study, all of which had been involved in serious improvement efforts for a minimum of three years.

Schools were selected for the study through a two-step process. In the first step, school-district administrators, Ministry of Education officials, and Faculty of Education professors were asked to nominate schools in their jurisdictions that had experienced significant improvement over the past several years and were now considered to be exemplary schools. As a second step, we developed and administered a brief questionnaire that asked staffs in each nominated school to indicate the extent of the change that had taken place in their schools, key factors contributing to the change, the extent of planning involved, and the nature of the improvement that has resulted, to date. Everyone who nominated a school was also asked to complete the same screening questionnaire as the relevant district administrators. Data about each school were collected from an average of eleven people, a total of 133 people.

The procedure used to analyze the interview data was adapted from the work of Miles and Huberman (1984) on qualitative analysis. Following a series of intermediate data-analysis steps (described in detail by Leithwood and Jantzi, 1991) a 'causal network' was produced for each school. These networks identified the variables involved in school improvement in each case and the relationship among these variables. Based on these analyses, we now address the three questions of interest in this chapter.

What Accounts for Variation in the Degree to which Schools Achieve Collaborative Cultures?

> My colleagues are really good. When I was on the grade 1 team and teaching grade 1 for the first time the team took me under their wing; for example, they would leave work in my mail box. They're not hoarders. In our team planning we all took a share; we all pulled our weight.... There's more sharing and communication among teachers about students, their needs, progress and problems. More teachers are aware of student problems and styles that will make a difference.

This teacher's remarks lent weight to the claim that, within her school, there was a collaborative or 'shared, technical' staff culture. Similar remarks can be found in teacher transcripts for all case schools. However, since this study was concerned to discover what school-leaders did to foster such cultures, more systematic assurance that collaborative cultures had been achieved to a substantial degree was necessary.

To provide this assurance, we adopted six indicators of collaboration from the work of Judith Little, 1982, p. 331). Her research suggested that in exceptionally effective schools with shared technical cultures:

- teachers engage in frequent, continuous and increasingly concrete and precise talk about teaching practices
- teachers are frequently observed, and provided with useful (if potentially frightening) critiques of their teaching
- teachers plan, design, research, evaluate, and prepare teaching materials together
- teachers teach each other the practice of teaching

These and other features of such schools, Little found, could best be explained by two prevailing norms shared by staff:

- a norm of collegiality (the meaning of which is nicely illustrated in the quotation beginning this section)
- a norm of continuous improvement: staff are motivated to grow professionally and to contribute where possible to school improvement

Given these four specific and two more general indicators of collaboration, a content analysis was carried out of the transcribed interviews conducted with the principal and all teachers in each of the twelve case schools. Its purpose was to estimate the degree of collaboration within each school. Results suggested that the cultures of the twelve schools, as a whole, were characterized by relatively high degrees of collaboration. Across all criteria, an average of approximately 70 percent of staff provided evidence of collaboration. This average rises to 80 percent if the observation criterion is not included. Teachers provided little evidence of frequent classroom observation and feedback (Mean = 16 percent consistent with evidence reported earlier by Little, 1982). Observation and especially *critical* feedback may violate what Corbett, Firestone and Rossman (1987) refer to as a 'sacred' norm of teaching. This non-evaluative norm, with respect to one's peers, is often reinforced in codes of ethics promoted by teachers' professional associations. The greatest percentage of teachers provided evidence of continuous, practical, concrete talk about teaching practice (M = 95 percent).

In spite of the high levels of collaboration evident in the schools as a whole, there was significant variation across the schools. To better understand reasons for variation, the three schools with the lowest levels of collaboration were compared with the three schools having the highest levels. This comparison suggested two reasons for variation in levels of collaboration. First, in the three lowest scoring schools, there was little indication, in the initial stages of the improvement projects, of strong motivation among staff members to participate. Their commitment to the project emerged in all cases but much later in the process. In contrast, staff motivation to participate was strong from the beginning in two of the three high-scoring schools; in the third, the principal quite quickly replaced staff who were not keen to participate with staff who were. Early and sustained motivation of teachers to engage in school improvement, therefore, may be a crucial determinant of at least the speed with which collaborative cultures develop. Actions by school-leaders to foster early enthusiasm among teachers for the school-improvement effort may contribute significantly to their predispositions toward collaboration.

A second reason for differences in levels of collaboration across schools may be found in the variable we label 'goal clarification'. The three schools which achieved the most collaborative cultures arrived at a set of clear, shared goals for school improvement in the context of substantial staff cohesiveness and/or collaborative decision-making. Goal clarification in two of the other three schools, in contrast, was stimulated directly by the school-leader or a leadership team prior to the development of much staff cohesiveness or collaborative decision-making. In the third school, goal clarification did not occur (we comment in more detail later on the importance of goal clarification).

The nature of collaboration varied across the schools in different ways as well. For example, in one school there was much evidence of joint work but this was mostly work in pairs and almost all of it involved the principal as one member of the pair. While this form of collaboration seems to have been useful in meeting the immediate school-improvement goals, it leaves the school culture especially vulnerable, should there be a change of school-leader. Collaboration in the three secondary schools also seemed different than in elementary schools. In these schools, joint work was usually within departments; they were 'Balkanized' in some respects (Hargreaves, 1990). Nevertheless, in-service work was frequently carried out across departments as was talk about teaching. Overall, the norms of collegiality and continuous improvement were as evident in secondary as in elementary schools.

In sum, we interpret these data as evidence of school cultures showing relatively extensive collaboration, although variation among schools existed for several reasons.

How Significant is the Larger Context for Cultural Change?

The (School Improvement Project) gave a more integrated and united focus on what every individual teacher would try to do, things that normally wouldn't be spelled out. It helped unify the school's instructional focus and the things we wanted to do through learning were important for everyone ... we had support all along the way, we just talked to each other for support (Teacher).

The larger context within which each of the school-leaders in our sample of twelve schools worked to develop more collaborative cultures was a school-improvement project. The specific purpose of these projects was determined by each school, sometimes in conjunction with district staff, and varied widely. Some projects focused on staff development, some on the implementation of new curricula, others attempted to use library resources more effectively and increase teachers' repertoire of instructional strategies. One secondary school was involved in a massive effort to individualize instruction, an initiative that touched on virtually every aspect of the school's program, administration, physical organization, and culture. Most improvement initiatives were much more modest than this.

To clarify the larger context in which school-leaders worked to develop a more collaborative culture, we have selected one of the twelve case studies of school improvement as an illustration. This was a suburban, K–8 (kindergarten to grade 8) school with an ethnically and socially diverse school population of about 400 and a teaching staff of twenty-one members. At the beginning of the project (early 1987) the principal had been at the school for three years. She was encouraged to develop the project, initially, by a senior administrator, after she had expressed some unease about instruction in the school. At the outset, teachers also expressed concern about lack of staff cohesiveness. The focus for school improvement became mastering the use of inquiry teaching methods and using them appropriately in the classroom.

Figure 9.1 is a causal network depicting the twenty-eight variables involved in the school-improvement processes that took place over three years in this school. Complete definitions of these twenty-eight variables, as well as others which appeared in the twelve cases as a whole, are available from the authors. For present purposes, variables referenced directly in the text are briefly defined when they are discussed. Figure 9.1 also depicts the relationships among variables. Based on the frequency with which variables were mentioned by the ten staff interviewed for this case, an estimate is provided of whether the influence of the variable was low, moderate, or high. In cases where the relationship is negative, a '(–)' appears next to the line joining the variables. Because the present

Figure 9.1: School-improvement processes: Causal network for one school

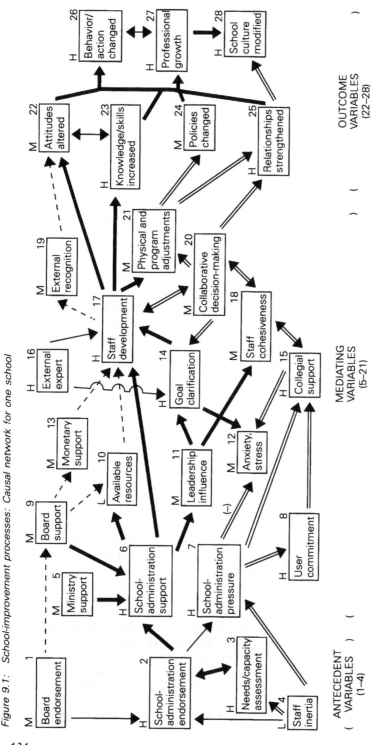

Developing Expert Leadership for Future Schools

134

study is focused on the development of collaborative cultures, it is useful to note that five of these twenty-eight variables constitute aspects of such a culture: collegial support (15), collaborative decision-making (20), staff cohesiveness (18), strengthened relationships (25), and modification of school culture (28).

A brief narrative will help the reader understand the processes depicted in Figure 9.1. There were four antecedent variables, of which three had differing but overlapping paths through the mediating variables to the outcomes. District-level endorsement (1) of the Ministry School-Improvement Project (SIP) and its invitation to this school was a factor in school-administration endorsement (2) as was the principal's perception of staff inertia (4), which had led the school administration to undertake a needs/capacity assessment (3) and to create pressure for change (7).

The first path begins with board endorsement (1) of the school being designated a SIP school. This endorsement led to board support (9) as a mediating variable in the change process. This support was manifested in available resources (10) as board consultants provided some support, and in monetary support (13), particularly for release time. Both the monetary support and the resources contributed to staff development (17). During the process of their staff-development activities, teachers had made revisions to the board curriculum document that resulted in some external recognition (19). This acknowledgment of their work was a factor in teacher's altered attitudes (22) to greater confidence in their professional abilities. The staff-development variable was related to other outcome variables in patterns that will be described below.

The second and most significant path through the causal network begins with school-administration endorsement (2) interacting with the needs/capacity assessment (3) to initiate the school-improvement effort. This endorsement was reflected in the mediating variable, school-administration support (6), which was reinforced by both Ministry (5) and board support (9). School-administration support contributed directly to staff development (17) as well as contributing indirectly through the principal's efforts to obtain whatever limited resources (10) that were available. School-administration support (6) also resulted in the development of leadership influence (11) with the formation of the school-improvement team (SIT) which connected with the third path through collaborative decision-making (20). Leadership influence from the School Improvement Team (SIT) led to increased goal clarification (14), which helped to alleviate anxiety and stress (12), as teachers developed greater certainty about what they could do; the clarification process also contributed to staff development (17). An external expert (16) was also crucial in developing greater clarity about goals (14) and in staff development (17). As an outcome of staff development, attitudes altered (22) and knowledge and skills increased (23), leading to changed behavior and actions (26) as well as professional growth (27). These outcomes, in turn, contributed to modification of the school culture (28). Staff development contributed to physical and program adjustments (21) to accommodate the inquiry teaching model. These adjustments led to policy changes (24) and strengthened relationships (25) with staff engaged in joint planning. These outcomes also affected professional growth (27), behavior and action (26), as well as school culture (28).

The final path through the network begins with the antecedent variable, staff inertia (4), which influenced the principal to initiate a needs/capacity assessment

(3), and led to school-administration pressure (7); staff were given a choice of making a three-to-five-year commitment to the SIP or transferring to another school, and new staff were hired only if they supported the SIP. This pressure resulted in a high level of user commitment (8) that contributed to collegial support (15), since teachers were willing to help others so the SIP would be a success. Some of the collegial support was the result of school-administration pressure (7) to form planning partners. The pressure to be active in the SIP also resulted in some anxiety and stress (12), as teachers were uncertain how to proceed. The anxiety was partially offset by increased collegial support (15). As staff supported each other in their SIP activities, there was an increase in staff cohesiveness (18), with new and previous staff pulling together as a team. Cohesiveness had a reciprocal relationship with collaborative decision-making (20), which was supported by leadership influence (11) from the SIT. Greater collaboration in decision-making was part of the process for developing clarity of goals (14), and contributed to staff development (17). Staff development, in turn, enhanced collaborative decision-making among staff colleagues and within class-rooms, as staff became more proficient in use of the inquiry teaching method. Collaborative decision-making (20) along with staff development (17) contri-buted to physical and program adjustments (21) to support the new teaching strategy. In this interaction with the second path, policies were changed (24) and relationships strengthened (25), as noted above. Collaboration also resulted directly in strengthened relationships among staff, among students, and between staff and students. Change in relationships was reflected in behavior and action changes (26), and teachers' professional growth (27), as well as contributing directly to school culture.

Figure 9.1 depicts a comprehensive set of school-improvement processes similar, in many respects, to processes found in the other eleven case studies. What significance does this larger context have for the development of collabora-tive cultures? First, it is important simply to recognize that while 'restructuring schools' (in this case their cultures) is a worthwhile reform objective, it is unlikely that people will be motivated to pursue it as an end in itself. Consistent with the results of other research (e.g., Huberman and Miles, 1982), our case studies suggested that most people were motivated to change by goals much more directly concerned with curriculum and instruction.

Second, the larger context for school improvement, usually focused on 'educationally compelling' changes, potentially neutralizes the primary disincen-tive for increased collaboration with colleagues: the significant additional costs of collaboration, particularly in the initial stages. Increased costs are a function of the time required for group deliberation, as distinct from individual decision-making. This time may be added onto the normal work time of staff or require the direct outlay of money to free people from duties during their normal work time. The incentive for collaboration is the perception that these costs are at least balanced by significant benefits. Such perceptions depend on collaboration being viewed, eventually at least, as a powerful means for coping with problems attendant upon implementing 'educationally compelling' changes.

A third way in which the larger context for school improvement has signi-ficance for developing collaborative cultures is the multiple and diverse opportu-nities it affords to reinforce the benefits of collaboration. This can be illustrated with reference to Figure 9.1, for example, by examining the relationships with collegial support (15). This variable emerges as a direct response to pressure from the school administration (7) to begin to implement inquiry teaching strategies, and a parallel commitment to that goal by many teachers (8). The development of collegial support, in this case, initiates a process which eventually increases staff cohesion (18) and results in collaborative decision-making. (20). But the perception that collegial support is valuable is usefully reinforced by its ability also to help teachers cope with an unintended by-product of school-administration pressure: increased anxiety and stress (12).

Finally, as Figure 9.1 also illustrates, at least understanding the larger context for school improvement allows us to appreciate how significant a force school-leaders can be in the development of more collaborative cultures. For example, the principal's support for instructional change (6) in this case study was followed by delegation of leadership responsibilities to others and a school-improvement team (11), and the need for staff development (17). Both of these variables subsequently fostered a need for collaborative decision-making (20). School-administration pressure (7) was similarly pivotal in the development of other aspects of a collaborative culture.

What Strategies Were Used by School-Leaders to Influence School Cultures?

Understanding the larger context within which a collaborative culture develops draws attention, as we have noted, to the extent of school-leaders' potential influence on that process. In addition, such understanding helps clarify more specifically what school-leaders can do in exercising such influence. This matter is addressed here in two stages. First, variables most directly linking school-leaders' actions to collaborative cultures are discussed. Then, a more detailed analysis of specific leadership strategies is provided.

The relationship between strategies initiated by school-leaders and school culture is neither simple nor direct (as Figure 9.1 illustrates). To better understand the nature of the 'space' between the two, we developed a series of cross-case causal fragments (Miles and Huberman, 1984) focused, however, on only selected subsets of variables and relationships to best represent the twelve cases, as a whole.

We first examined the most direct chains of relationships between school-leaders' actions, and one central attribute of collaborative cultures strengthened interpersonal relationships among staff that contributed to changes in school cultures. School-leaders' actions, for this purpose, were considered to be of only two types: those intended to be helpful, supportive or facilitative (e.g., provision of resources) and those intended to exert pressure for change on teachers (e.g., persuasion of reluctant participants).

The space between supportive school-leader actions and strengthened staff relationships is filled with six variables, two of which, leadership influence and collaborative decision-making, appeared most frequently. Collegial support and organizational adjustments, appearing moderately often, facilitate the development of collaborative decision-making directly. Collegial support interacts with staff development and user commitment in a few cases. The space between school-leader pressure and strengthened relationships is filled with four variables, none of which appeared in many of the cases.

These two causal fragments suggested, in sum, that:

- the most direct contributor to the development of strengthened relationships is for staff to be involved in collaborative decision-making
- the likelihood that staff will participate authentically in such decision-making is a function of the amount of support they perceive from colleagues, their commitment to accomplishing their school-improvement goals, and the opportunities for collaboration provided through adjustments to the organization (e.g., time to meet, suitably structured groups)
- school-leaders have at their disposal activities which are reasonably effective in creating user commitment and suitably adjusting to the organization ... delegating power to others in the school seems likely to lead to greater collegial support and forms of staff development that assist in building collegial support

In order to identify more specific leadership strategies, we relied on the twelve causal networks as well as the content analysis of the interviews with the twelve school-leaders reflecting on their own actions to influence their schools' cultures. In reporting results, we assume high levels of interdependence between strategies used by school-leaders to help implement the 'educationally compelling' changes in their schools and strategies influencing school cultures. Justification for this assumption can be found in the twelve causal networks.

Results suggested that six broad strategies were used to influence school cultures. School leaders:

- strengthened the school's culture
- used a variety of bureaucratic mechanisms to stimulate and reinforce cultural change
- fostered staff development
- engaged in direct and frequent communication about cultural norms, values, and beliefs
- shared power and responsibility with others
- used symbols to express cultural values

Each of these broad strategies manifested itself in a range of specific actions. While all school administrators in the study used most strategies, their different choices of methods illustrate this range reasonably well. Each of these strategies will be examined in more detail in the remainder of this section.

Strengthen the School's Culture

Initially the SIT [School Improvement Team] got together to talk about goals for the SIP [School Improvement Project] and then we decided to take everything back to the staff to see what kind of general direction they wanted. We [the whole staff] brainstormed what we needed to do with resource-based learning in the school. We broke into groups and decided on a variety of very tight recommendations and after discussion were able to reduce all our ideas to the six subgoals under RBL. We then took on the commitment of working each of these through, until we were comfortable they had been achieved (Teacher).

School cultures are typically weak (Firestone and Wilson, 1985). As such, they remain of little consequence in bringing about significant school reform even when they reflect aspects of collaboration. Firestone and Wilson claim that such weakness is a function of (a) ambiguous, excessive, poorly specified purposes; (b) the isolation of teachers from one another and from administrators; and (c) low levels of commitment by staff to the school's purposes. The causal networks (Figure 9.1, for example) suggested that most school-leaders, at least implicitly, recognized the need to strengthen their schools' cultures and acted in a variety of ways to ameliorate sources of cultural weakness.

All school-leaders in this study, as in the study by Deal and Peterson (1990) engaged in some process to clarify and prioritize a set of shared goals for the school-improvement initiatives (variable 14 in Figure 9.1), although variations among schools in how this was done have been noted already. This often involved entire school staffs in a process for setting goals, initially, sometimes using a consultant to assist. It also involved efforts throughout the life of many projects to block competing priorities and systematically orient new staff to the goals for school improvement.

Rosenholtz's (1989) research has depicted a central role for shared goals in helping to foster a shared, technical culture. For this reason, we examined more closely the relationships associated with this variable in our study and found that the relationship between school-leaders' actions and such goals is quite direct. Establishing collaborative decision-making procedures was a moderately frequent prerequisite to goal clarification. In more than half of the case schools, such procedures were used to identify goals and priorities. In most schools, the power to establish goals for school improvement was delegated to or shared with others, usually a school-improvement team. This fostered greater participation in the process and prevented the principal's goals from dominating the process (or from being seen to dominate the process). Rosenholtz (1989, p. 15), explaining similar relationships in her data, suggests that 'principals who involve teachers in generating information about the goals of teaching, in scanning and choosing the best alternatives, grant teachers a part in constructing school reality'.

Reducing teacher isolation, a second method of strengthening school culture, was accomplished by creating opportunities for staff to influence one another (e.g., creating time for joint planning, holding staff retreats, asking staff to offer workshops to colleagues, encouraging teachers to visit one another's classes) and which sometimes required interaction (e.g., creating working committees with specific tasks assigned).

Finally, teacher commitment was stimulated quite directly and forcefully in at least four of the cases. Teachers were given the option, after reasonable opportunities to understand the school's purposes, to stay in the school and devote themselves to those purposes, or transfer to another school, with the principal's assistance. In most cases, as well, only new teachers were hired who expressed a prior commitment to the schools' purposes, an action Rosenholtz (1989) also found related to the development of shared goals.

Use of Bureaucratic Mechanisms

> The principal encouraged us to meet with other people at our own grade level. I found that one of the best ways was to get down to business and do some planning because it gives you a different way of looking at things. This year two of us are working together on some units. Initially it was time consuming and we just plodded along doing so much talking, but by the time we were finished we really understood how to go about it (Teacher).

Bureaucratic mechanisms, as Firestone and Wilson (1985, p. 278) point out, 'establish constraints on and opportunities for how teachers teach'. Such mechanisms will sometimes support cultural changes by making such changes easier to accomplish or more rewarding in which to engage. School-leaders reported using a number of such mechanisms to foster directly implementation of school-improvement goals and to create more collaborative cultures. Theses mechanisms included, for example:

- money (e.g., reallocating existing money for the project, finding new money, buying needed materials)
- planning and scheduling (e.g., providing time for collaborative planning during the workday, timetabling students to allow teachers to work together, keeping school improvement on the forefront of meeting agendas)
- decision-making structures (e.g., establishing divisional and committee structures, pairing teachers for planning)
- staffing procedures or, more specifically, what Sashkin and Sashkin (1990) termed 'value-based' staffing (e.g., selecting new staff based on improvement priorities and willingness to collaborate, involving staff in hiring decisions)
- evaluation (e.g., progress with school improvement across school, supervise improvement efforts in individual classrooms)

The last three mechanisms, especially teacher evaluation, Rosenholtz (1989, p. 27) found to contribute significantly to teachers' commitment to school goals. This contribution occurs, in her view, when teachers believe 'that evaluation criteria are ... central to their work, applied frequently and capable of being influenced by their own effort'.

Staff Development

> Our principal shares new knowledge and is always questioning where we are, what our strengths and difficulties are. She finds resources for us

if she doesn't have the answer. She monitors us and pulls together across divisions. She gets outside help if she sees any need ... Sharing is the key thing here. Because I was new I had extra help with planning. I took my planning to my colleagues and my principal and discussed where the problems lay (Teacher).

Activities designed 'to improve teachers' skill, knowledge, understandings or performance in present or future roles', (Fullan's, 1990, p. 3, definition of staff development), appeared prominently in all twelve causal networks. While staff development and increased collaboration were not linked by any logical necessity, they were linked empirically to at least some aspect of collaboration in all cases. The reasons for such a link are evident in Little's (1982, p. 339) research which suggested that:

> To the extent that school situations foster teachers' recourse to others' knowledge and experience, and to shared work and discussion, teachers are likely to favor some participation in staff development – staff development appears to have the greatest prospects for influence when there is a prevailing norm of collegiality.

Staff development which acknowledges what can be learned from one's immediate colleagues, as well as others, fosters a collaborative culture and is, in turn, nurtured by that same culture. This reciprocity is evident in the chains of variables that form the causal fragment between school administrators' actions and staff development. The chains consist of eight variables, six of which have been discussed previously, as they bear on the development of collaborative cultures. Two variables, monetary support and other available resources, are not related in any way to collaboration but are directly linked to the creation of useful staff development, as is supportive action by the school-leader. Furthermore, school-leaders have considerable influence on these two variables directly. This causal fragment suggests, in sum, that useful staff development depends most directly on the commitment of the staff to school-improvement goals, the perception of collegial supports, and the availability of money and other sources to support staff-development activities. School-leaders help create useful staff development directly, by providing the needed resources, and indirectly, by fostering staff commitment and a supportive collegial environment. Both of these findings are similar to results reported by Rosenholtz (1989) and by Little (1982, p. 334). Finally, delegating power to others (leadership influence) is a key strategy for building the kind of collegial support that makes staff development relatively meaningful.

School-leaders reported fostering staff development in both direct and indirect ways. They acted directly by themselves giving workshops to staff in areas of their expertise, assisting teachers in their own classrooms, attending in-service sessions with staff, and sharing information from conferences or workshops which they had attended. Through such actions school-leaders modeled values considered important in the school (Sashkin and Sashkin, 1990). Less directly, school-leaders informed staff of in-service opportunities and encouraged participation, invited 'experts' into the school to assist staff, and sent staff to relevant conferences. They also encouraged use of board consultants and provided reading to staff and follow-up with discussion. Because these activities brought teachers into contact with either the school-leader, other colleagues in the school, or other adults outside the school, they encouraged the use of collaboration as a means for problem-solving.

Direct and Frequent Communication

In actual planning in half day sessions I was actively involved with a planning team working with consultants. It's important to work through with the teacher to understand each unique classroom setting and the problems that may arise.... I think the thing I've learned [in this process] is that a principal needs to learn as much as she can about a teacher. You need to know your staff thoroughly, listen and show people you truly care about them. When they realize you are ready to help them realize their goals, you will find a positive and favourable response (Principal).

Firestone and Wilson (1985) hypothesize that active communication of the culture is an especially opportune strategy for principals because of the large proportion of their time spent in interpersonal contact. Some research estimates that up to 75 percent of a principals' time is spent in such contact (Willower and Kmetz, 1982, Martin and Willower, 1981). School-leaders in our study frequently used such words as 'informing', 'persuading', 'directing', 'writing', 'negotiating', 'counseling', 'visiting', and 'discussing' to indicate the prevalence of this strategy and the importance they attached to it in pursuing school improvement and greater collaboration. This strategy is not clearly distinguishable from others we have discussed since all, to this point, include an important role for communication. What is different in this case (aside from staff development) is that the school-leader is the source of the communication and, as a result, controls its content more directly than in the cases of previously examined strategies.

Share Power and Responsibility with Others

The SIT [School Improvement Team] was involved in planning where we are going, looking to the future and getting input from staff in terms of where we think we need to change (Principal).

Central to the concept of a collaborative culture is the more equitable distribution of power for decision-making among members of the school. Especially when the focus of the decision-making centers on cross-classroom and school-wide matters, this will involve school administrators in at least delegating, if not giving away, sources of power traditionally vested in their positions. Without school-leaders' willingness to do this and teachers' willingness to accept the power thus offered, true collaboration seems unlikely. With power, of course, comes the responsibility for decisions and actions. This has the potential for making the teacher's role in the school not only much more meaningful, but also more complex. Teachers, under these circumstances, are professionally more 'empowered' – a goal of many school-reform advocates at present (e.g., Maeroff, 1989).

The most obvious way school-leaders in this study went about sharing power and responsibility was through the establishment of school-improvement teams, of which they were sometimes members. These teams shared the responsibility for project coordination with principals and assisted principals in many of the strategies already mentioned. Also, these teams served as important links between staff and administration, testing plans and soliciting reactions and ideas. Individual members of these teams often acted as mentors or role models for their colleagues; they shared expertise, tried out new ideas in their classes, and encouraged conversation about the school-improvement effort.

Use Symbols and Rituals to Express Cultural Values

> Every staff meeting starts with 'good news' about the school, something I've seen in the classroom or they tell us ... at the end of the year we always have a celebration of sorts where we look back at achievements and celebrate what we've achieved. Our newsletter mentions teachers and talks about their accomplishments ... Children have been involved in things like the safety patrol, assemblies, and daily announcements. A strong sense of community has been developed in the school because the children identify with their mascot (Principal).

Sashkin and Sashkin (1990), Deal and Peterson (1990), and Firestone and Wilson (1985) suggest this strategy as a promising one through which principals can influence school culture. As others point out, symbols are visible expressions of the content of an organization's culture (Peters, 1979, Pfeffer, 1981, Shein, 1985). Manipulating such symbols and rituals, therefore, is a way to make more visible those aspects of the culture that school-leaders believe are valuable.

In our study, school-leaders explicitly mentioned three ways in which they used symbols and rituals to foster collaboration. At staff meetings and assemblies they celebrated and publically recognized the work of staff and students which contributed to their school-improvement efforts. This action invited others to share in the successes of their colleagues. School-leaders also wrote private notes to staff, expressing appreciation for special efforts. This action demonstrated to individuals the value attached to some practices by the principal and the possibility of recognition by an esteemed colleague. Staff were encouraged, third, to share experiences with their colleagues, both as a source of stimulation for colleagues and also for recognition by other adults.

Each of these ways of using symbols and rituals has the potential of contributing to an increase in teachers' professional self-esteem. This is a pivotal variable, influential in building a collaborative culture, according to Rosenholtz's (1989) research, a variable which increases the likelihood that teachers will feel 'safe' in revealing their work to others.

Our study suggests, in sum, that school-leaders used six strategies to influence the culture of their schools and to foster greater collaboration. They strengthened the culture, modified bureaucratic mechanisms, and engaged in staff development. In addition, school-leaders communicated frequently and directly with staff, shared power, and used symbols to express cultural values. A wide range of specific actions were taken by school-leaders to pursue each strategy and some actions served multiple purposes.

Summary and Further Insights about the Process of Culture Change

Compelling evidence suggests that collaborative school cultures contribute significantly to teacher development. Such cultures, which are 'shared and technical' appear to foster practices most conducive to the types of staff (and student) development which are the focus of current school-reform efforts. We also believed that evidence, in support of the claim that school administrators can have a significant impact on schools, was compelling but not available specifically in relation to school culture. Indeed, in our own recent research with secondary school administrators, the relationship between their practices and their schools' cultures was extremely weak (Lawton and Leithwood, 1988). 'Why was this the case?', we wondered. 'Was it because school culture has not been a focus of their work? Or have they tried to influence school culture and failed?' These questions stimulated our inquiry into what nine elementary and three secondary principals did to help develop collaborative cultures in their schools. These were schools known to have such cultures and also to have experienced success in their school-improvement efforts over at least a three-year period.

After identifying sources of variation in collaboration in each school, the study inquired about the significance of the larger school-improvement context for the development of collaborative cultures. We found that this larger context provided important incentives for initiating collaboration, and continuously reinforced the value of collaboration over time. We then asked what strategies principals used to foster greater collaboration and were able to identify six. These included strengthening the culture, using bureaucratic mechanisms, fostering staff development, frequent and direct communication, sharing power and responsibility, and using rituals and symbols to express cultural values. These strategies seem quite teachable and ought to be developed within the repertoire of leaders of future schools.

The study provided support for the claim that school-leaders have access to strategies which are 'transformational' in effect and, hence, assist in the development of collaborative school cultures. This means two things in our view: significant changes in staff members' individual and shared understandings of their current purposes and practices; and an enhanced capacity to solve future professional problems, individually and collegially.

The transformational effect of the strategies identified in the study may be explained by the ways in which they alter the patterns of interaction among staff. Because meaning is socially constructed (Berger and Luckmann, 1965), differences in the patterns of interactions experienced by school staff will result in differences in the meanings which they associate with their work. The meaning that individual staff members bring to their work is a product of the schemata (concepts or related ideas) they possess in relation to that work. Borko and Livingston (1989), for example, identify the specific scripts, mental scenes and propositional structures that make up the schemata which expert teachers bring to their instructional practices. Such schemata are the cognitive guides to action, growing out of the teacher's assumptions, norms, values and beliefs about, for example, the role of teacher and the nature of effective instruction. Alterations in the school culture and accompanying changes in staff practices, therefore, depend on changes in the individual schemata guiding a staff member's practices. Such alterations in cognitive structure, however, must eventually coalesce around schematic content that is common, in some optimum measure, across individuals. This recapitulation of similar cognitive processes at different levels of social structure (Mehan, 1984) is a more complex type of change to assist with than schematic change within an individual alone. This is especially so, since each staff member's starting points will necessarily be different.

In a traditional, isolated, professional culture, these schemata are adapted, extended, and linked together in new ways primarily in response to students. Such social negotiation of meaning will usually take place indirectly: teachers will have to infer the implications for their purposes and practices from students' responses. These responses rarely challenge teachers to reflect directly on their basic assumptions and values. Indeed, relying primarily on the negotiation of meaning with students, as Rosenholtz (1989) found, seems likely to encourage a gradual narrowing of purpose, a reducing of the teacher's aspirations for students, and an increased weight given to practices which are successful in managing classroom behavior. Rarely, in an isolated professional culture, will teachers' assumptions, norms, values, and beliefs be challenged by significantly more ambitious visions of what is possible.

Collaborative cultures, on the other hand, potentially confront teachers with a different order of dissonance about purposes and practices to which they must adapt their classroom schemata. The social negotiation of such meaning will often be quite direct; it also has the power to challenge the teacher to reconsider basic assumptions and values. Unlike students, other peers (including principals as well as teachers) are much more likely to stimulate the teacher to consider more ambitious purposes and non-trivial modifications in their practices, as a way of achieving such purposes.

The potential effect of the six strategies, used by school administrators to influence school culture, which we identified in this study, can be explained from this theoretical perspective. Three of these strategies provide principals and other teachers with opportunities to clarify explicitly the preferred content of relevant schemata from their point of view: using symbols and rituals to express cultural values; direct and frequent communication; and staff development. More interactive versions of these strategies allow for the negotiation of schematic content between school-leaders and teachers or among teachers. Several of the six strategies appear to constrain the range of schematic content available to the teacher, rather than to dictate its precise form. This seems the case, for example, with the use of bureaucratic mechanisms. Finally, sharing power and responsibility may provide a stimulus for developing shared meaning (effecting the strength of the culture) without necessary reference to the meaning itself (the content of the culture). If school-leaders share power with those who hold similar points of view, however, this strategy is more prescriptive of the schematic content possessed by school-leaders.

Conclusion

Experiences aimed to develop leaders for future schools ought to include opportunities to appreciate and carry out the strategies for fostering more collaborative school cultures, as discussed in this chapter. Such strategies encourage and permit the expertise of colleagues within the school to serve as powerful stimulants for teacher development.

Part 3

Developing Expert Leadership for Future Schools

Chapter 10

The Socialization of School-Leaders

The term 'socialization' conveys quite different meanings to people in different cultural settings. To some, the term is almost synonymous with brainwashing or, at the least, 'swallowing' in an uncritical fashion the purposes and procedures of one's organization or group of colleagues. To be socialized, from this perspective, is to become simply a cog in the organizational wheel, a mindless bureaucrat serving the policies of the organization, which are interpreted in a literal fashion and without a sense of personal empowerment.

In this chapter, the term socialization is intended to convey a quite different meaning. After Merton (1963), the term *socialization* encompasses those processes by which an individual selectively acquires the knowledge, skills and dispositions needed to perform effectively the role of school-leader. Such processes may range from carefully planned, formal education programs, for example, through less formal but still planned experiences (e.g., working with a mentor), to informal, usually unplanned on-the-job leadership experiences. One need not become a cog in the organizational wheel as a result of experiences like these. Indeed, it is possible to imagine such processes fostering the individual's critical capacity as he or she gets 'closer' to the organization and better able to see blemishes on the corporate body. Whether or not 'getting closer' magnifies the corporate blemishes and encourages a disposition toward change, or blurs one's sight and creates blind acceptance, also depends on the nature of the socialization process. The ideal socialization process positions one at the point of sharpest focus: not so close as to render the corporate image a fuzzy blur; nor so far away as to make the detailed features of the image unrecognizable.

As we have argued in Part 1 of this book, leaders of future schools will need to possess a detailed, well focused picture of their school organizations. They will also require a capacity to envision ever more productive forms that those schools might take and the disposition to embark on changes, driven by a desire to approximate those more productive forms. The overriding question of interest in this chapter is: What kinds of socialization experiences contribute most to the development of such qualities in school-leaders (effectiveness on the high ground and expertise in the swamp)?

Together, Tables 10.1 and 10.2 summarize the framework for the chapter and the research on which it was based. This framework took as its point of departure results[1] of the small body of theory[2] and empirical research[3] relevant to

Table 10.1: Socialization patterns experienced by aspiring principles

Dimensions of Socialization Experiences	Socialization Patterns	
	Not Helpful	Very Helpful
1. Relationships (a) Superordinates	– (Aspiring Principal) discouraged from entering role; exposed to models of ineffective practice; no communication networks developed for organizational problem-solving	– (Aspiring Principal) receives active sustained encouragement and sponsorship to enter role; exposed to models of effective school administration; increase in the organization's communication networks which foster more successful problem-solving
(b) Peers	– interacts with peers primarily about social matters; has infrequent or no opportunities to assume leadership roles with peers on school-wide and and district issues influencing schools	– interacts regularly with peers about classroom, school-wide and district issues; has many opportunities to assume leadership role with peers on school-wide and district issues influencing schools; develops a network of peers sharing aspirations for the principalship
2. School-System Policies, Procedures and 'Control Mechanisms'	– establishes a reward system (e.g., promotion) in which merit is frequently subordinated in favor of loyalty, personal relationships and other 'political' criteria	– establishes a reward system which acknowledges merit through promotion
3. Formal Training	– university-sponsored field-experience is short-term and perfunctory	– focused on the understandings required to exercise instructional leadership; opportunities to reflect on relationship between own school problems and knowledge provided in formal training programs; opportunities to experience the world of the principal first-hand over an extended time period; availability of frequent short programs focused on particular skills and issues; opportunities provided by district to learn 'how things are done' in the district
4. Outcomes (a) Image of Role	– adoption of image of role as 'building manager' by those not in role; lack of clear image of role by those not in the role	– adoption of image of role as instructional and curriculum leader
(b) Skills	– minimal development of skills required for entry to role	– significant development of skills required for entry to role
(c) Norms and Values	– decreased sharing of values and norms of behavior with superiors	– increased sharing of values and norms of behavior with superiors

Table 10.2: Socialization patterns experienced by practicing principals

Dimensions of Socialization Experiences	Socialization Patterns	
	Not Helpful	Very Helpful
1. Relationships (a) Superordinates	(Practicing Principal) – receives feedback when school problems become visible; exposed to models of ineffective practice in both school and school-system leadership; communication networks developed are designed to protect self-interest and school interests (damage control) in the face of system-wide decisions	(Practicing Principal) – receives continuous feedback, support, collaborative planning, and clear, realistic expectations, exposed to models of effective practice in both school and school-wide leadership; increase in the organization's communication networks which foster more successful problem-solving
(b) Peers	– occasionally interacts with peers about district issues; has occasional opportunities to assume leadership role with peers on district issues influencing schools; develops a network of peers to provide advice, as needed	– regularly interacts with peers about social, classroom, school-wide and district issues; has many opportunities to assume leadership role with peers on district issues influencing schools; develops a network of peers to provide advice and coaching
(c) Subordinates	– has few requests for advice from subordinates aspiring to the school administration; remains distant from the perspective of subordinates on classroom and school-wide matters	– encouraged to develop a mentoring relationship with subordinates who show potential for school administration, actively encouraging their development; has regular opportunities to better appreciate the perspectives of subordinates on classroom and school-wide matters; receives regular feedback from experienced teachers about how they are doing; works with teachers on school-improvement projects
(d) Students	– most contacts with students concern discipline and school-routine issues	– maintains close contact with students
(e) Self	– has no strategies to foster self-reflection	– maintains case records of significant problems encountered

2.	School-System Policies and Procedures	– explicitly focuses close to half the principals' time on non-instructional matters in the school; severely constrains opportunities to address school-based needs, giving the major priority to system-wide needs and rewards; reinforces a 'building manager' image of the role	– focuses a large proportion of the principals' time on school improvement; encourages principals to address school-wide needs in conjunction with district-wide needs; consistently reinforces and rewards an 'instructional leadership' image of the role; encourages greater experimentation and risk-taking by principals; provides opportunities for mentoring, apprenticeships, and the shadowing of other principals
3.	Formal Training	– no ongoing training available routinely in the school system and little effort made to find training elsewhere	– multiple opportunities available and taken, which provide access to increased skill, current educational knowledge, and attitudes of continuous learning
4.	Outcomes		
	(a) Image of Role	– increased commitment to image of role as 'building manager'	– increased commitment to image of role as instructional and curriculum leader
	(b) Skills	– refinement of a narrow range of school-management skills not directly related to school improvement	– significant refinement of existing skills and addition of new skills especially useful for school improvement
	(c) Norms and Values	– decreased sharing of values and norms with superordinates; lack of procedural skills in day-to-day management of school; insufficiently developed skills in interpersonal relations; lack of knowledge about how school system really operates and what procedures to follow	– increase in values and norms hared with superiors

the socialization of formal school-leaders. Table 10.1 summarizes differences in socialization processes experienced prior to appointment as a vice-principal or principal. Table 10.2 is directed at socialization processes experienced after selection as a formal school-leader.

Four dimensions of socialization are included in the framework. The first dimension is the nature of the experiences provided by the relationships engaged in by those being socialized. These are experiences provided, for example, by relationships with peers, superordinates and subordinates (for those already in the role) in the school district. Experiences resulting from contact with district policies and practices is the second dimension. Especially relevant to this dimension are policies and practices related to administrator selection and promotion, performance appraisal, and professional development. Formal education experiences and outcomes of socialization experiences are the final dimensions of the framework.

As Figures 10.1 and 10.2 indicate, the small amount of theory and empirical evidence which is available suggests that there are, at present, different patterns of socialization experiences and that each pattern has different effects on those being socialized. Such differences are summarized in a bipolar way as being 'not helpful', and 'very helpful' in developing qualities associated with effective school-leadership. The 'very helpful' socialization pattern contributes to the adoption and maintenance of an instructional leadership image of the role much like the program manager and systematic problem-solver described in Chapter 4; it fosters, as well, the development and refinement of knowledge and skills required to carry out such curriculum and instructional leadership. Very helpful socialization contributes to consensus about central organizational norms and values among administrators, at the school and district levels.

Taken together, Tables 10.1 and 10.2 also acknowledge that there are predictable stages in the socialization process and that the perspectives and needs of people may well differ depending on the stage in which they find themselves. Ronkowski and Iannaccone's (1989) review of studies using a conceptualization of socialization stages (initiation, transition and incorporation), drawn from the work of van Gennep (1960) and from Becker and Carper (1956), supports the usefulness of such a conceptualization. At the initiation stage people are concerned primarily about how others judge their adequacy. The standard for comparison at the transition stage is some sense of required job performance. At the incorporation stage comparisons are with oneself (how much 'I' have changed from my previous self toward becoming an effective school-leader). Table 10.1 is intended to describe forms of socialization primarily relevant to those somewhere in the initiation and transition stages of their socialization. Table 10.2 is relevant to those at the incorporation stage.

Given this framework, our general interest in this chapter about the most useful forms of socialization seems best served by seeking answers to four specific questions: Do school-leaders experience significantly different patterns of socialization? If so, what are the effects of these different patterns? Which specific socialization activities do school-leaders perceive to be most useful in their own development? Are different career paths associated with different socialization experiences? Differences related to gender, stage of socialization, and district or region also will be explored as part of several of these questions. It is worth noting that the results of the research described below bear most directly on the development of effective leadership on the high ground. More tenuous, from these results, is the link between what we describe as helpful forms of socialization and expertise in the swamp. That link needs considerably more scrutiny than we are able to give it in this chapter.

Answers to the specific questions addressed in the remainder of this chapter are based on the results of a series of four related studies. Results of the third of these studies are used as the primary evidence in answering the specific questions of interest in this chapter. Study One (Leithwood, Steinbach and Begley, in press) used a thirty-two item survey-questionnaire to collect data from a sample of forty-nine aspiring and thirty-eight practicing school-leaders drawn from many different school systems in Ontario. Study Two (Leithwood and Steinbach, in progress) was based on lengthy interviews with twenty-six practicing school-leaders, probing, in some depth, questions left uncertain or unanswered by the first study; these school-leaders were also drawn from many different school systems, all in Ontario.

The third study, of primary interest in this chapter, was a survey, as in Study One, with a forty-item instrument refined and extended to take into account what had been learned in the two previous studies. In order to examine possible regional differences, respondents were practicing school-leaders (principals and vice-principals) from one school system in the eastern Canadian province of Nova Scotia (113 respondents), one school system in the central Canadian province of Ontario (seventy-eight respondents) and a group of twenty-seven respondents from a number of school systems in British Columbia, the most westerly Canadian province.

The fourth study (Begley, Campbell-Evans and Brownridge, 1990) was conducted in the context of a school-leader preparation program jointly developed and run by the Northwest Territories Department of Education and the OISE Centre for Leadership Development. Eighty-seven aspiring and practicing school-leaders enrolled in this program, provided material for the survey, acting as participant observers, and supplied journal data to the study. Survey and interview techniques were combined for the last study in this series with aspiring and practicing school-leaders in one large school system in south central Ontario (Leithwood *et al.*, in progress). The discovery from previous studies of significant district effects on school-leaders' socialization experiences and a desire to redesign such experiences through some action research was the reason for conducting this study within a single school system. Subsequent results are drawn from Study Three unless otherwise noted.

Question 1: Do School-Leaders Experience Different Patterns of Socialization?

In order to inquire about differences in administrators' socialization experiences, each respondent was first classified depending on his or her opinion on socialization activities, as having a pattern of socialization that was either 'not helpful', 'mixed', 'moderately helpful', 'high mixed', or 'very helpful'. This classification was based on responses to ten questions. Each of these questions concerned a single socialization activity (e.g., extent of exposure to effective role-models) and required respondents to identify, from a fixed set of alternatives, the nature of that activity as they had experienced it. These alternatives ranged from those likely to contribute least (rated as 1) to the respondents' administrative development to those likely to contribute most (rated as 3), as suggested by Tables 10.1 and 10.2. Similar ratings on six or more of the ten items qualified a person to be assigned to one of three socialization patterns: six or more ratings of 1 led to assignment in the 'not helpful' pattern and a similar number of ratings of 2 resulted in assignment to the 'moderately helpful' pattern. Assignment to the 'very helpful' pattern required ratings of 3 on six or more of the ten items. The 'mixed' patterns were reserved for respondents who did not rate at least six items in a similar manner. Those assigned the 'high mixed' category had five items of the ten rated as 3, with at most one item rated as 1.

Table 10.3 identifies the ten items used for determining socialization patterns, reports the means and standard deviations for responses in Study Three to each item by those assigned to each pattern, and indicates the number of people assigned to each pattern. The number assigned to each item corresponds to the question about this item as it was numbered in the survey instrument (the same practice is followed for Tables 10.3 and 10.4).

As the last line of Table 10.3 indicates, only nine people (4 percent) appeared to have experienced the 'not helpful' socialization pattern. Relatively few people (eighteen or 8 percent) reported a 'very helpful' pattern, although when these people are combined with those experiencing the 'high mixed' pattern (twenty-four), almost a fifth of the respondents appear to have had relatively positive experiences. The bulk of respondents (167 or 77 percent) were classified as having received a 'moderately helpful' (42 percent) or 'mixed' (35 percent) pattern. These results are very similar to findings in Study One, with a somewhat smaller proportion of respondents reporting 'high mixed' or 'very helpful' socialization experiences – about 5 percent fewer.

Sources of difference in the socialization experiences of respondents are evident in all of the items in Table 10.3. These results are very similar to those found in Study One; in that study, 'opportunity to interact with peers' (item 11) was the only experience in which there did not seem to be differences across socialization patterns. Ratings for the same ten items were also examined for possible differences related to gender and stage of socialization. Statistically significant differences ($p < 0.05$ = the probability of these differences occurring by chance is less than 5 in 100.) were evident in the responses of women and men to two items. Men reported receiving encouragement to consider the role of school administrator earlier in their careers than did women (item 7), a trend also evident in Study One. Unlike Study One, women reported more frequent opportunities to assume leadership roles on school or board-wide committees (item 22). Study Three did not find (as was the case in Study One) a tendency for women to report greater participation in a network of peers also aspiring to school-leadership positions (item 19). Two statistically significant differences were also evident when the responses of those in the earlier stage of their socialization (vice-principals) were compared with those in the later stage (principals). Principals reported earlier encouragement to consider a school-administration role (item 7). Vice-principals reported more frequent exposure to effective role-models (item 15), a difference favoring women over men in Study One. Study One reported statistically significant differences favoring principals on items related to the intent of board hiring and promotion practices, evaluation

Table 10.3: *Patterns of school-leaders' socialization experiences*

Socialization Patterns
Mean ratings for each activity per group (scale: 1–3)

Socialization Activities	Not Helpful Mean *S.D.		Mixed Mean S.D.		Moderately Helpful Mean S.D.		High Mixed Mean S.D.		Very Helpful Mean S.D.	
(6) Extent of encouragement to pursue administrator role	1.56	0.88	2.24	0.77	2.18	0.60	2.67	0.48	2.71	0.47
(7) Stage in career, encouragement received	2.00	0.87	2.24	0.77	2.28	0.61	2.75	0.44	2.82	0.39
(11) Extent of opportunity to interact with peers	1.89	0.60	2.37	0.54	2.35	0.48	2.75	0.44	2.94	0.24
(15) Extent of exposure to effective role models	1.67	1.00	2.03	0.57	2.02	0.53	2.29	0.46	2.71	0.47
(19) Extent of participation in peer network of aspirants	1.22	0.44	1.33	0.60	1.64	0.59	1.96	0.55	1.88	0.78
(22) Extent of opportunity to assume leadership roles	1.67	1.00	2.24	0.62	1.97	0.56	2.44	0.51	2.88	0.33
(25) Intent of hiring and promotion practices	1.22	0.67	1.48	0.69	1.85	0.55	2.22	0.67	2.18	0.73
(26) Effect of hiring and promotion practices	1.11	0.33	1.60	0.66	1.91	0.33	2.17	0.38	2.35	0.61
(28) Intent of administrator-evaluation practices	1.25	0.71	1.52	0.63	1.83	0.51	2.13	0.69	2.00	0.87
(30) Nature of system's preparation programs	1.44	0.73	1.79	0.86	2.14	0.70	2.83	0.48	2.88	0.33
Number of respondents in each pattern (percentage of population)	9 (4%)		76 (35%)		91 (42%)		24 (11%)		18 (8%)	

Notes: Data estimate the degree of helpfulness of socialization activities using results of previous research about effective socialization experiences.
*S.D. = Standard Deviation

Table 10.4: Relationship between importance of socialization activities and socialization patterns

Socialization Activities	Socialization Patterns Mean ratings for each activity per group (scale: 1–4)											Mean Response for Each Activity
	Not Helpful *(N = 9)		Mixed (N = 76)		Moderately Helpful (N = 91)		High Mixed (N = 24)		Very Helpful (N = 18)			
	Mean	S.D.	Mean	S.D.	Mean	S.D.	Mean	S.D.	Mean	S.D.		
• (9) Encouraged to pursue administrator role	3.40	1.34	2.93	0.99	3.01	0.85	3.65	0.57	3.17	0.99		3.23
• (12) Opportunities to interact with peers	2.67	1.41	2.81	1.03	2.97	0.97	3.52	0.59	3.83	0.38		3.16
• (14) Having a mentor	3.50	0.71	3.39	0.86	3.17	0.78	3.50	0.71	3.86	0.36		3.48
• (16) Exposure to effective role models	3.00	1.31	3.04	0.96	3.09	0.75	3.25	0.79	3.78	0.43		3.23
• (17) Preparation for teaching	1.88	1.13	1.80	1.00	1.69	0.92	1.86	1.04	1.75	0.93		1.80
• (18) Teaching experience	2.43	1.13	3.09	0.95	3.00	0.90	3.14	0.83	3.18	1.02		2.97
• (21) Participation in peer network of aspirants	2.33	0.58	2.82	1.10	2.53	1.08	2.94	1.03	3.18	0.75		2.76
• (23) Opportunities to assume leadership roles	3.00	1.41	3.03	0.86	2.86	0.88	3.30	0.77	3.94	0.24		3.23
• (27) Perception of hiring and promotion practices	1.29	0.76	1.89	1.05	2.25	1.13	2.55	1.06	2.63	1.31		2.12
• (29) Perception of administrator-evaluation practices	1.14	0.38	1.30	0.61	1.67	0.94	1.91	1.00	1.88	1.05		1.58
• (31) Administrator-preparation programs	2.88	0.76	2.69	0.77	2.62	0.70	2.55	0.53	2.46	0.52		2.64
• (34) Overall perception of readiness	3.33	1.00	3.42	0.76	3.46	0.62	3.65	0.65	3.75	0.45		3.52
Mean Response for Each Pattern	2.50	0.80	2.55	0.47	2.62	0.48	2.92	0.25	3.06	0.40		

Note: Data estimate the value of socialization activities using respondents' perceptions.
*N = Number of respondents

practices, and preparation programs (items 25, 28, 30). Such trends were also evident in Study-Three data but the differences were not statistically significant.

Although not evident from Table 10.3, about twice as many principals as vice-principals (25 percent vs. 13 percent) reported the two most helpful patterns of socialization. This difference is largely attributable to the Ontario sample where 55 percent of principals compared with 36 percent of vice-principals classify their socialization experiences as either 'high mixed' or 'very helpful'. Study One also found similar differences; in that study, the comparison was between aspiring and incumbent school-leaders, with incumbents generally reporting more helpful patterns of socialization. Also relevant, but not evident from Table 10.3, were differences in the patterns of socialization experienced by those in different districts and/or regions of the country. A much larger proportion of respondents from the Ontario school system reported either 'high mixed' or 'very helpful' patterns of socialization than did respondents from other regions: 48 percent of Ontario respondents as compared with 12 percent in British Columbia and only 2 percent in Nova Scotia. The two least helpful patterns of socialization were reported by 23 percent of the Ontario sample, 37 percent of the British Columbia sample and 50 percent of the Nova Scotia sample.

Do school-leaders experiences different patterns of socialization? The answer from Studies One and Three, in sum, is: definitely yes. These studies lend support to claims that:

- Most aspiring and practicing school-leaders experience a 'moderately helpful' pattern of socialization (in their own opinion); few experience a uniformly negative socialization pattern whereas 19 percent experience a quite helpful pattern (High Mixed + Very Helpful)
- District effects on socialization experiences are very strong; differences in activities at the district level may be capable of determining whether virtually no school-leaders or as many as 48 percent count their socialization experiences as relatively helpful in their own development (High Mixed + Very Helpful)
- Women and men experience very similar socialization patterns although men appear to receive earlier encouragement to consider the role, whereas women perceive more frequent leadership opportunities available to them
- School-leaders in the later stage of their socialization generally perceive having experienced a more helpful pattern of socialization than those in the earlier stage

Question 2: What are the Effects of Different Patterns of Socialization?

Among the most important reasons for our interest in socialization patterns is the expectation that differences in such patterns account for a substantial amount of the variation observed among school-leaders in their orientation to the role and effectiveness in it. Increasingly helpful patterns, as described in this chapter, should contribute to an orientation to the role generally consistent with what was described in Chapters 4 and 5 as effectiveness and expertise. To inquire about this relationship, it was assumed that indicators of a school-leader's orientation to the role could be found in responses to four open-ended questions. These questions concerned 'overall image of the role', 'most important tasks' associated with the role, and tasks in which respondents were most and least confident in their ability to carry them out.

In order to interpret responses to the question about overall images of the role, the four-fold conception of dominant orientations of school-leaders to problem-solving on the high ground, described in Chapter 5, was used initially. Eventually, we combined the two orientations considered most effective on the high ground and those considered least effective.

Overall, 44 percent of the total sample of respondents (as well as the principal and vice-principal sub-samples) identified images of the role, consistent with the most effective patterns of leadership. As with Study One, results of Study Three suggested that as socialization patterns became increasingly helpful, larger percentages of respondents expressed images consistent with the most effective orientations to problem-solving. 11 percent, 39 percent and 45 percent of respondents experiencing the three least helpful patterns held such images, in comparison with 58 percent and 56 percent of those who had experienced the two most helpful patterns ('high mixed' and 'very helpful'). Among the 19 percent (forty-two) of respondents who reported the two most helpful socialization patterns, 69 percent (twenty-nine) were principals and 31 percent (thirteen) were vice-principals. About half of these principals but more than three-quarters of these vice-principals expressed images consistent with the most effective orientations to problem-solving.

A content analysis of responses to the open-ended questions concerning most important tasks and tasks which one had most and least confidence resulted in the identification of nine categories of tasks. Five of these tasks were directly associated with the emphasis one would associate with effective problem-solving on the high ground: instructional leadership; having a student focus; effective administrative problem-solving; providing leadership (e.g., role modeling, motivating, facilitating); and continuing to acquire new knowledge. Three of the remaining four tasks were primarily interpersonal in nature: communication; developing a positive climate; and personnel relations (e.g., staff development, being supportive). A final task identified was the management of routines (e.g., budget, discipline). (To be clear, and as we explained in Chapter 5, all of these tasks are required of school-leaders. But the preoccupation of less effective school-leaders tends to be with tasks like the last four described above. Highly effective leaders, in contrast, carry out such tasks but consider tasks like the first five mentioned above to be priorities for their attention.)

Based on previous research, one might expect those experiencing increasingly helpful socialization patterns and espousing images of the role consistent with effective orientations to problem-solving, to award more importance to those tasks directly associated with such problem-solving. Those experiencing the two most helpful patterns differed only marginally from those experiencing the three least helpful patterns, however. Each set of respondents identified about equal numbers of tasks associated with effective problem-solving and not so associated, a finding similar to Study One. Further, there were no regional differences evident in these results. In a similar fashion, respondents, experiencing the two most helpful patterns combined, had less confidence in their ability to carry out tasks preoccupying less effective problem solvers as compared with tasks of priority to highly effective problem solvers; 72 percent vs. 28 percent in the case of least confidence and 60 percent vs. 40 percent in the case of most confidence. Respondents who experienced the three least helpful socializations patterns reported very similar tendencies: identical in the case of most confident tasks and 63 percent vs. 37 percent in the case of least confident tasks. These results are also similar to the results of Study One. Differences based on region or district were very small.

Among all tasks, respondents expressed least confidence in their ability to perform what we have been calling 'managerial' tasks. Included in this category were such matters as office procedures, discipline of students, report writing, processing paper work, and interpreting legal acts and regulations and the like. About 34 percent of all statements, made about least confident tasks by the total of 157 who responded to this question, as well as by Ontario and Nova Scotia respondents, concerned this category. A much smaller proportion of British Columbia principals (10 percent) demonstrated this pattern.

Acknowledging the correlational and, therefore, only suggestive nature of the evidence, what are the effects, in sum, of different patterns of socialization? Results of our research (both Studies One and Two) suggest that:

- There is a predictable relationship between school-leaders' images of their role and the patterns of socialization which they experience. Increasingly helpful patterns are associated with a tendency to adopt images of the role, consistent with effective forms of school-leader problem-solving
- Independent of the socialization pattern experienced and image of the role adopted, school-leaders award about equal importance to interpersonal and managerial tasks, as to tasks more central to effective problem-solving on the high ground. These interpersonal and managerial categories of tasks also contain a higher proportion of specific tasks in which school-leaders are least confident. Managerial tasks are a source of greatest uncertainty for all school-leaders. The region or school district in which school-leaders work does not seem to affect these results.

Question 3: Which Socialization Activities Do School-Leaders Perceive to be Most Helpful?

Data reported in Table 10.3 estimate the degree of helpfulness of selected socialization activities using, as the standard, results of previous research about effective socialization experiences. Data summarized in Table 10.4 help estimate the value of most of these same socialization activities, using respondents' perceptions rather than previous research results as the standard. These perceptions are useful in helping to confirm or disconfirm results of previous research. So, for example, if respondents who indicated receiving sustained early encouragement to become administrators also indicated that it was not important in their decision to pursue the role, that would be considered a challenge to the validity of previous research findings concerning effective socialization activities.

Table 10.4 reports the school-leaders' perceived importance to their administrative development of the socialization activities appearing in Table 10.3 (plus three additional factors: teaching experience, preparation for teaching and having a mentor). Respondents' perceptions of their overall readiness for an administrative role is also reported (respondents rated importance on a four-point scale, 4 being very important, 1 being not important).

In general, support for previous research results concerning the value of a socialization activity would be evident where ratings increased, as socialization patterns became more helpful. Such an interpretation of the data seems warranted, based on the mean ratings of all activities assessed by respondents ('Mean Response', Table 10.4). While respondents in the 'not helpful' pattern provided the lowest mean rating (2.50), there are virtually no differences in mean ratings for respondents in the 'mixed' (2.62), and 'moderately helpful' (2.62) patterns. Those respondents in the 'high mixed' and 'very helpful patterns', however, awarded greater value (2.92 and 3.06 respectively) to their overall socialization experiences, as would be predicted by their generally more helpful socialization pattern; they also perceived themselves to be readier for the challenges of school administration (item 34). These results replicate findings from Study One.

Support for previous research results is also provided in relation to four specific socialization activities: exposure to effective role models, having a mentor, opportunities to interact with peers, and opportunities to assume leadership roles. They were seen, on average, as being very important aids to leadership development. Across all socialization patterns, opportunities to assume leadership roles were rated as most helpful, a finding similar to evidence reported in Study One. Among the twelve socialization activities reported in Table 10.4, ratings for six fell below 3.0: preparation for teaching (Mean Response = 1.80), teaching experience (M.R. = 2.97), participation in peer networks (M.R. = 2.76), perception of administrator evaluation practices (M.R. = 1.58), administrator preparation programs (M.R. = 2.64) and perception of hiring and promotion practices (M.R. = 2.12).

Differences between women and men in the perceived importance of the twelve socialization activities were also examined. Having a mentor (item 14) was rated highest by both groups. Other activities, rated highly by both, included encouragement to pursue the role (item 9), exposure to effective role models (item 16), and opportunities to assume leadership roles (item 23). Women rated seven of the twelve activities higher than did men, but none of the differences were statistically significant. In spite of this, women rated their overall readiness for the position lower than did men. This difference approached statistical significance (p = 0.078) and reinforces the statistically significant result reported in Study One.

Those in the earlier stage of their socialization (vice-principals) attributed much greater importance to teaching experience (item 18) although this difference did not quite reach statistical significance. Mean ratings, given the twelve socialization activities, were marginally higher overall for those in the earlier, as compared with the later, stage of their socialization, as was also the case in Study One.

Data reported in Table 10.4 give some indication of the perceived value of only a small number (twelve) of socialization activities. However, the survey contained four open-ended questions bearing on this issue as well. These questions asked respondents to list other people, experiences or factors contributing to the aspiration to become a school administrator, identify most and least helpful experiences, and describe experiences which they would recommend to others. Responses to these four questions were summarized around categories which emerged naturally from what was written on the surveys.

As in the earlier study, specific, on-the-job leadership activities were cited as most helpful more frequently than any other category of activity (29 percent of all responses). Having experience in as many professional settings as possible (breadth of experience) was viewed as the second most helpful kind of activity (25 percent). Taken together, these two categories account for 54 percent of all responses and suggest that these respondents feel that experience is the best teacher. However, the experiences must be seen as worthwhile since they can also be counted as relatively useless when they are meaningless and trivial (e.g., counting books). For example, breadth of experience and on-the-job leadership experience were considered to be the second and third least helpful kinds of activities (10 percent and 7 percent respectively). Respondents felt that formal training was the least helpful preparatory experience they had had, with 70 percent of all responses falling in that category. Again, though, depending on the specific form it takes, formal training can be seen as very helpful; it was the third most helpful experience cited with 16 percent of responses.

In the same vein, relationships with superordinates was the fourth most frequently mentioned category on both lists accounting for 15 percent of responses to the most helpful experience question and 7 percent of responses to the least helpful question. The other most helpful experiences were personality factors such as be a self-starter, be a risk-taker, have a sense of humor (6 percent); relationships with peers (6 percent); and personal history or family relationships (2 percent). District policies were never mentioned as being helpful to becoming a school-leader but it accounted for 3 percent of all responses to the least helpful question. Lengthy or poor interviews and lack of specific policies or initiations are examples of the types of activities cited here.

The responses to the open-ended questions showed consistency across districts with one exception: in answer to the question regarding most helpful experiences, British Columbia was half as likely to report relationships with peers, as the other two districts (British Columbia, 4 percent of responses; Nova Scotia, 8 percent; Ontario, 9 percent).

Both Studies One and Three centered their inquiry about sources of socialization on what might be termed external sources – sources outside the individual. A useful perspective on the importance of these sources is provided by Study Four. In addition to a concern for external sources, this study also examined the role played by 'factors' internal to the individual, particularly as such factors influenced decisions to pursue a school-leadership career and the training required. Results of this study confirm an important role for the external sources identified in Studies One and Three. However, internal sources, such as the need for challenge, pursuit of knowledge and skill, interest in a new role, and the need for additional responsibility, were even more frequently identified. As Begley *et al.* (1990) also point out, these factors provided practicing school-leaders in Duke's (1987) study with their greatest sources of satisfaction and, at the same time, were the main causes of them leaving the job (e.g., excessive challenge). Study Four suggests that internal sources may be especially influential in the decision to pursue a school-leader career and the attendant training: external sources of the sort evident in Studies One and Three may be of particular importance after those decisions are made.

Based on the data described in this section of the chapter, the following claims about most helpful socialization activities seem warranted:

- Sources most influential in giving rise to the decision to become a school-leader and prepare for the role appear to include such internal or personal qualities as the need for challenge, a thirst for knowledge and the like
- Those forms of socialization valued most after the decision to pursue a school-leadership position appear to be embedded in the context of school life. On-the-job leadership experiences and having broadly-based school experiences (e.g., holding a variety of teaching positions in various grades) are seen as being very helpful activities; however, depending on the specific form, they can also be of little use
- Formal preparation programs for aspiring and practicing administrators appear to vary widely in their perceived value. They are capable of being very helpful or extremely unhelpful, presumably depending on their quality. Such variation may also be the case, in a less pronounced way, for relationships with superordinates

Question 4: Are Different Career Paths Associated with Differences in Socialization Experiences, Gender, or Socialization Stage?

One question on the survey asked respondents to indicate the roles which they had occupied over the course of their careers to the principalship and to identify with numbers the sequence in which they had occupied such roles. Options included: (a) job outside education; (b) elementary teacher; (c) middle-school teacher; (d) secondary-school teacher; (e) consultant, coordinator, or the like; (f) department head; (g) elementary-school teacher; (h) vice-principal; and (i) other (to specify).

Responses were classified in relation to four alternative career paths. Path 1 included those who had begun their careers with a job outside education and had then occupied a series of in-school roles through to their current job. Path 2 included those who had arrived at their current job through a series of exclusively in-school roles. Path 3 included people who had experience in a district-level role (e.g., consultant), irrespective of the nature and sequence of other roles which they had occupied. Path 4 involved taking a job outside of education in the middle of one's educational career (e.g., leave an education position but return later). These four paths were chosen as the basis for analyzing responses because they seem likely to help develop different skills or to contain experiences leading to potentially different perspectives on the principalship. For example, a job outside education may provide one with an opportunity o appreciate the uniqueness of the school's responsibility to society; a coordinator's job may provide opportunities to understand the stimuli giving rise to district initiatives and to acquire significant curriculum-management skills.

Of interest in analyzing the data were dominant career paths, as well as the relationship between career path and socialization pattern, gender and stage of socialization. Results indicated that Path 2 (in-school to administration) was the dominant pattern including 45 percent of respondents. Paths 1 and 3 were each followed by about 25 percent of respondents. Only 5 percent of the respondents followed Path 4. Paths 2 and 4 respectively were the most and least dominant patterns found in Study One.

As in Study One, also, there was a distinct tendency for those experiencing more helpful socialization patterns to have career paths including some out-of-school role, about three-quarters (74 percent) of those experiencing 'very helpful' or 'high mixed' patterns, as compared with less than half of the rest (46 percent). Men and women did not demonstrate large differences in their career paths although a larger proportion of men than women followed Path 2 (48 percent vs. 36 percent); the reverse was the case with Path 3 (23 percent vs. 36 percent). These tendencies were in evidence more dramatically in Study One. Only marginal differences in career path were apparent between vice-principals and principals, replicating Study One results for those at earlier and later socialization stages.

One difference in career path appeared to be related to the district or region. The Ontario sample of respondents demonstrated a much greater tendency to follow Path 3, involving some district-level experience (54 percent in Ontario vs. 8 percent in Nova Scotia and 19 percent in British Columbia). Such a pattern is not surprising, given the encouragement in the district to consider such experiences as extremely valuable preparation for school-leadership. This career path emphasis in Ontario was mostly offset by a disproportionately small number in Ontario (13 percent vs. 34 percent in Nova Scotia and 33 percent in British Columbia) following Path 1.

These results suggest, in sum, that:

- Once aspiring administrators and principals begin their careers in education they rarely experiment with careers in other fields
- The most frequently chosen career path to the principalship includes in-school roles only
- A significant minority of aspiring administrators and principals have had career experiences outside schools, either in district roles (more often for women) or roles outside education (more often for men). These career experiences are related to socialization experiences more helpful in preparing administrators for instructional leadership
- Districts are able to use career paths as preparation for school leadership through conscious and visible attention to leadership-selection criteria.

Conclusions and Implications

By way of conclusion, we explore some of the implications of two issues central to our study: variations in the helpfulness of different socialization patterns and the socialization experiences of women.

Socialization patterns experienced by respondents in the study were at least moderately helpful in contributing to instructional leadership. While this is good news, it is also clear that there is much room for improving the quality of socialization experiences. Since such experiences seem likely to account for much of the variation in the quality of leadership available to schools, they are a potent vehicle for school improvement. Furthermore, it is possible, with the greatly increased demand for new school administrators over the next decade (due to retirements), that socialization experiences may actually deteriorate. This is likely if previous amounts of attention and effort given to socialization are spread across many more people. One possible explanation for our finding that administrators in the later stages of socialization experienced more helpful patterns than those in earlier stages is that such dilution may be occurring already.

Several suggestions for improving the socialization experiences of aspiring and practicing principals emerge from this study. One suggestion concerns formal training programs. Greenfield (1985) has suggested that such programs are the primary vehicle for developing the technical knowledge and skill which administrators require. Yet their quality and impact is extraordinarily uneven (see, for example, Leithwood, Stanley and Montgomery, 1984, and Leithwood and Avery, 1987). Devoting more time to programs which deliver substantially meaningful content, in a form consistent with good principles of adult education, is one promising suggestion for improving socialization experiences. The characteristics of such programs are examined in the subsequent two chapters. It is also worth noting the results of our research which indicated a lack of confidence in performing managerial tasks; this might be due to our zeal to focus school-leaders on 'educational' aspects of their role, which would cause their managerial preparation to be badly neglected.

A recent study by Papke (1989) supports the claim, made in this chapter, that on-the-job leadership activities are viewed as among the most helpful of all socialization activities. Our second suggestion is designed to make this activity even more productive. Papke (1989), among others, proposes to do this by ensuring that principals and vice-principals negotiate job responsibilities so that vice-principals have experience with a comprehensive array of principals' responsibilities, not simply the mundane, routine, maintenance tasks. We recommend taking this a step further by formally including in the criteria, used to evaluate principals, responsibility for the leadership development of their vice-principals.

On-the-job leadership experiences could be increased in their potency in several additional ways. For some school districts, routinely favoring the selection of administrative applicants with experience in curriculum-consulting roles is the most promising. As Ross (1989) has also observed, such roles offer unique opportunities to acquire many of the attributes associated with instructional leadership. These include, for example, the development of curriculum-management skills, the reliance on authority grounded in expertise rather than position, refinement of communication and other interpersonal skills, development of group problem-solving processes, and acquisition of a more comprehensive perspective regarding district-school relationships.

Finally, on-the-job leadership experiences could become more potent, by systematically selecting those who have expressed an interest in school administration, to chair district-level committees working on any problem which requires the exercise of leadership. In addition, it would be worthwhile to provide this opportunity for those who have not yet expressed an interest but who seem to be likely candidates for administrative positions. This tactic would not only encourage those who haven't yet considered such a position, but would also build confidence and enable them to make judgments about their suitability for, and interest in, administration.

The five studies alluded to in this chapter included at least equal numbers of women and men. It appears that women are now preparing to become school administrators in record numbers although the Study-Three sample of existing administrators was weighted more than three-to-one in favor of men. This is a dramatic change over one decade, judged by the available evidence (e.g., Haven, Adkinson and Bagley, 1980). Results of our studies suggest that this may be due, in part, to the greater encouragement women are receiving to consider administration (although still not as early in their careers as men). Undoubtedly, the broader social recognition of discriminatory practices and generally enhanced female career expectations account for much of this change, as well. Notwithstanding such rapid progress, these studies point to an anomaly worth noting. Whereas women generally considered their socialization experiences, as a whole, to be at least as helpful, if not more helpful, than did men, they expressed much less confidence than men in their readiness to assume an administrative role. One possible explanation for this apparent contradiction may be found in gender-based differences in confidence about one's abilities in relation to tasks and roles traditionally associated closely with only one gender. Linn and Hyde (1989), for example, have demonstrated this phenomena in relation to mathematics and science abilities, abilities traditionally associated more closely with males. Even when gender groups perform equally, evidence suggests that males are much more confident about such abilities. Because formal school-leadership roles have traditionally been dominated by men, results of our studies may be indicating a lack of self-confidence on the part of women, unrelated to actual administrative ability.

This explanation, however, has little practical import and is premised on assumptions consistent with what Shakeshaft (1989) describes as the third of six stages of research on women in educational administration: women as disadvantaged or subordinate. We find more helpful a perspective on these data, consistent with Shakeshaft's (1989) fourth stage: women studied on their own terms. From this perspective, it becomes, especially important to inquire further into the reasons for women's 'only modest' levels of self-confidence and to develop forms of support that address these reasons, to be provided in the transition stages of their socialization. Following this line of reasoning, it seems worthwhile to investigate also the role that personality characteristics in general (for both men and women) play in socialization.

Notes

1 We wish to acknowledge Cisco Magagula's help with statistical analysis.
2 Theoretical sources used to develop the framework included: Greenfield (1985), Peterson (1986), Silver (1986), and Kline (1988).
3 Empirical sources used to develop the framework included: Cooper (1989), Daresh (1986), Marshall (1984), Crowson and Morris (1985).

Chapter 11

Characteristics of Formal Programs for Developing Expert School Leadership on the High Ground

In Chapter 10 we outlined the array of experiences which, at least potentially, shape the readiness of individuals for the practice of school leadership. We reported a wide range of opinion with respect to the perceived relevance of formal preparation programs. For some school-leaders, experiences with such programs proved very helpful; for many others the experience was perceived as a waste of time. While these results may come as no surprise to many familiar with such programs, they ought to be viewed as alarming for at least two reasons. Although seriously underfunded, for the most part, formal preparation programs are sufficiently institutionalized in many provinces, states, and countries that they are likely to remain a part of school-leaders' experience during the 1990s. Moreover, in light of the hectic and unreflective context characteristic of the school-leaders' work environments, such programs continue to offer a more or less unprecedented oasis of opportunity, free from the 'press for action' for the development of key skills, knowledge, and dispositions.

Given the probable continuation of formal programs and their significant potential for leadership development, program quality should be a primary concern. To address this concern, as it bears on preparation for the high ground, we pursue answers to three questions in this chapter: Why have so many formal preparation programs failed to live up to the expectations of their developers and clients? What accounts for the success of one set of formal preparation programs which have been widely implemented and systematically evaluated? What guidelines can be offered to those wishing to develop and implement formal, high-ground preparation programs for school-leaders?

Why Many Formal Preparation Programs Fail

Reasons for the failure of many formal preparation programs, most of which aim to develop high-ground expertise, have been described in some detail (e.g., Hallinger and Murphy, 1991, Blum and Butler, 1989, Griffiths, Stout and Forsyth, 1988, Pitner, 1987, Leithwood and Avery, 1987). According to Murphy (1990), the weakness of many formal programs can be classified as attributable to either program content or program delivery. For present purposes, we touch on them briefly to set the stage for describing a program which addresses many of these weaknesses.

Program-Content Weaknesses

Three weaknesses attributable to course content are especially noteworthy. First, such content often makes questionable contributions to school-leaders' school-improvement abilities by virtue of the outcomes it helps to achieve:

> Encompassed by this criticism are programs in which such outcomes are not convincingly linked to school improvement; depend primarily on the expressed needs of participants; are entirely 'issues dependent', not addressing the principals' role in the issue; and/or do not recognize the scope of the principals' job as a whole. (Leithwood, Stanley and Montgomery, 1984, p. 51)

A second content-based weakness is characteristic of courses organized along a thematic or issues approach, or those which allow candidates relative freedom in selecting their learning experiences. Such programs are less likely to be founded on a particular image of the role which integrates and brings professional coherence to the various bodies of knowledge, skills, and attitudes required. Many university-based programs, for example, have been criticized as an eclectic selection of courses that add up to neither a clear image of the role nor a reliable set of relevant skills. This is an important consideration for course candidates who have little or no leadership experience to use as a basis for identifying and selecting appropriate learning experiences. In contrast, basing a preparation program on a comprehensive and integrated image of school leadership allows candidates to move beyond just the mastery of discrete skills. For example, there is little doubt that the development of time-management skills is important to school-leaders, but aspiring leaders should be able to answer the question: 'Time management, to what end?'

A third weakness in the content of many programs is their failure to come to grips adequately with the full scope of the school-leader's role. Given the constraints of time and place, and the complexity of the role, it is unrealistic to expect any preparation program to fully prepare the aspirant for the position. Presenting and maintaining a balanced program is difficult at the best of times. Some types of activities have traditionally tended to be over-represented in preparation courses while others have been ignored or given short shrift. For example, knowledge and skills related to building management functions, information about legislated acts and regulations, and timetabling procedures are usually well represented. This reflects the 'rear-view' perspective of many course designs which are based on traditional practices and expectations rather than current organizational needs. Moreover, such traditional content is easier to teach than some of the more pro-active, open-ended, higher-order skills such as, implementing an entry plan when assigned to a new school, or developing positive school culture.

Program-Delivery Weaknesses

Three shortcomings are especially evident in the delivery of many programs. A great many programs fail to consider the developmental aspects of the school-leader's role and particularly the varying stages of readiness manifested by individual candidates. Program candidates vary considerably in prior experience and most preparation programs are not sensitive to such variation. Begley, Campbell-Evans and Brownridge (1990), in their research on factors which influence the socialization of aspiring principals in the Northwest Territories, have found that individuals enroll in preparation programs for a variety of reasons, with a variety of prior experiences and qualifications, as well as varied expectations for the program. More significantly, course candidates, who were surveyed and interviewed in this study, apparently began their preparation programs with vague or varied images of the principal's role.

A second consideration is that program participants, many without previous administrative or leadership experience, cannot be expected to become full-blown school-leaders simply by imitating the actions of course instructors who are exemplary practitioners or by learning sets of procedures passed on by instructional staff, presenters or academics. The incorporation of a school-based practicum component as part of the preparation experience begins to address this shortcoming. However, to be effective, skill-application experiences must be properly supervised or coached and be of sufficient duration and substance to assure significant learning. This is often not the case.

A third program-delivery weakness arises out of a tendency, given the constraints of time and place, for programs to be focused on what principals do, or at best, on generalized procedures for carrying out their responsibilities. Little attention is typically devoted to encouraging reflection by candidates on why such actions are appropriate, and on the intent of such actions or the variations in approach necessitated by situational factors. Several authorities on principal development, for example Barnett and Brill (1990), have become increasingly interested in building such reflection into administrative training programs.

One further characteristic of most formal programs, which perhaps transcends the categories of content and delivery, is what Gaines-Robinson and Robinson (1989) describe as the 'training for activity' trap. This trap arises when program designers and implementors are held responsible, as is typical, for the 'activity' of the program, but not for its results. Accountability in the training sector (whether education or industry) is restricted to such criteria as the number of programs offered, the number of participants enrolled, and the relative cost of programs. Program designers become preoccupied with the design and delivery of programs, leaving little or no incentive to do needs' assessments beforehand or research on program outcomes. Similarly, there is a frequent and equal absence of identified management responsibility for the results of training programs. Ultimately, no one person or group has accepted accountability for ensuring that particular knowledge, skills or attitudes viewed as desirable will be applied by the course participants when they carry out their professional roles.

As a consequence of this lack of accountability, the degree of skill transfer from the program context to the classroom and school is usually unknown or absent. The primary concern of the course implementor is providing a high-quality learning environment and producing high candidate satisfaction with the program. Program activities frequently lack a clear link or alignment with either what school administrators do on the job or the particular professional needs of individuals. Traditional university-based courses tied to graduate degree programs add insult to injury, by not necessarily being sensitive to the canons of good pedagogy or candidate-satisfaction levels. As Gaines-Robinson and Robinson (1989) point out, course activities are more likely to reflect a stereotyped requirement of a course, which has developed a life of its own through repetition, rather than any identified need expressed by candidates or perceived by the program sponsors. Furthermore, course candidates, who may or may not have need for a particular skill activity, must typically participate in all activities because of expectations for a uniform-preparation course experience.

Clearly, the design and delivery of school administrator pre-service programs is a complex business fraught with shortcomings and challenges. Subsequent sections of this chapter give consideration to the characteristics of formal programs most helpful to the development of leadership on the high ground.

Characteristics of Successful Programs: An Illustrative Case

Overview

The program used in this chapter to describe characteristics of successful formal programs for preparing school-leaders on the high ground is one offered by OISE's Centre for Leadership Development. It is a program leading to certification or eligibility to be considered for a school-administration position: principal or vice-principal. The program is offered in three sections. Part 1 and Part 2 consist of approximately 125 hours of instruction each. The 'practicum', which typically intervenes between Parts 1 and 2, involves school-based leadership experiences which take place in parallel with one's normal job. A special version of the practicum awarding credit toward a graduate degree is also available.

This certificate program was first initiated in 1985. At the time of writing this chapter, approximately 600 participants from three different sites in Ontario had completed the program. Through a contract with the Department of Education in the Northwest Territories, an adapted-version program has also been offered to approximately 200 participants in that region of Canada since 1987. During the five-year period of the operation, each cycle of the program has been evaluated both formatively and summatively. Components of this evaluation process have included pre-course surveys or other needs-assessment strategies, assessment by candidates at regular intervals (usually weekly) throughout the program, end-of-course 'summative' evaluations by candidates and staff, participant observation by a full-time course evaluator, and evaluation by a Ministry-of-Education-designated external monitoring team. While all five of these components have been incorporated as evaluation procedures for all OISE-sponsored courses since 1985, variations in procedure and process have occurred. For example, pre-course surveys have ranged from a one page opening-day exercise to a full-blown needs' assessment process as was conducted prior to the development of the first North-West-Territories-principal-certification course in 1987.

Although not reported in detail in this chapter, it is a synthesis of these evaluations on which we base our claim that the program is an 'exemplary case'.

A similar claim has also been made independently by Blum and Butler (1989), based on comparing the program with many others available elsewhere in North America and Europe.

The Context in which The Case Program Was Designed and Implemented

All formal leadership programs are influenced by conditions or constraints in their context. That is certainly the case for the program described in this chapter. Some understanding of those forces is required if the lessons learned from this program are to be usefully applied in other venues.

The certification of principals is currently mandatory in only three regions of Canada: New Brunswick, Ontario and, as of 1989, the North-West Territories. In the United States virtually all states report some form of principal certification although there is considerable variety in the nature of qualifications necessary for accreditation. In many North American states or provinces, prospective school-leaders are expected to have taken, or be willing to take, additional qualification courses which may or may not form part of a degree-granting program. American state requirements usually include at least some graduate-level university credit courses in educational administration. Preparation programs in Canada and many American states are delivered by faculties of education, at various sites, under contract with the local, provincial, or state education agency. Thus most regions of Canada and the United States make available varying levels of pre-service training and in-service professional development. However, in many cases, these programs are not legislated requirements and may not result in government certification.

Requirements for candidate entry into formal training programs can vary widely. In the United States there is an increasing trend towards the requirement for a Master's degree. In fact the report of the National Policy Board for Educational Administration (1989) recommends that a Doctor-of-Education degree be the requisite for principal certification throughout the United States. In Ontario, entry requirements include certification in three of the four divisions of the school program (primary, junior, intermediate, senior), program-specialist qualifications in two subject areas or completion of a Master's level graduate degree. Candidates must also hold an Ontario teaching certificate and possess a minimum of five years teaching experience, two of which must be in Ontario schools. The North-West Territories' (NWT) newly legislated program requires that course candidates hold a valid NWT teaching certificate, have at least a year of teaching experience in the NWT, and must secure the recommendation of their regional superintendent for enrollment in the program.

In any given province or state there can be considerable variation in emphasis among the objectives and methods of instruction across course sites. For example, some programs focus on a specific conception of the principal's role (e.g., instructional leader) or a generalized approach to carrying out that role (e.g., school-improvement procedures). Other programs are structured by the National Association of Secondary School Principals (NASSP) leadership-skills model. Still other courses take a more traditional, thematic, 'issues dependent' or participant-controlled approach, sometimes termed the 'smorgasbord' approach by critics. Until recently such variations in approach were considered quite acceptable. For example, the Ontario Ministry of Education tolerates and even encourages such variations in approach, providing that they are perceived as stemming from legitimate differences in regional contexts and/or sincere efforts to experiment with innovative course designs. However, the recent report of the National Policy Board for Educational Administration (1989) illustrates an increasing consensus that reforms are required to establish a uniform set of standards for the preparation of school administrators.

Principal-preparation programs in Ontario and the North-West Territories are typically delivered as two separate courses scheduled during the summer months. As a result, candidates tend to become certified over a two-year period. In recent years, winter courses have been offered in some regions. These winter courses operate on weekends and/or evenings between October and April. An in-school practicum project is usually completed between courses during the school year following completion of the Part 1 program. Summer courses are of two to four weeks in duration. Shorter courses, such as the ten-day NWT program or the three-week University of Western Ontario program, are very intensive and require full-time residency. The longer, more relaxed four-week format employed by most Ontario faculties usually operates four days per week and may or may not be residential. All Ontario courses, as well as the North-West Territories courses, make use of a variety of small and large group activities. They also profess a sensitivity to the special needs of the adult learner.

Preparation courses in the United States are more typically tied to graduate-degree program where candidates enroll in a set of credit courses. Considerable variation in the number and nature of required courses exists among institutions. Similarly, field-based practicum projects are required in some states and not in others. Typically, these are taken on a part-time basis rather than through a sustained residency of a year or more, as has been recommended by the National Policy Board for Educational Administration.

Instructors and presenters in both the Ontario and North-West Territories programs available in Canada are, typically, practicing administrators. Ministry personnel, senior district administrators, trustees, social workers and other professionals often participate as presenters. University faculty play a significant role in the design of these programs and frequently contribute to the implementation of selected components. Ministry or Department of Education personnel also usually perform course-monitoring functions. The patterns are similar in some states of the United States, however, in other regions instruction is entirely in the hands of university faculty with minimal involvement of practitioners from the field. This often gives rise to questions of the relevancy of these programs as preparation for administrative practice.

Program Goals: The Nature of Problem-Solving Expertise on the High Ground

As noted earlier, the content of many formal programs has been criticized for being unrelated to the achievement of valued outcomes in schools, not projecting a coherent image of the role, or not acknowledging the full range of demands on school-leaders. The case program has avoided these limitations partly through its research base.

The program objectives of our pre-service program are derived from the research findings described in Chapter 5 and subsequent research specifically focused on school-improvement procedures. The former paints a multi-level description of growth in high ground problem-solving expertise among school-leaders. By way of review, the four-component model of high ground problem-solving included:

- Goals: the long-term, internalized aspirations held by school-leaders which form the basis for their decisions and actions; such goals might be derived from a school-leader's vision
- Factors: those aspects of the school, experienced directly by students, which significantly influence what they learn and which can be influenced by school-leaders
- Strategies: clusters of related actions or procedures used by school-leaders to influence factors
- Decision-making: processes used to identify and choose from alternative goals, factors, and strategies

For a summary of the problem-solving processes associated with each component of the model, the reader is referred back to Table 5.1 in Chapter 5. Those qualities associated with the more expert levels of practice, as summarized in Table 5.1, served as general goals for Part 1 of our program, in particular.

Table 11.1 illustrates the type and specificity of objectives used to guide the program. In this case the objectives are based on the goals' dimension of the high ground problem-solving model which is concerned with the nature, sources, and uses of school-leaders' goals.

While the four-component model of high ground problem-solving provides a framework for the certification program, as a whole, Part 2 of the program incorporates a set of knowledge and skills about school improvement. These are conceptualized within a five-phased school-improvement procedure (Leithwood, Fullan and Heald-Taylor, 1987), intended as a guide for school-leaders. The phases of the procedure include:

- Establishing the climate for change
- Identifying goals for school improvement
- Selecting and/or developing strategies or programs for achieving goals
- Implementing selected strategies or programs
- Institutionalizing selected strategies or programs

Each phase includes a set of general steps to be taken by the school-leader, identifies probable obstacles the school-leader might expect to encounter and provides advice about how to respond to such obstacles. The features of each phase have been distilled from a systematic review of recent school-improvement research. Traditional school-leader tasks such as program and teacher evaluation, relations with district staff and selection of curriculum materials are treated as part of the school-improvement process. Much of the knowledge and skill acquired during Part 1 of the program about 'Goals, Factors, Strategies and Decision-making' is applied as part of the school-improvement process, as well. In this sense, the major purpose of Part 1 is to give participants a clear image of

Table 11.1:   Objectives for Week One – July 4–7

Goals
Candidates will:
1   Analyze the Ontario Goals of Education
2   Compare the Ontario Goals of Education with other goals proposed for public education
3   Identify potential problems or discrepancies among such goals and objectives
4   Examine the principal's moral and ethical responsibilities in relation to educational goals
5   Know how to derive a set of educational goals suitable for a school, given the differences in religious, cultural, and racial contexts

what expert school-leaders do on the high ground; Part 2 helps show them *how* to do it.

Program Means: Justifying the Choice of Instructional Strategies

The delivery of many formal preparation programs has been criticized, as mentioned earlier, for the use of generally weak or inappropriate forms of instruction. As a whole, such instruction is transmission-oriented: that is, based on an 'empty vessel' model of the learner. Knowledge and skill are conveyed to the learner with limited interaction and too few opportunities for the learner to make the knowledge personally meaningful. In contrast, the case program has evolved from one which had significant reliance on transmission instruction in its beginnings, to one which is now highly transactional.

Both this chapter and Chapter 12 make explicit the conception of learning which underlies the formal programs described in those chapters. Then we describe the specific instructional strategies used in the programs and illustrate how those strategies are incorporated in a slice of the life of each program.

The starting point for our conception of learning is the type of knowledge the programs are intended to develop. In the case of the program described in Chapter 12, we call this 'useful, strategic' knowledge; in this chapter, we call this 'declarative and procedural' knowledge. In fact, both programs share some similar intents but different emphases with respect to types of knowledge. More emphasis is devoted in this chapter to declarative knowledge and more in Chapter 12 about useful, strategic knowledge. Useful strategic knowledge is also procedural knowledge. The difference of consequence is that in this chapter we are concerned with how a school-leader acquires already developed and condified procedures for solving routine problems. In Chapter 12, we are concerned with how school-leaders develop their own, often unique, procedures for solving non-routine problems. Such distinctions notwithstanding, these two chapters develop one, not two, conceptions of learning. Differences between chapters reflect the type of knowledge of greatest emphasis in the program being described. This chapter presents a relatively simple, skeletal model of learning appropriate to the development of all the types of knowledge addressed in both chapters. Chapter 12 presents a relatively well developed extension of that basic model as it bears on the acquisition of useful, strategic knowledge.

The most direct source of the learning model outlined here is contemporary information-processing theory. Such theory admits to no definitive formulation. It is still rife with unresolved problems, as one would expect of any field of study, subject to the amount of current work characteristic of this one. Nevertheless, the brief synthesis provided here is generally consistent with more extensive formulations that are to be found, for example, in Schuell (1986) and Calfee (1981). We present this brief summary of relevant information-processing theory to explain our instructional methods. Its application within formal programs is covered in the succeeding section entitled 'Instructional Strategies'. Those readers less interested in the theoretical underpinning may wish to skip to that section.

Acquisition of Declarative and Procedure Knowledge

Contemporary accounts of information processing stress the goal-oriented nature of human functioning and describe mental structures and processes associated with the resolution of problems standing in the way of goal achievement. Three structures dominate this description: the Executive, Short-Term Memory (STM) – also called working memory, and Long-Term Memory (LTM). The Executive is the primary location of both short and long-term goals (or aspirations). Once perceived, information from the external environment is screened or assessed by the Executive to determine its relevance for goal achievement. Information judged to be irrelevant is given no further attention; if judged to be potentially relevant, information is passed on to STM. Beyond the limited processing space of STM or working memory and its capacity to integrate bits of information for treatment as a single piece, little is known about the functioning of STM. Its purpose, however, is to make sense of information passed on to it by the Executive. It does this by searching through the virtually unlimited storage space in LTM. Structurally, this space is represented as clusters or nodes of information, typically referred to as schemata, many of which are associated in networks, sometimes organized hierarchically. Relatively undemanding forms of sense-making take place when, through simple matching processes, STM locates existing schemata or schematic networks capable of assimilating new information. More demanding forms of sense-making – for instance, problem-solving – usually demand modification of existing schemata or schematic networks to accommodate novel aspects of information.

There is considerable debate about the nature of schemata. For present purposes, two distinct types are distinguished in LTM. 'Knowledge schemata' encompass facts, concepts, principles, and personal theories as well as affective dispositions toward these elements. STM seeks out relevant schemata of this type in its attempts both to identify those elements or factors in the environment which influence goal achievement and to determine the conditions within each factor that must be met if goals are to be achieved. Such conditions having been determined, action may be required to meet them. Actions are guided by 'procedural schemata': structures which indicate how to act and the steps to take.

Superordinate procedural schemata (sometimes called executive strategies) exist to coordinate highly complex sets of actions.

Knowledge structures or schemata become increasingly sophisticated as they are reorganized to incorporate additional pieces of related information and as the associations among such schemata increase. Such sophistication is a function of active attempts to make meaningful more and newer information. And as new information is subsumed by existing knowledge schemata, the potential for meaningfully processing subsequent information increases. Actions become more skillful (effective) as procedural schemata become potentially more adept in accomplishing their ends, as overt behaviors reflect more accurately the image of skilled performance encapsulated in such schemata, and as the use of procedural schemata becomes less conscious and more automatic. High levels of automaticity permit effective responses to environmental input without the need for processing such input through STM; this reduces response time and leaves the severely limited information-processing space of STM available for handling other problems.

Information-processing explanations of motivation begin with those internalized goals located in the Executive. People are normally motivated to engage in behaviors that they believe will contribute to goal achievement. Strength of motivation to act depends on the importance attached to the goal in question and judgment about its achievability. Motivational strength also depends on judgments about how successful a particular behavior will be in moving toward goal achievement (Bandura, 1977).

An information-processing view of the learning process is at the core of the model of learning, underlying the prototype curriculum for school administrators. Nevertheless, there are two additional theoretical threads that serve not so much to add to this view of learning as to emphasize and highlight several of its features. The first such thread is social-interaction theory (e.g., Simpson and Galbo, 1986). This theory stresses the dynamic nature of communication between people in the creation of personal meaning. Because each of those involved in communication actively brings different intellectual 'histories' to bear in their attempts to construct such meaning, the outcomes of communication can never be entirely pre-determined. This has significant implications for the role of instructor as well as for the choice of instructional techniques, elaborated later in this chapter. In brief, however, the implication is stated succinctly by Simpson and Galbo (1986) (although they have a normal classroom context in mind):

> The quality of a particular interaction is not entirely predictable, for the ultimate form is determined by the participants at the time of encounter ... [Instructors] must rely upon information gained through interacting with students ... to determine some of the ultimate specifics of instruction. Some parts of the instructional process may be directed more by the interaction of students and teacher than by the consciously determined behavior of the teacher. The process is most useful in enhancing a carefully derived general lesson plan, especially in the hands of a superior teacher with very clear objectives in mind. (pp. 45–50)

This position stresses the importance of interaction during learning – not only between the learner and the formally designated instructor but with the learner's peers, as well.

A second theoretical thread is adult-learning theory (e.g., Merriam and Caffarella, 1991). While this is a highly derivative body of theory at present, it does provide a compelling argument for special attention to the greater accumulated contents of adult learners' long-term memory in comparison with that of younger learners. This reservoir of knowledge, skill, and affect is at once a potentially vast resource for sense-making and a relatively firm 'substance' to modify and extend. Adult-learning theory also draws attention to:

- the relatively complex and richly integrated organization of the contents of long-term memory
- the relatively high ego investment of adult learners in their past experiences and accomplishments
- the relatively well established, clearly defined, personal goals the adult learner brings to the educational experience

As did social-interaction theory, this position stresses the importance of interaction during learning. In addition, adult-learning theory supports instructional strategies that allow learners a significant role in shaping the nature and direction of their own instruction.

Instructional conditions which foster learning

While a model of learning, such as the one just outlined, is not synonymous with a model of instruction, its 'implications' for instruction are relatively obvious and some have already been noted. In this section, nineteen such implications are assembled; they are conditions that can be met with an array of instructional strategies examined below. These conditions are loosely associated with the mental structures hypothesized by contemporary cognitive psychologists to account for mental functioning and, taken together, constitute what can be referred to as 'transactional' instruction: instruction designed to be as personally meaningful to the student as possible. Instruction is increasingly effective to the extent that it:

– The Executive –

1 Provides opportunities for the learner to clarify goals to self and to the instructor
2 Demonstrates relevance of new information to the learner's internalized goals

– Short-Term Memory –

3 Helps the learner organize information into related 'chunks' for more efficient processing
4 Introduces new information to the learner in small, manageable increments
5 Provides the learner with immediate opportunities for making links to contents of long-term memory

– Long-Term Memory (general) –

6 Diagnoses contents of the learner's long-term memory relevant to use in making sense of new information

– Long-Term Memory (declarative knowledge schemata) –

7 Assists the learner in matching new information with as many existing knowledge schemata as possible
8 Assists the learner in expanding, modifying, or adapting existing schemata in order to make new information meaningful
9 Assists the learner in linking together previously independent schemata in order to make new information meaningful
10 When no relevant knowledge is stored in long-term memory, assists the learner to build new schemata and practice its retrieval

– Long-Term Memory (procedural knowledge schemata) –

11 Provides the learner with initial procedural schemata by modeling, verbal description, and the like
12 Provides the learner with opportunities to act (perform) in accordance with initial procedural schemata
13 Stimulates the learner to reflect on the discrepancies between his/her performance and his/her procedural schemata
14 Provides the learner with feedback designed to increase the sophistication of procedural schemata and reduce the discrepancy between performance and procedural schemata
15 Extends the learner's opportunities for practice with feedback until performance is sufficiently skillful

– Motivation (multiple structures) –

16 Clarifies for the learner the relationship between new information and his/her own goals
17 Formulates the goals for learning in a sufficiently incremental way that the learner sees their achievement as feasible
18 Convincingly demonstrates the value of achieving the goals for learning as contributing to achievement of the learner's own, internalized goals
19 Establishes a relationship between what is to be learned and stored knowledge and/or skill about which a person feels positively

Instructional Strategies

In this section, we address six components of instructional strategy. These are: objective-referenced instruction, the role of instructors, techniques of instruction, program evaluation procedures, the critical role of practicum, and selection of materials.

Objective-referenced instruction
Experience with our program suggests that using specific defensible objectives to structure program design and delivery allows instructional staff, as well as course candidates, to focus their efforts on the attainment of specific course outcomes. OISE programs, for example, are typically organized into four or five components, each of several days' duration, with clearly stated objectives keyed to assigned readings, small group activities and plenary presentations. One feature that appears to be crucial to the success of the programs is that instructional staff and candidates regularly make reference to and use the course objectives.

Objectives are used in the program to reinforce and clarify the intended focus of the course, measure the progress of the course, evaluate the extent to which objectives have been attained, and tie the diverse readings, discussions and activities to a specific image of the principalship which candidates are intended to internalize. This reliance on clearly articulated program objectives for program development and evaluation purposes was a distinctive characteristic of the original OISE program in 1985. However, what has evolved since that time is an increased dependence on the daily or weekly objectives by candidates and staff as a means for renewing the course focus as well as linking together the various components of the course experience into a consistent image of effective practice.

Instructor roles
The 'relevance' of programs for school-leaders hinges on the extent that course objectives reflect the knowledge, skills, and affect required for expert school leadership. It is possible, however, for the substance of a program to be 'relevant' yet for the program still to suffer from lack of utility. Utility is a function of not only program objectives but also the nature of instruction designed to achieve those objectives.

Often, criticism of program utility is expressed in terms of excessive attention to theory and not enough concern for practice. More precisely, however, utility means 'capable of being put to use'. And while it is true that bad theory cannot be put to use with much advantage, good theory has great potential utility through its power to predict and control. This is especially so in otherwise highly uncertain environments like those inhabited by school-leaders. Indeed, many school-leaders have developed quite elaborate, although often implicit, 'theories in use' (as Argyris, 1982, would call them) to guide their work. Unpacking the meaning of utility in this way raises the question: What is 'good' theory from the perspective of the school-leader's job? How can the job be done more expertly? What can be done to ensure that a program as implemented reflects these features of good theory and is, thus, useful?

Part of the answer to this question about good theory is to be found in three features of some of those 'theories in use' already guiding many school-leaders. Such theories, first of all, are theories for action; they are designed for the purpose of prescribing what ought to be done in response to some problem. By far the bulk of current, formal administrative theory has as its purpose description and explanation; this is a sometimes helpful but never sufficient basis for action. The objectives of our program for the high ground, in contrast, are based on theories for action, ones which conceptualize how school-leaders can be effective in bringing about school improvement. Second, 'theories in use' have usually been subjected to considerable empirical verification, albeit a highly personal, unsystematic form of verification. While there is a long history of prescriptive theory in administration (theories for action), its empirical verification is woefully limited.

One response to the importance of basing a school-leader program on verified theory has already been discussed; the bulk of our program's objectives for the high ground remain well rooted in empirical research data. This grounding, however, was necessarily limited to the sites in which data were collected. Extensive use of practicing school administrators as program instructors is an additional form of verification. These instructors are able to relate the generalized theory for school-leader action to their own work and convey its utility, through interaction with participants, from that perspective. They are also able to supplement the generalized theory, when interaction suggests that is necessary, from the stock of their own professional experience.

The same response, having practicing school administrators as instructors and co-developers of the program, is a way of recognizing a third powerful feature of school-leaders' 'theories in use'. Many school-leaders' 'theories in use' are sufficiently operationalized so that their implications for application to specific problems in each school-leader's own school context are extremely clear, at least to the holder of the theory. In contrast, much formal administrative theory is remote from specific action and often ambiguous in the guidance it provides for action in a particular context. Instructors need to be able to add specificity to the general theory for action guiding the course and help students make meaningful applications to their own context.

The selection of appropriate instructional staff is an especially critical factor for ensuring the effectiveness of a formal preparation course. A number of insights have been gained by OISE personnel in these matters as a result of five years experience. The selection of the course principal or coordinator is particularly critical. A course principal must be willing to do more than just manage the course. He or she must be knowledgeable about, and committed to, the conceptual framework of the course and take steps to ensure that it is honored. The course principal, as well as group leaders, must model effective practice and, when necessary, do whatever is required to guarantee the integrity of the course. All group leaders should ideally be experienced practitioners, although this is often not the case in formal training programs offered in a university setting. The justification for this assertion is the aspirants' need for appropriate modeling. Beyond this important requirement, course staff should be representative in a number of ways. Group leaders should be highly experienced principals, although one or two relative newcomers to the principalship may also be desirable in the interest of providing a fresh perspective. Gender, racial and religious factors should also be balanced. Above all, group leaders must understand that their role is chiefly to facilitate group processes, to act as a resource when required, and to model effective practice. They are not there to dominate discussion, pass along war stories or launch an independent course process.

There is another side to the utility dilemma which cannot be adequately addressed, simply by modeling the features of school-leaders' implicit theories. While many educational programs have been accused of being 'too theoretical', others have been described as trivial and mundane (the most common criticism leveled at principal-certification programs in Ontario prior to about 1980). This criticism implies that there is an excessive focus on individual school-leader's espoused theories (Argyris, 1982). The value to others of such espoused theories depends on their congruence with 'theories in use'. Espoused theories which do not closely capture 'theories in use' do not benefit from the empirical verification they are normally associated with.

The value of individual school-leader's espoused theories to others also depends on their external validity. Espoused theories of no demonstrable effect in multiple school contexts are probably of interest only to the espousers and their immediate families. The process used in both designing and implementing our program attempted not only to recognize, but actively to foster productive tension between theory and practice. Researcher-participants were forced to clarify the meaning of their research in specific cases and contexts. Instructors were forced to examine the relationship between their 'theories in use' (and espoused theories) and the general theory for school-leader action, reflected in research-based descriptions of expert problem-solving.

Instructional techniques
A review (e.g., Sparks, 1983, Silver and Moyle, 1984, Hutson, 1981, Daresh and LaPlant, 1984) of pre-service and in-service education programs for teachers and administrators generated a significant number of promising instructional techniques. These techniques, which are potentially available to meet the learning conditions identified earlier, are as follows:

- (a) Opportunities for learners to identify some of their own needs and to participate in some program planning
- (b) Lectures (giving information)
- (c) Private reading and reflection
- (d) Independent study
- (e) Demonstration of skills by 'experts' (live, video)
- (f) Opportunities for practice and feedback (coaching)
- (g) Role playing
- (h) Guided group-discussion
- (i) Case analyses
- (j) Simulated case problem-solving
- (k) Site visits
- (l) Participant presentations
- (m) Opportunities for subgroup leadership
- (n) Provision of individual diagnosis and counseling
- (o) Clarification and extension of ideas with peers through discussion

Table 11.2 indicates which of these techniques seem most suitable in meeting each of the nineteen learning conditions discussed earlier. Some of the attributes in Table 11.2 are speculative and might change, depending on more specific information concerning how the instructional technique is to be applied; a number of these techniques could be used with widely varying consequences.

Using the course process itself as a simulation of school-leadership activities has proven to be a particularly useful technique to minimize the 'training for activity' trap previously described in this chapter. Such an approach might involve the rotation of the small group chairperson's role on a daily basis whereby one person, or occasionally two working collaboratively, manage the group's affairs for a day. They may be required to chair group discussions,

Table 11.2:   Relating instructional techniques to learning conditions

Learning Condition	Technique
The Executive	
1. Clarify goals to self and instructor	a, c, h, n
2. Demonstrate relevance of new information to internalized goals	a, h, n
Short-Term Memory	
3. Organize information into related chunks	b, c, d, i, o
4. Introduce new information in small manageable increments	b, c, e, g, i
5. Immediate opportunities for making links to contents of long-term memory	f, g, h, j, o
Long-Term Memory (general)	
6. Identify contents of long-term memory relevant to making sense of new information	c, d
Long-Term Memory (declarative knowledge schemata)	
7. Matching new information with as many existing knowledge schemata as possible	a, c, d, f, o
8. Expand, modify, or adapt existing schemata in order to make new information meaningful	a, c, d, e, f, g, j, m
9. Linking together previously independent schemata	c, d, f, g, o
10. Build new schemata and practice its retrieval	f, g, i, j, m, o
Long-Term Memory (procedural knowledge schemata)	
11. Provide initial procedural schemata by modeling and verbal description	b, e, k
12. Provide opportunities to act in accordance with initial procedural schemata	f, g, j, m
13. Stimulate reflection on discrepancies between performance and procedural schemata	f, g, j, n
14. Feedback to increase sophistication of procedural schemata and reduce discrepancy	f, g, j, m, n
15. Practice with feedback until performance is sufficiently skillful	f, m, n
Motivation (multiple structures)	
16. Clarify relationship between new information and goals	a, n, o
17. Formulate goals incrementally to foster perceptions of feasible attainment	e, f, g, j, m, n
18. Demonstrates value of learning to achievement of internalized goals	a, c, m
19. Establish relationship between learning and valued prior knowledge and/or skill	a, n

schedule activities, manage time and solve problems as they occur. In these settings, the group group-leader becomes a resource rather than a director of activity. Course instructional staff can further model effective practices by openly describing their perceptions and responses to real problems which crop up during the course. Candidates quickly catch on that the course process is an ideal testing ground for their newly-learned management and leadership skills.

Although the objectives of a formal preparation program resulting in accreditation should be relatively non-negotiable once the course design has been validated, candidates can still be given considerable freedom, particularly in small group sessions, to make choices about what and how they will learn, and how they will use their time. Indeed, it is arguable that more alternate activities should be made available than time would permit addressing. This forces candidates to participate in interesting simulations of the priority setting and time-management exercises principals frequently encounter in real schools.

Through a candidate-committee system established as part of the course process, participants soon recognize that control of the course experience is shared with them to a considerable extent. For example, in OISE programs, four committees are typically established: program, communications, evaluation, and social. A final strategy frequently employed in formal preparation programs involves encouraging candidates to share any special expertise they may possess through candidate-organized workshops. These workshops can be a regular part of the course which is usually scheduled towards the end of the program. This strategy has been found to be particularly useful when delivering courses in isolated areas (e.g., the North-West Territories of Canada) where the inclusion of cultural issues is a critical requirement and the availability of expert presenters can be limited.

Most of these techniques are probably better thought of as: general approaches to instruction that can be further developed once one is clear about the objectives to be met, some of the preferred learning styles of students, the amount of variety required to maintain energy and interest over the entire period of the program, and the skills and preferences of instructors (although the selection of instructors should be done so as to avoid restricted choices of techniques, for this reason).

Evaluation procedures

Five or more components can be recommended for inclusion in the evaluation procedures for a state-of-the-art leadership-development program. These may include pre-course surveys or other needs assessment instruments, assessment by candidates at regular intervals throughout the course, end-of-course 'summative' evaluations by candidates and staff, participant observation by an objective course evaluator, and Ministry-monitoring team reports.

An important consideration concerning evaluation of pre-service programs has to do with the purpose of evaluation. Course-delivery personnel typically maintain a strong interest in two predominant purposes for course evaluation. First, the issue of accountability, particularly given contractual arrangements with the departments or ministries of education is a primary concern. For the most part, end-of-course 'summative' evaluations and ministry or department monitoring have been successful in meeting such accountability demands. Instruments which provide course-delivery personnel with 'satisfaction-level' data concerning various program components (e.g., meeting of objectives, readings, plenary sessions) are another example. These data derive primarily from responses to rating scales and associated comments. At the completion of each course, a summary can be made of responses to these items. The summary is useful not only from the standpoint of meeting accountability needs but in providing information for the second major purpose of course evaluation.

The second major focus, one which has been more central to ongoing operations, is 'formative' evaluation or evaluation for course improvement. The needs assessment practices referred to earlier have served to sensitize course coordinators to the specific needs of a particular client group. Program modifications based on these data can be readily made. Participant observation and daily course-evaluation data and comments on end-of-course instruments have also proven to be useful for modifying programs. Such instruments can provide program-delivery personnel with a wide range of comments and suggestions, the careful analysis of which, in view of participant observation data, can lead to some rather immediate, and responsive, mid-course changes. Suggestions associated with end-of-course evaluation instruments can also help course coordinators prepare and plan for upcoming programs.

The evaluation process allows for another major use of formative data. That purpose is to promote among candidates 'collective reflection' about things that have been learned, thoughts that have been generated, and perceptions that have been shared. For example, in OISE-sponsored courses, an evaluation committee is typically formed to assume responsibility for evaluation tasks. A major function of the committee is to analyze the evaluation data, but another function is to feed that information back to the group. This has typically been done in the form of a short verbal summary by a committee member, prior to having candidates engage in the next day's activities. This type of feedback tends to be very positively received by candidates. It helps them to consolidate information by observing how their peers have perceived it. Such information is viewed as very relevant by participants, especially those who have limited leadership experience from which to draw (Cousins and Leithwood, 1986). Finally, this process also carries with it the side benefit of motivating candidates to complete the daily evaluation forms.

A continuing problem with the evaluation of pre-service courses relates well to Gaines-Robinson and Robinson's (1989) notion of the 'training for activity' trap. How does one measure the extent to which pre-service training impacts on performance (current or future) in the schools? In a recent in-service program, OISE personnel used a more elaborate instrument for collecting end-of-course data. The instrument not only asked for the usual 'satisfaction with course components' data and suggestions for course improvement, but also posed questions about the school-level impact of the course experience.

These data, albeit self-report and limited for that reason, permit a statistical assessment of the relationship between course processes and course outcomes. The applicability to pre-service delivery of this approach is limited, due to the nature of the client. For the most part, candidates are not currently in leadership roles and would be unable to assess impact at the school level as a consequence. Nonetheless, linking evaluation data to field-based practice is a goal worthy of pursuing in the interest of meeting both accountability and course-improvement demands.

The practicum
Some aspect of formal training programs should be close to or in schools and the program should normally be sustained over a relatively long period of time. Unfortunately, virtually all Canadian and American pre-service courses are conducted away from the candidates' normal work environment. This pattern is perhaps a matter of academic tradition unlikely to change for at least two reasons. First, centralized delivery may afford ministries (departments) substantial

opportunities to monitor and maintain a level of control over from and content. Second, lumping people together in central locations for short intensive experiences is probably fiscally and pedagogically more efficient. Most school districts have neither the desire nor the resource capacity to run their own programs.

School-based practicum projects, as employed in Ontario and the North-West Territories, for example, begin to attend to this issue in some respects. However, while they provide opportunities for in-school application of formal course learning, the quality of the practicum experiences has been found to vary greatly depending on the suitability of the project, the commitment of the candidate and supervisor to the exercise, and the appropriateness of the local school setting for such a project.

The practicum experience scheduled between Parts 1 and 2 of the OISE certification program is intended to accomplish three general purposes. First, it aims to assist participants in applying and refining the decision-making and problem-solving schemata required for the effective use of developed procedures in the contingent world of their own schools. This purpose is accomplished to the extent that the practicum instructor (e.g., an experienced principal) models, provides opportunities for practice, and gives feedback to the participants about their decisions and decision processes. Second, the practicum instructor may further develop the procedural knowledge that participants bring to the practicum situation and extend the repertoire of procedures possessed by them. Both these purposes are possible in the practicum to the extent that effective procedures and problem-solving processes can be made relatively explicit.

The third purpose, while more difficult to accomplish, is a traditional expectation for the practice of practicum experiences in other types of education. Such experiences include the clinical work of medical interns under the guidance of a senior practitioner, the articling experience of the novice lawyer, and apprenticeship activities associated with skill development in the fine arts and in craft-based vocations. These practices share in common the goal of acquiring the more tacit components of the experienced practitioner's repertoire of knowledge and skill – those components that permit such practitioners to deal effectively with problems 'in the swamp' or 'situations of uncertainty, uniqueness and conflict' (Schön, 1983, p. 16). Chapter 12 provides a more complete analysis of what is required to develop expertise in the swamp.

Schön (1987) accounts for the 'artistic aspects of practice' by reference to this tacit knowledge and skill. He suggests that these aspects of practice are acquired in professional studios and conservatories by creating certain necessary conditions which he identifies as the:

> freedom to learn by doing in a setting low in risk, with access to coaches who initiate students into the traditions of the calling and help them by the right kind of telling to see on their own behalf and in their own way what they need most to see. (p. 17)

What does this view of a practicum mean in the context of our certification program? To accomplish the three general purposes discussed above, the practicum attempts to:

- Provide a significant portion of time to observe experienced principals at work on a range of non-trivial problems and to discuss with principals their intentions, how they link their overt actions to those intentions, and how they manage their problems

- Provide an opportunity for the participant to become involved in an administrative problem on the high ground, with close coaching from an experienced principal. This coaching is intended to foster what Schön (1983) refers to as 'reflection in action' in order to refine procedural knowledge and problem-solving processes
- Provide an opportunity for the participant to become involved, with an experienced principal, in an administrative problem in the swamp. Frequent discussion of the process used by the experienced principal and implications for solving other problems should foster 'reflection in action'

Selection of appropriate course materials

Our experience with the OISE program also recommends special attention to the selection of course materials. In Ontario and some parts of the United States, many candidates typically have graduate degrees which were previously earned. These individuals are likely to have a relatively high capacity for academic reading as compared to course participants in other regions without graduate school experience. For the latter group, substitute readings from popular professional journals can provide a good alternative. Alternatively, when difficult journal articles or research reports must be used, the inclusion of a reading-guide cover page detailing and highlighting important points is a good strategy. Small group discussion of important readings in a seminar setting is also good practice in that candidates are able to increase comprehension through discussion and debate. Course duration is another factor which influences the amount of reading that can be realistically assigned. There is little point in assigning readings that candidates will not or cannot read. Attention to preferred learning styles and a multi-media approach to the presentation of material is a preferred strategy; increased focus in this direction has characterized recent OISE programs.

Summary and Implications

In this chapter, we identified characteristics of formal programs for developing expert school-leaders on the high ground. We used five years of experience and data collection in the delivery of a school-leader certification program in Ontario.

A number of issues central to high-quality programs have arisen throughout this description. Nine of these are selected as especially in need of emphasis, or as noteworthy implications for others designing formal programs for developing high-ground expertise.

1 A Coherent Research-based Image of School Leadership

Several problems may be overcome if the program builds from a research-based conceptual framework; candidates are able to develop a comprehensive conception of the role of school-leader; segments of the course may be tied together in a coherent pattern; the relevance of course objectives becomes apparent; individual issues are viewed in the context of the larger picture of the role; candidates will develop a sense that the validity of key issues and practices is justified by research; and finally, unanticipated objectives determined or contributed by course participants are more likely to be congruent with the goals of the course. Course instructors should be knowledgeable about, and committed to, the particular framework used. Provision should be made to review the framework periodically and to update it, based on emerging research.

2 Systematically Assess Client Needs

Knowledge and skills that are demonstrably relevant to clients' needs from the clients' point of view are likely to be much more useful. Within the confines of a conceptual framework, program implementors should systematically collect information prior to course delivery and should use that information to modify the program. Variation in stages of development in candidates' leadership knowledge and skills is likely to be enormous at the pre-service level. Instructors should be prepared to assess and respond to such variation. Data from previous versions of the program, participant observations, and such programs and informal contacts can serve to refine more formally collected needs' assessment data.

3 Maintain Objectives-based Focus

Candidates should regularly be made aware of the purposes of the program, and within bounds, have an opportunity to shape such purposes. Program objectives should be linked directly to the underlying conceptual framework but should be sufficiently flexible to allow for continued review and adaptation as the need arises. Where possible, variation in course objectives should overlap with candidates' stage of development.

4 Adhere to Principles of Effective Instruction

Appreciation of different learning styles, transactional curriculum delivery, multi-media presentation materials, and continual involvement of course participants in course delivery are important features of effective pre-service delivery. Candidates have little tolerance for being lectured to extensively, although, in recognition of the need for content input, an appropriate mix of instructional strategies is recommended. Candidates find extremely valuable opportunities to share with peers relevant experiences and to learn how others would handle particular problem situations. Learning materials should be sensitive to the candidates' stage of development and they should be provided with a healthy amount of 'hands-on' material.

5 Simulate Role Responsibilities

As part of the course-delivery process, candidates should be actively involved in chairing small group discussions, organizing workshops, assuming course administrative responsibilities, and otherwise engaging in leadership functions. Activities designed to simulate school-leaders' responsibilities can enhance the development of procedural knowledge and minimize the apparently abstract nature of some program topics. This is particularly an important consideration where leadership expertise is limited and candidates do not have extensive experience from which to draw.

6 Include Practicum

Candidates typically work in environments where high-quality, supervised practica can be readily undertaken. It is important to practice and reinforce program learnings in on-the-job experiences. This type of activity provides candidates with opportunities to refine procedural knowledge and to reflect on, and analyze, such experiences. Program-delivery personnel should be sensitive to candidates' motivation to 'fast-track' and take steps to ensure that practical experiences are adequately reflected upon.

7 Promote Social and Professional Interaction

Candidates probably learn as much from interacting and participating with one another as they do from course readings and presenters. Opportunities for interaction with one another in either structured (e.g., home group) or unstructured (e.g., social occasion) situations should be provided regularly. These opportunities not only enable candidates to gain valuable insight from the experience of others but may serve to consolidate information in their own minds.

8 Use Evaluation Processes for Multiple Purposes

Valuable insights concerning course development can be gleaned from evaluation conducted for accountability reasons. The sophisticated use itself of formative evaluation to improve course delivery can meet accountability needs. But evaluation can be used for at least one purpose other than accountability or development: it can be used to stimulate reflection among candidates. Thinking about one's own perceptions and feelings about a program experience is certainly one way to stimulate reflection. Thoughtfully completing a daily evaluation task; becoming involved in analyzing and reporting evaluation data to one's peers; and receiving daily evaluation reports (either written or verbal) are all processes which are likely to stimulate, among candidates, reflection about important issues.

9 Work Toward Assessing Course Impact

Many course evaluations are too focused on process and pay little, if any, attention to outcome. Course developers would do well do give serious consideration to defining real course outcomes (e.g., other than course satisfaction) and in some way attempting to measure these. The very nature of pre-service delivery, inasmuch as most candidates are not in positions to implement administrative strategies learned, stands as an obstacle to collecting data on impact. Nonetheless, this is an obstacle with which it is worth struggling. For the present, even in state-of-the-art pre-service programs, the value of particular practices espoused by the program are justified by research findings on effective administrative practices rather than by empirical evidence of improved performance in the role of program candidates.

Conclusion

This chapter reviewed current practice in the delivery of pre-service programs for aspiring school administrators in Canada and, to a lesser extent, the United States. A critical analysis of traditional practices was also presented. Based on five years of experience in the delivery of principal pre-service training programs and extensive evaluation data accumulated over the years, the evolution of OISE programs and how developers have attempted to meet the challenges of pre-service delivery were discussed as an illustration of a formal program for developing effective leadership on the high ground.

Traditional programs were described as being predominantly 'issues-oriented' and lacking in coherence and an adequate conception of the school-administrator role. The case was made for structuring pre-service delivery according to a research-based conceptual framework. Key implementation and evaluation elements of the OISE program were described as delivery strategies that meet the developmental needs of candidates, encourage reflection among candidates as courses proceed, address ill-defined or swampy role responsibilities that principals face daily, and attempt to 'train for outcome' as opposed to course satisfaction. Consideration was given to problems that emerge when course-delivery personnel attempt to implement these strategies.

The chapter concluded with a set of recommendations based on what the authors believe to be principles of effective pre-service delivery practice. The appropriateness of individual recommendations and the weight each carries will vary from one preparation program to the next. Nonetheless, serious attempts to adhere to them seem likely to result in improved pre-service programming.

Chapter 12

Characteristics of Formal Programs for Developing Expert School Leadership in the Swamp

As Chapter 11 indicated, there is a relatively large body of well examined experience on which to draw in determining the characteristics of formal programs that will be successful in preparing future leaders for the high ground. Much less experience has been had in preparing school-leaders for the swamp. Nevertheless, that experience has been instructive with regard to program characteristics and gives rise to optimism about the possibility of improving expertise in the swamp.

The program characteristics described in this chapter are based most directly on research related to versions of a four to five-day program we have designed, implemented and refined through four iterations over a three-year period. Several different types of data were collected each time the program was implemented. The most comprehensive research was undertaken in conjunction with the first iteration of the program. On this occasion, the program was implemented with twenty-two school-leaders (fourteen principals, eight first-year vice-principals) and changes in their expertise were compared with a matched group of sixteen principals and vice-principals. Data collected before and after the program from both groups included the participants' own appraisals of changes in their expertise, and written solutions to case problems which were analyzed in detail by the researchers and holistically by two expert school-leaders working independently of one another. The same types of data were collected from the ninety experienced school-leaders in the second iteration of the program but there was no matched control group included in this study. Only participants' self-appraisals of change were collected for the third and fourth iterations.

Each time the program has been implemented, three sets of questions have served as the focus for data collection. First, can school-leaders' expertise in solving swampy problems be improved? Second, will an instructional focus on general problem-solving processes used by expert school-leaders enhance the problem-solving capacities of others? Finally, what are the most promising program characteristics for improving school-leader expertise in the swamp? This last question is the main focus of this chapter. Nevertheless, unless the first two questions can be answered affirmatively, it is a meaningless question. Our data, in line with evidence provided through research in other fields (e.g., Nickerson, 1988–89) strongly suggest such affirmative answers. In this chapter, we do not provide a detailed report of the results of our data analysis. For those wishing to review these data see Leithwood and Steinbach (1991).

The remainder of the chapter describes the central characteristics of a formal program for developing expert school leadership in the swamp. These characteristics are of two types: characteristics related to the purposes or goals of the program and characteristics of the instructional strategies used in the program. In each case, the theoretical justification for each characteristic is described in some detail. Some readers may consider this unnecessary for them and may wish to read only the conclusions of our theoretical musings, the 'practical' stuff. In fact, we believe these theoretical musings to be highly relevant for anyone interested in their own development or in assisting with the development of others. Our goal is to insert a 'light bulb' into the 'black box' of the school-leader's mind. Being able to see better how the insides of the 'black box' work increases our flexibility and effectiveness as instructors by reducing our dependency on instructional prescriptions from others. It also allows us to exercise more productive control over our own learning.

Program Goals: The Nature of Problem-Solving Expertise in the Swamp

Expert Processes Identified in the Research

Problem-solving processes which our experimental program aimed to develop emerged most directly from research partly described in Chapters 6 and 7. As noted there, this research has: examined school-leaders' problem classification and management processes (Leithwood and Stager, 1986, Leithwood, 1988); developed a grounded model of school-leader problem-solving alone (Leithwood and Stager, 1989) and in groups (Leithwood and Steinbach, in press b); examined the flexibility of school-leaders' cognitions (Stager and Leithwood, 1989); and inquired about the role of values in problem-solving (Begley and Leithwood, 1989, in press, Campbell, 1988). Differences in problem-solving processes due to differences in role or organizational context (Leithwood and Steinbach, 1989) have been examined. As readers of Chapters 6 and 7 will know, much of this research has examined differences in the problem-solving processes of 'expert' and 'non-expert' school-leaders. As in the research of many others, using expert vs. novice designs (reviewed by Alexander and Judy, 1988) our long-term purpose has been to clarify those aspects of expertise that might become a productive focus for selection, evaluation, and professional development of principals.

By way of quick review, a central result of this research has been a six-component model of problem-solving including:

- **Interpretation**: principals' understanding of the specific nature of the problem, often in situations where multiple problems may be identified
- **Goals**: the relatively immediate purposes that the principals are attempting to achieve in response to their interpretation of the problem
- **Principles/Values**: the relatively long-term purposes, operating principles, fundamental laws, doctrines, values, and assumptions guiding the principals' thinking

- **Constraints**: 'barriers or obstacles' which must be overcome, if an acceptable solution to the problem is to be found
- **Solution Processes**: what the principals do to solve a problem in light of their interpretation of the problem, principles, goals to be achieved, and constraints to be accommodated
- **Affect**: the feelings, mood and sense of self-confidence the principals experience when involved in problem-solving

For a summary of the problem-solving processes associated with each component of the model, the reader is referred back to Table 6.1 in Chapter 6. Those processes associated with experts summarized in Table 6.1 served as general goals for the instructional program. As is evident in Table 6.1 and discussed extensively in Chapter 7, values play an integral role in problem-solving as do the problem solver's moods or affective states through their influence on problem-solving flexibility. While both of these components of problem-solving merit instructional attention, our experimental program touched on them only lightly. This was because we were not confident in the instructional approaches available to us. Instruction was limited to making participants aware of research results concerning the nature and role of values and mood in the problem-solving of experts. The program also encouraged self-instruction and self-evaluation as a means of regulating mood, techniques which seem to be helpful for this purpose (Meichenbaum, 1977, Wine, 1971).

Justifying a Focus on General Processes

Greatest emphasis in the program on which this chapter is based was focused on the other components of the model, which are a set of general cognitive skills and problem-solving strategies (e.g., problem interpretation, goal setting, identifying constraints, and solution processes). The focus is important to acknowledge because of the long standing, continuing debate about the relative contribution to expertise, in many fields, of domain-specific (or local) knowledge (e.g., knowledge about teacher evaluation) as compared with generalizable, content-independent skills and strategies (e.g., Ogilvie and Steinbach, 1988).

Evidence brought to bear on either side of this debate is reasonably compelling: on the 'domain-specific knowlege' side, see Chi, Glaser and Farr (1985) and Lesgold (1984), for example; examples of evidence on the 'general skills side' include Brown and DeLoache (1978) and Nisbett and Ross (1980). As Nickerson (1988–89) points out, however, this controversy is primarily a question of emphasis with widespread acknowledgment, in recent research, that both general thinking skills and domain-specific knowledge are important. In the absence of domain-specific knowledge, one has nothing to think about. In the absence of reasonably well developed general thinking skills, one's knowledge may well remain inert: that is, not be applied in circumstances where it has potential use. For instructional purposes, it seems reasonable to approach the matter in a conditional way. The probability that a school-leader will successfully solve a problem is a function of both the availability of problem-relevant knowledge and general thinking skills or heuristics and so both are addressed in the program.

The primary focus of instruction is on general problem-solving strategies with domain-specific knowledge provided by colleagues in the course of solving real-life administrative problems.

A general strategies focus was chosen for three related reasons. First, expert practice in many professions is centrally concerned with solving ill-structured problems for which there is relatively little available content knowledge and no readily available solution. As Schön (1983) suggests and as we discussed in Chapter 6, it is problems 'in the swamp' that are of greatest interest to experienced practitioners in many professions, and there is a corresponding need to learn how to respond to such problems in an effective manner. Evidence reviewed in Chapter 4 suggests that as many as ˙one in five problems faced by school administrators are ill-structured from their point of view. Second, we believe that experienced school-leaders at the present time, contrary to Perkins' (1985) assertion, are likely to have more opportunity to acquire domain-specific knowledge than general problem-solving skills. Descriptions of the content of contemporary preparation programs provide one source of evidence in support of this belief (Leithwood, Rutherford and Van der Vegt, 1987, Blum and Butler, 1989). Hence, improvements in present school-leaders' practices seemed likely by improving their capacities to use their existing knowledge more effectively through increasing their problem-solving skills. Finally, since our research showed that expert practitioners could be differentiated from their less expert colleagues on the basis of their problem-solving skills, it seemed appropriate to at least try to teach those expert processes.

We believe our choice of focus on general problem-solving skills for the experimental program is justified by the case outlined above. Nevertheless, the term 'general thinking or problem-solving skills' conveys an incomplete impression of the knowledge we attempted to develop through the program. A more comprehensive impression is conveyed by the term 'useful, strategic knowledge'.

Interpreting General Processes as Useful, Strategic Knowledge

In the case of the experimental program, 'useful, strategic knowledge' refers to the explicit strategies and heuristics associated in our research with expertise, as well as the (usually) tacit knowledge required for its actual use in real-life school leadership contexts. Our meaning of 'useful, strategic knowledge' is essentially the same as Sternberg and Caruso's (1985, p. 134) definition of practical knowledge: 'procedural knowledge that is useful in one's everyday life'. Such knowledge is strategic or procedural in the sense that it is knowledge concerned with *how* to solve problems (e.g., how to clarify school goals) rather than knowledge *about* problem-solving (declarative knowledge).

The strategic knowledge of concern to us also had to be useful in two senses. First such knowledge had to be sufficiently detailed so as to be of direct use in the context of school-leaders' practices. This meant that the explicit problem-solving strategies identified in our research had to be combined with an extensive body of 'ordinary' (Lindblom and Cohen, 1979) knowledge, usually tacit, in the mind of the learner; the importance of this type of knowledge is often overlooked in discussions of expertise. This combination acknowledges both the limited cognitive guidance provided by explicitly described, general strategies and the conditional nature of practical knowledge (e.g., knowledge that: 'although your teachers need more time to plan, Harry Smith doesn't want to be out of his class during school hours any more than he is already'). With respect to strategic knowledge, expert practice requires explicit general strategies, detailed knowledge about how to use them, and knowledge of the circumstances under which their application is appropriate. For our purposes, 'useful' also meant that the knowledge provided by the experimental program had: to be relevant to solving a wide range of school-leaders' problems, to contribute significantly to their success in solving problems, and to be potentially teachable. Perkins and Salomon (1988) argue that four conditions must be met for knowledge to be useful in this sense. The research from which this program emerged (see Chapter 6) indicates that the program does meet them. That is, the program's focal strategies: appeared to be used by experts in solving problems; played an important role in problem-solving; were transferable across many problems; and were commonly absent among non-expert school-leaders.

Program Means: Problem-Based Instruction

Initial Acquisition of Useful, Strategic Knowledge

Our conception of how useful, strategic knowledge develops was partially informed by what cognitive scientists refer to as schema theory and such related conceptions of how knowledge is organized and stored inside one's mind as scripts (Shank and Abelson, 1977) and production systems (Sternberg and Caruso, 1985). According to this perspective, learners commonly acquire an initial understanding of (or primitive schema explaining) how to carry out some practice, like solving a swampy problem, by experiencing the practice, being carried out by others. This experience may take the form, for example, of a verbal description or the observation of modeled behavior (e.g., watching a fellow principal give feedback to a teacher after observing a lesson). Following Sternberg and Caruso (1985), the learner's initial schema or understanding is pieced together by identifying those elements of experienced information considered relevant to carrying out the practice (e.g., identifying teachers' strengths as well as weaknesses) and putting this information together as an integrated structure or understanding. This new structure or understanding is then related to other information already stored in memory. The resulting primitive schema or picture then serves as a guide for the learner's initial performance (e.g., attempting, oneself, to give a teacher helpful feedback).

As a result of initial performances, the learner is provided with information potentially useful in refining the initial schema. This is information about discrepancies between the actual performances and learners' schema-dependent understandings of what ought to have happened. Such information may indicate to the learners that: (a) their guiding schema requires further refinement and elaboration (e.g., 'I didn't describe what I saw the teacher doing in enough detail'); or (b) their ability to perform does not yet match their understanding of what performance entails (e.g., 'I know what needed to be said but I didn't choose the right words'); or (c) both.

Development of increasingly skilled performances, based on increasingly sophisticated cognitive schemata, depends on opportunities for repeated practice and the quality of the feedback provided as a result of practice. A skilled coach (perhaps a more experienced colleague) already possesses a sophisticated schema to guide performance and knowledge of how best to provide feedback. As a consequence, such a person is likely to facilitate improvement in the learner's guiding schema and actual performance much faster than if the learner has available only his own analysis of discrepancies. Burton, Brown and Fischer (1984), using the teaching of skiing as a model of instruction, conceptualized the conditions provided by a skilled coach in terms of 'Increasingly Complex Microworlds' (ICMs). The learner is exposed to a sequence of environments or microworlds in which the task demands become increasingly complex. By manipulating the physical setting, the equipment (where appropriate), and the task specifications, the coach maintains a gap between the learner's initial capabilities and the requirements for performance that is challenging but manageable. Such a gap nourishes optimal development and refinement of guiding schemata. As Burton, Brown, and Fischer (1984, p. 148) point out: 'The goal of a sequence of microworlds is not to remove all chances for misconceptions but – to increase the possibility that a student will learn to recognize, learn from, and correct her mistakes'.

Based on this partial conception of how useful strategic knowledge develops, it is reasonable to infer that instruction in expert school-leader problem-solving in the swamp will be productive to the extent that it provides:

- models of expert school-leader performance
- multiple opportunities for practicing problem-solving in the swamp
- a sequence of increasingly complex requirements for problem-solving
- feedback about the adequacy of performance and the sophistication of school-leaders' guiding cognitive schema

While schema theory contributes to an understanding of how strategic knowledge develops, it is not sufficient. Nor does such theory speak directly to the usefulness of such knowledge. We relied on research concerned with the context in which learning takes place to complete our conception. This research explores the effects on learning of both the social context in which learning takes place and the purposes such learning is intended to help achieve; treatment of this former dimension of context will clarify our interest in developing useful strategic knowledge.

Most problems perceived by school-leaders to be ill-structured or swampy are defined as such as a consequence of their social rather than technical character, as we pointed out in Chapter 4. Further, most such problems have to be solved by school-leaders in some form of collaboration with others, as discussed in Chapter 6. It is particularly important, for these reasons, to understand better the significance of the social context for school-leader problem-solving. One defensible way of thinking about the relationship between individual learning and social contexts accepts, as its point of departure, Berger and Luckman's (1966) well known thesis that knowledge is socially constructed, as we described in our discussion of culture change in Chapter 9. This means that what counts as knowledge is socially defined, and that many of the most helpful processes used by individuals to acquire knowledge in practical settings involved considerable social interaction. As Rogoff (1984, p. 4) explains:

> Central to the everyday contexts in which cognitive activity occurs is interaction with other people and use of socially provided tools and schemas for solving problems. Cognitive activity is socially defined, interpreted, and supported. People, usually in conjunction with each other and always guided by social norms, set goals, negotiate appropriate means to reach the goals, and assist each other in implementing the means and resetting the goals as activities evolve.

For purposes of the experimental program, it was most important to conceptualize the nature of the contributions that social interaction could make to individual problem-solving capacity, as well as the conditions under which those contributions seemed most likely. One potential contribution of directed social interaction is the improvement of individuals' problem-solving expertise. Conditions required for this potential to be realized are evident, for example, in Vygotsky's (1978) concept of a 'zone of proximal development'. This zone is the gap between the problem-solving capacity of the individual learner and the capacity demonstrated by those with whom the learner interacts – like colleagues within a group. Sensitive instruction, as Rogoff (1984) explains, at the learner's cutting edge of understanding, encourages participation at a comfortable yet challenging level. It also provides a bridge for generalizing strategies from familiar to more novel situations. In this way, the problem-solving processes of the group are internalized by the individual. This is the same perspective used in Chapter 6 to understand the conditions of group problem-solving that would improve the capacity of individuals within the group.

Social interaction also has the potential for increasing the individual's capacity to contribute more effectively to joint problem-solving. In Mehan's (1984, p. 64) observations of committee deliberations, problem-solving was socially distributed: 'The information upon which decisions are made is in the collective memory of the group, not in any individual's memory'. In the case of the individual learner being stimulated by the group to develop better processes for solving problems individually, the group models performance from which more sophisticated guiding schemata can be inferred and provides socially compelling feedback about adaptations of existing schemata. In the case of becoming a more skillful contributor to a group's problem-solving processes, the individual is stimulated to acquire another, higher order set of schemata or understandings to guide their participation in the group.

As we pointed out also in Chapter 6 in reference to teachers, conditions likely to foster development of such expertise among school-leaders include:

- provision of group problem-solving processes likely to be more sophisticated than processes used by the individual
- opportunities for the individual to reflect on or to recover the elements of the groups' problem-solving processes
- stimulation for individuals to compare their own processes to those of the group

- opportunities for the group to reflect critically on the roles played by individual members and to provide feedback to individuals about how their contribution could be improved

Social interaction, we argued, is a crucial feature of the context in which problem-solving expertise is learned (and practiced). A second crucial feature of the context is the nature of the problems used as vehicles for developing expertise. For purposes of developing practical or useful strategic knowledge among school-leaders, such problems must be approximately the same as the problems they encounter in real life and perceived as authentic by them. There are several compelling reasons for this to be the case. The 'situated' nature of useable knowledge is one reason for using authentic problems as vehicles for developing expertise. As Brown, Collins and Duguid (1989) argue, for example, with respect to what is learned, the activity in which knowledge is developed is neither neutral nor separable from it. 'Situations' (or problems used as instructional vehicles) along with the social context for instruction co-produce knowledge. While the instructor is not uninfluential in the process, often mediating the learning, it is the learner, finally, who is doing the selecting. What the learner selects, from the situation in which learning takes place, as the basis for developing meaning, is unpredictable, at best. Furthermore, there will be substantial variation among learners in their selections depending on the nature of those existing cognitive structures used in the creation of meaning.

The situation (or activity) in which learning takes place, therefore, cannot be separated from the knowledge to be learned; it is part of the knowledge that is stored in memory by the learner. The most certain way of ensuring appropriate understanding of what is learned, therefore, is to create situations the learner will encounter in practice. This not only aids in the initial creation of meaning, it also helps ensure appropriate application of knowledge subsequently: 'knowledge will be retrieved only if the retrieval cues available at the time of access match the cues that were encoded with an item of knowledge' (Tulving and Thomson, cited in Sternberg and Caruso, 1985, p. 149). Bransford, Franks, Vye and Sherwood (in press) extend this idea in their analysis of conditions for knowledge transfer (discussed later).

A second reason why instructional situations and problems should be authentic has to do with the large amounts of usually tacit and/or 'ordinary' knowledge (Lindblom and Cohen, 1979) required actually to use a general problem-solving strategy in practice. Authentic situations increase the probability that learners will make connections with existing tacit knowledge. Artificial situations decrease this probability. When learners take advantage of social interactions among peers (as when a group of five or six school-leaders try to solve an authentic problem together), the opportunities are increased for tacit knowledge to become explicit and thereby examined. Further, it is then possible to acquire the formerly tacit knowledge of one's colleagues developed through hard experience. This formerly tacit knowledge of one's colleagues may be easily as important a contribution to problem-solving expertise as the research-based knowledge more typically the exclusive focus of formal instruction.

Finally, authentic situations are simply more motivating for learners than are situations abstracted from the context in which knowledge is to be used (Sternberg and Caruso, 1985). Besides being easier to relate to, familiar or real-life problems provide the usually enjoyable opportunity for sharing relevant and often humorous anecdotes. Our experience suggests, as well, that the use of authentic problems under conditions discussed to this point, also adds to the domain-specific knowledge and to the strategic knowledge of some participants. Receiving specific pointers about how to deal with possible problems may also be part of what is motivating about authentic situations.

Conditions to be met by an instructional program, based on these views include:

- providing instructional situations which authentically approximate the circumstances of actual school-leader practice
- encouraging the recovery, sharing, and evaluation of relevant knowledge which would normally remain tacit

Additional Interventions to Foster Transfer

The transfer of knowledge from the instructional setting to the real-life administrative setting is assisted through some conditions already examined: in particular, the use of authentic problems and settings. More can be done, however, to ensure appropriate application of strategic knowledge by drawing from results of research on transfer of training.

For purposes of designing the experimental program, transfer refers to:

the impact of learning a behavior [broadly defined] on the same performance in another context or on a different performance not simply containing the first in the same or a different context (Salomon and Perkins, p. 5, mimeo)

In order to design the program for greatest transfer, we were guided by an orientation to transfer, recently proposed in a series of papers by Perkins and Salomon (Perkins and Salomon, 1988, 1989, Salomon and Perkins, mimeo). Two types of transfer are distinguished in this formulation: 'high road' and 'low road' – each produced by different ways of thinking and stimulated by different instructional approaches. Because each type of transfer produces valuable although different outcomes, Perkins and Salomon (1988) argue that instructional programs ought to attempt to foster both. In general, transfer of any sort appears to depend on how one initiates a search through one's memory for already stored clusters of knowledge that might usefully be applied to the task one faces. Transfer also depends on the extent to which such stored knowledge is linked to other potentially relevant clusters of knowledge also stored in memory.

Low-road transfer is characterized by the ready application of well-learned knowledge and/or skills to the same performance, in contexts very similar to ones in which the knowledge and skills were originally learned, or in performances only modestly different from the originally learned performances (e.g., transferring what you know about running a staff meeting to the task of chairing a district-curriculum committee). Such transfer occurs as a consequence of extensive practice in varied contexts until the application of the learned knowledge and skill becomes automatic: that is, until the presence of a situation or condition elicits the application of relevant knowledge and skill, with little or no conscious cognitive mediation. Practice extends the application of what has been learned from its initial performance or context to other similar performances and contexts. Variation in the application contexts or performances (e.g., chairing many different groups) during practice gradually stretches the boundaries of application, as the learner adapts to partially new circumstances in minor and largely unconscious ways. The advantage of low-road transfer is smooth and reliable application of mastered performances with little expenditure of cognitive resources (e.g., you don't have to think much consciously). This suggests that low-road transfer is most appropriate for knowledge and skills subject to routine and frequent use. The 'automaticity' associated with low-road transfer, on the other hand, inhibits analytic reflection on matters such as when the application of existing skills and knowledge is appropriate.

Whereas low-road transfer is relatively 'mindless', high-road transfer is 'mindful'. It involves applying a set of rules or principles extracted from one or more contexts and/or performances, to other, quite novel, contexts and/or performances (e.g., using what you know about how to chair a meeting in order to conduct a group seminar in a graduate class). The greater the degree of abstraction, the larger the range of instances such rules and principles subsume and to which they can be applied. High-road transfer depends on 'both the decontextualization and representation of the decontextualized information in a new, more general form subsuming other cases' (Salomon and Perkins, pp. 10–11, mimeo). This is not critically fostered by practice, although evidence suggests that limited amounts of practice are helpful. Rather, such transfer depends on bringing considerable thought to bear on determining the generalizable features of the information. Not only must these generalizable features be determined by the learner, but they must also be genuinely understood, evoked in the transfer context and effectively applied (e.g., beginning to understand that 'giving everyone air time in a meeting' is a way of diagnosing the existing understanding each person has of the issue being discussed).

Salomon and Perkins (mimeo) also point out that, because of the relatively mindless automaticity that comes with practice and expertise, experts may have difficulty mindfully transferring well mastered skills and knowledge to novel contexts. This suggests that, especially with people who have considerable expertise, guided abstraction from (or reflection on) well-rehearsed practices may be quite important in helping them make better use of what they already know in responding to novel problems.

This conception of the transfer process implies a number of conditions to be met for successful transfer of problem-solving skills. In the case of frequently and routinely used skills (e.g., information collection), most suitable for low-road transfer, it will be important to:

- provide many opportunities for application or practice across a wide variety of problem types
- provide feedback about the adequacy of performance and opportunities for further guided practice

For general principles and skills most suitable for high-road transfer, it will be helpful to:

- provide assistance in decontextualizing and abstracting generalizable features of existing problem-solving practices
- provide direct instruction in the key components of effective problem-solving practices and coaching in the application of such components to specific cases

Fostering Metacognition

School-leader expertise is partly a function of applying useful, strategic knowledge to the solution of swampy problems. To this point in the explanation of our framework, the nature of that knowledge and how it is initially developed has been described. We have also described how to help ensure that useful, strategic knowledge developed in a formal instructional setting, for example, will be applied in appropriate, real-life school-leader settings.

The strategic components of administrative expertise are not limited to the use of problem-solving strategies alone, however. Argyris' conception of double and single-loop learning help illustrate why this is the case (e.g., Argyris, Putnam and Smith, 1985, Argyris, 1982). The term 'single-loop learning' is applied by Argyris to a process in which the learner responds to a problem by initiating a chain of actions intended to resolve the problem. If that chain of actions proves less effective than desired, the learner chooses another chain of actions in a further attempt to resolve the problem, as the problem was originally conceived. So, while the solutions change as part of single-loop learning, the variables, governing the learner's understanding of the problem and the setting, remain the same. In instances of double-loop learning, the governing variables are themselves objects of conscious scrutiny and, as a consequence, the nature of the problem and the setting may be significantly redefined (e.g., 'maybe this isn't a discipline problem after all, maybe it's a sign of a deficiency in our program'). Individuals engaged in double-loop learning are also actively aware of their own thinking; they are involved in managing their own cognitive resources, and monitoring and evaluating their own intellectual performance. This is metacognition (Nickerson, 1988–89). Some would also refer to this process as a form of reflection in which experience is reconstructed in such a way as to enable one to transform one's own practice (Grimmett, 1989). During such reflection, the learner engages in a 'conversation' with the setting in an effort to understand it better and the meaning that it has for the assumptions underlying the problem-solving activity.

Conditions which seem likely to foster the development of metacognition include:

- the provision of cues to the learner which are likely to stimulate self-questioning
- the modeling of metacognitive thinking by others
- direct instruction about the value of metacognition (since metacognitive activity is unlikely in the absence of a belief in its value) and the kinds of questions one might use as aids to self-reflection

Instructional Strategies Used in the Program

Table 12.2 summarizes the instructional strategies used in the experimental program to address those conditions we have identified as contributing to the development of useful, strategic knowledge. As a whole, these strategies constitute our version of 'problem-based instruction' (Hallinger and McCary, in press, Boud, 1985, Bransford *et al.*, in press). Currently used with promising results in a small number of institutions but across a wide range of professions (e.g., medicine, management, agriculture, architecture), problem-based instruction acknowledges especially well the situated nature of cognition and dilemmas associated with inert knowledge and lack of transfer. It does this by centering instruction around key problems of practice. Students acquire both domain-specific and useful, strategic knowledge in the context of working through such problems. The contribution of problem-based instruction can be explained in terms of readier accessibility of knowledge acquired through such instruction, for application in practice. Such accessibility is a function of the way knowledge is organized and stored in memory initially, around problems of practice.

The experimental program required participants to work on parts, or all, of a total of nine problems. These problems varied in their degree of structure, although all were perceived to be relatively unstructured. In addition to degree of structure, two other variables were manipulated in order to provide 'Increasingly Complex Microworlds'. One variable was the number of components in our problem-solving model (i.e., interpretation, goals, principles, etc.). Participants were asked to address from one to all six of these components in relation to a given problem. A second variable was the function participants were asked to perform in relation to the components. These functions included: (a) describing how a model of problem-solving (e.g., a principal talking about how he or she solved a problem) addressed the component(s), the simplest function; (b) evaluating the model's performance; and (c) addressing the component(s) oneself, the most complex function.

Other variables manipulated through the program were the social context for problem-solving (individually, in pairs, in groups) and the form in which thinking was communicated (orally, in writing or audio-taped). Participants were required to evaluate the program at the end of each instructional day and a summary of their opinions was reported to them at the beginning of the next day, along with an indication of adjustments made to the program, in response to these opinions. This was intended, in part, to stimulate thinking about the types of experience most helpful in stimulating thinking.

A Summary of One Day's Activities in the Experimental Program

To illustrate more clearly how the conditions for optimal learning were met, we provide a more detailed picture of a typical day in the life of our experimental program. The numbers in parentheses indicate the item on Table 12.1 of which the commentary is an example. The agenda for each day was distributed to all participants when they arrived. Each session was organized around a theme – usually one or two of the components in the model. On Day 2, the focus was on setting goals and dealing with constraints.

Table 12.1: *Development of useful, strategic knowledge: Instructional strategies and conditions*

Conditions	Instructional Strategies
1. provide models of expert problem-solving	• audiotaped examples of expert administrators describing the process they use to solve a case problem • 'live' administrators tell how they solved a real problem they faced
2. provide practice opportunities across wide variety of problem types	• ask individuals to write solution to own selected problem; colleague critique • ask individuals to solve colleagues' problem; colleague critique • groups of 5/6 participants solve problems together
3. sequence increasingly complex task demands	• problem-solving tasks for individuals and groups manipulated in terms of: evaluate other's solution vs. solve oneself; number of problem-solving components to consider; complexity of case problems
4. provide performance feedback on individual problem-solving	• response by individual colleague, group, instructor to processes described in writing and described verbally
5. insure participation in sophisticated group problem-solving processes	• careful instruction to groups prior to engagement in problem-solving task
6. encourage individual reflection on own and group problem-solving	• individual participants required to think aloud about their own solving of problems or to write solutions to problems. Peers and instructors discussed, with individuals, their processes
7. provide performance feedback on contribution of individual to group problem-solving processes	• not done in this program
8. provide authentic instructional settings and problems	• instructional problems identified through research on problems encountered by principals and by having case problems written (or orally presented) by administrators as they encounter them
9. assist in recovering, sharing and evaluating tacit knowledge	• work with a peer or group of peers to solve problems collaborative, discussing alternative proposals based on experience and the thinking leading to such proposals
10. assist individuals in decontextualizing and abstracting general features of existing problem-solving practices	• most case problem-solving by individuals or groups followed by 'debriefing' in which the components of the problem-solving model were used as the framework for discussion • use of check-lists of general strategies to be considered
11. provide direct instruction in effective strategies and coaching in their application	• brief presentations by instructors on characteristics of effective problem-solving as identified in research; readings provided to students describing effective problem-solving
12. provide cues to stimulate self-questioning	• instructors continuously monitored group problem-solving processes and intervened as warranted to provide cues or orienting questions • check-lists

Table 12.1 (cont.)

Conditions	Instructional Strategies
13. model metacognition and provide reasons for metacognition	• 15 percent of program devoted to looking at same problem from four different perspectives (legal, political, financial, educational) • each perspective presented by a person with special training or experience in the perspective (lawyer, trustee, business administrator, principal) • different, justified approaches to problem-solving and solutions evident through observation of different perspectives • daily evaluation of program

Introduction

Each day began with a summary of the results of the previous day's evaluation. Participants received a handout showing the frequency counts of responses to the forced-choice questions and typical responses (with frequency counts) to the open-ended questions. They were also told how the program was adjusted in response to their opinions. By showing them that the evaluations were important and had some effect, the participants were encouraged to reflect seriously on the day's events (13). The second part of the introduction reviewed the proceedings to date and the plan for the day was unveiled.

Solution to Case Problem

On Day 1, groups had discussed how to interpret a problem that had actually occurred (8) and there had been various interpretations offered. On Day 2, the area superintendent directly involved with that problem was on hand to provide the actual interpretation and eventual solution (1). A listening guide comprised of questions related to the problem-solver's use of each component in our model was provided to focus participants' thinking (10, 12). Afterwards, the whole group had the chance to analyze the superintendent's solution by comparing their own previous interpretations with those of the expert (6) and by discussing their understanding of how the other components were dealt with (10).

Individual Writing: Solving a Swampy Problem

Capitalizing on the belief that writing crystalizes one's thoughts and enhances the likelihood that learning takes place, participants were asked to write the solution to a swampy problem they had encountered during the preceding few weeks and which they had described as part of a homework assignment. For this session, each participant was asked to write the solution to a colleague's swampy problem and then critique each other's solution with a main focus on the interpretation component (learned on Day 1) but also touching on all of the components (which had been described briefly). This activity provided an opportunity to work on a new problem (2), was moderately complex in terms of the number of components addressed and the difficulty of the task (3), and provided performance feedback on individual problem-solving (4). The discussions between colleagues encouraged reflection about problem-solving in general (6), provided an opportunity to share tacit knowledge (9), and also provided direct instruction about specific strategies that worked well or failed miserably (11). Additionally, the problems dealt with were obviously authentic (8). This activity also met a criterion for optimal learning not considered on Table 12.1: the participants found these discussions enormously enjoyable.

Setting Goals

This section represents our typical method for presenting new information. A general description of the meaning and importance of the goals' component was delivered orally by an instructor; the group also received a one-page handout summarizing the talk (11). A written case problem which was particularly appropriate for illustrating the importance of identifying goals was distributed (2) and possible solutions were discussed in small groups according to instructions at the bottom of the one-page case description (5). Those instructions pertained especially to the goals that a solver would set but asked for consideration of all other components (3), as well. Following this, a check-list detailing the kinds of thinking in experts engage which regarding goals was distributed (12). Small groups reanalyzed the 'implementation problem' in light of these specific cues. These reactions were then shared with the whole group (10). A similar procedure was used for the 'constraints component' using another problem entitled 'the Marks Secnario' (2). Two errors commonly committed by non-expert problem-solvers were described (11) and the groups' solutions to the 'Marks Scenario' problem were examined for evidence of them (10). Finally, an expert problem-solver and educational leader described how he would have solved this problem (1) with the group engaged in focused listening, using the guide described earlier (10, 12). The entire group was invited to ask specific, content questions (9) and discuss the strengths and weaknesses of the solution process (10). To end the day, homework related to the next day was assigned, a relevant article was distributed (11), and participants evaluated the day's events (13).

In one day, all of the conditions we have listed for stimulating learning had been arranged for at least once (and most more than once). What is missing from this narrative is the importance of keeping the group keenly motivated. Careful pacing of activities to keep interest high and a wealth of illustrative cartoons were essential elements of the program.

Conclusion

Evidence collected to evaluate the program described in this chapter (e.g., Leithwood and Steinbach, in press) supports the claim that even quite experienced school-leaders are able to increase their expertise in solving swampy problems given the right conditions. While the amount of evidence is quite limited, there is considerable theoretical support for the instructional conditions incorporated into our experimental program. On these grounds, it seems quite appropriate to build formal programs for improving expertise in the swamp, taking care to monitor their effects at the same time.

Chapter 13

Performance Appraisal and Selection of School-Leaders: Performance Appraisal for Growth

Formal programs, as described in the two previous chapters, are obvious and quite direct strategies for fostering school-leader development. School-leader selection and appraisal policies and procedures, while possibly less obvious development strategies, are also quite direct.

In the case of selection procedures, it is the school's rather than the individual's leadership capacity which is being developed most directly through the choice of the greatest actual or potential expertise. Especially during periods, such as the 1990s, of unusually rapid turnover in school-leaders due to retirement (Leithwood and Begley, 1985, Musella and Lawton, 1986, Peterson, Marshall and Grier, 1987) these choices are of enormous consequence to the quality of leadership which will be available to schools as they enter the twenty-first century.

Appraisal policies and procedures, as they are used 'summitively' to assist with dismissal, promotion, and transfer decisions, influence the school's leadership capacity in approximately the same way as do selection practices. When appraisal policies are used 'formatively,' they are capable of fostering the growth of individual school-leaders in precisely the manner we outlined for teacher-appraisal policies in Chapter 8.

This chapter and Chapter 14 apply a single framework to issues involved in using appraisal and selection processes to foster the development of leaders for future schools. In the case of each set of processes, we review research describing current practices and then explore ways of increasing the contribution of such practices to leader development. Such improvement is often considered to be a matter of improving the quality of the information available to appraisers and selectors. And, as we shall see, there is much to be done to bring typical appraisal and selection processes 'up to speed' with regard to such quality. A major emphasis throughout these two chapters, however, will be on making effective use of the information that is available. Compelling evidence suggests that information generated during appraisal and selection processes is often not used or is misused (see, for example, Hickcox, Lawton, Leithwood and Musella, 1988). Under such conditions, the contribution of appraisal and selection processes to school-leader development is likely to remain severely blunted. Greater attention to use, we argue, is a promising avenue for improving appraisal and selection processes.

This chapter is concerned exclusively with performance appraisal. We begin by examining thoroughly current practice, by reviewing recent literature on the topic, and then report on some of our own research concerned with identifying effective practices. In Chapter 14 we examine current selection processes and then consider a number of issues involved in the measurement of school-leader performance. These issues, while they may not appeal to all readers due to their inherently technical nature, have significant implications for both school-leader appraisal and selection. A summary of guidelines for improving both sets of processes is left to the end of Chapter 14.

Knowledge about current school-leader selection and appraisal practices is quite limited. Our attempt to find and review relevant knowledge included the use of computerized searches (ERIC), and scanning recent issues of relevant periodicals and bibliographic follow-up. Only a few comprehensive, descriptive surveys of selection and appraisal practice were found. Most studies focused on the utility of participant forms of selection and/or appraisal (e.g., performance-assessment centers) rather than engaging in more comprehensive reviews of practice. Furthermore, most of what has been written about selection and appraisal practices might best be termed 'opinion' literature. It may be that the bulk of this writing is based on valuable and illuminating practical experience but the reader rarely has a way of making this determination. Hence, mention is made of this literature only sparingly and when judged to overlap significantly with research findings.

Our reviews of both the appraisal and selection literature are organized around a conceptual framework used to guide the research of Lawton, Hickcox, Leithwood and Musella (1986). The framework includes five process-oriented components:

- **Preparation**: planning, purposes, criteria, and standards for selection and appraisal. Essentially activities that occur prior to the evaluation that determine its form and substance
- **Data Collection**: sources and types of information, methods of collection, who collects data and how much time is spent in doing so
- **Reporting and Follow-up**: the nature of the report, the form it takes, its destination, the development of plans of action and other consequences of the data-collection process
- **Evolution of Policy**: processes by which policies are developed, implementation activities, and whether policies are reviewed and revised on a periodic basis
- **Impact**: degree of compliance with policy, commitment to implementation and administration, and the nature and degree of impact within the system, including especially 'use'.

The Current Status of School-Leader Appraisal

Much has been written about the appraisal of school-leaders but, as with the literature on selection, research in the area is not well developed. Based on a comprehensive literature review, Ginsberg and Berry (1990) suggested that much of what is written on school-leader evaluation concerning models, procedures, and instruments is description of local practice and not explicitly supported by empirical research. Results of the few significant and relevant studies which were available support Ginsberg and Berry's (1990) suggestion that school-leader evaluation practices are in the 'stone age'.

The description of current assessment practices presented in this section relies most heavily on the study by Lawton *et al.* (1986). This study included an analysis of existing policies in Ontario, a survey of thirty school systems with data from 4092 teachers, 879 principals, 114 supervisory officers, and twenty-six chief education officers (CEOs). Also included were a series of case studies based on interview data with local administrators and teachers in thirteen school districts. Also reflected in our description of current appraisal practices are the results of a comprehensive (but still descriptive) study reported by Duke and Stiggins (1985). They surveyed one district administrator with responsibility for school-leader evaluation and two principals (one elementary and one secondary) from each of thirty school districts. Other studies reviewed for this section include Ginsberg and Berry (1990), Berry and Ginsberg (1988), Bolam (1990), Duhamel, Cyze, Lamacraft and Rutherford (1981), Harrison and Peterson (1986), Janey (1988), Murphy, Peterson and Hallinger (1986), Peters and Bagenstos (1988), and Redfern (1986). Comments from advocates of various approaches to school-leader evaluation (Ingle, 1975, Rentsch, 1983, Valentine, 1987) are interjected where appropriate.

Preparation

Preparation for school-leader appraisal includes planning, perceived purpose, and criteria-setting activities. Ginsberg and Berry (1990) reported that not many school systems had formal policies. This was corroborated by Lawton *et al.* (1986) although these authors believed that the trend was quickly changing. Documentation for school-leader appraisal policies was found to be more prevalent than for other roles, and most districts either supplied formal policies or individuals responding to the survey were able to describe policies in written form.

Considerable variation existed in the procedures for informing school-leaders about the district's appraisal process (Duke and Stiggins, 1985). These include relevant communication mechanisms, handbooks, written instructions, and verbal explanations. Lawton *et al.* (1986) found that over half of the principals they surveyed received personal notification that a formal appraisal was pending and that pre-conferences between principals and appraisers were quite common (over 70 percent) Pre-conferences were used primarily as methods for setting objectives for the impending observation period (usually throughout the course of the year).

Ginsberg and Berry (1990) reported that the most common purpose of school-leader appraisal was performance improvement (formative). This purpose also appeared to be most common among those engaged in headmaster-appraisal pilot projects currently underway in the UK (Bolam, 1990). Ingle (1975) suggested that although improvement and decision-oriented (summative) purposes for administrative evaluation can be separated conceptually, this cannot be done in practice. Indeed, research on current practice showed that there may be considerable confusion about these fundamental functions of school-leader appraisal. But not all available data support the claim that improvement was the acknowledged purpose of performance appraisal. When asked about actual and preferred purposes for appraisal, principals were strongly inclined to indicate that although performance improvement (variously referred to, as supervision for growth, formative evaluation, developmental evaluation, etc.) was highly valued, it did not appear to be the most commonly acknowledged function in practice (Duke and Stiggins, 1985, Lawton *et al.*, 1986). Lawton *et al.* found that 'comply with policy' was the most frequently identified actual purpose. Some would suggest that 'comply with policy' is not a purpose at all and interpret this finding as revealing principals' lack of true understanding of the intended purposes of the policy and/or cynical attitudes toward organizational control and accountability (Hickcox, 1990). They found, and others as well (e.g., Duke and Stiggins, 1985, Peters and Bagenstos, 1988), that considerable weight was given to summative purposes such as tenure, transfer, promotion, certification, and retention remediation. Harrison and Peterson (1986) reported that principals' and superintendents' views were somewhat discrepant about principal appraisal. Whereas superintendents were quite positive and more consistent in their perceptions, principals were less clear about the intentions of the process and in less agreement about them. Finally, in many states in the US merit-pay plans were being implemented (Duke and Stiggins, 1985, Berry and Ginsberg, 1988). Such evaluation plans constituted another example of decision-oriented or summative purposes for appraisal.

Criteria for evaluating school-leaders were extremely varied both across and probably within school systems. Murphy *et al.* (1986) found that in effective school districts, school-leaders were held accountable for school objectives, an observation they believed may be attributable to an instructional management orientation of supervisors. Other authors observed that 'management by objectives' models were the most popular forms of principal appraisal (e.g., Ginsberg and Berry, 1990, Peters and Bagenstos, 1988, Redfern, 1986). Ginsberg and Berry (1990) indicated that, in addition to outcome-oriented evaluations, a popular focus for principal appraisal appeared to be observable behaviors or processes in which principals engage. The development of behavioral rating inventories for use in appraisal activities is consistent with this orientation to evaluation. Variation in criteria and lack of defined performance standards were common in current practice:

> no consensus among districts exists concerning the precise nature of instructional leadership or school management. Forty-two percent of the respondents ... cited inadequate performance standards as a shortcoming of the existing principal evaluation system. (Duke and Stiggins, 1985, p. 92)

The findings of Lawton *et al.* (1986) were consistent with these results since appraisal criteria were shown to be vague, ambiguous, and not necessarily linked to any existing conception of expert practice. On the other hand, they did observe that as compared with other roles, the criteria used for principal appraisal were more broad and focused on activities both in and outside the school. Also, they reported a tendency for standards or performance expectations to be developed collectively with appraisers, a practice commonly associated with more improvement-oriented appraisal. Other studies reported criteria and standard-setting activities to be unclear, inconsistent and troublesome (Ginsberg and Berry, 1990, Harrison and Peterson, 1986). As several authors have suggested, in addition to outcome and process, other criteria for evaluating principals might fall into a category called 'presage' which would include interpersonal skills (e.g., appearance, personal characteristics, and traits). The use of such criteria, it would appear, is rapidly diminishing (Duhamel *et al.*, 1981, Ginsberg and Berry, 1990, Rentsch, 1983). Some advocated approaches to principal evaluation underscore the need to link process variables to outcomes (e.g., Valentine, 1987). It is not clear, however, to what extent this has been accomplished in practice.

Data Collection

Typically, school-leaders are formally appraised, on an annual basis, by their immediate supervisor (Lawton *et al.*, 1986). Some variation in this tendency exists and informal ongoing supervision by immediate supervisors is becoming much more prevalent (Duke and Stiggins, 1985): it is also characteristic of processes in effective school districts (Murphy *et al.*, 1986). School-leaders play a central role in providing data for their own appraisal, according to Lawton *et al.* (1986). Data from supervisory officers was found to be a distant second source of information about principals. Relatively infrequently, teachers, parents, and students were sources of data. This finding corroborates observations by Ginsberg and Berry (1990) and Redfern (1986) who noted that rarely do appraisal processes include multiple data sources as a standard feature for data collection. In cases where this occurs it is likely to be optional (Redfern, 1986). Bolam (1990) reported that peers are used in the newly developing, national appraisal processes in the UK but that confusion exists concerning the role to be played by various individuals. Keck and Hampton (1987) advocate a portfolio-based peer-assessment model where multiple assessors help to ensure adequate reliability and validity.

Janey (1988) advocated the use of parents as a source of data for principal appraisal but showed that current school-leaders are not comfortable with this approach, presumably because they would question the validity of parent observations. Harrison and Peterson (1986) reported discrepancies in views held by principals and supervisors concerning sources of data for current appraisal practices. While supervisors made the claim that they used multiple sources of data and, especially, information derived from the principals themselves, principals suggested that observations from the community were the appraiser's primary source of information. Indeed Murphy *et al.* (1986) confirmed that such data, in addition to student-achievement data, were used to evaluate principals in effective school districts. However, the authors acknowledged that these sources were used as 'perception-checking activities' as opposed to assistance in making judgments. For the latter, superintendents tended to rely on their own observations of the principal and available quantitative data. For this reason, supervisors in the effective districts in the study necessarily made frequent visits to the schools.

The most frequently identified types of data were school-evaluation reports prepared by principals followed by notes taken by supervisors, and documents such as school-community newsletters, according to Lawton *et al.* (1986). Several other types of data including behavior check-lists, written self-evaluations, school budgets, timetables, and handbooks were also examined but much less frequently. Duke and Stiggins (1985) reported that planned and unplanned observations by superintendents were the most frequently identified types of evidence used for appraisal but that these were less likely to be used than informal input from teachers, other school personnel, and especially parents. Principals were most likely to be observed in meetings with community organizations and faculty meetings (see also Murphy *et al.*, 1986). Bolam (1990) reported that head-teachers were generally observed for both management and teaching performance, since teaching represents a significant component of their responsibilities. Bolam also indicated that interviews with colleagues appeared to be a popular method of collecting data in the early stages of the national-assessment program they studied. As Ginsberg and Berry (1990) noted, there are many instruments and check-lists in existence and probably in use but not an abundance of information concerning their use. School-leaders often believed that instruments such as check-lists and behavior inventories are used too much in practice; in contrast, district administrators preferred to see them used more (Lawton *et al.*, 1986).

In the Lawton *et al.* (1986) study, information was generally collected and evaluated by a single district administrator, usually the principal's area superintendent'. In addition, information was usually collected in one day or less. Although there was some variability in this trend, over 50 percent of the sample reported this to be the case. In a few cases, a team of supervisors or appraisers (in some instances CEOs were part of the team) were responsible for the evaluation: data were usually collected over about a week in a very intensive effort by the team.

Reporting and Follow-up

Duke and Stiggins (1985) and Lawton *et al.* (1986) both reported heavy reliance on the use of post-conferences between the appraiser and principal following the formal evaluation. Typically, a written report was prepared and either forwarded to the principal prior to the conference or brought to the meeting by the supervisory officer. This written report, which generally did not exceed one or two pages (Lawton *et al.*, 1986) formed the basis for discussion during the meeting. It gave the principal an opportunity to counter or even refine observations by the appraiser. The usual length of the post-conference was approximately one hour, on average, and in some cases more than one district administrator was present.

Lawton *et al.* (1986) reported that principals' perceptions of post-conferences were very favorable. For the most part, principals found their appraisers to be fair, sincere, and to take the process seriously. The post-conferences were found to be positive and non-threatening experiences. On the other hand, principals did profess to take the process seriously. These findings leave one with the sense that the post-conference is basically a 'summing up' of the supervisors' observations and that no surprises were typically apparent. Ingle (1975) noted that trust between appraiser and school-leader is an important feature of reporting and follow-up but suggested that a certain amount of pressure is necessary if performance improvement is expected to occur.

Bolam (1990) noted that statements about head-teachers were being prepared and sent to CEOs following the appraisal and that head-teachers were feeling somewhat anxious about this. Finally, Ginsberg and Berry (1990) indicated that the quality of communication between appraiser and principal was typically not very high.

Evolution of Policy

Lawton *et al.* (1986) observed that principal-evaluation policies were generally developed by district administrators with some input from principals. Such policies were typically less specific than teacher-evaluation policies but more specific than policies developed for superordinate roles. Systematic revision or even cyclical review of policies appears to be lacking in most districts according to the authors. There was neither much evidence of systematic monitoring of how well such policies were implemented nor much effort to 'fine tune' policies once developed. Some policies took years to develop where others had been constructed in a hurried fashion by adapting policies developed in other districts. The authors concluded that impact was likely to be higher where policies were constructed from the ground up or where significant local energy was invested in their design and implementation.

Other than the Lawton *et al.* study, we were unable to locate data on the evolution of principal-appraisal policies.

Impact

One of the most interesting findings of the Lawton *et al.* (1986) study was that, although 'satisfaction' with the appraisal process was comparatively high, impact was low. The extent to which performance improvement was believed to be a consequence of the appraisal was minimal, as reported by both principals and district administrators. This is not surprising since in only about 25 percent of the cases were individual development plans developed by, or for, the school-leaders as a consequence of the process. Such lack of attention to follow-up helps explain the results mentioned earlier, that appraisal for performance improvement was perceived by many as the desirable but not the actual purpose for doing the appraisal in the first place.

In addition, in very few cases were administrative actions (e.g., promotion, dismissal) a consequence of the process. Less than 2 percent of principals were placed on review as a result of the process and about as many received some sort of recognition or award as a consequence. These data largely corroborate those of Duke and Stiggins (1985). Perhaps the most frequently observed outcomes of the appraisal processes they studied were individual and private acknowledgements of satisfactory or more than satisfactory performance. Even though principals tend to be very satisfied with the processes used in their appraisal, the impact of these processes is almost non-existent. No news, it seems, is better than bad news. And good news seems not to be expected.

Finally, Berry and Ginsberg (1988) reported that principals believed that evaluation systems structured around the merit-pay concept have neither the sensitivity to detect substandard performance nor the integrity to identify only deserving school-leaders as meritorious.

Summary

To this point, we have reviewed the small amount of empirical research that was available, describing current school-leaders' appraisal practices. This evidence suggests that until recently such practices have been poorly developed and have not been the object of systematic attention by a large proportion of school districts. This portrait of neglect may well be changing rapidly, as we speak, however. The increasing importance attached to school leadership and its development seems likely to be a central force in stimulating such change. Nevertheless, even the best of current practice has some distance to go if it is to contribute to school-leader development as it has the potential to. Much greater effort will need to be devoted to reshaping these practices so that they reinforce a defensible image of future school leadership and so that they become more powerful stimulants to school-leader growth. We now turn to issues involved in bringing about such changes.

Factors Influencing the Impact of Principal-Appraisal Systems

Much of the research concerning the appraisal of school administrators, as we have noted, is exploratory, descriptive, and, at best, correlational in design. These studies are very useful for describing current practice and investigating practitioner-based knowledge about what should be happening. But essentially, the consumers of such research are left to decide if the recommendations offered are sensible and worthy of serious consideration. Very little research of a more tightly controlled or causal nature has been carried out. There is a significant need in the field to conduct at least quasi-experimental and preferably longitudinal studies that investigate relationships, linkages, and causal patterns among appraisal policies and practices, and various measures of impact. In some of our own research and work we have conducted with colleagues we have attempted to address some of these concerns.

In this section, we examine a small series of studies, each contributing to the identification of ways in which school-leader appraisal practices can be shaped to enhance school-leader development.

Study One: Lawton, Hickcox, Leithwood and Musella (1985)

While the primary purpose of Study One was to describe current evaluation practice, a secondary purpose was to determine if some evaluation practices were seen by those involved in the process as being more effective than others.

Although data were exploratory and correlational in nature, 'a pattern of activities and procedures emerges from the data that indicates generic techniques and strategies do exist which are more likely to succeed than other widely used practices' (p. 2). Summarized here are the results that specifically apply to the evaluation of principals.

In this study, data were aggregated to the district level (number of districts = 30) and two sets of impact measures were constructed based on data from various sources. The first set of impact measures concerned 'intervening effects' including satisfaction with report form, fairness of appraiser's judgment, and fairness of procedures. Intervening effects also included: skillfulness of appraiser, how seriously the principal took the appraisal, and how seriously the appraiser took the appraisal. The second set of impact measures concerned the 'final effects' of school-leader appraisal and involved data from teachers and superintendents in addition to school-leaders. Included as 'final effects' were the effectiveness of the principal appraisal reported by CEOs, and the extent of improvement in the principal's performance, as reported by the principal, teachers, and CEOs. Lawton *et al.* used the framework described in Figure 13.1 to summarize the findings.

Preparation
The existence and length of pre-conferences with principals were positively correlated with a number of intervening and 'final effect' variables. Other variables such as method of notification and use of 'objective-based' evaluation did not yield consistent results. A variable that correlated positively with all intervening effect variables was whether purposes for the appraisal were clearly given to principals. Interestingly, although correlated with satisfaction measures, this variable did not correlate with 'final effect' variables.

Criteria such as administrative performance, school/community relations and personnel management were not found to yield interpretable patterns of relationship. However, if principals' contributions at the district level were included as criteria, there appeared to be a tendency for the appraiser's judgment to be perceived as fair and for the superintendent to perceive the performance-appraisal system as being effective.

Data collection
Several variables in the categories: types of information used, who collected information, and time spent collecting it, were tested against the impact measures. In districts where teachers were called upon to provide information for the principal's appraisal, there were positive relationships with both satisfaction and outcome variables. General and specific note-taking appeared to be a data-collection practice that was accepted as satisfactory and correlated with principals' perceptions of performance improvement due to the appraisal. Findings were mixed concerning the use of student disciplinary records as a basis for appraisal. Principals appeared to take the process more seriously when such data were used but there was a negative correlation with performance improvement. Other types of data such as check-lists, self-evaluation questionnaires, school handbooks, and goal packages did not yield interpretable patterns of correlations.

The use of a team of appraisers appeared to have a strong relationship with the seriousness with which the principal took the process, as well as with the

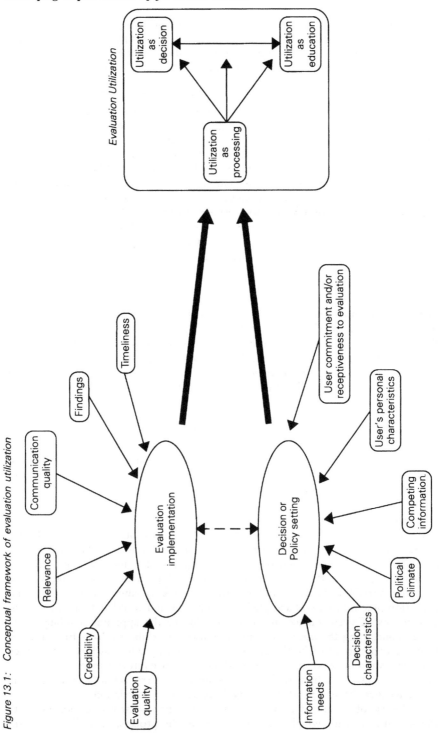

Figure 13.1: Conceptual framework of evaluation utilization

superintendent's perceptions about performance improvement. Greater teacher involvement, beyond the level of providing information, also correlated positively with perceived fairness of the process and the skill with which it was carried out. Where more time was spent collecting data, both appraisers and appraisal-subjects appeared to have taken the process more seriously. A similar, yet stronger relationship was found where post-conferences were held. This was related to principal satisfaction and perceived improvement.

Reporting and follow-up
Clearly, provision for holding a post-conference at the conclusion of the process turned out to be a worthwhile activity, especially in relation to its effectiveness (performance improvement, CEOs perception). As noted above, longer conferences seemed to be more worthwhile. There was mild evidence associated with effects concerning the form in which communication of results occurred. On the one hand, semi-structured and unstructured statements about principals' performance appeared to have a positive relationship to several outcomes, but the use of rating scales was found to correlate negatively with principals' propensity to take the process seriously. Finally, although the existence of an appeal process did not correlate significantly with measures of impact, the development of a plan for performance improvement correlated with several measures of both intervening and performance-improvement effects.

Evolution of policy
Lawton *et al.* reported that steps taken to develop and implement policy had a modest relationship to its effectiveness. Specifically, the fidelity of implementation documentation, training, and commitment of resources appeared to be important.

The authors urged caution in interpreting the findings of their study for two reasons. First, the sample size of thirty school systems may be representative of systems in Ontario but it poses restrictions on the statistical analyses employed. Second, the analyses are only correlational and are therefore only suggestive of possible causal relationships. Nonetheless, the study was very comprehensive and allowed for a test against impact of a wide range of features and activities in school-leader performance appraisal.

Perhaps the significance for performance-appraisal practice of findings from this study might best be summed up in the words of one of its authors:

> I've developed a strong sense that what is imbedded in these findings for both teachers and principals is that what they look for in performance appraisal is contact with someone who has an interest in their work. It is the conferencing aspects, pre and post, that are crucial, in the eyes of these respondents. If this is accurate, it has a whole lot to say about how appraisal procedures should be carried out and about the supervisory roles. (Hickcox, 1990)

To be sure, as we shall see below, the role played by the dynamics of the relationship between supervisor and principal is crucial. Credibility, trust, openness, and willingness to share information appear to be integral components of especially growth-oriented appraisals.

Study Two: Cousins (1988)

Cousins' (1988) study inquired about factors that influence the use of performance-appraisal data for developmental purposes by school-leaders. Do principals use performance-appraisal data concerning their own performance? If so, under what conditions? The research consisted of three substudies conducted in sequence, each probing more deeply into the utilization process.

Substudy A: Current knowledge about evaluation utilization

In Substudy A (also reported by Cousins and Leithwood, 1986) we sought to develop a justifiable conception of how evaluative information (of any sort) is used and what determines the likelihood that it will be used. To do this, we reviewed and synthesized a large body of original research (eighty studies) under the general topic of 'evaluation utilization'. Most of these studies were about the use of information resulting from program, student, course, and curriculum evaluation; very few studies dealt with the use of personnel-evaluation data. Studies were identified through computer searches and bibliographic follow-up. Each study was systematically analyzed and information such as measures of use, variables affecting use, sample, instruments, theoretical framework, and results was summarized. As a product of this analysis, we constructed a framework (Figure 13.1) for understanding knowledge use that could be applied to the more specific domain of performance appraisal.

In this study 'utilization' meant both use for decision-making (instrumental use) and use for less direct, educative purposes (conceptual use). In our definition of use, we also included: just thinking about the information (cognitive processing) – a minimum condition for use. Two clusters of factors were identified as major influences on use: characteristics of how the evaluation is implemented and characteristics of the decision or policy setting. Factors associated with each of these categories include the following:

Characteristics of the Evaluation Implementation

- **Evaluation quality**:
  Characteristics of the evaluation process including its sophistication, rigor, availability of follow-up, and the like. An evaluation that attempts to link program components to program outcomes, for example, is considered to be more sophisticated than one that merely describes outcomes.
- **Credibility**:
  Credibility of the evaluator and/or the evaluation process defined by objectivity, believability, appropriateness of criteria, and so on. A well-seasoned evaluator with a proven track record is attributed higher levels of credibility than a novice, for example.
- **Relevance**:
  The extent to which the evaluation is relevant (usually meaning practical) to the needs of the audience. Do the purposes of the evaluation meet the explicit and implicit needs of the audience for whom the evaluation is conducted? Do evaluators working within the organization tend to produce evaluations that are more relevant?

- **Communication quality**:
  The clarity, style, readability, flair, and the like, with which the evaluation information is communicated to the intended audience. Communication can be oral, written, visual, and so forth and evaluator advocacy of findings and recommendations, and follow-up activities are activities that improve communication quality.
- **Findings**:
  The nature of the actual information (data) being disseminated: consistency with existing knowledge, congruence with expectations, positiveness, scope, value for decision-making, and the like.
- **Timeliness**:
  The extent to which evaluation information is disseminated in a timely fashion. Sometimes this means whether information is delivered in time for impending decisions or on an ongoing basis, depending upon purpose.

Characteristics of the Decision or Policy Setting

- **Information needs**:
  The type of information sought, number of evaluation audiences with differing information needs, time pressure, and perceived need for evaluation. To what extent are explicit and implicit needs for evaluation information shared among different audiences?
- **Decision characteristics**:
  Characteristics of decisions associated with the evaluation problem including decision-impact area, type of decision, program novelty, and significance of the decision, among other examples. Decisions regarding politically sensitive or controversial issues are of relatively high significance.
- **Political climate**:
  Characteristics associated with political climate such as political orientation of commissioners of the evaluation, dependence of decision makers on external sponsors, inter and intraorganizational rivalries, budget fights, and power struggles. Is it politically prudent for decision makers to decide in a manner that is consistent with the evaluation results?
- **Competing information**:
  Information from sources beyond the evaluation, relevant to the research problem and competing with evaluation data to inform decisions. Personal experience, informal observations made by decision makers, and 'working knowledge' are examples.
- **User's personal characteristics**:
  Decision makers' organizational role, information-processing style, organizational experience, and social characteristics, among other variables, fall into this category. Decision makers who carefully plan for the future and take preventative actions are distinguished from 'crisis managers' who operate on a more 'reactive' basis.
- **User's commitment/receptiveness to evaluation**:
  The extent to which decision makers are open-minded about decisions and about the evaluation findings. Are the decision makers dogmatic

217

about the decision? Are they predisposed to attitudes about the utility of evaluation?

Substudy B: Multiple-case study

In Substudy B, the framework was applied in an actual performance-appraisal setting. An independent judge (district adminstrator) selected principals in four elementary schools for the study. Two were selected because they were thought to be 'high users' of their own appraisal data, the remaining two were thought to be 'low users'. At each of the four schools we conducted interviews about the principal's actions. We talked with principals, vice-principals, superintendents, teachers, and parents with a reasonable knowledge of the principal's daily activities. The interviews and subsequent analyses of them were directly guided by the framework developed in the preceding study. We used analytic procedures outlined by Miles and Huberman (1984). Also, questions were asked about the performance-appraisal policy used to guide each principal's appraisal, in addition to its implementation and its usefulness to the principal (impact). We then attempted to identify factors that enhanced and/or inhibited impact.

The use of appraisal data by principals in this study was found to be, at best, only moderate. Very little conceptual development regarding performance improvement was observed, even though the data appeared to be taken seriously (e.g., processed) by principals. Learning that did occur was typically a reinforcement of the principals' existing knowledge as opposed to them learning something new. Speaking about a year-end summation of a specific appraisal, an appraiser said,

> I think the appraisal process was a confirmation of what [the principal] already thought. All we did was confirm each other's impressions in that experience. There were really no surprises.

Similarly, decisions based on appraisal data usually confirmed impressions about existing school-level programs and directions. A principal decided, for example, to carry on with staff-development initiatives focused on standardizing student evaluation within and across grades. In some instances, there were decisions to move in new directions. One principal decided to pursue Ontario supervisory-officer certification partially because of constant encouragement from her appraiser.

In sum, although principals tended to take the process seriously, they did not generally learn anything from, nor base decisions upon, appraisal information concerning their own performance. Why was this the case? Why didn't principals use appraisal data? As part of the answer, we found that principals' motivation, experience, and attitude toward appraisal limited learning attributable to it. According to one seasoned principal:

> I don't remember looking forward to the appraisal process as a learning experience for me. I looked forward knowing it was going to be there and very confident of the way it would be scored.

In contrast, a superintendent spoke of a somewhat less experienced and more motivated principal:

[The principal's] attitude is much more of 'What can I learn from the evaluation? Let's not even do the evaluation unless it's going to help me to do my job'.

Other reasons had to do with whether an open, honest, and trusting relationship existed between principal and appraiser. Principals who knew they would not be reprimanded for making mistakes were relatively open about discussing problems and ideas with supervisors. They felt confident that the purpose of the appraisal process was to help them to improve and were not concerned about things they had disclosed 'coming back' on them. Finally, the appraisers' persistence and the positive manner in which they communicated their findings had relatively small but positive effects on use.

Perhaps one of the more interesting findings of this study was that we identified variables that influenced use that could not readily be accommodated by our framework. These variables were associated with the relationship between appraiser and appraisal-subject, and had to do with trust and willingness to disclose performance-related information. It is likely that these variables emerged because the user of the appraisal information is also the focus for evaluation in a 'performance appraisal for improvement' context.

Substudy C: Statistical reanalysis

Finally, we wanted to assess the confidence one could have in the results of Substudy B by using independent data. In this study, we reanalyzed a set of questionnaire responses from almost 900 principals in the Lawton *et al.* (1986) study. As we noted earlier, one of the more dramatic findings of the survey was that although principals believed their appraisal policies to be fair and were reasonably satisfied with them, they were perceived to have little or no impact on performance.

From the survey data, we examined some of the findings from our multiple-case study by investigating relationships between measures of use and variables believed to affect them. We used LISREL (Joreskog and Sorbom, 1981, Version 6) to conduct path analyses on the survey data. Our knowledge-utilization framework and findings from Substudy B guided the statistical analyses. The markedly low degree to which appraisal data were used by principals for the purposes of performance improvement was confirmed by Substudy C. Such information was taken seriously but nothing much happened beyond that. The positive manner in which information was communicated to principals, and principals' positive attitudes or receptiveness to the process were found to lead to greater impact. Perhaps more to the point, where these variables were negative, use of the information was minimal or non-existent.

It is evident from these studies that although the context in which appraisal occurs is important, there are features associated with the implementation of performance-appraisal policies that can determine whether or not they contribute to the development of school-leaders. This is encouraging news for those responsible for implementing such policies. In addition, the studies underscore the need to work hard at developing positive interpersonal dynamics between supervisor and principal. Improvement along these lines seems likely to predict more effective growth-oriented appraisal practice.

Conclusion

The sequence of studies reported in the last half of this chapter offer promising insights regarding the improvement of school-leader appraisal practices. We leave a summary of these insights to the last part of the next chapter.

Chapter 14

Performance Appraisal and Selection of School-Leaders: Selection Processes and Measurement Issues

This chapter continues our analysis of how performance appraisal and selection processes can be carried out so as to contribute significantly to the development of future school-leaders. The first section of the chapter reviews research literature about selection processes using, as a framework, the same categories of activities which structured our analysis of appraisal processes: preparation, data collection, reporting and follow-up, evolution of policy, and impact. The second and third sections of the chapter explore, respectively, issues in measuring school-leader performance and guidelines for improving school-leader selection and appraisal.

The Current Status of School-Leader Selection Processes

Given the loss of leadership experienced by a school district as a consequence of a 'wrong' selection decision and the problems often associated with terminating or demoting individuals from a post, one would expect research on the topic to be extensive. However, our search located relatively little. Schmitt and Schechtman (1990) encountered the same vacuum in their evidently careful and thorough search: they were able to locate only six studies that reported predictive validity data; most of the empirical work they found was descriptive in nature. Two such studies (Baltzell and Dentler, 1983, Bryant, Lawlis, Nicholson and Maher, 1978) were included in our review. In a province-wide survey of practice in Ontario, Musella and Lawton (1986) analyzed both existing policies and documents concerned with the selection of school-leaders (as well as other roles), and survey data about policy implementation and impact. Archival data were obtained from ninety-nine of 136 districts in the Province, and 1353 department heads, vice-principals, principals, and district administrators submitted completed questionnaires.

Two other descriptive studies originated from the United Kingdom. Morgan, Hall and Mackay (1983) observed actual selection processes and conducted a comprehensive survey about secondary head-teacher selection practices in the UK. Elkins (1987) focused more directly on what appeared to be occurring at the level of the local education authority (LEA). In a study by Parkay and Currie (1989) desired and actual sources of support for secondary-school principals during selection and entry were examined. Several other studies dealt specifically with the use of assessment-center technology in the selection and development of school administrators (Allison and Allison, 1989, 1990, Allison 1989, Bryant, 1990, Gomez and Stephenson, 1987, Milestein and Fiedler, 1989; Nagy and Allison, 1988, Schmitt, Noe, Meritt, Fitzgerald and Jorgensen n.d., Schmitt, Noe, Meritt and Fitzgerald, 1984, Tracy and Schuttenberg, 1989) or with other issues such as effective criteria (Gips, 1985) and comparative cost effectiveness of alternative approaches to selection (Hogan and Zenke, 1986). Finally, some authors provided models of selection processes for school administrators based on practical experience (Musella, 1983, Parkay, 1987). A particularly interesting approach to selection was described in detail by Jantz, Hellervik and Gilmore (1986). These authors developed a technique called 'behavior-description interviewing'. Although designed for application in business and industry, this technique has significant implications for selection of school-leaders. Jantz *et al.* provided a research-based argument for their set of procedures.

Preparation

Based on available evidence, school-leader selection procedures are typically multi-step processes. A pool of aspirants become applicants and enter what Musella (1983) called a 'decision-point funnel' with fewer and fewer individuals achieving candidate, and eventually 'selected' status. In the UK this process was described as long-listing, short-listing, preliminary interview, and final interview (Morgan *et al.*, 1983).

There appeared to be considerable variation in selection processes across districts (Baltzell and Dentler, 1983, Schmitt and Schechtman, 1990). In Ontario, for example, the process ranged from a single interview with the chief education officer (a rather short funnel) to very elaborate, structured procedures that might include mandatory participation in locally sponsored leadership courses or attendance at assessment centers (Musella and Lawton, 1986). Considerable variation across districts also exists in terms of the decision mechanisms installed at each critical point in the funnel. Depending upon supply and demand, the majority of applicants were 'screened out' at very early stages of the process. Elkins (1987) reported that up to 80 percent of applicants were eliminated after the first screen in at least one LEA in the UK.

Musella and Lawton (1986) reported that written policies and procedures were more prevalent in Ontario for principal and vice-principal selection than for any other role. Most such documents had been developed only recently, however. In the UK, the written description of selection policies and procedures was much less prevalent. Many of the processes observed were fairly unsystematic and non-explicit. There appeared to be a focus on individualism and 'felt need' supporting the selection of teachers for specific schools (Morgan *et al.*, 1983). Elkins' (1987) data confirmed these findings. He argued that the typically consensual process of developing a profile of the ideal applicant was of questionable validity. Criteria for selection were often obscure or only loosely defined in current practice. Frequently used criteria included biographical information, career track record, communication and interpersonal skills, knowledge of administration, knowledge of the position, education/training, and appropriate philosophy of education (Baltzell and Dentler, 1983, Bryant *et al.*, 1978, Elkins, 1987, Morgan *et al.*, 1983, Musella and Lawton, 1986, Schmitt and Schechtman, 1990). Many of these indicators have been criticized as being 'inevitably subjective' (Morgan, *et al.*, 1983, p. 58) and poor predictors of successful future performance (Jantz *et al.*, 1986, Parkay, 1987). There is considerable support for use of criteria that are more job relevant and directly linked to performance in the role. Indeed, the courts' insistence on such criteria have finessed professional deliberations on this matter. Several authors advocate the use of systematic and thorough position analysis as a way of identifying such criteria (Jantz *et al.*, 1986, Musella, 1983, Parkay, 1987). Analysis of this sort, it is claimed, would inform the interviewer about what to look for, ensure that all important dimensions of performance are covered, and reduce the likelihood that selection is based upon an unjustifiably narrow set of criteria (Parkay, 1987).

Assessment centers have become quite popular in the US, parts of Canada, and elsewhere. They are used by many districts as part of the school-leader selection process. One model of the assessment-center concept designed especially for school-leaders has been developed by the National Association of Secondary School Principals (NASSP). Versions of this model are now being implemented in over fifty locations in the US and Canada. Their features, advantages and disadvantages have been described in detail (e.g., Allison, 1989, Gomez and Stephenson, 1987, Hersey, 1986, Milstein and Fiedler, 1989, Schmitt *et al.*, n.d., Schmitt *et al.*, 1984). Participants' responses to a series of simulated school-administration tasks are evaluated by a panel of trained assessors. Principles of performance-based evaluation and high objectivity lie at the heart of the assessment-center concept.

The tasks and assessment procedures associated with NASSP centers (see Figure 14.1) were developed around a set of twelve criteria or dimensions of performance which emerged from an extensive job-analysis study conducted in the United States. While job analysis is a systematic way of identifying criteria, it has not gone without criticism. For example, the content validity of the NASSP assessment-center dimensions or criteria have been the subject of debate. The results of several studies appear to support claims that these criteria are valid reflections of expert school leadership (e.g., Schmitt *et al.*, 1984, Gomez and Stephenson, 1987) but concerns persist, nevertheless. Allison (1989, p. 4), for example, suggested that 'scholars inclined toward more global conceptions of administration ... might well take serious issue with the conceptual framework'. Bryant (1990, pp. 358–9) claimed that:

> If the NASSP Assessment Center is to be trusted as an employment screen, it should be able to capture the accumulation of expertise that ... is the logical by-product of the knowledge gained through varied and repetitive experience. The results of the investigator's analysis ... would suggest that the NASSP Assessment Center does not capture the assumed expertise (experience) possessed by participants on many dimensions.

Another concern regarding the NASSP dimensions of performance has to do with the method used to derive them. The use of job-analysis technology entails the generation of a comprehensive list of relevant dimensions of performance,

Figure 14.1:   *Assessment-center dimensions and descriptions*

---

1.   Problem analysis: Ability to seek out relevant data and analyze complex information to determine the important elements of a problem situation; searching for information with a purpose.

2.   Judgment: Skill in identifying educational needs and setting priorities; ability to reach logical conclusions and make high-quality decisions based on available information; ability to evaluate critically written communications.

3.   Organizational ability: Ability to plan, schedule, and control the work of others; skill in using resources in an optimal fashion; ability to deal with a volume of paper work and heavy demands on one's time.

4.   Decisiveness: Ability to recognize when a decision is required and to act quickly (without an assessment of the quality of the decision).

5.   Leadership: Ability to recognize when a group requires direction, to get others involved in solving problems, to interact effectively with a group, to guide them to the accomplishment of a task.

6.   Sensitivity: Ability to perceive the needs, concerns, and personal problems of others; tact in dealing with persons from different backgrounds; skill in resolving conflicts; ability to deal effectively with people concerning emotional issues; knowing what information to communicate and to whom.

7.   Range of interests: Competence to discuss a variety of subjects (educational, political, economic, etc.); desire to actively participate in events.

8.   Personal motivation: Showing that work is important to personal satisfaction; a need to achieve in all activities attempted; ability to be self-policing.

9.   Educational values: Possession of well-reasoned education; philosophy; receptiveness to change and new ideas.

10.   Stress tolerance: Ability to perform under pressure and opposition; ability to think on one's feet.

11.   Oral-communication skills: Ability to make a clear oral presentation of ideas and facts.

12.   Written-communication skills: Ability to express ideas clearly in writing; to write appropriately for different audiences such as students, teachers, parents, or other administrators.

Source: Schmitt *et. al.* (1984) *Journal of Applied Psychology*

which are then rated for importance by a representative sample of job incumbents. A potential problem with this method lies in the sampling strategy. Failure to distinguish between expert and non-expert job incumbents means that ratings of importance reflect the views of non-expert to expert school-leaders with the weight of opinion favoring the non-experts, since experts, as we have defined them in this book, usually represent only a small proportion of the school-leader population. This was the case in the development of the NASSP framework. It is considerably more desirable to derive importance ratings from expert job incumbents, especially when the purpose is the selection of future leaders. Results of the type of research reported in earlier chapters of this book (especially Chapters 5 and 6) provide, in our view, a more viable source of criteria for the selection of future school-leaders. While the research directly supports the validity of some of the NASSP criteria appearing in Figure 14.1 (e.g., problem analysis) and rules out very few, it also identifies criteria which do not appear in Figure 14.1 or are not given adequate weight: for example, in the case of high-ground expertise, goals [or vision] and the extensive knowledge of curriculum and instruction subsumed by factors.

Nonetheless, the NASSP criteria are the result of a systematic attempt to move away from less well grounded criteria often used for selection purposes. Assessment centers are growing in popularity and recent evidence suggests that they are used for development purposes (e.g., Milestein and Fiedler 1989, Tracy and Schuttenberg, 1989). Further, they are rarely the only source of evidence used for the purpose of selection (Allison and Allison, 1990, Hersey, 1986).

Data Collection

Although a wide variety of data appear to be gathered for the purpose of school-leader selection, the interview is clearly the most popular source of information for making decisions about candidates (Baltzell and Dentler, 1983, Bryant *et al.*, 1978, Morgan *et al.*, 1983, Musella and Lawton, 1986, Schmitt and Schechtman, 1990). Interviews were found to be used quite extensively at both short-listing and final-decision points. While many districts undoubtedly utilize structured interview questions that are applied to all candidates, open-ended or unstructured interviews are still fairly common in practice. Morgan *et al.* (1983) observed a considerable amount of unstructured interviewing in their study in the UK. Baltzell and Dentler (1983) also reported substantial variation in interview structure over school districts in the US.

The dangers in using unstructured interviews have been well documented (Jantz *et al.*, 1986, Morgan *et al.*, 1983). A tendency to rely on subjective criteria and to collect data that are not comparable across candidates are the two chief concerns. The use of structured interviews, as a minimum, helps to ensure that comparable data are collected.

Next to personal interviews, resumes and references appeared to be the sources of information with the highest perceived value to selectors (Baltzell and Dentler, 1983, Musella and Lawton, 1986, Schmitt and Schechtman, 1990). Other sources included application forms (usually requiring education, experience, and certification information), written statements by candidates about their personal philosophy of education, and schedules and summary sheets. Bryant *et al.* (1978) reported that superintendents ascribed importance to neat, grammatical, business-like letters of application.

No research evidence was available about current practice to suggest that standardized instruments were being used to measure potential expertise in the school-leader role. However, several such instruments have been developed in recent years (e.g., Cousins and Leithwood, 1987a, Hallinger and Murphy, 1985, Ellett, 1978, Vandenberghe, 1988). While many of these (often behavior rating scales) instruments have been designed specifically for appraisal (and research) purposes, they offer promise as screening mechanisms in school-leader selection (more on this in the next section of this chapter).

In NASSP assessment centers, assessors observe a small number of candidates performing various tasks under very intense circumstances, usually for about a two-day period. Then, individually and collectively, assessors review data for each candidate and develop a consensus about his or her performance. Candidates are assigned scores on each of the twelve performance dimensions and a summary score is calculated. Although not as high as for assessment centers in business and industry, 'inter-rater' reliability for performance judgments was reported to be quite high (Schmitt *et al.*, n.d.).

Who is involved in the selection process? There is considerable variation within and across districts regarding those responsible for selection, variation which depends upon the point in the decision-making funnel. Musella and Lawton (1986) observed that prior to having one's application for a formal school-leadership position taken seriously, a favorable recommendation from the applicant's current principal must have been submitted. They also noted that in some cases 'pre-consideration interviews' might be held. From that point, selection committees consisting of district administrators, current school-leaders, trustees and even CEOs assumed responsibility for coordinating the selection process. Final decisions about candidates were most often made by elected officials or by the CEO with trustee approval.

Evidence from US research suggested that the final decision also rested with the CEO, with rather unstructured screening processes being conducted by personnel directors and senior assistants to the CEO (Baltzell and Dentler, 1983, Bryant, *et al.*, 1978, Schmitt and Schechtman, 1990). Similarly, in the UK, elected LEA members, governors, and advisory officers were typically involved in the selection process (Morgan *et al.*, 1983). The extent to which advisory officers had selection as part of their portfolio was found to vary across systems. Different selector groups were found to be active at different 'stages of elimination'. Sometimes this resulted in a completely new group of selectors being present for the final phases of the selection process (Elkins, 1987, Morgan *et al.*, 1983). Candidates might have been required to face a panel of up to thirty selectors. Generally, CEOs and governors assumed responsibility for final decisions about head-teachers' appointments.

In the case of assessment centers, assessors were typically district administrators from the school systems that were active members of the centre. Indeed, such contribution of district-administrator time was usually a requirement of membership. This requirement helped to ensure that assessors were never responsible for assessing someone from their own district, thus reducing various types of potential bias in the process. The extent to which these data were used for selection was quite variable, as well as who at the system level was responsible for evaluating the information (Allison and Allison, 1990). As noted earlier, when assessment-center data were used for selection purposes, such data were among a larger set collected from other sources too.

Reporting and Follow-up

We have noted that selection decisions were usually made by trustees, CEOs and other district administrators. Procedures for reporting such decisions were varied, depending upon the needs of the district and the decision process in place. Personnel files, with accumulated bits of information about candidates and sometimes summary sheets, were used to support the final decision-making process. The extent to which these documents convey the most useful information about candidates can be limited. This was especially the case where those making the final selection decisions did not participate in earlier stages of data collection and decision-making (Morgan *et al.*, 1983).

Jantz *et al.* (1986) called for the systematization of note-taking during the selection process. They recommend that notes be reviewed and clarified after each interview and that some measure of standardization over candidates is practiced. With the exception of assessment centers, we were unable to find evidence of such practice in the current literature on school-leader selection. Following the assessment process, assessors typically reached agreement on a candidate's performance and a standardized summary report was prepared. The report was shared with the candidate and with the sponsoring school-system officials. Musella (1983) advocated the use of training in the selection process at three different levels. First, training should be provided for those aspiring to the role. Second, training or debriefing should be provided for those who have been screened out of the process so that they can work toward developing the required qualities for future consideration. Finally, training should be provided on an ongoing basis for candidates once they are selected. Parkay and Currie (1989) provided evidence revealing that principals perceived a gap in the availability of such training opportunities. The extent to which such training occurred is unclear. Musella and Lawton (1986), on the other hand, found that several Ontario districts have their own training programs designed to develop leadership among their own staffs. The quality of these programs, however, remains unclear. Some districts sent candidates to assessment centers for the purpose of professional development, as reported earlier. Also, as described in Chapter 11, some regions in Canada required certification for the principalship prior to securing such a position. On the other hand, Elkins (1987) found that very few candidates for head-teacher ever began their teaching career with such a goal in mind and that teachers usually had very little knowledge about what heads did, let alone how to prepare for the role. Training opportunities appeared to be very limited for those aspiring to the role of head-teacher in the UK. Current research revealed that very little follow-up of this nature was occurring in practice.

Evolution of Policy

There was little evidence about how selection policies were developed, who participated in their development and whether they were subject to review and revision. As mentioned earlier, Musella and Lawton (1986) found that documentation for school-leader selection was more prevalent than for any other role in Ontario. With respect to the UK, we were unable to find evidence of change since the rather dismal picture provided by Morgan *et al.* (1983). There appeared to be a strong need to integrate, into existing policy and practice, a review mechanism consciously to examine the utility and effectiveness of school-leader selection.

Impact

Two questions are central to considerations about the impact of selection procedures: 'To what extent do data derived from the selection process support the
decisions made?' and 'To what extent does the information gathered and used for
decision-making predict success in the role at a later point in time?'

On the first question, there was substantial variation depending upon the
sophistication of the process used. Where criteria were not well specified and data
were not systematically processed, the influences of local political processes,
patronage, favoritism, and individual advocacy remained unchecked (Baltzell and
Dentler, 1983, Elkins, 1987, Morgan *et al.*, 1983). Where use was made of more
explicit processes with multiple decision points, checks, balances, and provisions
for data integration, it was likely that more objective, fair, and valid decisions
were going to result (Musella, 1983, Parkay, 1987). Inasmuch as non-job-related
criteria are in frequent use, we can assume that the quality of data for selection
purposes often will predict future performance on the job very poorly indeed.
Elkins (1987) reported this to be the case especially for the early screening stage
of the selection process. Jantz *et al.* (1986) described the inadequacy of such
criteria as biographical facts, technical knowledge, experience and activity descriptions, and self-evaluative statements. They claimed that grounding criteria in
the performance base of candidates will improve substantially the predictive
validity of selection data.

As we indicated above, the predictive validity of NASSP assessment-center
data has been the object of considerable debate. While some concluded that the
predictive validity of the centers has been demonstrated to be satisfactory (Gomez
and Stephenson, 1987, Hersey, 1986, Schmitt, *et al.*, n.d., Schmitt *et al.*, 1984),
others remained skeptical (Allison, 1989, Bryant, 1990). However, an additional
chief concern corresponding to the utility of assessment centers for selection
purposes has to do with costs (Milestein and Fiedler, 1989). Costs to individual
systems were substantial, given fees for candidates and the time requirements of
providing assessors. Hogan and Zenke (1986) conducted a cost-benefit analysis
that favored the use of assessment centers and performance-assessment tasks for
selection purposes as compared to traditional interviews and paper and pencil
inventories. The estimate of predictive validity they used in their formula seems
substantially higher than estimates reported elsewhere, however. Allison and
Allison (1990) reported that school systems were not often in a fiscal position to
send all potential candidates for selection to assessment centers and, as a consequence, the use of such data for selection purposes became highly limited. The
developmental benefits of assessment centers may outweigh their use as aids to
the selection process. Clearly, reports from candidates (Allison and Allison, 1989,
Nagy and Allison, 1988, Tracy and Schuttenberg, 1989) and personnel of school
systems sponsoring candidates (Allison and Allison, 1990) tended to support this
claim. As yet, there was limited systematic evidence to support this claim (e.g.,
Tracy and Schuttenberg, 1989).

Summary

The review of evidence concerning current school-leader selection processes
paints a bleak picture of such processes. Under typical circumstances, for exam-

ple, selection processes may include the use of inappropriate, ambiguous and/or invalid criteria, and the collection of data which are both an unreliable and invalid reflection of such criteria. Assessment-center processes, especially those developed by NASSP, offer promising responses to the limitations of typical selection processes. In practice, however, assessment centers are subject to criticisms, especially regarding their choice of criteria and the predictive validity of their results. Perhaps of even more consequence is their cost, which is clearly prohibitive to many districts.

While the review of current selection practices in this section of the chapter contains a number of implications for improvement, much work needs to be done before selection processes can be relied on to contribute to the development of leadership expertise in future schools. At the heart of much of this work are a series of issues regarding the measurement of school-leader expertise: these issues, of course, are also important to performance-appraisal processes.

Measuring School-Leader Expertise

In this section, current approaches to measuring school-leader expertise are described. This is followed by an analysis of several especially critical measurement issues. We then examine in more detail the measurement of expertise on the high ground. Research to validate one instrument, the Principal Profile-Based Instrument (PPBI), is summarized briefly and the advantages of the instrument are noted. Finally, an agenda for further development work in this area is outlined. Special attention is given to the challenges of assessing expertise in the swamp. Those readers less interested in the inherently technical issues explored here may wish to skip directly to 'Implications for Improvement'.

Instruments for Measuring School-Leader Expertise

Ginsberg and Berry (1990) identified instruments and approaches that have been used in the selection and appraisal of school-leaders. Undoubtedly their sample was incomplete because thousands of school districts have developed their own check-lists and inventories and only a fraction of these are reported in the research or professional literature.

Our search for existing instruments was guided by two criteria. The report had to:

- show that the instrument was either designed for, or adaptable to the problem of school-leader assessment
- describe the instrument in terms of its
  - format
  - origins and/or development, and
  - psychometric properties (however meager the description).

Using these criteria, fourteen instruments, aspects of which are described in Table 14.1, were identified primarily through a computerized (ERIC) search and bibliographic follow-up. While this set of fourteen is clearly not exhaustive, it is

Table 14.1: *Instrument for measuring school-leader expertise*

Source(s)	Instrument	Description	Validity	Reliability	Comments
Andrews, Soder and Jacoby (1986)	1. Staff-Assessment Questionnaire (SAQ)	– 19 items from 167-item questionnaire – 5 point scale	– Based on review of instructional leadership literature (Moderate)	Alpha = 0.93 (High)	
Cousins and Leithwood (1987a) Cousins (1989)	2. Principal Profile-Based Instrument (PPBI)	– 68 items – BARS – 4 subscales – 6 point scale	– Based on Principal Profile – Effectiveness research, – literature review, empirical validation (Moderate – High)	Alpha = 0.98 Subscales 0.91 to 0.96 (High)	Requires further empirical validation
Ebmeier and Wilson (1989)	3. School-Principal Effectiveness-Diagnostic Instrument	– 5 questionnaires (student, staff, parent, principal, supervisor) – 213 items – 5 and 6 point scales	– Based on conceptual framework and subjective determination of items (Moderate – Low)	Projected to be 0.80+ (Inconclusive)	Still in early development stage
Ellett (1978)	4. Principal-Performance Description Survey (PPDS)	– 4 questionnaires (principal, teacher, external, observer, supervisor) – 100 items	– Based on extensive content-validation procedure – job analysis (Moderate)	Not reported	
Hallinger and Murphy (1985, 1987)	5. Principal Instructional Management-Rating Scale (PIMRS)	– 71 items – BARS – 11 subscales – 5 point scale	– Based on review of literature on instructional leadership – empirical validation (High)	Alpha = 0.75+ (Moderate – High)	

Citation	No.	Instrument	Description	Validity	Reliability	Purpose
Knoop and Common (1985)	6.	Performance-Review Analysis and Improvement System for Education (PRAISE)	– 81 items – 9 subscales – 5 point scale	– Based on review of effectiveness literature and extensive content-validation procedure (High)	Alpha = 0.88 to 0.98 Test-retest 0.59 to 0.80 (Moderate – High)	
Krysinski et al. (1987)	7.	N/A	– 34 items – 5 point scale	– Based on Power theoretical framework of Spady and Mitchell (1977) (Inconclusive)	Test-retest and expert-novice data reported in non-traditional manner (Inconclusive)	– for use in analyzing responses to performance-assessment tasks
Larsen (1987) reported in Heck et al. (1990)	8.	Instructional Activity Questionnaire	– 34 items – 3 subscales – 5 point scale	– Based on review of literature and empirical validation (Moderate – High)	Alpha = 0.7 to 0.9 (Moderate – High)	
Leithwood and Montgomery (1986), Leithwood (1987)	9.	Principal Profile	– Multidimensional, multi-staged description of growth in practice – interview-assessment technique	– Based on review of literature and empirical validation (Moderate – High)	Inter-rater agreement 0.50 to 1.00 (Moderate – High)	– for use primarily as a diagnostic tool
Leithwood and Steinbach (1990)	10.	N/A	– Performance-assessment instrument for rating response to problem-solving tasks – 4 point scale – holistic ratings by 2 experts	– Showed past intervention gain in problem-solving skill (Inconclusive)	Inter-rater agreement 71% to 95% (Moderate – High)	– for use in analyzing responses to performance-assessment tasks

Table 14.1 (cont.)

Source(s)	Instrument	Description	Validity	Reliability	Comments
Pitner and Hocevar (1987)	11. Yukl's Management-Behavior Survey	– 115 items – 23 subscales – 5 point scale	– 9 subscales eliminated due to non-response – confirmatory factor validity established (Moderate)	Alpha = 0.78 to 0.93 (Moderate – High)	Instrument adapted from business and industry
Tucker and Bray (1986)	12. Profile for the Assessment of Leaders (PAL)	– 88 items – 8 subscales	– Items drawn from initial list of 10,000+ – empirical validation (teachers, principals) (Moderate)	Not reported	Items initially drawn from behaviors identified by Project ROME (Ellett, 1978)
Valentine and Bowman (1986)	13. Audit of Principal Effectiveness	– 80 items – 3 domains – 9 subscales	– Review of literature (not cited) – factor validity (Inconclusive)	Alpha = 0.79 to 0.93 (Moderate – High)	
Vandenberghe (1988)	14. Change-Facilitator Style Questionnaire (CFSQ)	– 77 items – 3 domains – 6 subscales – 6 point scale	– Based on policy implementation literature – empirical validation – factor validity (Moderate – High)	Alpha = 0.64 to 0.95 (Moderate)	

probably sufficiently representative of the field to sustain our subsequent observations.

All fourteen of the instruments examined have been developed in recent years. The Principal Performance Description Survey (PPDS) reported upon by Ellett (1978) was the earliest to be developed of the instruments (4 in Table 14.1) that came to our attention. The majority of the instruments were rating scales and most had versions designed for self-ratings and for ratings of school-leaders by others such as teachers, superordinates, parents and students. The ratings are generally 'Lickert' type scales ranging from 4 to 6 points. Some instruments take the form of behavior-observation scales (BOS) (e.g., Cousins and Leithwood, 1987a, Hallinger and Murphy, 1985; 2 and 5 in Table 14.1) while others included ratings of attitudes, competencies or knowledge. Two instruments (Krysinski, Reed, Gougeon and Armstrong, 1987, Leithwood and Steinbach, 1990; 7 and 10) were designed specifically for the purpose of helping to assess the performance of school-leaders on simulated tasks.

There was considerable variation in the length and comprehensiveness of the instruments. Some were quite long (e.g., 115 items, Ellett, 1978, 100 items, Pitner and Hocevar, 1987; 4 and 11) but the average length was between sixty to ninety items. Others consisted of a battery of questionnaires designed for completion by different groups of raters (e.g., Ebmeier and Wilson, 1989, Ellett, 1978; 3 and 4) Most also had several subscales corresponding to dimensions or components of school-leader expertise.

Validity data were highly variable. At least two different approaches to the question of content validity were employed. Some instrument developers focused on effective school-leader practices identified through reviews of effectiveness literature (e.g., Andrews, Soder and Jacoby, 1986; 1) or empirical validation employing panels of 'experts' as judges of content (e.g., Cousins and Leithwood, 1987a, Larsen, 1987; 2 and 8). Other developers derived sets of items from reviews of research and obtained ratings of importance from representative samples of practitioners including supervisors, principals, and teachers (e.g., Ellett, 1978, Hallinger and Murphy, 1985, Knoop and Common, 1985; 4, 5 and 6). Yet others relied on statistical validation usually employing exploratory factor analysis (e.g., Knoop and Common, 1985 Valentine and Bowman, 1986, Vandenberghe, 1988; 6, 13 and 14) to make decisions about how variables clustered together. Pitner and Hocevar (1987; 11) used confirmatory factor analysis, a procedure that requires *a priori* decisions about factor structure and variable loadings. Some developers were less rigorous in their pursuit of validity evidence and were content to generate and informally field-test items based upon a conceptual framework (e.g., Ebmeier and Wilson, 1989; 3). Several studies employed tests of different types of validity including content, construct and discriminant validities (Cousins, 1989, Hallinger and Murphy, 1985; 2 and 5).

The reliability of these instruments was generally found to be quite good, but often this could be attributed to the large number of items and raters in the sample. Internal consistency using Cronbach's Alpha was the most popular test of reliability. Coefficients ranged from about the 0.70 to 0.95+ range with some variation over subscales. In some cases, reliability data were not reported (e.g., Ellett, 1978, Tucker and Bray, 1986; 4 and 12) or were reported in a casual manner (Krysinski *et al.*, 1987; 7). In other cases, test-retest reliability was reported (e.g., Knoop and Common, 1985; 6). None of the reports cited inter-rater reliability analyses.

Most developers claimed multiple purposes for their instruments such as research, appraisal, and selection. Some instruments were designed specifically for the purpose of providing diagnostic information for growth (Leithwood and Montgomery, 1986, Leithwood, 1987; 9). Other instruments were designed as aids for the analysis of performance data (e.g., Krysinski *et al.*, 1987, Leithwood and Steinbach, 1990; 7 and 10).

Key Issues in the Measurement of School-Leader Expertise

While there appear to be a number of promising instruments to help in the selection and appraisal of school-leaders, careful attention needs to be devoted to some of the limitations and potential dangers in such use.

The Joint Committee on Standards for Educational Evaluation has recently published a set of standards for personnel evaluation practice (Joint Committee, 1988). Prior to this publication, we participated in the public hearings' process coordinated by the Joint Committee (Cousins and Leithwood, 1987b). This participation gave us the opportunity to compare a pre-publication version of the standards against, among other things, the knowledge-utilization framework described in Chapter 13 (see Figure 13.1). Figure 14.2 summarizes the results of our comparison of the standards against our knowledge-utilization framework and demonstrates a high level of consistency between the two.[1]

Most of the standards apply to and can be categorized according to the appraisal-implementation dimension of the knowledge-utilization framework. Also, most are associated with factors that have a direct connection to measurement issues, specifically accuracy standards such as valid measurement, reliable measurement, systematic data control, sufficient sample of performance (this standard has since been deleted by the Joint Committee), biased control, and defined role. Several of the utility standards, further, are associated with factors from the implementation dimension of the knowledge-utilization framework including defined uses, valuational interpretation, and evaluator credibility.

However terse, this analysis supports the use of the standards to assist in improving the measurement of school-leader expertise, improving not only reliability and validity but also impact (use). But the task of measuring school-leader expertise is complex, and 'measuring up' to the standards set by the Joint Committee will not be easy. We turn now to a more direct examination of some key issues involved in achieving such a goal.

Definition and specification of what is to be measured
Murphy (1988) provided a comprehensive analysis of problems involved in measuring instructional leadership. Many of the instruments that were described earlier, as well as the criteria employed by the NASSP assessment centers were based on job-analysis techniques, an approach that Murphy considered to be flawed for two reasons. First, the results of job analysis often do not provide clear definition of the qualities required of the job. Second, instruments based on job analysis are unrelated to any coherent theory of expert practice. This second problem is likely to be the more serious. Unclear definition of job qualities influences instrument reliability but the reliability of at least the instruments which were reviewed earlier in this chapter was quite high. Lack of a coherent

Figure 14.2: Personnel evaluation standards by knowledge-utilization factors

Evaluation-implementation Factors

1) Evaluation quality	F-1 Practical procedures
	A-4 Valid measurement
	A-5 Reliable measurement
	A-6 Systematic data control
2) Credibility	U-3 Evaluator credibility
	* Valuational interpretation
	* Sufficient sample of performance
	A-7 Biased control
3) Relevance	U-2 Defined uses
	* Valuational interpretation
	A-1 Defined role
4) Communication quality	U-4 Functional reporting
5) Timeliness	U-4 Functional reporting
	U-5 Follow-up and impact
6) Nature of results (Findings)	U-1 Constructive orientation
	U-5 Follow-up and impact

Decision or Policy-setting factors

1) Information needs	U-2 Defined uses
2) Significance of decision (Decision characteristics)	None
3) Political climate	F-2 Political viability
	P-3 Conflict of interest
4) Competing information	A-2 Work environment
5) Personal characteristics	None
6) User commitment	None

Appraiser/evaluation-subject dynamics | F-2 Political viability
| | P-5 Interaction with subjects of evaluation

Note: *From previous draft of The Standards
Source: Adapted from Cousins and Leithwood (1987b) JCSEV, Washington, DC

theory, however, calls into question the construct validity of instruments. According to Murphy, the job-analysis approach yields lists of variables that are descriptive of 'typical' practice. If there is a need to measure expert practice, a conception of such expertise is needed to generate items for the instrument. Hence, instrument development will need to include, as part of the process of reviews, research on expertise and/or empirical validation using panels of experts. A coherent conception of expert school leadership such as that provided in Chapters 5, 6 and 7 should form the basis of any instrument to be used for the purpose of measuring school-leadership expertise.

Assessment
Murphy (1988) also expressed concerns about the use of behavior-based instruments in isolation. Results of such instruments alone ignore the contextual realities of schools. Organizational conditions, symbolic and cultural activities, and established organizational routines are important parameters of the school-leader's role which should be considered in concert with instrument data. Failure to do so may give a distorted impression of a school-leader's true expertise.

Two other issues concerning assessment are also worth noting. First, as Hazi

(1989) reminded us, there is a tendency to trivialize our conception of performance in complex roles and to fall prey to the illusion that instruments are error free. Instruments do involve human judgment and subjectivity does enter into the processes of administering an instrument. This underscores the need to collect multiple types of data from multiple sources. No single measure of a schoolleader's expertise is likely to be a truly valid picture of his or her capabilities. Second, and more fundamentally, it is necessary to consider those aspects of school leadership that do and do not lend themselves to measurement. Consider, for example, aspects of expertise on the high ground. Strategies used by schoolleaders and elements of their decision-making are more directly suited to measurement with the kinds of instruments that are currently available. But when the focus shifts to other aspects of expertise – the nature and role of values, for example – what are the implications for measurement? A call for a fundamental shift in our approach to the measurement problem, one that adheres to performance-assessment technologies is supported.

Potential for misuse

Cousins, Begley and Leithwood (1988) have explored the question of potential misuse of instruments for the purposes of school-leader selection and appraisal. Given the information needs of decision makers and the need of school-leaders for professional development, what are the possible or probable misuses of available instruments? A useful framework for responding to this question was provided by Alkin and Coyle (1988). Patton (1988), (cited by Alkin and Coyle) identified two dimensions relevant to our analysis of this question: utilization and misutilization. Utilization of performance data varies from use for decisionmaking or conceptual development (depending on purpose) at one extreme and non-utilization (e.g., failure for users to process data) at the other. Similarly, variation in misuse may be plotted along a continuum ranging from misutilization to justifiable action.[2] As a heuristic for differentiating types of misuse, it might be helpful to consider these dimensions to be completely independent of one another as shown in Figure 14.3.

Alkin and Coyle (1988) described several distinct variations of misutilization. Data derived from an instrument may be expected to vary in technical quality. It may be more or less free of measurement error (reliable), and derived from multiple raters such as school-leaders, district administrators, and teachers (valid). If information about an individual is known to be of superior technical quality but is suppressed by a potential user (e.g., selection-committee member) for whatever reason, we have an instance of what Alkin and Coyle refer to as *abuse*: a clear case of non-utilization of the data that can readily be described as misutilization.

But some instances of non-utilization may be legitimate. For example, if a selector was aware that the results of an assessment were technically flawed or erroneous, he or she would be justified in not incorporating the information into the selection process. This would constitute an example of *justified non-use*, an appropriate and responsible action. If, on the other hand, the data are of sufficient technical quality but potential users are unaware of their existence, or inadvertently fail to process the information, this is a case of *unintentional non-use*. While this is not misutilization, it is certainly not a desirable outcome.

The best possible outcome is one in which good-quality instrument data are

Figure 14.3:   Conception of misutilization

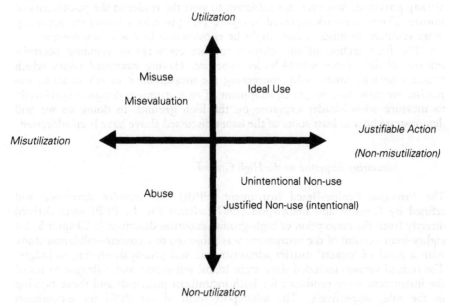

Source: Adapted from Alkin and Coyle (1988), *Studies in Educational Evaluation.*

thought about by users and subsequently lead to further conceptual development of the users and/or assist them in making specific decisions. This would be use in the *ideal*. A less satisfactory, but nonetheless legitimate form of use, would be for potential users to actively think about the meaning of data provided through an instrument but, subsequently, not to learn from them nor base decisions upon them. Such use can be quite legitimate. For example, a school-leader might fully understand the information provided by an instrument used in his or her apprais-al but consider it 'old news'. There is nothing new to be learned that would be helpful in fostering further self development.

Finally, Alkin and Coyle differentiated between two types of misutilization when data are processed. The first they described as *misuse*, a term that corres-ponds to the deliberate manipulation of, say, instrument scores to serve some particular purpose (e.g., support or non-support for a school-leader candidate). Clearly, this situation is an example of intentional misutilization of the data, since the data are used in an inappropriate fashion. The second type of misutilization is *misevaluation*. One type of misevaluation occurs when test developers do not take the necessary steps to prevent misutilization. Incomplete scoring information, absence of normative data, poor administrative instructions, and the like, are possible sources of error that could ultimately lead to misevaluation. Of course, the responsibility for misevaluation need not necessarily reside with the instru-ment developer. Misevaluation could be the result of careless instrument admin-istration, scoring, and the like. Cousins *et al.* (1988) identified a number of additional, potential misuses of data about school-leader expertise. The examples already provided, however, are sufficient to alert the reader to the possibilities of misuse. The framework captured in Figure 14.3 provides a means for becoming more sensitive to misuses that might be encountered in one's own context.

The final section of this chapter touches on ways of avoiding potential misuses of data about school-leader expertise. Having examined issues which appear especially noteworthy concerning the measurement of school-leader expertise, we now turn to the development of an instrument designed specifically to measure school-leader expertise on the high ground. In doing so we will demonstrate how at least some of the issues discussed above have been addressed.

Measuring Expertise on the High Ground

The Principal Profile-Based Instrument (PPBI) was initially developed and refined by Cousins and Leithwood (1987a). Items for the PPBI were derived directly from the conception of high-ground expertise described in Chapter 5. An eighty-item version of the instrument was subjected to a content-validation study with a panel of 'expert' district administrators and principals serving as judges. The refined version included sixty-eight items; self-report and colleague forms of the instrument were produced for both incumbent principals and those aspiring to the role, respectively. The self-report form of the PPBI for incumbents appears in Appendix A. We consider this version of the instrument to be 'content valid': that is, the items were judged to be representative of high-ground school-leader expertise (Cousins and Leithwood, 1987a). Additional evidence supporting the reliability and validity of the instrument was collected in a study by Cousins (1989). Specifically, this study aimed at following objectives concerning the PPBI: (1) to establish a central data base for the PPBI; (2) to examine normative response distributions of the instrument for both principals and colleagues; and (3) to provide further evidence about the validity and reliability of the instrument. Results of this study are reasonably encouraging from a psychometric point of view. The reliability of the instrument was found to be very high and there was some (less convincing) support for its construct validity. These are not conclusive analyses, however, and several limitations should be kept in mind.

First, the sample upon which these analyses were based was selected out of convenience. As such, the external validity of the results may be questioned. Clearly, further work is required to collect information from a sample of school-leaders more demonstrably representative of their colleagues. This step precedes any confidence in 'norming' the PPBI. Second, other aspects concerning validity should be examined. Specifically, more rigorous and sophisticated tests of predictive validity and concurrent validity should be conducted. Also, a more direct test of the extent to which subscale scores do measure different constructs (factor validity) would provide valuable information concerning the PPBI.

The PPBI is potentially useful as part of a set of school-leader selection or appraisal procedures (or as a tool for school-leader research). Our studies to date provide encouraging results concerning the psychometric properties of the instrument. Further work seems likely to yield useful results for measuring school-leader expertise on the high ground.

Measuring Expertise in the Swamp: Challenges Ahead

Accurately measuring expertise on the high ground is a task which has been seriously underestimated in school districts. Nonetheless, as we have demonstrated, research about expertise on the high ground is sufficiently well developed to be quite informative to the measurement process. Measuring expertise in the swamp has received much less attention to date and, for this reason, we are farther from being able to provide dependable, well-tried advice. Nevertheless, Murphy (1988, p. 122) raised some concerns that apply to the measurement of expertise in the swamp such as for example, his criticisms of job analysis described above, and a focus on:

> behaviors that are directly observable, technical in nature, directly linked
> to curriculum and instruction, visible in the short term and close in
> proximity to the consequent action or effect.

While many of the qualities associated with high-ground expertise are overlooked by such approaches, this is even more the case in relation to expertise in the swamp. A clear advantage to the use of behavior-rating scales, however, is 'the conceptual clarity with which the performance domain is defined' (Borman, 1986, p. 113). But, as we have argued, such conceptual clarity may not pertain to all aspects of the role of future school leaders.

How then can one go about the business of assessing expertise in the swamp? Our response to this question is limited to the answers which have been developed in the course of our research program. In that context, one instrument has been developed which offers the beginnings of a solution to the measurement problem. This instrument (broadly defined) is based on observing school-leaders' responses to simulated job tasks. Such simulations are, in fact, the cornerstone of the NASSP assessment center described earlier in this chapter. Also outlined were the elaborate procedures employed by the centers and how relatively objective measures of performance are obtained. The basic technology for measurement of this nature is described by Stiggins (1987) in his instructional module titled 'Design and development of performance assessment'. It is this approach that we recommend as the beginnings of an approach to measurement in the swamp.

The fundamental principle of performance assessment is that measurement is based on professional observation and judgment. It calls for the use of trained raters and when used carefully can produce reliable and valid results. As Stiggins (1987, p. 33) suggested, 'the keys to success ... are (a) to make the judgment-based evaluation as systematic and objective as it can be while (b) focusing on the most important attributes of performance'.

Performance-assessment techniques are useful where the assessor is interested in measuring the translation of knowledge and understanding into action. They typically involve a written response to a natural event (problem) framing the kind of performance required. Scoring is usually done by more than one rater and then ratings are compared for agreement. In the NASSP model, for example, several raters reach a consensus agreement about scores for a particular assessment-candidate. Data provided by Schmitt *et al.* (n.d.) indicated that inter-rater reliability is usually quite high for these ratings. Perhaps the main reason for this outcome is the extensive training that assessors undergo. This is an essential element of performance-assessment technology.

As Stiggins (1987) indicated, a major advantage of performance assessment is that it provides rich evidence of the use of skills and knowledge one is interested in assessing. The technology is performance-based and as such transcends the simple regurgitation of knowledge about how one might perform. This, the reader will recall, is a key feature of behavior-description interviewing described previously (Jantz *et al.*, 1986).

An additional requirement of performance assessment is that criteria are specified precisely and that they can be communicated to raters. This calls for the use of a valid framework to guide the scoring. In the NASSP model and the 'behavior-description interviewing' approach, the frameworks are derived from job analysis but criteria need not be restricted to this source. Our own scoring procedures were derived from our research-based framework for school-leader expertise in the swamp described in Chapter 6. A bit more detail about our instrument will help to demonstrate the application of performance-assessment technology to the problem of measuring school-leader expertise in the swamp.

In the study alluded to in Chapter 12, we had experimental and control school-leaders provide written solutions (called 'protocols') to four hypothetical case problems. Respondents received different problems for which they wrote solutions before and after the program was conducted. These written protocols were rated holistically for the quality of both the problem-solving process used and the product or solution generated. Protocols were also analyzed for evidence of the strategies explicitly taught in the experimental program. Two expert raters were trained to rate (on a 4-point scale) the protocols for the quality of both process and product. Raters did not know which of the two groups the protocols were from or whether a protocol was generated before or after the experimental program was conducted. The scoring yielded overall results as well as ratings of individual components of the problem-solving framework (e.g., interpretation, goals, values, etc.). This illustrates the application of performance-assessment technology to the measurement of expertise in the swamp. As noted by Stiggins (1987), the keys to success are: carefully prepared performance exercises; clear performance expectations; and careful, thoughtful rating (something that requires a fair bit of time).

Our own work in this area is in the early stages but we are encouraged by the results, so far. Of course, the Joint Committee's Standards apply to measurement of expertise in the swamp as well as to measurement of expertise on the high ground. Depending on training, reliability can reach sufficient levels; validity is heavily dependent upon the underlying theory or framework used in generating performance criteria. 'Feasibility' is another standard that must be considered, especially in the context of selection and appraisal. Certainly, a significant investment must be made in the training of raters and the time they require for their tasks. Given the potential contribution of appraisal and selection to developing expertise in the swamp, these are resources well spent.

Summary and Implications for Improvement

Both appraisal and selection processes result in judgments: judgments about needed growth, promotion, dismissal, transfer, and the like. Even in the case of appraisal for growth, school-leaders need to reflect upon, and make judgments about, their own performance. The adequacy of these judgments depends, critically, on the quality of the information available to those making judgments and the use of that information. This chapter and Chapter 13 have been preoccupied with both of these matters. But the most unique aspect of these chapters is their emphasis on the use of information. This emphasis has emerged from our own growing awareness that a great deal of personnel-evaluation information appears not to be used. Lack of use of such information means not only that the significant resources devoted to its collection are wasted but also that there is no possibility for such information to contribute to school-leader development – our main concern in this book.

The guidelines outlined in this section for improving appraisal and selection processes reflect our preoccupation with increasing the use of information collected as part of these processes. These guidelines are organized around the same framework used to describe current practices throughout these two chapters. Appraisal and selection processes are treated as one kind unless otherwise indicated.

Preparation

● **Specify policies and procedures**:
Selection and appraisal policies and procedures should be well specified, documented, and available for consumption by all interested parties. Specification should include criteria and expectations, process, timeliness, appeal procedures, and so forth. Selection policies should be multi-step with screening mechanisms and/or a decision-point funnel should be installed. Responsibilities ascribed at each decision point should be clearly outlined.

● **Differentiate purposes and emphasize growth**:
Purposes for selection and appraisal should be clearly understood by both evaluators and those being assessed. While it is possible conceptually to separate the two fundamental purposes (to support decision, to improve performance) for school-leader appraisal, it is rarely feasible to do so in practice. School-leaders should come to understand that although needs for accountability and for data to support personnel decisions exist, the central purpose for evaluation is performance improvement. Even in selection situations, where a decision clearly hangs in the balance, it is important to specify and make known that the process is oriented toward professional development. The selection processes should, in fact, be a learning experience for candidates regardless of their success; for unsuccessful candidates the process should direct them to avenues in which they can better prepare themselves for future selection. For the most part, it should also support them emotionally so that they remain committed to further application.

● **Base criteria on a coherent conception of growth**:
Knowledge about what it means to be an expert school-leader is becoming reasonably robust and offers the most promising source of criteria for selection and appraisal. Conceptions of growth should begin with well specified minimum levels of expertise but should clarify not only expectations for expert practice but also manageable steps toward such practice. Expectations for expert practice

should rely on research-based, practical and professional sources of knowledge, and the goals of the organization. In decision-oriented situations the entire set of criteria need to apply to all. Where developmental purposes are the focus, a subset of criteria should be selected. These should be negotiated between appraiser and the one to be appraised (in a pre-conference, for example).

- **Train selectors and appraisers**:
Those with responsibility for selection and/or appraisal duties should be well trained in three special domains. First, they should have a clear conception of growth. Second, they should be knowledgeable about local selection and appraisal procedures, especially including criteria related to expert school leadership. Finally, they should be competent in the skills required to implement the policy. Examples of such skills include, interviewing techniques, observation/data-recording techniques, and inter-personal skills. Responsibilities for school-leader selection and appraisal should be clearly outlined in supervisory job descriptions and incumbents should be held accountable for them.

- **Selection procedures should be sensitive to motivational characteristics of candidates**:
Perhaps the single best predictor of whether or not principals used information from their own appraisals is hunger for such information. Although, in practice, it is difficult for selection committees to measure motivational qualities validly or reliably, it would be useful for them to look for evidence of candidates' propensity toward self-evaluation, reflection, and an affinity for continuous, professional growth. It seems likely that evidence of such motivation prior to selection would predict, reasonably well, continued motivation of the same type throughout a candidate's tenure as a school-leader.

Data Collection

- **Selection procedures should make use of 'formal' instruments as early screening devices**:
Instruments such as the PPBI should be used as early screening mechanisms for selection procedures. In order to ensure fairness, data from self-evaluation and colleague forms (supervisor, peers) should be submitted for each candidate. District norms should be established to provide a basis for comparison.

- **Selection procedures should employ 'behavior-description interviews'**:
'Behavior-description interview' techniques (Jantz *et al.*, 1986) should be adopted in order to ground candidate responses in actual, past performance. Even if inappropriate decisions made by respondents are revealed in the interview, the process allows for a more fair and accurate basis for decisions (as well as carrying with it the benefit of stimulating reflection on the part of the candidate). The technique should be guided by questions that are applied to all applicants and grounded in the criteria identified prior to the process.

- **Use multiple data sources, collection intervals, and instruments**:
Valid and reliable data are essential, especially to decision-oriented evaluation situations. The use of multiple sources of data (e.g., teachers, peers, self-evaluation, supervisor observations, parents, documentation/archives, portfolio, etc.) will greatly enhance the believability of conclusions drawn about indi-

viduals. Comparable information should be available for all candidates and mechanisms for efficient and accurate processing, and summarizing of the data should be included. Data will need to be collected at different intervals to ensure reliability of 'observations.' In development-oriented appraisals it is not necessary to be as rigorous in establishing the validity of the data but it is necessary that findings are viewed as credible by the candidate. Data should be collected on an ongoing basis with an appropriate mix of informal and formal methods used. Agreement about data to be collected should be reached by the appraiser and appraisal-subject prior to the growth-oriented process.

Reporting and Follow-up

● **Use multiple selectors/appraisers:**
Selection decisions and other personnel decisions should not be left to single individuals, in the interest of guarding against susceptibility to real or perceived political influence and bias. Using a panel of decision makers, especially involving people from different roles, will help to ensure fairness and the perception of fairness. This practice is somewhat less necessary in growth-oriented appraisal situations. Although it will likely be advantageous to the principal being appraised, the development of credible and trusting relationships between individuals is more important.

● **Appraisers should communicate with school-leaders continuously:**
Just as an appraiser dropping in for a 'quick scan' to justify his or her impending appraisal report can have detrimental effects frequent, albeit brief, visits or phone calls can have very positive effects on school-leaders' propensity to take appraisal information seriously. The focus for conversation should be pertinent to the school-leader's objectives but should be timely and connected to current concerns or issues. The conversation should not only be viewed as a progress report but as an opportunity to share prior experience and knowledge.

There is a danger that too much communication may pose a threat to a school-leader's sense of autonomy. With each case, an appropriate balance between too much and too little interaction should be sought. School-leaders are more likely to make appraisers aware that they are overdoing it than they are to be openly critical about inattention. On the other hand, lack of attention can lead to cynicism, an outcome that can erode the trust and credibility required for appraisal information to be used. Developing trust and credibility are important objectives.

● **School-leaders should be encouraged to participate in the appraisal process:**
School-leaders who take the time and effort to add to the appraiser's knowledge by compiling different sorts of evidence about themselves (e.g., behavioral check-lists gathered anonymously from staff, self-assessments, school documents, etc.) stand to gain significantly more from the process. Not only will appraisers be better informed when time comes for discussing performance, but it is likely school-leaders will have engaged in more reflection about their own performance.

● **Develop plan for growth:**
In both decision-oriented and growth-oriented evaluation situations, constructive feedback should be provided. The most useful outcome of this feedback is a

negotiated plan for further development. Individuals that are unsuccessful in selection processes should be debriefed and a plan for growth should be developed. If appropriate and effective criteria are employed, strengths and weaknesses should be readily identifiable and suggestions for growth should become apparent.

• **Appraisers should strive to include unexpected results in the assessment:**

Appraisals that tell individuals what they already know may serve as a source of satisfaction and reward. But appraisals that point out, in a constructive fashion, not only legitimate strengths but also weaknesses, previously not known or fully understood by the school-leader, make a greater contribution to development. Appraisers should endeavor to teach school-leaders something about themselves every time the process occurs, while at same time taking great care not to be 'nit-picky'.

Evolution of Policy

• **Promote local ownership of policy**:

Key stakeholders should be involved in policy development and revision processes. For policies to have substantial impact, there must be significant commitment to the philosophy, rationale and spirit of them, and direct involvement in their development by, for example, those responsible for their implementation. Additionally, efforts can be made in mounting the policy to sustain this source of local ownership through promotion and advocacy.

• **Monitor ongoing implementation of policy**:

The implementation process should be monitored closely until satisfactory evidence accumulates, suggesting that implementation has taken a form that approximates what was intended. From that point, regular, periodic reviews of the policy should take place. Of key concern in such monitoring is the extent of the policy's impact (defined particularly in terms of utilization). Also of interest in monitoring are the components or features of the policy, as viewed within the context of its implementation, that foster impact. It is through such monitoring that fine tuning can take place. Evidence of impact emerging from such monitoring activities will sustain commitment to the processes by those responsible for their implementation.

Conclusion

Following all of the guidelines outlined in this chapter for improving appraisal and selection processes would be a formidable challenge, not a challenge many school districts are likely to consider realistic, in the short run. We appreciate this and consider the guidelines, rather, as worthwhile directions for the future, directions to be pursued incrementally. It seems important at the outset, however, to acknowledge the size of the task of developing and implementing defensible appraisal and selection processes. Quite candidly, we are trying to create a problem where many believe none exists, apparently. Evidence reviewed in these chapters, however, suggests that current practices are, in some instances, 'downright shocking!' Not only is there a problem but it is a problem about a set of school-district processes that crucially affect school-leader development. Poor practices in these areas do not just have 'no effect'. They have a significant negative effect on the development of future school leadership. For example, where selection processes in a district are perceived to be based on invalid information, promising potential candidates often choose not to become actual candidates – a considerable loss to the district and its future schools. When appraisal information is not used because it is not timely or is provided by an appraiser who lacks credibility, the accumulated result, in time, contributes to the continuation of school-leader practices that gradually become counter-productive because of changed expectations.

The quality of leadership for future schools depends, in a significant way, on our willingness to acknowledge 'the problem' and gradually adopt guidelines of the sort spelled out in this chapter.

Notes

1 The category 'appraiser/evaluation-subject' dynamics corresponds to the expansion of our framework for the use of personnel-evaluation information due to findings reported in Cousins (1988), Substudy B (see chapter 13).
2 Patton uses the term 'non-misutilization' to indicate justifiable action. We have substituted purely in the interest of avoiding the double negative.

Chapter 15

Conclusion: Implications for District Leaders

The role of district leaders in developing leaders for future schools has arisen many times throughout the book; sometimes as an impediment and sometimes as a significant part of the solution. Research reported in Chapters 2 and 4, for example, suggested quite forcefully that current school-leaders most often see district administrators and the policies and procedures which they manage as hurdles in their efforts to be more effective. The list of hurdles is quite long. On the other hand, some district initiatives are especially helpful for some school-leaders. Non-experts find the planning and support of the district especially useful when implementing externally-initiated policies about which they know little. In Chapter 10, we also noted a dramatic 'district effect' in the pattern of socialization experiences reported by school-leaders. This research suggested that while many districts may not contribute helpfully to the socialization of their school-leaders, targeted and sustained efforts by a district can be of considerable consequence.

The remainder of this chapter outlines five 'macro-strategies' which we believe would be helpful for district leaders to use in their efforts to foster the development of leaders for future schools. Several of these macro-strategies incorporate, and then further extend, specific implications for district leadership identified in earlier chapters. The first three macro-strategies are interdependent; they address similar aspects of the district from subtly but usefully different perspectives.

Design School-District Work as a Curriculum for School-Leaders

Chapters 11 and 12 were devoted to school-leadership development through formal 'instruction' of several sorts. Evidence from Chapter 10 about the range of experiences which contribute to the socialization of school-leaders, however, placed the contribution of such instruction in perspective. Under the best of circumstances, formal programs contribute importantly but modestly to school-leaders' development. More significant contributions are made by the myriad of experiences naturally created by school-leaders' work. Because this work is, by definition, 'authentic' and 'situated' (the importance of which was discussed in

Chapter 12), its impact on the development of school-leaders is paramount. Indeed, the tasks encountered by school-leaders in their schools and districts constitute the curriculum of most significance in their career-long professional education. These tasks may, in fact, constitute two quite separate curricula, one partly explicit and the other hidden.

A 'hidden curriculum' is a set of unplanned experiences. These experiences, usually encountered in the context of, or in parallel with, an explicit, planned, set of experiences, may have consequences which are helpful or not so helpful. Sam Sieber's (1981) review of the actual consequences of a broad range of social innovation offers compelling evidence of the frequent disjuncture between intention and reality. Social innovations can be viewed as a curriculum for those involved. And, as the title of Sieber's book suggests, they are often 'fatal remedies'.

Like social innovations, the experiences generated by the school district for school-leaders is also a curriculum. While most district leaders engage in a good deal of planning, this planning is rarely premised on a view of the experiences generated by the planning as a curriculum for those involved. Nor is there a concern for the hidden curriculum which develops in parallel.

Both of these limitations ought to be addressed by district leaders wishing to contribute to the development of leaders for future schools. The explicit, planned curriculum, applying Gordon's (1988) thesis about education as 'text' to our concerns, may be viewed as a story the district tells about itself. This being the case, district leaders need to examine their plans, policies, and procedures to determine whether the story which they tell school-leaders is useful to their development. For example, do school-leader selection and appraisal criteria reflect the qualities to be developed in leaders of future schools? Are the purposes of professional development programs consistent with the qualities associated with such leaders?

Conscious efforts to tell the right story through plans, policies, and procedures are ways in which district leaders can be teachers of school-leaders in often subtle and indirect, but invariably powerful, ways.

Our advice regarding the districts' hidden curriculum can best be understood by considering the symbolic function of district leaders. A symbol, according to Ricoeur is:

> any structure of signification in which a direct, primary, literal meaning designates, in addition, another meaning which is indirect, secondary and figurative and which can be apprehended only through the first. (1974, pp. 12–13)

This 'other meaning' is an interpretation or an inference drawn from the apparent or literal meaning. District leaders, especially those occupying formal roles of authority, are symbols of what their districts believe to be important, the norms to be used in guiding and judging behavior. The practices of such leaders are often the object of intense scrutiny, analysis, and discussion among school-leaders in their efforts to draw inferences about directions and expectations bearing on their own work. A school-leader might ask herself or himself: 'What does the superintendent's regular attendance at school-community meetings mean for my own school-improvement goals next year?' or 'What does the assistant superintendent's allocation of 50 percent of his time to the performance appraisal of principals this year say about the priority I should assign to teacher appraisal?' or 'How important for me is this in-service program on leadership, at which the superintendent offered words of initial greeting and was never seen thereafter?'

While school-leaders are, for the most part, a relatively autonomous bunch, like everyone else they are creatures of their social environment. From the environment, whether intended or not, they discern cues that shape the meaning of their work, give it definition and provide a basis for judging what is useful to do. The words and deeds of district leaders are symbols from which much is inferred. District leaders, therefore, need to ask themselves what their deeds and words signify. Do they symbolize a kind of leadership, consistent with, or exemplary of, the leadership they wish to develop for future schools? Are their espoused theories-of-action for school-leaders (to use Schön's 1983 distinction) discrepant with the theories-in-use symbolically evident in their own practices. When such discrepancies exist, district leaders' theories-in-use become an especially visible component of the district's 'hidden curriculum'. As Martin (1976) queried: 'What should we do with a hidden curriculum when we find one?' The answer depends on what it looks like. When the hidden curriculum symbolized by district leaders' practices reinforces the planned curriculum, a lot of applause and performance bonuses would be warranted. Significant change in district leaders' practices is warranted if the hidden curriculum appears to detract from the desired development of school-leaders.

In sum, given an image of future school-leaders appropriate for the district, it is vital for district leaders, then, to capture and assess the value of the curriculum created by the tasks required of school-leaders in the district. Are the tasks for school-leaders required by the district an obvious element of the type of school leadership the district is helping to develop? Does at least a significant proportion of these tasks stretch school-leaders in desired directions, and stimulate the type of growth which is desired? Or are these tasks largely routine and unchallenging (as suggested by evidence in Chapter 4) or even direct impediments to more effective school leadership (as suggested in Chapter 2)? The helpfulness of school-leaders' socialization experiences is largely dependent on the curriculum created by the tasks required of leaders in the district.

Develop an Appreciation for the Organizational Context within which Leadership Development Occurs

A classic teacher prototype, in the mind of some school-leaders, is the older, experienced staff member who resists implementing innovations being proposed for the classroom. The 'laggards' (to use an ironically pejorative term first applied by Rogers, 1962) do not respond to the school-leader's call for change for reasons that the school-leader prefers to think of as stubbornness, laziness, early unannounced retirement, lack of professionalism, and the like. Insights available from the past twenty years of research on school improvement, however, suggest that the truth of the matter is quite different. Many of these teachers have experienced previous failed attempts at innovation due to, for example, lack of leader support at crucial points, the withholding of promised resources, or the failure of highly-touted practices to deliver their claimed benefits. These teachers also may have experienced negative appraisals for implementing practices not understood or endorsed by the appraiser and lack of in-service opportunities needed to master the new practices. In a nutshell, teachers often decide not to change because they quite reasonably and correctly believe that their school organizations are not designed to support such change and their experience tells them that redesign is unlikely. These teachers have learned that their enthusiasm and good intentions will carry them through the early stages of change, but much more is required for a change to be sustained. Continued professional growth for teachers depends on an organizational context which values such growth and which provides opportunities for and rewards such growth. For teachers, that organizational context is most obviously the school.

What is true for teachers is also true, analogously, for those who would become leaders of future schools – especially those occupying a formal administrator role. In the case of developing school-leaders, however, the organizational context more obviously includes the school district. Chapters 10 through 14 addressed a number of matters relevant to the redesign of a supportive organizational context for developing school-leaders. District leaders need to incorporate those matters and others into a coherent framework for district-level action.

Evidence about external influences on school-leaders, reviewed as part of Chapter 2, suggested that such action is badly needed. This evidence indicated that the context created by the district in which the school is located often creates substantial constraints on school-leaders' efforts to improve their schools. The district is also perceived by the majority of school-leaders as blunting their efforts to develop and exercise the sort of leadership considered in Chapter 5 to be effective on the high ground. As Goldman *et al.* concluded from their research 'when other factors are controlled, district constraints reduce [school] leadership impact' (1990, p. 15). Examples of district constraints typically cited in this research are: conservative stances toward school-initiated change; advocacy of priorities in conflict with school priorities; actions eroding school autonomy; lack of recognition of school-leaders' work; nature of in-service provided to school-leaders; and lack of support for implementing new practices (e.g., Leithwood and Montgomery, 1984, Trider and Leithwood, 1988).

While district 'factors' are viewed by many school-leaders as especially vexing to their efforts, the negative impact of these factors seem even greater for those with less effective patterns of problem-solving. Trider and Leithwood (1988), for example, found that factors such as quality of district planning, district staff relations with school staffs, and the symbolic support provided or not provided by the district office outweighed personal beliefs and values in shaping non-expert principals' policy-implementation efforts. Expert school-leaders, in contrast, were quite autonomous: their own beliefs, values, and know-how outweighed or displaced district factors in most cases. What this means, in sum, is that not only do district factors often appear to inhibit the development of effective school leadership (at least in the minds of school-leaders) but also that this inhibition is strongest for those whose continued growth as school-leaders is most crucial. Donaldson's (1990) study of the dilemmas or paradoxes identified by school-leaders in moving from 'manager' to 'instructional leader' gives additional force to this claim. These paradoxes were:

1 establish clear, unassailable goals for students but be responsive to their needs and idiosyncrasies (the 'high expectations' paradox)
2 set and use high professional standards for faculty but create strong morale and teacher participation (the 'accountability' paradox)
3 be accessible, responsive and informed but establish and maintain mission and an efficient organization (the 'agenda' paradox)
4 authority: Now you have it, now you don't (the 'authority' paradox).
5 be a successful principal ... but we don't agree on what that is (the 'success' paradox).

The district has a more or less obvious role to play in either reducing or increasing the difficulty school-leaders will encounter in responding to each of these paradoxes during their transition toward more effective forms of problem-solving. Districts might help, for example, by:

- defining a core curriculum (a response to paradox 1)
- modeling participative decision-making and collaborative cultures (a response to paradox 2)
- communicating those elements of the district mission common to all schools (a response to paradox 3)
- clarifying the roles and responsibilities of principals and the nature of the relationships between them and other leaders – school and district (a response to paradoxes 4 and 5)

In sum, our advice to district leaders responsible for developing future school-leaders, then, is to become more sensitive to the way in which the district as a whole serves as a context of the work of school-leaders. This context can encourage and sustain or negatively reinforce the practices believed to be appropriate for leaders of future schools.

Identify and Eliminate Sources of Organizational Incoherence, Schizophrenia and Double Binds

'Organizational incoherence' is an evocative term. It is understood immediately, in our experience, by almost anyone who has lived in an organization long enough to understand how it works beyond what is depicted on the organizational chart. Several years ago, after a brief explanation of the term, we asked about eighty teachers, school administrators and central office resource staff from one school district, who had come together for some in-service, to identify examples of incoherence which they had experienced in their district. After two hours of small-group work, the walls of the room we were in were covered in chart paper with long lists of examples. And the groups were far from finished. The music consultants pointed to some of the special skills required to implement the new music curriculum and lack of any attention to those skills when music teachers were being hired by administrators. Almost all groups pointed to the heavy emphasis awarded to higher-order thinking skills in the district's curricula, and their complete neglect in the only standardized tests used to collect district-wide data. A teacher of gifted students mentioned that all of her time in school was scheduled with students, yet her job description called for meetings with teachers to coordinate instructional initiatives being taken with such students. Organizational incoherence, as these examples illustrate, exists when two or more parts of what ought to be a single whole don't fit together (e.g., the explicit and the hidden district curriculum).

Double binds and organizational schizophrenia are phenomena closely related to incoherence, although somewhat more complex. Hennestad offers this illustration of a double bind:

> Managers, for example, urge the members of the organization to show one kind of behaviour, but they tend to reward another [so far, this is 'only' incoherence]. Simultaneously, they make it hard for subordinates to point this out, partly because to do so would imply a criticism of their leaders. They could be punished for that, or they think they could. (1990 p. 266)

Double binds like this for school-leaders are not uncommon in school districts. The superintendent espouses an image of the principalship as autonomous, self-directed and entrepreneurial, yet promotes only those who adhere closely to the central offices' priorities and preferred procedures. In this example, pointing out the inconsistency appears to risk non-promotion in the future. It is the inability to talk openly about inconsistencies that makes a double bind out of a source of incoherence.

The major consequence to an organization of double binds is a loss of capacity to question underlying assumptions and to reconceptualize problems in new and more fruitful ways. To use Argyris's (1983) framework, 'double loop' learning is unlikely and the organization is confined to solving, better and better, the same problems (single-loop learning). These problems may become less and less relevant to the continuing health of the organization. The obvious result of continuing to view increasing levels of absenteeism from a secondary-school history class as a truancy problem (single loop) rather than reinterpreting it as an instructional or curricular problem (double loop), illustrates the point. In the long run, organizations that continue to operate with many double binds stand a good chance of becoming truly schizophrenic. Organizational schizophrenia occurs where practices consistent with two quite polar values are allowed to develop side-by-side, each to a mature level of coherence (e.g., where norms of cooperation and collaboration become a guiding ethic for school-level leadership and culture, and norms of competition and individual achievement become a guiding ethic for district-level leadership culture. Schizophrenic school districts offer contexts in which continuing professional growth for school-leaders is virtually impossible because the definition of growth itself is contested.

Our advice, in sum, is to encourage all staff, especially school-leaders, in the identification of sources of incoherence in the district. District leaders should provide convincing evidence that they value and reward overt, public discussion and elimination of such incoherence and that they consider the reduction of incoherence the collective responsibility of all school and district staff.

To this piece of advice we append an important qualification. Incoherence is not all bad: in one form or another it is, after all, usually the stimulant for change. Obversely, too much coherence is not good. As Geertz observed: There is nothing so coherent as a paranoid's delusion or a swindler's story (cited in

Gordon, 1988, p. 435). The task for district leaders is to find the optimum level of coherence, the point at which the organization is capable of both making significant progress towards its vision, and refining and revising the vision as well.

Think Developmentally

With an interest in the development of pedagogical expertise, Berliner (1988) has offered a five-stage theory of skill learning. Beginning as a 'novice', according to this theory, a teacher then proceeds to the 'advanced beginner' stage. This is followed by stages labeled 'competent', 'proficient', and 'expert'. At the novice stage, teachers are learning context-free rules about teaching (e.g., don't smile till Christmas) and are following those rules somewhat inflexibly, as they accumulate actual classroom experience; this real world experience is by far the most important contribution to their development to this stage. Advanced beginners start to learn how to modify the rules in light of particular classroom conditions, thus becoming more flexible in their practices. Such teachers are not yet consciously making decisions about their practices, however, and so may still not accept personal responsibility for their instruction. As teachers move through stages of competence and proficiency to the most expert forms of pedagogical practice, they, first, engage in more deliberate forms of decision-making. Eventually, they move to intuitive and highly automatic forms of practice. Expert teachers, like their counterparts in other fields (including school-leaders), engage in fluid performance, which is the object of conscious guidance only when it produces unexpected responses (of course, teachers like school-leaders frequently need to devote substantial cognitive energy to swampy problems).

While Berliner's theory remains to be formally tested, it has a great deal of intuitive appeal. It also mirrors important aspects of school-leader development described in Chapters 5 and 6. Two implications of the theory for district leaders, therefore, are of more than passing interest. One implication concerns professional development. As Berliner points out, because of novices' inexperience, it makes sense to focus their development on such things as standard-lesson forms and scripts, the particular assignments they will face in the immediate future, and practice in classroom routines. As was pointed out in Chapter 8, as well, these are the basic professional tasks that must be mastered as stepping stones to the next stage of expertise. Mastery of such tasks provides the novice with time to think about the more demanding problems which are embedded in the classroom but which may otherwise be left unattended. This fosters growth to an advanced-beginner stage and beyond.

Some of the data about school-leader socialization reported in Chapter 10 helps justify a parallel implication for their professional development. All school-leaders, no matter what the image of the role, pattern or stage of socialization or gender reported, feel least confident about their mastery of managerial routines. We pointed out, in Chapter 10, that this finding might be explained by a premature focus in their preparation on the higher-order competences associated with the role, and a lack of attention to basic management skills. Thinking developmentally, then, raises for district leaders the need to be more discriminating in the focus of the professional development provided to school-leaders. Such discrimination should lead to planning school-leader professional development with their full career cycles in mind. It should also lead to including, in the professional development of novice school-leaders, significant opportunities for the development of basic management skills.

Thinking developmentally also has consequences for school-leader appraisal if appraisal is to function as an instrument for professional growth, as we advocated in Chapters 13 and 14. Berliner (1988) points out in relation to teachers, that any given set of uniform appraisal criteria, standards and/or data collection procedures are likely to be inappropriate for teachers at several stages in their development. Novices need to be appraised, for example, in relation to their directly observed mastery of specific classroom routines. Experts, on the other hand, would benefit from a critique of their performance which is more open-ended. Such a critique might even attend to aesthetic aspects of their performance. As discussed in Chapter 8, it would certainly consider their contribution to the growth of their colleagues, as reported by their colleagues. Similarly, routine management practices might well be the centerpiece in appraising a novice school-leader; for an expert, the range of stakeholders satisfied by his or her responses to especially swampy problems and the 'elegance' of the responses would form a legitimate criterion for appraisal. Such criteria would be especially helpful if arrived at through a process of negotiation between the appraiser and school-leader.

A relatively clear, public, and detailed picture of school-leader development (such as begun in Chapters 5 and 6) is a prerequisite for district leaders who wish to realize the benefits of thinking developmentally. This parallels the requirement we asserted in Chapter 8 for school-leaders who would contribute to teacher growth.

Look After Yourself: Don't Spend Too Much Time at 'Home'

David (a pseudonym) was one of the most effective district leaders with whom we have ever worked. He was a rung below a chief education officer in a position labeled 'superintendent' in Ontario, in a district of about twenty-two elementary and secondary schools. Trustees, principals, teachers, and other district staff all knew David well and accorded him great respect for his professional judgment and the leadership with which he provided the district. This judgment and leadership, so far as we could see, were based on two qualities: an unquestioned commitment to solve the problems that came with his job, and state-of-the-art knowledge relevant to solving those problems. In addition to this commitment and knowledge, the other thing that David was best known for was the proportion of his time spent outside his district. There were, of course, many hypotheses (rumors) about how David spent that time, and some of the more 'socially interesting' ones were true. What was also true, however, was that by far the majority of out-of-district time was spent in the collection of information about how to solve his districts' problems. The fund of knowledge acquired in this way, in combination with his considerable intellect and self-confidence (these qualities feed on one another) made David an invaluable resource to others when he was in his district. He modeled expert problem-solving, espoused a vision of what the district could be, assisted others in overcoming their immediate obstacles, and provided opportunities for others to improve their capacities for problem-solving.

The moral of this (true) story is quite simple. It's lonely at the top. Teachers, principals, trustees and others in a school district have someone else in a similar role in the district from whom to collect advice, commiserate and share successes and failures. Often, they also have district personnel who count, among their duties, fostering the professional development of teachers, principals, and the like. But there is only one chief education officer and relatively few other district-level senior administrators. Yet the practices of those in such positions touch a great many people and have a considerable bearing on what happens in schools (Peterson, Hallinger and Murphy, 1987, Coleman and LaRocque, 1991). It is in everyone's interests to insure the continuing growth of district leaders as well as school-leaders. This growth is in capacities for both high ground and swampy problem-solving, for, surely, it makes good sense to view district, as well as school leadership as a problem-solving process. Such continuing growth is necessary if district leaders are to be symbols of what the district stands for.

Some Final Reflections

Our intention in this book was to offer an image of expert leadership for future schools and some insights about how such expertise might be developed. In doing so, we adopted a ten-year horizon on our meaning of 'the future', because of the inherent unpredictability of anything beyond that. Within such a time-frame, we argued, research about current, expert leadership practices offers a useful basis for imaging leadership for future schools when several other relevant sources of information are also considered.

Expert problem-solving was the image of leadership developed in the book and we offered research-based models of such leadership in response to both routine or 'high ground' problems and non-routine or 'swampy' problems. Such an image of leadership incorporates the range of transactional to transformational leadership acts presently considered part of school leadership. This image makes largely meaningless the traditional distinction between management and leadership. Indeed, we spent considerable effort in showing how expert school leadership depends on how one carries out tasks normally considered managerial in nature. It depends as well on the consistency one brings to the impact of these tasks on the direction of the school, a consistency born of a widely shared, defensible vision of what the school should be.

Most chapters of the book attempted to offer some insights about the development of school-leaders, although the last six chapters were most directly aimed at the development challenge. These insights came either directly or indirectly from the results of the last four years of our continuing research program at the OISE Center for Leadership Development. These years of research have produced significant growth in our own understanding of school leadership and its development. We claim to know very little for sure, but what we know now, as reflected in the book, is much more useful than what we knew four years ago. We also expect to add considerably to our current understandings and to change our minds about some aspects of leadership development over the next four years.

Like the image we espouse for expert leaders of future schools, we aspire to be expert problem solvers in our own domain. What is especially important for us and we think for future school-leaders, is a willingness to view our current understandings as tentative and improvable, and a passion for engaging in the struggle to improve our understandings. There is no final destination – there is only the journey. The journey toward becoming an increasingly expert school-leader should be an enormously rewarding one for both leaders' colleagues and leaders themselves. What could offer more satisfaction than an open-ended, relatively self-directed, intellectually challenging and emotionally rich occupation aimed at fostering the growth of one's fellow human beings. It is a role which should be occupied only by those who consider it a privilege.

Appendix A
The Principal Profile-Based Instrument

Self Assessment Form 3b, September 1988

Your Current Position (please print) _____

Instructions

Indicate how likely you feel you are to exhibit each of the following behaviors. Do so by circling the appropriate number. Circle one number only or 'N.A.' where items are either not applicable or where you have insufficient knowledge upon which to base your ratings. Try to use the 'N.A.' response as infrequently as possible.

1. GOALS

1.1 Source of Goals

How likely [1 = Not Likely; 6 = Extremely Likely] are you to:

1. establish goals for the school which reflect Ministry policy?
    1   2   3   4   5   6   N.A.
2. establish goals for the school which reflect school system priorities?
    1   2   3   4   5   6   N.A.
3. establish goals for the school which reflect community and student needs (including data on student achievement)?
    1   2   3   4   5   6   N.A.
4. involve staff in setting school goals?
    1   2   3   4   5   6   N.A.
5. work toward a set of goals which accommodate as many legitimate interests as possible?
    1   2   3   4   5   6   N.A.

1.2 Nature of Goals

How likely [1 = Not Likely; 6 = Extremely Likely] are you to:

6. maintain goals that support an image of the learner as a self-directed problem solver?

    1   2   3   4   5   6   N.A.

7. have as a goal the provision of the best education and best experiences possible for students?

    1   2   3   4   5   6   N.A.

8. include goals that recognize the importance of student development in knowledge and skill as well as effect?

    1   2   3   4   5   6   N.A.

9. translate educational goals into concrete objectives when needed?

    1   2   3   4   5   6   N.A.

1.3 Use of Goals

How likely [1 = Not Likely; 6 = Extremely Likely] are you to:

10. communicate the school goals to the school staff?

    1   2   3   4   5   6   N.A.

11. discuss the school goals with teachers at staff meetings?

    1   2   3   4   5   6   N.A.

12. refer to the school goals when making curricular decisions with teachers?

    1   2   3   4   5   6   N.A.

13. refer to the school goals in student assemblies and in meetings with those outside the school?

    1   2   3   4   5   6   N.A.

2. STRATEGIES

2.1 Staff Supervision

How likely [1 = Not Likely; 6 = Extremely Likely] are you to:

14. conduct formal observations in the classrooms on a regular basis?

    1   2   3   4   5   6   N.A.

15. conduct informal observations in classrooms on a regular basis (informal observations are unscheduled, last at least 5 minutes, and may involve written feedback)?

    1   2   3   4   5   6   N.A.

16. ensure that the classroom objectives of teachers are consistent with the stated goals of the school?

    1   2   3   4   5   6   N.A.

17. review student work when evaluating classroom instruction?

    1   2   3   4   5   6   N.A.

18. include objectives directly related to those of the school when evaluating teachers?
    1   2   3   4   5   6   N.A.

19. point out specific strengths in teacher instructional practices in post-observation conferences?
    1   2   3   4   5   6   N.A.

20. point out specific weaknesses in teacher instructional practices in post-observation conferences?
    1   2   3   4   5   6   N.A.

21. note specific strengths of the teacher's instructional practices in written evaluations?
    1   2   3   4   5   6   N.A.

22. note specific weaknesses of the teacher's instructional practices in written evaluations?
    1   2   3   4   5   6   N.A.

23. note specific instructional practices related to the stated classroom objectives in written evaluations?
    1   2   3   4   5   6   N.A.

2.2 Program Planning

How likely [1 = Not Likely; 6 = Extremely Likely] are you to:

24. make clear who is responsible for coordinating the curriculum across grade levels (e.g., the principal, vice principal, or teacher)?
    1   2   3   4   5   6   N.A.

25. ensure that the school goals are translated into common curricular objectives?
    1   2   3   4   5   6   N.A.

26. ensure that the objectives of special programs are coordinated with those of the regular classrooms?
    1   2   3   4   5   6   N.A.

27. monitor the classroom curriculum to see that it covers the school curricular objectives?
    1   2   3   4   5   6   N.A.

28. visit classrooms to see that instructional time is used for learning and practicing new skills and concepts?
    1   2   3   4   5   6   N.A.

2.3 Direct Relations with Students

How likely [1 = Not Likely; 6 = Extremely Likely] are you to:

29. take time to talk with students during recess and breaks?
    1   2   3   4   5   6   N.A.

30. attend or participate in cocurricular or extracurricular activities?
    1   2   3   4   5   6   N.A.
31. consistently model for students behaviors valued by the school?
    1   2   3   4   5   6   N.A.
32. provide opportunities for students to express their views on how well the school meets their needs?
    1   2   3   4   5   6   N.A.
33. use student discipline situations to foster student growth?
    1   2   3   4   5   6   N.A.

2.4 Providing Staff with Knowledge and Skill

How likely [1 = Not Likely; 6 = Extremely Likely] are you to:

34. inform teachers of opportunities for professional development?
    1   2   3   4   5   6   N.A.
35. select in-service activities that are consistent with the school goals?
    1   2   3   4   5   6   N.A.
36. support teacher's requests for in-service that are directly related to the school goals?
    1   2   3   4   5   6   N.A.
37. actively support the use in the classroom of skills acquired during in-service training?
    1   2   3   4   5   6   N.A.
38. provide time to meet individually with teachers to discuss instructional issues?
    1   2   3   4   5   6   N.A.
39. set aside time at faculty meetings for teachers to share ideas on instruction or information from in-service activities?
    1   2   3   4   5   6   N.A.
40. develop among staff a team approach to problem solving?
    1   2   3   4   5   6   N.A.

2.5 Providing Incentives for Learning

How likely [1 = Not Likely; 6 = Extremely Likely] are you to:

41. recognize students who do superior academic work with formal rewards such as an honor roll or mention in the principal's newsletter?
    1   2   3   4   5   6   N.A.
42. recognize outstanding individual effort by students?
    1   2   3   4   5   6   N.A.
43. ensure that parents are contacted to communicate improved student performances in school?
    1   2   3   4   5   6   N.A.

3. FACTORS

3.1 Factors of Most Concern

How likely [1=Not Likely; 6 = Extremely Likely] are you to:

44. promote the appropriate assignment of students to teachers?
    1   2   3   4   5   6   N.A.
45. have some desirable impact on program objectives and emphasis?
    1   2   3   4   5   6   N.A.
46. affect in a favorable way the instructional behaviors of teachers?
    1   2   3   4   5   6   N.A.
47. influence, in positive ways, materials and resources in the classroom?
    1   2   3   4   5   6   N.A.
48. have some positive impact on the assessment, recording and reporting procedures of teachers?
    1   2   3   4   5   6   N.A.
49. affect teachers' time/classroom management in desirable ways?
    1   2   3   4   5   6   N.A.
50. positively influence the content of the teacher's program?
    1   2   3   4   5   6   N.A.
51. have some favorable impact on interpersonal relationships in the classroom?
    1   2   3   4   5   6   N.A.
52. positively affect the physical environment of the classroom?
    1   2   3   4   5   6   N.A.
53. influence favorably integration across subjects and grades?
    1   2   3   4   5   6   N.A.
54. have some positive impact on human resources in the school?
    1   2   3   4   5   6   N.A.
55. favorably affect relationships with community?
    1   2   3   4   5   6   N.A.
56. influence in desirable ways extracurricular and intramural activities?
    1   2   3   4   5   6   N.A.
57. have some positive impact on relationships with out-of-school staff?
    1   2   3   4   5   6   N.A.
58. affect relationships among staff in desirable ways?
    1   2   3   4   5   6   N.A.
59. influence, in desirable ways, student behavior while at school?
    1   2   3   4   5   6   N.A.
60. have some favorable impact on relationships outside of the classroom between teachers and students?
    1   2   3   4   5   6   N.A.

3.2 Nature and Source of Expectations

How likely [1 = Not Likely; 6 = Extremely Likely] are you to:

61. have concrete, specific expectations regarding those factors that significantly affect student learning (e.g., factors listed in items 44–60)?

     1   2   3   4   5   6   N.A.

62. base expectations on competent professional judgments?

     1   2   3   4   5   6   N.A.

4. DECISION MAKING

How likely [1 = Not Likely; 6 = Extremely Likely] are you to:

63. be able to use a variety of forms and procedures for decision making?

     1   2   3   4   5   6   N.A.

64. choose the focus for decision making and decision making procedures after a careful analysis of such things as the nature of tasks and the skills of others involved?

     1   2   3   4   5   6   N.A.

65. involve staff in those decisions that affect them when appropriate *and* when their skill and/or willingness permits?

     1   2   3   4   5   6   N.A.

66. base decisions on the best available information?

     1   2   3   4   5   6   N.A.

67. consistently use professional goals as a basis for making decisions?

     1   2   3   4   5   6   N.A.

68. have a well developed set of principles or values which are regularly used for decision making?

     1   2   3   4   5   6   N.A.

References

Chapter 1

BACHARACH, S.B. (1988) 'Four themes of reform: An editorial essay', *Educational Administration Quarterly*, **24**, 4, pp. 484–96.

BASS, B.M. (1981) *Stogdill's Handbook of Leadership*, New York, The Free Press.

BASS, B.M. (1985) *Leadership and Performance Beyond Expectations*, New York, The Free Press.

BENNIS, W.G. (1959) 'Leadership theory and administrative behavior: The problem of authority', *Administrative Science Quarterly*, **4**, pp. 259–60.

BENNIS, W. and NANUS, B. (1985) *Leaders: The Strategies for Taking Charge*, New York, Harper and Row.

BURNS, J.M. (1978) *Leadership*, New York, Harper and Row.

COLEMAN, P. and LaROCQUE, L. (1989, April) 'Loose coupling revisited' Paper presented to the Annual Meeting of the American Educational Research Association, San Francisco.

CORBETT, D., WILSON, B. and ADUCCI, L. (1990) 'District leadership for restructuring', Paper presented at the Annual Meeting of the American Educational Research Association, Boston, April.

CROWSON, R.L. and MORRIS, V.C. (1990) 'The superintendency and school leadership' Paper presented at the Annual Meeting of the American Educational Research Association, Boston, April.

DRUCKER, P.F. (1989) *The New Realities: In Government and Politics, in Business, Technology and World View*, New York, Harper and Row.

DUKE, D.L. (1987) *School Leadership and Instructional Improvement*, New York, Random House.

ILLICH, I. (1971) *Deschooling Society*, New York, Harper and Row.

IMMEGART, G.L. (1988) 'Leadership and leader behavior', in BOYAN, N.J. (Ed.), *Handbook of Research on Educational Administration*, New York, Longman, pp. 259–78.

KLEMP, G.O. and McCLELLAND, D.C. (1986) 'What characterizes intelligent functioning among senior managers?', in STERNBERG, R.J. and WAGNER, R.K. (Eds) *Practical Intelligence*, Cambridge, Cambridge University Press.

LAWTON, S.B. and LEITHWOOD, K.A. (1988) *Student Retention and Transition in Ontario High Schools*, Toronto, Ontario Ministry of Education.

LIEBERMAN, A. and MILLER, L. (1990) 'Restructuring schools: What matters and what works', *Phi Delta Kappan*, June, pp. 759–64.

MARSH, C. (1988) *Spotlight on School Improvement*, Sydney, Allen and Unwin.

MITCHELL, B. (1990) 'Loss, belonging and becoming: Social policy themes for children and schools', in MITCHELL, B. and CUNNINGHAM, L.L. (Eds) *Educational Leadership and Changing Contents of Families, Communities, and Schools* (Eighty-ninth Yearbook of the National Society for the Study of Education), Chicago, The University of Chicago Press.

ORNSTEIN, R. and EHRLICH, P. (1989) *New World New Mind: Moving Toward Conscious Evolution*, New York, Doubleday.

PROVINCE OF BRITISH COLUMBIA (1989) *Policy Directions*, Victoria, BC, Ministry of Education.

REGAN, H.B. (1990) 'Not for women only: School administration as a feminist activity', *Teacher's College Record*, **91**, 4, pp. 565–78.

ROSENHOLTZ, S.J. (1989) *Teachers' Workplace*, New York, Longman.

RUMBERGER, R.W. (1987) 'High school dropouts: A review of issues and evidence', *Review of Educational Research*, **57**, 2, pp. 101–21.

SCHLECTY, P. (1990) *Schools for the Twenty-first Century*, San Francisco, Jossey-Bass.

SERGIOVANNI, T.J. (1987) 'The theoretical basics for cultural leadership', in SHIEVE, L.T. and SCHOENHEIT, M.B. (Eds) *Leadership: Examining the Elusive*, Alexandria, VA, The Association for Supervision and Curriculum Development.

SERGIOVANNI, T.J. (1990) *Value-Added Leadership*, San Diego, Harcourt Brace Jovanovich.

SMITH, W.F. and ANDREWS, R.L. (1989) *Instructional Leadership*, Alexandria, VA, The Association for Supervision and Curriculum Development.

SMYLIE, M.A and BROWNLEE-CONYERS, J. (1990) 'Teacher leaders and their principals: Exploring new working relationships from a micropolitical perspective', Paper presented at the Annual Meeting of the American Educational Research Association, Boston, April.

TERRY, G.R. (1960) *Principles of Management*, 3rd ed., Homewood, IL., Irwin.

VAIL, P.B. (1989) *Managing as a Performance Art*, San Francisco, Jossay Bass.

WALFORD, G. (1990) 'The 1988 education reform act for England and Wales: Paths to privatization', *Educational Policy*, **4**, 2, pp. 127–44.

WILSON, B. and CORCORAN, T. (1988) *Successful Secondary Schools*, New York, Falmer Press.

Chapter 2

ANDREWS, R.L., SODER, R. and JACOBY, D. (1986) 'Principal roles, other in-school variables, and academic achievement by ethnicity and SES', Paper presented at the Annual Meeting of American Educational Research Association, San Francisco, April.

BACHARACH, S.B., CONLEY, S.C. and SHEDD, J.B. (1987) 'A career development framework for evaluating teachers as decision makers', *Journal of Personnel Evaluation in Education*, **1**, 2, pp. 181–94.

BEGLEY, P. (1988) 'The influence of beliefs and values of principals on the adoption and use of computers in the school', Unpublished doctoral dissertation, University of Toronto (OISE Press).

BLASE, J., DEDRICK, C. and STRATHE, M. (1986) 'Leadership behavior of school principals in relation to teacher stress, satisfaction, and performance', *Journal of Humanistic Education and Development*, **24**, 4, pp. 159–71.

BOYAN, N.J. (1988) 'Describing and explaining administrator behavior', in BOYAN, N. (Ed) *Handbook of Research on Educational Administration*, New York, Longman.

BRADESON, P.V. (1986) 'Principally speaking: An analysis of the interpersonal communications of school principals', Paper presented at the Annual Meeting of American Educational Research Association, San Francisco, April.

BRADY, L. (1985) 'The supportiveness of the principal in school-based curriculum development', *Journal of Curriculum Studies*, **17**, 1, pp. 95–7.

BRUBAKER, D.L. and SIMON, L.H. (1987) 'How do principals view themselves and others?', *NASSP Bulletin*, **71**, 495, pp. 72–8.

CALDWELL, W.E. and PAUL, D.M. (1984) 'Principals' input on self-interest issues influencing perceptions of organizational climate', Paper presented at the Annual Meeting of American Educational Research Association, New Orleans, April.

CHATER, R. (1985) 'Aspects of decision-making in secondary schools', *Educational Management and Administration*, 13, 3, pp. 207–14.

COUSINS, J.B. (1988) 'Knowledge Utilization', Unpublished doctoral dissertation, University of Toronto.

CROWSON, R.L. and MORRIS, V.R. (1985) 'Administrative control in large city school systems: An investigation in Chicago', *Educational Administration Quarterly*, **21**, 4, pp. 51–70.

CUBAN, L. (1986) 'Principaling: Images and rules', *Peabody Journal of Education*, **63**, 1, pp. 107–19.

DARESH, J. (1987) 'The highest hurdles for the first year principal', Paper presented at the Annual Meeting of the American Educational Research Association, Washington, DC, April.

DAVIES, L. (1987) 'The role of the primary school head', *Educational Management and Administration*, **15**, pp. 43–7.

DWYER, D.C., LEE, G.V., BARNETT, B.G., FILBY, N.N. and ROWAN, B. (1984) *Instructional Management Program*, San Francisco, Far West Laboratory for Educational Research and Development.

EHIAMETALOR, E.T. (1985) 'Primary school principals' performance in critical administrative task areas', *Journal of Negro Education*, **54**, 4, pp. 566–74.

FARREL, J.P. (1989) 'International lessons for school effectiveness: The view from the developing world', in HOLMES, M., LEITHWOOD, K.A. and MUSELLA, D. (Eds) *Educational Policy for Effective Schools*, Toronto, Ont., OISE Press and Teachers College Press.

FULLAN, M., ANDERSON, S.E. and NEWTON, E. (1986) *Support Systems for Implementing Curriculum in Schools*, Toronto, The Queen's Printer for Ontario.

FULLER, B. (1987) 'What school factors raise achievement in the Third World', *Review of Educational Research*, **57**, 3, pp. 255–92.

GALLY, J. (1986) 'The structure of administrative behaviour: An international dimension in educational administration', Paper presented at the Annual

Meeting of the American Educational Research Association, San Francisco, April.

GLASMAN, N. (1985) 'Perceptions of school principals about their engagement in evaluation on the basis of student data', *Studies In Educational Evaluation*, **11**, 2, pp. 231–36.

GLEICK, J. (1987) *Chaos: Making a New Science*, New York, Viking.

GOLDMAN, P. and KEMPNER, K. (1990) 'School administrators' leadership impact: A view from the field', Paper presented at the Annual Meeting of the American Educational Research Association, Boston, April.

GOUSHA, R.P. (1986) 'The Indiana school principalship: The role of the Indiana principal as defined by the principal', Bloomington, IN, Indiana University, School of Education.

GUNN, J.A. and HOLDAWAY, E.A. (1986) 'Perceptions of effectiveness, influence and satisfaction of senior high school principals', *Educational Administration Quarterly*, **22**, 2, pp. 43–62.

HALL, G., RUTHERFORD, W.L., HORD, S.M. and HULING, L.L. (1986) 'Effects of three principal styles on school improvement', *Educational Leadership*, **41**, 5, pp. 22–31.

HIGH, R.M. and ACHILLES, C.M. (1986, April) 'Principal influence in instructionally effective schools', Paper presented at the Annual Meeting of American Educational Research Association, San Francisco.

HODGKINSON, C. (1978) *Toward a Philosophy of Administration*, Oxford, Basil Blackwell.

HOY, W.K. and BROWN, B.L. (1986) 'Leadership of principals, personal characteristics of teachers and the professional zone of acceptance of elementary teachers', Paper presented at the Annual Meeting of American Education Research Association, San Francisco, April.

JOHNSON, G.S. and VENABLE, B.P. (1986) 'A study of teacher loyalty to the principal: Rule administration and hierarchical influence of the principal', *Educational Administration Quarterly*, **22**, 4, pp. 4–27.

KINGDON, H.D. (1985) 'The role of the teaching elementary school principal', *Principal Issues*, **4**, pp. 20–3.

KOTKAMP, R.B. and TRAVLOS, A.L. (1986) 'Selected job stressors, emotional exhaustion, job satisfaction and thrust behavior of the high school principal', *Alberta Journal of Educational Research*, **32**, 3, pp. 234–48.

LARSEN, T.J. (1987) 'Identification of instructional leadership behaviors and the impact of their implementation on academic achievement', Paper presented at the Annual Meeting of the American Educational Research Association, Washington, DC, April.

LEITHWOOD, K.A. (1982) 'Research on the role of the principal in school improvement: State-of-the-art in Canada', in HORD, S. (Ed.) *Looking at the Principal and Internal Change Agents in the School-Improvement Process*, Proceedings of the Florida International School Improvement Project Conference, West Palm Beach, November.

LEITHWOOD, K.A. (1986) *The Role of the Secondary School Principal in Policy Implementation and School Improvement*, Toronto, The Queen's Printer for Ontario.

LEITHWOOD, K.A., BEGLEY, P. and COUSINS, B. (1990) 'The nature, causes and consequences of principals' practices, An agenda for future research, *Journal of Educational Administration*, **28**, 4, pp. 5–31.

LEITHWOOD, K.A. and MONTGOMERY, D.J. (1982b) 'The role of the elementary school principal in program improvement', *Review of Educational Research*, **52**, 3, pp. 309–39.

LEITHWOOD, K.A. and MONTGOMERY, D.J. (1986) 'Obstacles preventing principals from becoming more effective', *Education and Urban Society*, **17**, 1, pp. 73–88.

LEITHWOOD, K.A. and MONTGOMERY, D.J. (1982a) *Improving Principal Effectiveness: The Principal Profile*, Toronto, Ont., OISE Press.

LEITHWOOD, K.A. and STAGER, M. (1986) 'Differences in problem solving processes used by moderately and highly effective principals', Paper presented at the Annual Meeting of the American Educational Research Association, San Francisco, April.

LEITHWOOD, K.A. and STAGER, M. (1989) 'Components of expertise in principals' problem-solving', *Educational Administration Quarterly*, **25**, 1, pp. 126–61.

LOUIS, K.S. (1989) 'The role of the school district in school improvement', in HOLMES, M., LEITHWOOD, K. and MUSELLA, D. (Eds) *Educational Policy For Effective Schools*, New York, Teachers College Press.

MARSHALL, C. and GREENFIELD, W. (1987) 'The dynamics in the enculturation and in the work of the assistant principalship', *Urban Education*, **22**, 1, pp. 36–52.

McCOLSKEY, W.H., ALTSCHULD, J.W. and LAWTON, R.W. (1985) 'Predictors of principals' reliance on formal and informal sources of information', *Educational Evaluation and Policy Analysis*, **7**, 4, pp. 427–36.

MIKLOS, E. (1988) 'Administrator selection, career patterns, succession and socialization', in BOYAN, N. (Ed.) *Handbook of Research on Educational Administration*, New York, Longman.

MONTGOMERIE, T.C., McINTOSH, R.G. and MATTSON, N.A. (1987) 'The role of the principal: Superhero with a big stick?', Paper presented at the Annual Meeting of the Canadian Society for the study of Educational Administration, Vancouver, June.

PFEIFER, R.S. (1986) 'Enabling teacher effectiveness: Teachers' perspectives on instructional management', Paper presented at the Annual Meeting of the American Educational Research Association, San Francisco, April.

PITNER, N.J. and HOVECAR, D. (1987) 'An empirical comparison of two-factor versus multifactor theories of principal leadership: Implications for the evaluation of school principals', *Journal of Personnel Evaluation in Education*, **1**, 1, pp. 93–110.

SARROS, J.R. and FRIESEN, D. (1987) 'The etiology of administrator burnout', *The Alberta Journal of Educational Research*, **33**, 3, pp. 163–80.

SERGIOVANNI, T.J. (1984) 'Leadership and excellence in schooling', *Educational Leadership*, **41**, 5, pp. 4–13.

SHARMAN, R.G. (1987) 'Organizational supports for implementing an instructional innovation', *The Alberta Journal of Educational Research*, **33**, 4, pp. 236–46.

SPARKES, R.L. (1986) 'Principal job satisfaction in Newfoundland and Labrador', *Newfoundland Teachers' Association Journal*, **74**, 1, pp. 14–15.

STANARD, M. (1986) 'Rural principal: A case study of an effective disciplinarian', *Rural Education*, **8**, 1, pp. 16–21.

STEVENS, W. and MARSH, L.D.D. (1987) 'The role of vision in the life of elementary school principals', Paper presented at the Annual Meeting of the American Educational Research Association, Washington, DC, April.

TAYLOR, B.O. (1986) 'How and why successful elementary principals address strategic issues', Paper presented at the Annual Meeting of the American Educational Research Association, San Francisco, April.

TRACY, S.J. (1985) 'Career patterns and aspirations of elementary school principals: The gender difference', *Journal of NAWDAC*, **49**, 1, pp. 23–28.

TRIDER, D.M.A. and LEITHWOOD, K.A. (1988) 'Influences on principals' practices', *Curriculum Inquiry*, **18**, 3, pp. 289–312.

WILLIAMS, L. (1986) 'Principals' perception of their instructional leadership role', St. John's, Nfld., Memorial University.

Chapter 3

AREHART, J.E. (1979) 'Student opportunity to learn related to student achievement of objectives in a probability unit', *Journal of Educational Research*, **72**, 5, pp. 253–59.

BASS, B.M. (1981). *Stoqdill's Handbook of Leadership*, New York, Free Press.

COHEN, M. (1982, October) 'Effective schools: Accumulating research findings', *American Education*, **18**, 1, pp. 13–16.

COLEMAN, J.S. (1983) 'Families and schools', *Educational Researcher*, **16**, August–September, pp. 32–8.

COLEMAN, J.S. and HOFFER, T. (1987) *Public and Private High Schools*, New York, Basic Books.

CORBETT, D., WILSON, B. and ADUCCI, L. (1990) 'District leadership for restructuring', Paper presented at the Annual Meeting of the American Educational Research Association, Boston.

COUSINS, J.B. and LEITHWOOD, K.A. (1986) 'Current empirical research on evaluation utilization', *Review of Educational Research*, **56**, 3, pp. 331–64.

DUCKETT, W.R. (1980) 'Why do some urban schools succeed: The Phi Delta Kappan Study of exceptional urban elementary schools', *Phi Delta Kappan*, Bloomington, IN.

DUKE, D. and GANSNEDER, B. (1990) 'Teacher empowerment: The view from the classroom', *Educational Policy*, **4**, 2, pp. 145–60.

EDMONDS, R. (1979) 'Effective schools for the urban poor', *Educational Leadership*, October.

FARRAR, E., NEUFELD, B. and MILES, M.B. (1984) 'Effective schools', programs in high school: Social promotion or movement by merit', *Phi Delta Kappan*, **65**, 10, pp. 701–06.

FEIMAN–NEMSER, S. and FLODDEN, R.E. (1986) 'The cultures of teaching', in WITTROCK, M. (Ed.) *Handbook of Research on Teaching*, New York, MacMillan.

FIRESTONE, W.A. and HERRIOT, R.E. (1982) 'Prescriptions for effective elementary schools: Don't fix secondary schools', *Educational Leadership*, **40**, 3, pp. 51–3.

FORD FOUNDATION. (1984) *City High Schools: A Recognition of Progress*, New York, Ford Foundation.

FREDERICK, W.C., WALBERG, H.J. and RASHE, S.P. (1979) 'Time, teacher comments and achievement in urban high schools', *Journal of Educational Research*, **73**, 2, pp. 63–5.

FRYE, N. (1988) *On Education*, Toronto, Ont., Fitzhenry and Whiteside.

GOODLAD, J.I. (1984) *A Place Called School*, New York, McGraw-Hill.

GUNN, J.A and HOLDAWAY, E.A. (1986) 'Perceptions of effectiveness, influence and satisfaction of senior high school principals', *Educational Administration Quarterly*, **22**, 2, pp. 43–62.

HARNISCH, D.L. (1987) 'Characteristics associated with effective public high schools', *Journal of Educational Research*, **4**, 80, pp. 233–41.

HAY, L.E. and ROBERTS, A.D. (1989) 'Curriculum for the new millenium: Trends shaping our schools', Alexandria, VA, Paper prepared by the Connecticut Association for Supervision and Curriculum Development.

HUDDLE, E. (1986) 'Creating a successful secondary school', *NASSP Bulletin*, **70**, 491, pp. 64–9.

KEITH, T.Z. and PAGE, E.B. (1985) 'Do Catholic high schools improve minority student achievement?', *American Educational Research Journal*, **22**, 3, pp. 337–49.

KLEMP, G.O. and McCLELLAND, D.C. (1986) 'What characterizes intelligent functioning among senior managers?', in STERNBERG, R.J. and WAGNER, R.K. (Eds) *Practical Intelligence*, Cambridge, Cambridge University Press.

LEITHWOOD, K.A. and MONTGOMERY, D. (1982) 'The role of the elementary school principal in program improvement', *Review of Educational Research*, **52**, 82, pp. 309–34.

LEITHWOOD, K.A. and JANTZI, D. (1989) Organizational effects on student learning, to HUSEN, T. and POSTLETHWAITE, N. (Eds) *The International Encyclopedia of Education*, Second Edition. Oxford, Pergamon Press.

LIGHTFOOT, S.L. (1983) *The Good High School*, New York, Basic books.

LIPSITZ, J. (1984) *Successful Schools for Young Adolescents*, New Brunswick, NJ, Transaction Books.

LITTLE, J.W. 'Names of collegiality, and experimentation: Workplace conditions of school success', *American Educational Research Journal*, **19**, 3, pp. 325–40.

MACKENZIE, D.E. (1983) 'Research for school improvement: An appraisal of some recent trends', *Educational Researcher*, **12**, 4, pp. 5–16.

MADAUS, G.F., KELLAGHAN, T. and RAKOW, E.A. (1976) 'School and class differences in performance on the learning certificate examination', *The Irish Journal of Education*, **10**, 1, pp. 41–50.

McDONNELL, L. (1989) *Restructuring American Schools*, New York, National Center on Education and Employment.

McNEIL, L.M. (1986) *Contradictions of Control*, New York, Routledge and Kegan Paul.

MORGAN, E.P. (1979) 'Effective teaching in the urban high school', *Urban Education*, **14**, 2, pp. 161–81.

MORGAN, G. (1989) *Riding the Waves of Change*, San Francisco, Jossey-Bass.

MURPHY, J. and HALLINGER, P. (1985) 'Effective high schools – what are the common characteristics?', *NASSP Bulletin*, **69**, 477, pp. 18–22.

NATIONAL OPINION RESEARCH CENTRE (1980) *High School and Beyond, Information for Users: Base Year (1980) Data*, Chicago.

ROSSMAN, G., CORBETT, A. and FIRESTONE, W. (1985) 'Professional cultures, improvement efforts and effectiveness: Findings from a study of three high schools', *Research for Better Schools*, Philadelphia.

ROUECHE, J.E. and BAKER, G.A. (Eds) (1986) *Profiling Excellence in American's Schools*, Arlington, VA, American Association of School Administrators.

RUTTER, M., *et al.* (1979) *Fifteen Thousand Hows: Secondary Schools and Their effects on Children*, Cambridge, MA, Harvard University Press.

SCHLECTY, P. (1990) *Schools for the Twenty-First Century*, San Francisco, Jossey-Bass.

SLAVIN, R.E. (1987) 'Mastery learning reconsidered', *Review of Educational Research*, **57**, 2, pp. 175–214.

STEVENS, W. (1986) 'The role of vision in the life of elementary school principals', Unpublished doctoral dissertation, University of Southern California.

TERRY, G.R. (1960) *Principles of Management*, 3rd ed., Homewood, IL., Irwin.

VAIL, P.B. (1989) *Managing as a Performing Art*, San Francisco, Jossey-Bass.

WALBERG, H.J. and SHANAHAN, T. (1983) 'High school effects on individual students', *Educational Researcher*, **12**, 7, pp. 4–9.

WEIL, M., MARSHALEK, B., MITMAN, A., MURPHY, J., HALLINGER, P. and PRUYN, J. (1984) 'Effective and typical schools: How different are they?', Paper presented at a meeting of the American Educational Research Association, April.

Chapter 4

BAIRD, L.L. (1983) *Review of Problem Solving Skills*, Princeton, NJ, Educational Testing Services, Research Report.

BOYD, W.L. and CROWSON, R.L. (1981) 'The changing conception and practice of public school administration', in BEMINER, D.C. (Ed.) *Review of Research in Education*, **9**, Washington, DC, American Educational Research Association.

CROWSON, R.L. and MORRIS, V.C. (1985) 'Administrative control in large-city school systems: An investigation in Chicago', *Educational Administration Quarterly*, **4**, 21, pp. 51–70.

DUKE, D.L. (1988) 'Why principals consider quitting', *Phi Delta Kappan*, December, pp. 308–12.

FREDERICKSEN, N. (1984) 'Implications of cognitive theory for instruction in problem solving', *Review of Educational Research*, **54**, 3, pp. 363–407.

GOLDMAN, P., KEMPNER, K., POWELL, W.R. and SCHMUCK, R.A. (1990) 'School administrators' leadership impact: A view from the field', Paper presented at the Annual Meeting of the American Educational Research Association, Boston, April.

LEITHWOOD, K.A. (1988) 'How chief school officers classify and manage their problems', Paper presented at the Annual meeting of the American Educational Research Association, New Orleans, April.

LEITHWOOD, K.A. (1990) 'A description of the principals' world from a problem solving perspective: A Replication', Toronto, Ont., OISE Press (mimeo).

LEITHWOOD, K.A. COUSINS, B. and SMITH, M. (1989/90) 'A description of the principal's world from a problem solving perspective', *The Canadian School Executive*, **9**, 7/8, pp. 9–12.

LEITHWOOD, K.A. and JANTZI, D. (1989) 'Organizational effects on student outcomes', Toronto, The Ontario Institute for Studies in Education (mimeo).

LEITHWOOD, K.A. and MONTGOMERY, D.J. (1984) 'Obstacles preventing principals from becoming more effective', *Education and Urban Society*, **17**, 1,
pp. 73–88.

LEITHWOOD, K.A. and STAGER, M. (1986) 'Differences in how moderately and
highly effective principals classify and manage their problems', Paper presented at the Annual Meeting of the American Educational Research Association, San Francisco, April.

LEITHWOOD, K.A. and STAGER, M. (1989) 'Expertise in principals' problem
solving', *Educational Administration Quarterly*.

LEITHWOOD, K.A. and STEINBACH, R. (1990) 'Characteristics of effective secondary school principals' problem solving', *Educational and Administrative
Foundations Journal*, **5**, 1, pp. 24–42.

MARTIN, Y.M. and WILLOWER. D.J. (1981) 'The managerial behavior of high
school principals', *Educational Administration Quarterly*, **17**, 1, pp. 69–90.

MORRIS, V.C., CROWSON, R.L., PORTER-GEHRIE, C. and HURWITZ, E. (1984)
Principals in Action, Columbus, OH, Charles E. Merrill.

PAVAN, B.N. and REID, N.A. (1990) 'Building school cultures in achieving urban
elementary schools: The leadership behaviors of principals', Paper presented
at the Annual Meeting of the American Educational Research Association,
Boston, April.

SCHÖN, D.A. (1983) *The Reflective Practitioner*, New York, Basic Books.

SCHÖN, D.A. (1987) *Educating, The Reflective Practitioner*, San Francisco, Jossey-
Bass.

SHULMAN, L.S. and CAREY N.B. (1984) 'Psychology and the limitations of
individual rationality: Implications for the study of reasoning and civility',
Review of Educational Research, **54**, 4, pp. 501–24.

SMITH, W.F. and ANDREWS, R.L. (1989) *Instructional Leadership: How Principals
Make a Difference*, Alexandria, VA, Association for Supervision and Curriculum Development.

VAIL, P.B. (1989) *Managing as a Performing Art*, San Francisco, Jossey-Bass.

WILLOWER, D.J. and KMETZ, J.T. (1982) 'The managerial behavior of elementary
school principals', Paper presented at the Annual Meeting of the American
Educational Research Association, New York.

WOLCOTT, H.F. (1978) *The Man in the Principal's Office*, New York, Holt,
Rinehart and Winston.

Chapter 5

BEREITER, C. and SCARDAMALIA, M. (1986) 'Educational relevance of the study of
expertise', *Interchange*, **17**, pp. 10–19.

BERLINER, D.C. (1986) 'In pursuit of the expert pedagogue', *Educational Researcher*, **15**, 7, pp. 5–13.

BLOOM, B.S. (Ed.) (1985) *Developing Talent in Young People*, New York, Ballen-
tine.

BLUMBERG, A. and GREENFIELD, W. (1980) *The Effective Principal: Perspectives on
School Leadership*, Boston, Allyn and Bacon.

CALDWELL, W.E. and LUTZ, F.W. (1978) 'The measurement of principal rule administration behavior and its relationship to educational leadership', *Educational Administration Quarterly*, **14**, pp. 63–79.

CHI, M.T.H., FELTOVICH, P.J. and GLASER, R. (1981) 'Categorization and representation of physics problems by experts and novices', *Cognitive Science*, **5**, pp. 121–52.

DUKE, D. (1987) *School Leadership and Instructional Improvement*, New York, Random House.

DWYER, D.C., LEE, G.V., BARNETT, B.G., FILBY, N.N. and ROWAN, B. (1984) *Grace Lancaster and Emerson Junior High School: Instructional Leadership in an Urban Setting*, San Francisco, Far West Laboratory for Educational Research and Development.

EASTABROOK, G. and FULLAN, M. (1978) *School and Community Principals and Community Schools in Ontario*, Toronto, Ontario Ministry of Education.

GERSTEN, R., CARNINE, D. and GREEN, S. (1982, December) 'The principal as instructional leader: A second look', *Educational Leadership*, **40**, pp. 47–50.

HALL, G., RUTHERFORD, W.L., HORD, S.M. and HULING, L.L. (1984) 'Effects of three principal styles on school improvement', *Educational Leadership*, **41**, 5, pp. 22–31.

HECK, R.H., LARSEN, T.J. and MARCOULIDES, G.A. (1990) 'Instructional leadership and school achievement: Validation of a causal model', *Educational Administration Quarterly*, **26**, 2, pp. 94–125.

JOHNSTON, J.M. (1983) 'The myths and realities: Principals' classroom supervision', Saskatoon, University of Saskatchewan (mimeo).

LEITHWOOD, K.A. (1982) 'The principals' role in school improvement: State-of-the-art research in Canada', Paper presented to International School Improvement Project, West Palm Beach, FL, November.

LEITHWOOD, K.A. (1986) *The Role of the Secondary School Principal in Policy Implementation and School Improvement*, Toronto, Ont., Ministry of Education.

LEITHWOOD, K.A. and MONTGOMERY, D.J. (1982) 'The principals' role in program improvement', *Review of Educational Research*, **52**, pp. 309–40.

LEITHWOOD, K.A. and MONTGOMERY, D.J. (1985) 'The role of the principal in school improvement, in AUSTIN, G. and GARBER, H. (Eds) *Research on Exemplary Schools*, New York, Academic Press.

LEITHWOOD, K.A. and MONTGOMERY, D.J. (1986) *Improving Principal Effectiveness: The Principal Profile*, Toronto, Ont., OISE Press.

LICATA, J.W. and HACK, W.G. (1980) 'School administrator grapevine structure', *Educational Administration Quarterly*, **16**, pp. 82–99.

MARTIN, W.S. and WILLOWER, D.J. (1981) 'The management behavior of high school principals', *Educational Administration Quarterly*, **17**, 1, pp. 69–90.

MILES, M.B. (1988) *Thinking About Educational Change*, Toronto, OISE (a video tape).

MORRIS, V.C., CROWSON, R.L., PONTER-GEHRIE, C. and HURWITZ, E. (1986) *Principals in Action*, Columbus, OH, Charles E. Merrill.

NEWBERG, N.A. and GLATTHORN, A.A., (n.d.) Instructional leadership: Four ethnographic studies on junior high school principals, Phiadelphia, University of Pennsylvania (mimeo).

NORRIS S.P. (1985) 'Synthesis of research on critical thinking', *Educational Leadership*, **42**, 8, pp. 40–6.

PETERS, T. and AUSTIN, N. (1985) *A Passion for Excellence*, New York, Random House.

SALLEY, C., McPHERSON, R.B. and BAEHR, M.E. (1978) 'What principals do: A preliminary occupational analysis', in ERICKSON, D.A. and RELLER, T.L. (Eds) *The Principal in Metropolitan Schools*, Berkeley, CA, McCutchan.

SCHÖN, D.A. (1983) *The Reflective Practitioner*, New York, Basic Books.

SMITH, W. and ANDREWS, R. (1989) *Instructional Leadership*, Alexandria, VA, Association for Supervision and Curriculum Development.

STEVENS, W. (1986) 'The role of vision in the life of elementary school principals', Unpublished doctoral dissertation, Los Angeles, University of Southern California.

TOFFLER, B.L. (1986) *Tough Choices: Managers Talk Ethics*, New York, John Wiley and Sons.

TRIDER, D. (1986) 'Influences on the policy implementation behaviors of school principals', Unpublished doctoral dissertation, Toronto, Ont., OISE Press.

VOSS, J.F., GREENE, T.R., POST, T.A. and PENNER, B.C. (1983) 'Problem-solving skill in the social sciences', in BOWER, G.H. (Ed.) *The Psychology of Learning and Motivation*, New York, Academic Press, pp. 165–213.

WILLOWER, D.J. and KMETZ, J.T. (1982) 'The managerial behavior of elementary school principals', Paper presented at the Annual Meeting of the American Educational Research Association, New York.

Chapter 6

BANDURA, A. (1977) *Social Learning Theory*, Englewood Cliffs, NJ, Prentice-Hall.

BOLMAN, L.G. and DEAL T. (1984) *Modern Approaches To Understanding and Managing Organizations*, San Francisco, Jossey-Bass.

DAMON, W. and PHELPS, S.E. (1989) 'Critical distinctions among three approaches to peer education', *International Journal of Educational Research*, **13**, 1, pp. 9–18.

DUKE, D., GANSNEDER, B. (1990) 'Teacher empowerment: The view from the classroom', *Educational Policy*, **4**, 2, pp. 145–60.

ETTLING, J. and JAGO, A.G. (1988) 'Participation under conditions of conflict: More on the validity of the Vroom – Yetton model', *Journal of Management Studies*, **25**, 10, pp. 73–84.

FULLAN, M. (1990) 'Staff development, innovation and institutional development', in JOYCE, B. (Ed.) *Changing School Culture Through Staff Development*, Alexandria, VA, The Association For Supervision and Curriculum Development.

FULLAN, M. and CONNELLY, F.M. (1987) *Teacher Education in Ontario*, Toronto, Ministry of Colleges and Universities.

KANTER, R.M. (1983) *The Change Masters: Innovation and Entrepreneurship in the American Corporation*, New York, Simon and Schuster.

KLEMP, G.O. and McCLELLAND, D.C. (1986) 'What characterizes intelligent functioning among senior managers?', in STERNBERG, R.J. and WAGNER, R.K. (Eds) *Practical Intelligence*, Cambridge, Cambridge University Press.

LEITHWOOD, K.A. and STAGER M. (1986) 'Differences in how moderately and highly effective principals classify and manage their problems', Paper presented at the Annual Meeting of the American Educational Research Association, San Francisco, April.

LEITHWOOD, K.A. and STAGER, M. (1989) 'Expertise in principals' problem solving', *Educational Administration Quarterly*, **25**, 2, pp. 126–61.

LEITHWOOD, K.A. and STEINBACH, R. (1991a) 'Indicators of transformational leadership in the everyday problem solving of school administrators', *Journal of Personnel Evaluation in Education*.

LEITHWOOD, K.A. and STEINBACH, R. (in press b) 'Components of chief education officers' problem solving', in LEITHWOOD, K.A. and MUSELLA, D. (Eds) *Understanding School System Administration*, New York, Falmer Press.

LITTLE, J. (1982) 'Norms of collegiality and experimentation: Workplace conditions of school success', *American Educational Research Journal*, **19**, 3, pp. 325–40.

LOHMAN, D.F. (1990) 'Human Intelligence: An introduction to advances in theory and research', *Review of Educational Research*, **59**, 4, pp. 333–74.

MORINE-DERSHIMER, G. (1986) 'What can we learn from thinking?', Paper presented at the Annual Meeting to the American Educational Research Association, San Francisco, April.

NEISSER, U. (1976) 'General, academic, and artificial intelligence', in RESNICK, L. (Ed.) *The Nature of Intelligence*, Hillsdale, NJ, Erlbaum, pp. 135–44.

NISBETT, R.E. and ROSS, L. (1980) *Human Inference: Strategies and Shortcomings of Social Judgement*, Englewood Cliffs, NJ, Prentice-Hall.

ROSENHOLTZ, S.J. (1989) *Teacher's Workplace*, White Plains, NY, Longman.

SCHOENFELD, A.H. (1989) 'Ideas in the air: Speculations on small group learning, environmental and cultural influences on cognition, and epistemology', *International Journal of Educational Research*, **13**, 1, pp. 71–88.

SCHÖN, D.A. (1983) *The reflective practitioner*, San Francisco, Jossey-Bass.

SCHWAB, J.J. (1983) 'The practical 4: Something for curriculum professors to do', *Curriculum Inquiry*, **13**, 3, pp. 239–65.

SHOWERS, C. and CANTOR N. (1985) 'Social cognition: A look at motivated strategies', *Annual Review of Psychology*, **36**, pp. 275–305.

SHULMAN, L.S. (1984) 'The practical and the eclectic: A deliberation on teaching and educational research', *Curriculum Inquiry*, **14**, 2, pp. 183–200.

SHULMAN, L.S. and CAREY, N.B. (1984) 'Psychology and the limitations of individual rationality: Implications for the study of reasoning and civility', *Review of Educational Research*, **54**, 4, pp. 501–24.

SIMON, H. (1957) *Administrative Behavior: A Study of Decision-Making Process in Administrative Organization* (2nd ed.), New York, The Free Press.

STAGER, M. and LEITHWOOD, K.A. (1989) 'Cognitive flexibility and inflexibility in principals' problem solving', *Alberta Journal of Educational Research*, **35**, 3, pp. 217–36.

STERNBERG, R.J. and WAGNER, R.K. (1986) 'Tacit knowledge and intelligence in the everyday world', in STERNBERG, R.J. and WAGNER, R.K. (Eds) *Practical Intelligence: Nature and Origins of Competence in the Everyday World*, Cambridge, Cambridge University Press, pp. 51–83.

VYGOTSKY, L.S. (1978) *Mind in Society*, Cambridge, MA, Harvard University Press.

WEBB, N.W. (1989) 'Peer interaction and learning in small groups', *International Journal of Educational Research*, **13**, 1, pp. 21–40.

Chapter 7

BAYLES, M.D. (1981) *Professional Ethics*, Belmont, Calif., Wadsworth.

BECK, C. (1984a) 'The Nature of Values and Implications for Values Education', Toronto, The Ontario Institute for Studies In Education (mimeo).

BECK, C. (1984b) 'The Nature of Teaching of Moral Problem Solving', Paper presented at the meeting of the Institute for Logic and Cognitive Studies, University of Houston, TX, July.

BECK, C. (1984c) 'Our faith confronts differing life styles and value systems', Paper presented to the Islington United Church School of Religion, Toronto, Ont., November.

BEGLEY, P.T. (1988) The influence of personal beliefs and values on principals' adoption and use of computers in schools. Unpublished doctoral dissertation, The Ontareo Institute Studies in Education.

CAMPBELL-EVANS, G. (1988) 'The nature and influence of values in principal decision-making', Unpublished doctoral dissertation, University of Toronto.

ENGLAND, G.W. (1967) 'Personal value systems of American managers', *Academy of Management Journal*, **10**, pp. 53–68.

ERICCSON, K.A. and SIMON, H.A. (1984) *Protocol Analysis: Verbal Reports as Data*, Cambridge, MA, MIT Press.

EVERS, C.W. (1985) 'Hodgkinson on ethics and the philosophy of administration', *Educational Administration Quarterly*, **21**, 1, pp. 27–50.

GREENFIELD, T.B. (1986) 'The decline and fall of science in educational administration', *Interchange*, **17**, 2, pp. 57–80.

HAMBRICK, D.C. and BRANDON, G.L. (1988) 'Executive Values', in HAMBRICK, D.C. (Ed.) *The Executive Effect: Concepts and Methods for Studying Top Managers*, Greenwich, CT, JAI Press.

HODGKINSON, C. (1978) *Towards a Philosophy of Administration*, Oxford, Basil Blackwell.

HODGKINSON, C. (1951) 'The Value Bases of Administrative Action', Paper presented at Annual Meeting of the American Educational Research Association, San Francisco, April.

KLUCKHON, C. (1951) 'Values and value orientations in the theory of action', in PARSONS, T. and SHILS, E.Z. (Eds) *Toward a General Theory of Action*, Cambridge, MA, Harvard University Press.

LEITHWOOD, K.A. and STEINBACH, R. (1991) 'Components of chief education officers problem solving strategies', in LEITHWOOD, K.A. and MUSELLA, D. (Eds) *Understanding School System Administration: Studies of the Contemporary Chief Education Officer*, New York, Falmer Press.

LEITHWOOD, K.A. and STAGER, M. (1989) 'Expertise in principals' problem solving, *Educational Administration Quarterly*, **25**, 2, pp. 126–361.

MARTIN, W.J. and WILLOWER, D.J. (1981) 'The managerial behavior of high school principals', *Educational Administration Quarterly*, **17**, 1, pp. 69–90.

NISBETT, R.E. and WILSON, T.D. (1977) 'Telling more than we can know: Verbal reports on mental processes', *Psychological Review*, **84**, pp. 231–59.

ROKEACH, M. (1975) *Beliefs, Attitudes and Values*, San Francisco, Jossey-Bass.

SMITH, M.B. (1963) 'Personal Values in the Study of Lives', in WHITE, R.W. (Ed.) *The Study of Lives*, New York, Atherton Press.

STRIKE, K., SOLTIS, E. and HALLER, J. (1989) *The Ethics of School Administration*, New York, Teachers College Press.

TOFFLER, B.L. (1986) *Tough Choices: Managers Talk Ethics*, New York, John Wiley and Sons.

WILLIAMS, R.M. (1968) 'Values', in *International Encyclopedia of the Social Sciences*, New York, MacMillan.

WILLOWER, D.J. (1987) 'Inquiry into educational administration: The last twenty-five years and the next', *Journal of Educational Administration*, 25, 1, pp. 12–28.

Chapter 8

BACHARACH, S.B. (1988) 'Four themes of reform: An editorial essay', *Educational Administration Quarterly*, 24, 4, pp. 484–96.

BACHARACH, S.B., CONLEY, S.C. and SHEDD, J.B. (1987) 'A career developmental framework for evaluating teachers as decision-makers', *Journal of Personnel Evaluation in Education*, 1, pp. 181–94.

BAIRD, L.L. (1983) *Review of Problem Solving Skills*, Princeton, NJ, Educational Testing Services, Research Report.

BALL, S. and GOODSON, I. (Eds) (1985) *Teachers' Lives and Careers*, London, Falmer Press.

BOSSERT, S.T. (1988) 'School effects', in BOYAN, N. (Ed.) *Handbook of Research on Educational Administration*, White Plains, NY, Longman.

BRADESON, P.V. (1986) 'Principally speaking: An analysis of the interpersonal communications of school principals', Paper presented at the Annual Meeting of the American Educational Research Association, San Francisco.

BRANDT, R.S. (1987) 'On teachers coaching teachers: A conversation with Bruce Joyce', *Educational Leadership*, 44, 5, pp. 12–17.

CALFEE, R. (1981) 'Cognitive psychology and educational practice', *Review of Educational Research*, 56, 4, pp. 411–36.

CLARK, C.M. and PETERSON, P.L. (1986) 'Teachers' thought processes', in WITTROCK, M.C. (Ed.) *Handbook of Research on Teaching*, 3rd ed., New York, MacMillan.

CORBETT, H.D., FIRESTONE, W.A. and ROSSMAN, G.B. (1987) 'Resistance to planned change and the sacred in school cultures', *Educational Administration Quarterly*, 33, 4, pp. 36–59.

DARLING-HAMMOND, L., WISE, A.E. and PEASE, S.R. (1983) 'Teacher evaluation in the organizational context: A review of the literature', *Review of Educational Research*, 55, 3, pp. 285–328.

DAVIES, L. (1987) 'The role of the primary head', *Educational Management and Administration*, 15, pp. 43–7.

FULLAN, M. and CONNELLY, M. (1987) *Teacher Education in Ontario: Current Practice and Options for the Future*, Toronto, Ontario Ministry of Education.

GALLY, J. (1986) 'The structure of administrative behavior', Paper presented at the Annual Meeting of the American Educational Research Association, San Francisco.

GARMSTON, R. (1987) 'How administrators support peer coaching', *Educational Leadership*, 44, 5, pp. 18–28.

GERSTEN, R., CARNINE, D. and GREEN, S. (1982) 'The principal as instructional leader: A second look', *Educational Leadership*, **40**, 3, pp. 47–50.

GIDEONESE, H.D. (1988) 'Practitioner-orientated inquiry by teachers: Meaning, justification and implications for school structure', *Journal of Curriculum and Supervision*, **4**, 1, pp. 65–76.

GRAY, W.A. and GRAY, M.M. (1985) 'Synthesis of research on mentoring teachers', *Educational Leadership*, **43**, 3, pp. 37–43.

HANNAY, L. and CHISM, N. (1988) 'The potential of teacher transfer in fostering professional development', *Journal of Curriculum and Supervision*, **3**, 2, pp. 122–35.

HARVEY, O.J. (1970) 'Beliefs and behavior: Some implications for education', *The Science Teacher*, **37**, December, pp. 10–14.

HUBERMAN, M. (1988) 'Teacher careers and school improvement', *Journal of Curriculum Studies*, **20**, 2, pp. 119–32.

HUNT, D. (1966) 'A conceptual systems change model and its application to education', in HARVEY, O.J. (Ed.) *Experience, Structure and Adaptability*, New York, Springer-Verlag.

JOYCE, B. and SHOWERS, B. (1980) 'Improving in-service training: The message of research', *Educational Leadership*, **37**, pp. 379–85.

JOYCE, B. and WEIL, M. (1980) *Models of Teaching*, 2nd ed., Englewood Cliffs, NJ, Prentice-Hall.

KOHLBERG, L. (1970) *Moral Development*, New York, Holt, Rinehart and Winston.

LAWTON, S.B., HICKCOX, E.S., LEITHWOOD, K.A. and MUSELLA, D.F. (1986) *Development and Use of Performance Appraisal of Certified Education Staff in Ontario School Board*, Toronto, Ontario Ministry of Education.

LEIBERMAN, A. and MILLER, L. (1986) 'School improvement: Themes and variations', in LEIBERMAN, A. (Ed.) *Rethinking School Improvement*, New York, Teachers' College Press.

LEITHWOOD, K.A. (1988) *Description and Assessment of a Program for the Certification of Principals*, Toronto, Ontario Ministry of Education.

LEITHWOOD, K.A. (1990) 'The principal's role in teacher development', in JOYCE, B. (Ed.) *Changing School Culture Through Staff Development*, Alexandria, VA, Association for Supervision and Curriculum Development.

LEITHWOOD, K.A. and MONTGOMERY, D.J. (1982) 'The role of elementary school principals in program improvement', *Review of Educational Research*, **52**, 3, pp. 309–39.

LEITHWOOD, K.A. and MONTGOMERY, D.J. (1986) *Improving Principal Effectiveness: The Principal Profile*, Toronto, Ont., OISE Press.

LEITHWOOD, K.A., ROSS, J. and MONTGOMERY, D.J. (1982) 'An investigation of teachers' curriculum decision making', in LEITHWOOD, K.A. (Ed.) *Studies in Curriculum Decision Making*, Toronto, Ont., OISE Press.

LEVINSON, D.J., *et al.* (1978) *The Seasons of a Man's Life*, New York, Knopf.

LITTLE, J.W. (1982) 'Norms of collegiality and experimentation: Workplace conditions of school success', *American Educational Research Journal*, **19**, 3, pp. 325–40.

LITTLE, J.W. (1985) 'Teachers as teacher advisors: The delicacy of collegial leadership', *Educational Leadership*, **43**, 3, pp. 34–6.

LOEVINGER, J. (1966) 'The meaning and measurement of ego development', *American Psychologist*, **21**, pp. 195–206.

LORTIE, D. (1973) 'Observations on teaching as work', in TRAVERS, R. (Ed.) *Second Handbook of Research on Teaching*, Chicago Rand McNally.

MAEROFF, G.I. (1988) 'A blueprint for empowering teachers', *Phi Delta Kappan*, **69**, 7, pp. 472–77.

MARTIN, W.J. and WILLOWER, D.J. (1981) 'The managerial behavior of high school principals', *Educational Administration Quarterly*, **17**, 1, pp. 69–90.

McEVOY, B. (1987) 'Everyday acts: How principals influence development of their staffs', *Educational Leadership*, **44**, 5, pp. 73–7.

MORRIS, V.C., CROWSON, R., HOROWITZ, E. and PORTER-GEHRIC, C. (1986) 'The urban principal: Middle manager in the educational bureaucracy', *Phi Delta Kappan*, **63**, 10, pp. 689–92.

MURPHY, J.T. (1988) 'The unheroic side of leadership: Notes from the swamp', *Phi Delta Kappan*, May, pp. 654–9.

OBERG, A. and FIELD, R. (1986) 'Teacher development through reflection on practice', Paper based on presentations to the Annual Meeting of the American Educational Research Association, San Francisco.

OJA, S. (1979) 'A cognitive-structural approach to adult ego, moral and conceptual development through in-service education', Paper presented to the Annual Meeting of the American Educational Research Association, April.

OJA, S.N. and PINE, G.J. (1981) 'Toward a theory of staff development: Some questions about change', Paper presented at the Annual Meeting of the American Educational Research Association, Los Angeles.

PETERSON, K. and MITCHELL, A. (1985) 'Teacher-controlled evaluation in a career ladder program,' *Educational Leadership*, **43**, 3, pp. 44–9.

PFIEFFER, R.S. (1986) 'Enabling teacher effectiveness: teachers' perspectives on instructional management', Paper presented at the Annual Meeting of the American Educational Research Association, San Francisco, April.

RALLIS, S.F. and HIGHSMITH, M.C. (1986) 'The myth of the great principal: Questions of school management and instructional leadership', *Phi Delta Kappan*, **68**, 4, pp. 300–4.

ROSENHOLTZ, S.J. (1989) *Teachers' Workplace*, White Plains, NY, Longman.

SALLEY, C., McPHERSON, R.B. and BAEHR, M.E. (1978) 'What principals do: An occupational analysis', in ERICKSON, D. and RELLER, T. (Eds) *The Principal in Metropolitan Schools*, Berkeley, CA, McCutchan.

SARASON, S. (1971) *The Culture of the School and the Problem of Change*, Boston, Allyn and Bacon.

SCHÖN, D.A. (1983) *The Reflective Practitioner*, New York, Basic Books.

SCHUELL, T.J. (1986) 'Cognitive conceptions of learning', *Review of Educational Research*, **56**, 4, pp. 411–36.

SHAVELSON, R.J. (1973) 'What is the basic teaching skill?', *Journal of Teacher Education*, **14**, pp. 144–51.

SHAVELSON, R.J. (1976) 'Teachers' decision making', in GAGE, N.L. (Ed.) *The Psychology of Teaching Methods*, Seventy-fifth Yearbook of the National Society for the Study of Education, Chicago, The University of Chicago Press.

SIKES, P.J., MEASOR, L. and WOODS, P. (1985) *Teacher Careers: Crises and Continuities*, London, Falmer Press.

References

SPRINTHALL, N.A. and THEIS-SPRINTHALL, L. (1983) 'The teacher as an adult learner: A cognitive developmental view', in GRIFFIN, G.A. (Ed.) *Staff Development*, Chicago, The University of Chicago Press.

STEVENS, W. (1986) 'The role of vision in the life of elementary school principals', Unpublished doctoral dissertation, Los Angeles, CA, University of Southern California.

STIGGINS, R. and DUKE, D. (1988) *The Case for Commitment to Teacher Growth*, Albany, State University of New York Press.

SULLIVAN, E.V., McCULLOUGH, G. and STAGER, M. (1970) 'A developmental study of the relationship between conceptual, ego, and moral development', *Child Development*, **41**, pp. 399–411.

TRIDER, D. and LEITHWOOD, K.A. (1988) 'Exploring influences on principals' behavior', *Curriculum Inquiry*, **18**, 3, pp. 289–312.

WAGNER, L.A. (1985) 'Ambiguities and possibilities in California's Mentor Teacher Program', *Educational Leadership*, **43**, 3, pp. 23–9.

WILLOWER, D.J. and KMETZ, J.T. (1982) 'The managerial behavior of elementary school principals', Paper presented at the Annual Meeting of the American Educational Research Association, New York.

WILSON, B. and FIRESTONE, W.A. (1987) 'The principal and instruction: Combining bureaucratic and cultural linkages', *Educational Leadership*, September, pp. 18–23.

Chapter 9

BACHARACH, S.B. (1988) 'Four themes of reform: an editorial essay', *Educational Administration Quarterly*, 24, 4, pp. 484–96.

BERGER. P.L. and LUCKMAN, T. (1965) *The Social Construction of Reality*, Garden City, NJ, Doubleday.

BORKO, H. and LIVINGSTON, C. (1989) 'Cognition and improvisation: differences in mathematics instruction by expert and novice teachers', *American Educational Research Journal*, **24**, 4, pp. 473–98.

CORBETT, H.D., FIRESTONE, W.A. and ROSSMAN, G.B. (1987) 'Resistance to planned change and the sacred in school cultures', *Educational Administration Quarterly*, **23**, 4, pp. 36–59.

DEAL, T. and PETERSON, K. (1990) *Principal's Role in Shaping School Culture*, US Office of Educational Research and Improvement.

ERICKSON, F. (1987) 'Conceptions of school culture', *Educational Administration Quarterly*, **23**, 4, pp. 11–24.

FEIMAN-NEMSER, S. and FLODEN, R.E. (1986) 'The cultures of teaching', in WITTROCK, M.C. (Ed.) *Handbook of Research on Teaching*, New York, Macmillan.

FIRESTONE, W.A. and WILSON, B.L. (1985) 'Using bureaucratic and cultural linkages to improve instruction: the principal's contribution', *Educational Administration Quarterly*, **21**, 2, pp. 7–30.

FULLAN, M. (1990) 'Staff development, innovation and institutional development', in JOYCE, B. (Ed.) *Changing School Culture Through Staff Development*, Alexandria, VA, The Association For Supervision and Curriculum Development.

FULLAN, M. and CONNELLY, M. (1987) *Teacher Education in Ontario*, Toronto, Ministry of Colleges and Universities.

HARGREAVES, A. (1990) 'Individualism and individuality: Reinterpreting the teacher culture', Paper presented at the Annual Meeting of the American Educational Research Association, Boston, April.

HARGREAVES, A. and WIGNALL, R. (1989) 'Time for the teacher: A study of collegial relations and preparation time use among elementary school teachers', Toronto, OISE Press (mimeo).

HUBERMAN, A.M. and MILES, M.B. (1982) *Innovation Up Close: A Field Study in Twelve School Settings*, Andover, MA, The Network Inc.

JOYCE, B., BENNET, B. and ROLHEISER-BENNET, C. (1990) 'The self-educating teacher: empowering teachers through research', in JOYCE, B. (Ed.) *Changing School Culture Through Staff Development*, Alexandria, VA, The Association For Supervision and Curriculum Development.

LAWTON, S.B. and LEITHWOOD, K.A. (1988) *Student Retention and Transition in Ontario High Schools*, Toronto, Ontario Ministry of Education.

LEITHWOOD, K.A. (1990) 'The principal's role in teacher development', in JOYCE, B. (Ed.) *Changing School Culture Through Staff Development*, Alexandria, VA, ASCD.

LEITHWOOD, K.A. and JANTZI, D. (1991) 'Transformational leadership: How principals can help reform school cultures', *School Effectiveness and School Improvement*, **1**, 3.

LITTLE, J. (1982) 'Norms of collegiality and experimentation: Workplace conditions of school success', *American Educational Research Journal*, **19**, 3, pp. 325–40.

LITTLE, J. (1990) 'The mentor phenomenon and the social organization of leading', *Review of Research in Education*, **5**, 16, Washington, DC, American Educational Research Association.

MAEROFF, G.I. (1989) 'A blueprint for empowering teachers', *Phi Delta Kappan*, **69**, 7, pp. 472–7.

MARTIN, W.J. and WILLOWER, D.J. (1981) 'The managerial behaviour of high school principals,' *Educational Administration Quarterly*, **17**, 1, pp. 69–90.

MEHAN, H. (1984) 'Institutional decision-making', in ROGOFF, B. and LAVE, J. (Eds) *Everyday Cognition: Its Development in Social Context*, Cambridge, MA, Harvard University Press, pp. 41–66.

MILES, M.B. and HUBERMAN, A.M. (1984) *Qualitative Data Analysis: A Sourcebook of New Methods*, Beverley Hills, CA, Sage.

NIAS, J., SOUTHWORK, G. and YEOMANS, R. (1982) *Understanding the Primary School as an Organization*, London, Cassell.

PETERS, T.J. (1979) 'Symbols, patterns and settings: An optimistic case for getting things done', *Organizational Dynamics*, **7**, pp. 2–23.

PFEFFER, J. (1981) 'Management as symbolic action: The creation and maintenance of organizational paradigms', in CUMMINGS, L.L. and STAW, B.M. (Eds) *Research in Organizational Behaviour, Vol. 3*, Greenwich, CT, JAI Press.

ROSENHOLTZ, S.J. (1989) *Teachers' Workplace*, White Plains, NY, Longman.

SASHKIN, M. and SASHKIN, M.G. (1990) 'Leadership and culture building in schools', Paper presented at the Annual Meeting of the American Educational Research Association, Boston, April.

SCHNEIDER, B. and HOCHSCHILD, J. (1988) 'Career Teachers' Perceptions of the Teaching Culture', Chicago, The University of Chicago Press (mimeo).

SHEIN, E.H. (1985) *Organizational Culture and Leadership: A Dynamic View*, San Francisco, Jossey-Bass.

SHULMAN, L.S. and CAREY, N.B. (1984) 'Psychology and the limitations of individual rationality: Implications for the study of reasoning and civility', *Review of Educational Research*, **54**, 4, pp. 501–24.

SU ZHIXIN (1990, May), 'The function of the peer group in teacher socialization', *Phi Delta Kappan*, pp. 273–277.

WILLOWER, D.J. and KMETZ, J.T. (1982) 'The managerial behaviour of elementary school principals', Paper presented at the Annual meeting of AERA, New York, April.

Chapter 10

BECKER, H.S. and CARPER, J.W. (1956) 'The development of identification with an occupation', *The American Journal of Sociology*, **61**, 4, pp. 289–98.

BEGLEY, P., CAMPBELL-EVANS, G. and BROWNRIDGE, A. (1990) 'Influences on the socializing experiences of aspiring principals', Paper presented at the Annual Meeting of the Canadian Association for the Study of Educational Administration, Victoria, B.C., June.

COOPER, L. (1989) 'The principal as instructional leader', *Principal*, **68**, 3, pp. 13–16.

CROWSON, R.L. and MORRIS, V.C. (1985) 'Administrative control in large-city school systems: An investigation in Chicago', *Educational Administration Quarterly*, **21**, 4, pp. 51–70.

DARESH, J. (1986) 'Support for beginning principals: First hurdles are highest', *Theory Into Practice*, **25**, 3, pp. 168–73.

DUKE, D.L. (1987) *School Leadership and Instructional Improvement*, New York, Random House.

GREENFIELD, W.D. (1985) 'The moral socialization of school administrators: Informal role learning outcomes', *Educational Administration Quarterly*, **21**, 4, pp. 99–119.

HAVEN, E., ADKINSON, P.D. and BAGLEY, M. (1980) *Minorities in Educational Administration: The Principalship*, ERIC ED208485.

KLINE, W.A. (1988) 'Developing principals' leadership skills', *Journal of Staff Development*, **9**, 2, pp. 52–7.

LEITHWOOD, K.A. and AVERY, C. (1987) 'Inservice education for principals in Canada', in LEITHWOOD, K.A., RUTHERFORD, W. and VAN DER VEGT, R. (Eds) *Preparing School Leaders For Educational Improvement*, London, Croom Helm.

LEITHWOOD, K.A., STANLEY, K. and MONTGOMERY, D.J. (1984) 'Training principals for school improvement', *Education and Urban Society*, **17**, 1, pp. 49–72.

LEITHWOOD, K., STEINBACH, R. and BEGLEY, P. (in press) 'The nature and contribution of socialization experiences to becoming a Principal in Canada', in HALL, G. and PARKAY, F. (Eds) *Becoming a principal: The Challenges of Beginning Leadership*, New York, Allyn and Bacon.

LEITHWOOD, K. and STEINBACH, R. (in progress) 'Do socialization experiences account for success in acquiring a school administration position?', Toronto, The Ontario Institute for Studies in Education.

LINN, M.C. and HYDE, J.S. (1989) 'Gender, mathematics and science', *Educational Researcher*, **18**, 8, pp. 17–28.

MARSHALL, C. (1984) 'The enculturation of the vice principal', Paper presented at the Annual Meeting of the American Educational Research Association, San Francisco, April.

MERTON, R.K. (1963) *Social Theory and Social Structure*, New York, The Free Press.

PAPKE, D. (1989) 'The socialization of the elementary school vice principal: Making the transition from teaching to administration', Unpublished doctoral dissertation, The Ontario Institute for Studies In Education, Toronto.

PETERSON, K. (1986) 'Principals' work, socialization and training: Developing more effective leaders', *Theory Into Practice*, **25**, 3, pp. 151–5.

RONKOWSKI, S. and IANNACCONE, L. (1989) 'Socialization research in administration, graduate school and other professions: The heuristic power of Van Gennep and Becker models', Paper presented at the Annual Meeting of the American Education Research Association, San Francisco, April.

ROSS, P.N. (1989) 'Socialization in the preparation of principals', Unpublished manuscript, York Region Board of Education, Ontario.

SHAKESHAFT, C. (1989) 'The gender gap in research in educational administration', *Educational Administration Quarterly*, **25**, 4, pp. 324–37.

SILVER, P. (1986) 'Case records: A reflective practice approach to administrator development', *Theory Into Practice*, **25**, 3, pp. 161–7.

VAN GENNEP, A. (1960) *The Rites of Passage*, Chicago, University of Chicago Press.

Chapter 11

ALEXANDER, P.A. and JUDY, J.E. (1988) 'The interaction of domain-specific and strategic knowledge in academic performance', *Review of Educational Resarch*, **58**, 4, pp. 375–404.

ANDREWS, R.L., SODER, R. and JACOBY, D. (1986) 'Principal roles, other in-school variables, and academic achievement by ethnicity and SES', Paper presented at the Annual Meeting of the American Educational Research Association, San Francisco.

ARGYRIS, C. (1982) *Reasoning, Learning and Action: Individual and Organizational*, San Francisco, Jossey Bass.

BANDURA, A. (1977) *Social Learning Theory*, Englewood Cliffs, NJ, Prentice-Hall.

BARNETT, B.G. and BRILL, A.D. (1990) 'Building reflection into administrative training programs', *Journal of Personnel Evaluation in Education*, **3**, pp. 179–92.

BEGLEY, P.T. (1988) 'The influence of personal beliefs and values on principals' adoption and use of computers', Unpublished doctoral thesis, University of Toronto, Ont.

BEGLEY, P.T., CAMPBELL-EVANS, G. and BROWNRIDGE, A. (1990) 'Influences on the socializing experiences of aspiring principals', Paper presented at the

Annual Meeting of the Canadian Society For Studies in Education, Victoria, B.C.

BLUM, R.E. and BUTLER, J.A. (1989) *School Leader Development for School Improvement*, Leuven, Belgium, Acco.

CALFEE, R. (1981) 'Cognitive psychology and educational practice', *Review of Research in Education*, **9**, pp. 3–74.

CAMPBELL-EVANS, G. (1988) 'Nature and Influence of Values in Principal Decision-making', Unpublished doctoral thesis, University of Toronto, Ont.

COUSINS, J.B. (1988) 'Factors influencing knowledge utilization: Principals' use of appraisal data concerning their own performance', Unpublished doctoral dissertation, University of Toronto, Ont.

COUSINS, J.B. and LEITHWOOD, K.A. (1986) 'Current empirical research on evaluation utilization', *Review of Educational Research*, **56**, 3, pp. 331–64.

COUSINS, J.B. and ROSS, J.A. (1990) *Fostering Teacher–Teacher Interaction: Principals' Efforts to Improve Student Outcomes*, Final Report of OISE Transfer Grant Project No. 81-1083, Peterborough, Ont., OISE Trent Valley Centre.

DARESH, J.C. and LaPLANT, J. (1984) 'In-service for school administrators: A status report', Paper presented at the Annual Meeting of the American Educational Research Association, New Orleans, April.

GAINES-ROBINSON, D. and ROBINSON, J.C. (1989) *Training for Impact*, San Francisco, Jossey-Bass.

GREENFIELD, W. (1987) *Instructional Leadership: Concepts, Issues and Controversies*, Boston, Allyn and Bacon.

GRIFFITHS, D., STOUT, R. and FORSYTH, P. (Eds) (1988) *Leaders for America's Schools: The Report and Papers of the National Commission on Excellence in Educational Administration*, Berkeley, CA, McCutchan.

HALL, G., RUTHERFORD, W.L., HORD, S.M. and HULING, L.L. (1984, February) 'Effects of three principal styles on school improvement', *Educational Leadership*, **41**, 5, pp. 22–9.

HALLINGER, P. and MURPHY, J. (1987) 'Instructional leadership in the school context', in GREENFIELD, W. (Ed.) *Instructional Leadership*, Boston, Allyn and Bacon.

HALLINGER, P. and MURPHY, J. (1991) 'Developing leaders for tomorrow's schools, *Phi Delta Kappan*, **72**, 7, pp. 514–20.

HECK, R.H., LARSEN, T.J. and MARCOULIDES, G.A. (1990) 'Instructional leadership and school achievement: Validation of a causal model', in *Educational Administration Quarterly*, **26**, 2, pp. 94–125.

HIGH, R.M. and ACHILLES, C.M. (1986) 'Principal influence in instructionally effective schools', Paper presented at the Annual Meeting of the American Educational Research Association, San Francisco, April.

HUTSON, H.M. JR (1981) 'In-service best practices: The learnings of general education', *Journal of Research and Development in Education*, **14**, 2, pp. 1–10.

LAWTON, S.B., LEITHWOOD, K.A., BATCHER, E., DONALDSON, E.L. and STEWART, R. (1988) *Student Retention and Transition in Ontario High Schools: Policies, Practices and Prospects*, Toronto, Queen's Printer for Ontario.

LEITHWOOD, K.A., and AVERY, C. (1987) 'Inservice education for principals in Canada', in LEITHWOOD, K.A., RUTHERFORD, W. AND VAN DER VEGT, R. (Eds) *Preparing Schools Leaders for Educational Improvement*, London, Croom-Helm.

LEITHWOOD, K.A. (1988) 'A Review of Research on the School Principalship', Study commissioned by the World Bank, Washington, DC.

LEITHWOOD, K.A., BEGLEY, P.T. and COUSINS J.B. (1990) 'The nature, causes and consequences of principals' practices: An agenda for future research', *Journal of Educational Administration*, **28**, 4, pp. 5–31.

LEITHWOOD, K.A., FULLAN, M. and HEALD-TAYLOR, G. (1987) 'School level CRDI procedures to guide the school improvement process', Toronto, Ont., OISE Press (mimeo).

LEITHWOOD, K.A., LAWTON, S.B. and COUSINS, J.B. (1989) 'The relationship between selected characteristics of effective secondary schools and student retention', in CREEMERS, B., PETERS, T. and REYNOLDS, D. (Eds) *School Effectiveness and School Improvement*, Amsterdam, Neth. Swets and Zeithinger.

LEITHWOOD, K.A. and MONTGOMERY, D.J. (1986) *Improving Principal Effectiveness: The Principal Profile*, Toronto, Ont., OISE Press.

LEITHWOOD, K.A. and STAGER, M. (1986) 'Differences in problem-solving processes used by moderately and highly effective principals', Paper presented at the Annual Meeting of the American Educational Research Association, San Francisco, April.

LEITHWOOD, K.A. and STAGER, M. (1989) 'Expertise in principals' problem-solving', in *Educational Administration Quarterly*, **25**, 2, pp. 126–61.

LEITHWOOD, K.A., STANLEY, K. and MONTGOMERY, D.G. (1984) 'Training principals for school improvement', *Education and Urban Society*, **17**, 1, pp. 49–72.

LEITHWOOD, K.A. and STEINBACH, R. (1990) 'Improving the problem-solving expertise of school administrators: Theory and practice', Paper presented at the Annual Meeting of the Canadian Society for Studies in Education, Victoria, B.C.

LEITHWOOD, K.A., STEINBACH, R. and BEGLEY, P.T. (1990) 'The nature and contribution of socialization experiences to becoming a principal in Canada', in HALL, G.E., PARKAY, F.W. (Eds) *Becoming a Principal: The Challenges of Beginning Leadership*, Boston, Allyn and Bacon.

MERRIAN, S.B. and CAFFARELLA, R.S. (1991) *Learning in Adulthood*, San Francisco, Jossey-Bass.

MILLER, J. and SELLER, W. (1985) *Curriculum: Perspectives and practice*, White Plains, NY, Longman.

NATIONAL POLICY BOARD FOR EDUCATIONAL ADMINISTRATION (1990) *Improving the Preparation of School Administrators: An Agenda for Reform*, Charlottesville, VA, University of Virginia.

PITNER, N. (1987) 'Administrator preparation in the United States', in LEITHWOOD, K.A., RUTHERFORD, W.J. and VANDER VEGT (Eds) *Preparing School Leaders for Educational Improvement*, London, Croom Helm.

SCHÖN, D. (1983) *The Reflective Practitioner*, New York, Basic Books.

SCHÖN, D.A. (1987) *Educating the Reflective Practitioner*, San Francisco, Jossey Bass.

SCHUELL, T.J. (1986) 'Cognitive conceptions of learning', *Review of Educational Research*, **56**, 4, pp. 411–436.

SILVER, P.F. and MOYLE, C. (1984) 'The impact of intensive in-service programs on educational leaders and their organizations', *Planning and Changing*, **5**, 1, pp. 18–34.

SIMPSON, R.J. and GALBO, J.J. (1986) 'Interaction and learning: Theorizing on the art of teaching', *Interchange*, **17**, 4, pp. 37–52.

SMITH, W.F. and ANDREWS, R.L. (1989) *Instructional Leadership: How Principals Make a Difference*, Alexandria, VA, Association for Supervision and Curriculum Development.

SPARKS, G.M. (1983) 'Synthesis of research on staff development for effective teaching', *Educational Leadership*, pp. 65–72.

Chapter 12

ARGYRIS, C. (1982) *Reasoning, Learning and Action*, San Francisco, Jossey-Bass.

ARGYRIS, C., PUTNAM, R. and SMITH, D. (1985) *Action Science*, San Francisco, Jossey-Bass.

BEGLEY, P.T. and LEITHWOOD, K.A. (1989) 'The influence of values on the practices of school administrators', *Journal of Educational Administration and Foundations*, **4**, 2, pp. 26–39.

BEGLEY, P.T. and LEITHWOOD, K.A. (in press) 'The nature and role of values in principals' problem solving', *The Canadian School Executive*.

BERGER, P. and LUCKMAN, T. (1966) *The Social Construction of Reality*, Garden City, NJ, Doubleday.

BOUD, D. (Ed.) (1985) *Problem-based learning in education for the professions*, Sydney, Herdsa.

BLUM, R.E. and BUTLER, J.A. (Eds) *School Leader Development for School Improvement*, Leuven, ACCO.

BRANSFORD, J.D., FRANKS, J.J., VYE, N. and SHERWOOD, R. (in press) 'New approaches to instruction: Because wisdom can't be told', in VOSNIADOM, S. and ORTONY, A. (Eds) *Similarities and Analogical Reasoning*, New York, Cambridge University Press.

BROWN, A.L. and DELOACHE, J.S. (1978) 'Skills, plans and self-regulation', in SIEGLER, R. (Ed.) *Children's Thinking: What Develops*, Hillsdale, NJ, Erlbaum, pp. 3–35.

BROWN, J.S., COLLINS, A. and DUGUID, P. (1989) 'Situated cognition and the culture of learning', *Educational Researcher*, **18**, 1, pp. 32–42.

BURTON, R.R., BROWN, J.S. and FISCHER, G. (1984) 'Skiing as a model of instruction', in ROGOFF, B. and LAVE, J. (Eds) *Everyday Cognition: Its Development in Social Context*, Cambridge, MA, Harvard University Press, pp. 139–150.

CAMPBELL, G. (1988) 'The relationship between principals' values and their decision making processes', Unpublished doctoral dissertation, The Ontario Institute For Studies in Education, Toronto.

CHI, M., GLASER, R. and FARR, M. (1985) *The Nature of Expertise*, Hillsdale, NJ, Erlbaum.

GRIMMETT, P. (1989) 'A commentary on Schön's view of reflection', *Journal of Curriculum and Supervision*, **5**, 1, pp. 19–28.

HALLINGER, P. and McCARY, C.E. (in press) 'Developing the strategic thinking of instructional leaders', *The Elementary School Journal*.

LEITHWOOD, K.A. (1988) 'How chief school officers classify and manage their problems', Unpublished manuscript, The Ontario Institute for Studies in Education, Toronto.

LEITHWOOD, K.A., RUTHERFORD, W. and VAN DER VEGT, R. (1987) *Preparing School Leaders for Educational Improvement*, London, Croom-Helm.

LEITHWOOD, K.A. and STAGER, M. (1986) 'Differences in problem-solving processes used by moderately and highly effective principals', Paper presented at the Annual Meeting of the American Educational Research Association, San Francisco, April.

LEITHWOOD, K.A. and STAGER, M. (1989) 'Expertise in principals' problem solving', *Educational Administration Quarterly*, **25**, 2, pp. 126–61.

LEITHWOOD, K.A. and STEINBACH, R. (1989) 'Components of chief education officers' problem solving', Paper presented at the Annual Meeting of the American Educational Research Association, San Francisco, April.

LEITHWOOD, K.A. and STEINBACH, R. (1991a) 'Improving the problem solving expertise of school administrators: Theory and practice', *Education and Urban Society*.

LEITHWOOD, K.A. and STEINBACH, R. (in press b) 'Indicators of transformational leadership in the everyday problem solving of school principals', *Journal of Personnel Evaluation In Education*.

LEITHWOOD, K.A., STEINBACH, R. and BEGLEY, P. (in press) 'The nature and contribution of socialization experiences to becoming a principal in Canada', in HALL, G.E. and PARKAY, F.W. (Eds) *Becoming a Principal: The Challenges of Beginning Leadership*, New York, Allyn and Bacon.

LESGOLD, A. (1984) 'Acquiring expertise', in ANDERSON, J.R. and KOSSLYN, S.M. (Eds) *Tutorials in Learning and Memory*, New York, Freeman, pp. 31–60.

LINDBLOM, C.E. and COHEN, D.K. (1979) *Usable Knowledge*, New Haven, CT, Yale University Press.

MEHAN, H. (1984) 'Institutional decision making', in ROGOFF, B. and LAVE, J. (Eds) *Everyday Cognition: Its Development in Social Context*, Cambridge, MA, Harvard University Press, pp. 41–66.

MEICHENBAUM, D. (1977) *Cognitive Behavior Modification*, New York, Plenum Press.

NICKERSON, R.S. (1988–89) 'On improving thinking', in ROTHERKOPF, E.Z. (Ed.) *Review of Research in Education*, **15** Washington, American Educational Research Association, pp. 3–57.

NISBETT, R. and ROSS, L. (1980) *Human Inference: Strategies and Short-comings of Social Judgement*, Englewood Cliffs, NJ, Prentice–Hall.

OGILVIE, M. and STEINBACH, R. (1988) 'Learning across domains: The role of generalized strategies', Paper presented at the Annual Meeting of the American Educational Research Association, New Orleans, April.

PERKINS, D.N. (1985) 'General cognitive skills: Why not?', in CHIPMIN, S.F., SEGAL, J.W. and GLASER, R. (Eds) *Thinking and Learning Skills, Vol. 2: Research and Open Questions*, Hillsdale, NJ, Erlbaum, pp. 339–64.

PERKINS, D.N. and SALOMON, G. (1988) 'Teaching for transfer', *Educational Leadership*, **46**, 1, pp. 22–32.

PERKINS, D.N. and SALOMON, G. (1989) 'Are cognitive skills context-bound?', *Educational Researcher*, **18**, 1, pp. 16–25.

ROGOFF, B. (1984) 'Introduction: Thinking and learning in social context', in ROGOFF, B. and LAVE, J. (Eds) *Everyday Cognition: Its Development in Social Context*, Cambridge, MA, Harvard University Press, pp. 1–8.

ROSS, J. (1990) *Personal communication*.

SALOMON, G. and PERKINS, D.N. (n.d.) 'Rocky roads to transfer: Rethinking mechanisms of a neglected phenomenon', Tel Aviv, University of Tel Aviv (mimeo).

SCHÖN, D. (1983) *The Reflective Practitioner*, New York, Basic Books.

SHANK, R. and ABELSON, R. (1977) *Scripts, Plans, Goals and Understanding*, Hillsdale, NJ, Erlbaum.

STAGER, M. and LEITHWOOD, K.A. (1989) 'Cognitive flexibility and inflexibility in principals' problem solving', *Alberta Journal of Educational Research*, **35**, 3, pp. 217–36.

STERNBERG, R.J. and CARUSO, O.R. (1985) 'Practical modes of knowing', in EISNER, E. (Ed.) *Learning and Teaching the Ways of Knowing*, NSSE Yearbook, Chicago, University of Chicago Press, pp. 133–58.

VYGOTSKY, L.S. (1978) *Mind in Society*, Cambridge, MA, Harvard University Press.

WINE, J. (1971) 'Test anxiety and the direction of attention', *Psychological Bulletin*, **76**, pp. 92–104.

Chapter 13

BERRY, B. and GINSBERG, R. (1988) 'Legitimizing subjectivity: Meritorious performance and the professionalization of teacher and principal evaluation', *Journal of Personnel Evaluation in Education*, **2**, 2, pp. 123–40.

BOLAM, R. (1990) 'Principal evaluation and appraisal in England', Paper presented at the Annual Meeting of the American Educational Research Association, Boston.

COUSINS, J.B. (1988) 'Factors influencing knowledge utilization: Principals' use of appraisal data concerning their own performance', Unpublished PhD dissertation, Toronto, Ont., University of Toronto.

COUSINS, J.B. (1989) 'Validity and reliability of the Principal Profile-Based Instrument', Toronto, Ont., Institute for Studies In Education (mimeo).

COUSINS, J.B. and LEITHWOOD, K.A. (1986) 'Current empirical research on evaluation utilization', *Review of Educational Research*, **56**, 3, pp. 331–64.

DUHAMEL, R., CYZE, M., LAMACRAFT, G. and RUTHERFORD, C. (1981) 'The evaluation of principals', *Education Canada*, **21**, 2, pp. 20–7.

DUKE, D.L. and STIGGINS, R.S. (1985) 'Evaluating the performance of principals: A descriptive study', *Educational Administration Quarterly*, **21**, 4, pp. 71–98.

GINSBERG, R. and BERRY, B. (1990) 'The folklore of principal evaluation', *Journal of Personnel Evaluation in Education*, **3**, pp. 205–30.

HARRISON, W.C. and PETERSON, K.D. (1986) 'Pitfalls in the evaluation of principals', Paper presented at the Annual Meeting of the American Educational Research Association, San Francisco (ED 019 48), April.

HICKCOX, E.S. (1990) *Personal Communications*, September.

HICKCOX, E.S., LAWTON, S.B., LEITHWOOD, K.A. and MUSELLA, D.F. (1988) *Making a Difference Through Performance Appraisal*, Toronto, Ont., OISE Press.

INGLE, R.B. (1975) 'Administrative evaluation: A caveat', in GEPHART, W.J., INGLE, R.B. and POTTER, W.J. (Eds) *The Evaluation of Administrative Performance*, Columbus, OH, National Symposium for Professors of Educational Research, Ohio State University, pp. 239–44.

JANEY, C.B. (1988) 'The role of parents in the evaluation of principals', *Equity and Choice*, **4**, 2, pp. 24–9.

JORESKOG, K.G. and SORBOM, D. (1981) *LISREL: Analysis of linear structural relations by the method of maximum likelihood*, Versions 5 and 6, Chicago, IL, National Educational Resources.

KECK, D.B. and HAMPTON, B.R. (1987) 'An evaluation and incentive program for school administrators: A professional approach', Paper presented at the Annual Meeting of the Association of School Administrators, New Orleans (ED 281 311).

LAWTON, S.B., HICKCOX, E.S., LEITHWOOD, K.A. and MUSELLA, D. (1985) 'Successful techniques for evaluating teachers and principals'. Toronto, The Ontario Institute for Studies In Education (mimeo).

LAWTON, S.B., HICKCOX, E.S., LEITHWOOD, K.A. and MUSELLA, D. (1986) *The Development and Use of Performance Appraisal of Certified Education Staff in Ontario School Boards*, Toronto, The Queen's Printer for Ontario.

LEITHWOOD, K.A. (1986) 'School system policies for effective school administration', Toronto, The Ontario Institute for Studies in Education (mimeo).

LEITHWOOD, K.A. and BEGLEY, P. (1985) *School Management in Canada: A Description and Analysis of Selected Issues*, Technical report prepared for the International School Improvement Project, Organization for Economic and Cooperative Development.

MILES, M.B. and HUBERMAN, A.M. (1984) *The Analysis of Qualitative Data: A Sourcebook of Methods*, Beverly Hills, CA, Sage.

MURPHY, J., PETERSON, K.D. and HALLINGER, P. (1986) 'The administrative control of principals in effective school districts: The supervision and evaluation functions', *The Urban Review*, **18**, 3, pp. 149–75.

MUSELLA, D. and LAWTON, S. (1986) *Selection and Promotion Procedures in Ontario School Boards*, Toronto, Ontario Ministry of Education.

PETERS, S. and BAGENSTOS, N.T. (1988) 'State mandated principal evaluation: A report on current practice', Paper presented at the Annual Meeting of the American Educational Research Association, New Orleans, March.

PETERSON, K.D., MARSHALL, C. and GRIER, T. (1987) 'Academies for assistant principals', *Educational Leadership*, **45**, 1, pp. 47–8.

REDFERN, G.B. (1986) 'Techniques of evaluation of principals and assistant principals: Four case studies', *NASSP Bulletin*, pp. 66–74.

RENTSCH, G.J. (1983) 'Assessing administrative performance', in ZAPPULA, E. (Ed.) *Evaluating Administrative Performance: Current Trends and Techniques*, Belmont, CA, STAR Publishing.

VALENTINE, J.W. (1987) 'Performance/outcome based principal evaluation', Paper presented at the Annual Meeting of the American Association of School Administrators, New Orleans (ED 281 317).

Chapter 14

ALKIN, M.C. and COYLE, K. (1988) 'Thoughts on evaluation utilization, mis-utilization and non-utilization', *Studies in Educational Evaluation*, **14**, pp. 331–40.

ALLISON, D.J. (1989) 'Assessing principal assessment centres', *The Canadian Administrator*, **28**, 6, pp. 1–8.

ALLISON, P.A. and ALLISON, D.J. (1990) 'Playing PACman in Canada: Reflections on the introduction and use of NASSP principal assessment centres in Canada', Paper presented at the Annual Meeting of the American Educational Research Association, Boston.

ALLISON, P.A. and ALLISON, D.J. (1989) 'Playing PACman: Principal assessment centres as an addictive innovation', *Field Development Newsletter*, **18**, 2, pp. 1–29.

ANDREWS, R.L., SODER, R. and JACOBY, D. (1986) 'Principal roles, other in-school variables, and academic achievement by ethnicity and ses', Paper presented at the Annual Meeting of the American Educational Research Association, San Francisco, California, April.

BALTZELL, D.C. and DENTLER, R.A. (1983) *Selecting American School Principals: A Sourcebook for Educators*, Cambridge, MA, Abt Associates (ED 236 811).

BORMAN, W.C. (1986) 'Behavior-based rating scales', in BERK, R.A. (Ed.) *Performance Assessment: Methods and Applications*, Baltimore, MD, John Hopkins University Press.

BRYANT, B.J., LAWLIS, P., NICHOLSON, E. and MAHER, B.P. (1978) *Employment Factors Superintendents use in Hiring Administrators for Their School Districts*, Madison, WI., Association for School College and University Staffing.

BRYANT, M.T. (1990) 'A study of administrative expertise in participant performance on the NASSP assessment centre', *Journal of Personnel Evaluation in Education*, **3**, 4, pp. 353–63.

COUSINS, J.B. (1988) 'Factors influencing knowledge utilization: Principals' use of appraisal data concerning their own performance', Unpublished PhD dissertation, Toronto, Ont., University of Toronto.

COUSINS, J.B. (1989) 'Validity and reliability of the principal profile-based instrument' (PPBI) Peterborough, OISE Trent Valley Centre (mimeo).

COUSINS, J.B., BEGLEY, P.T. and LEITHWOOD, K.A. (1988) 'Safeguards against the misuse of instruments for the selection and appraisal of school administration', Paper presented at the Annual Meeting of the Canadian Association for the Study of Educational Administration, Windsor, June.

COUSINS, J.B. and LEITHWOOD, K.A. (1987a) 'Development of a Principal Profile-based Instrument (PPBI) for the selection and appraisal of school administrators', Paper presented at the conference: The Selection of School Administrators, Toronto, Ont, November.

COUSINS, J.B. and LEITHWOOD, K.A. (1987b) 'Planned educational change, evaluation utilization and the evaluation of educational personnel', Paper presented at the public hearings of the Joint Committee on Standards for Educational Evaluation, Washington, DC, April.

EBMEIER, H. and WILSON, A. (1989) 'Development of an instrument for client based principal formative evaluation', Paper presented at the Annual Meeting of the American Educational Research Association, San Francisco, March.

ELKINS, T. (1987) 'Longlisting for leaderships and deputy headships in secondary schools: The elimination of the majority', *Research Papers in Education*, **2**, 3, pp. 177–99.

ELLETT, C.D. (1978) 'Understanding and using the Georgia Principal assessment system', *CCBC Notebook*, **7**, February, pp. 2–14.

GINSBERG, R.S. and BERRY, B. (1990) 'The folklore of principal evaluation', *Journal of Personnel Evaluation in Education*, **3**, 3, pp. 205–230.

GIPS, C.J. (1986) 'Influential criteria in the initial selection of assistant principal candidates: A study of determining factors in résumé analysis', Paper presented at the Annual Meeting of the Midwestern Education Research Association, Chicago, October.

GOMEZ, J.J. and STEPHENSON, R.S. (1987) 'Validity of an assessment centre for the selection of school-level administrators', *Educational Evaluation and Policy Analysis*, **9**, 1, pp. 1–7.

HALLINGER, P. and MURPHY, J.F. (1987) 'Assessing the instructional leadership behavior of principals', *The Elementary School Journal*, **86**, 2, pp. 217–48.

HAZI, H.M. (1989) 'Measurement vs. supervisory judgement: The case of Sweeney vs. Tarlington', *Journal of Curriculum and Supervision*, **4**, 3, pp. 211–29.

HECK, R.H., LARSEN, T.J. and MARCOULIDES, G.A. (1990) 'Instructional leadership and school achievement: Validation of a causal model', *Educational Administration Quarterly*, **26**, 2, pp. 94–125.

HERSEY, P.W. (1986) 'Selecting and developing educational leaders', *The School Administrator*, **43**, 3, pp. 16–17.

HOGAN, J. and ZENKE, L.L. (1986) 'Dollar value utility of alternative procedures for selecting school principals', *Educational and Psychological Measurement*, **46**, pp. 935–45.

JANTZ, T., HELLERVIK, L. and GILMORE, D.C. (1986) *Behavior Description Interviewing: New, Accurate, Cost Effective*, Boston, Allyn and Bacon.

THE JOINT COMMITTEE ON STANDARDS FOR EDUCATIONAL EVALUATION (1988) *The Personnel Evaluation Standards*, Beverley Hills, CA, Sage.

KRYSINSKI, P.R., REED, D.B., GOUGEON, T.D. and ARMSTRONG, M.D. (1987) 'Assessing leadership qualities of school principals employing responses to case studies', Paper presented at the Annual Meeting of the American Educational Research Association, Washington, DC, April.

KNOOP, R. and COMMON, R.W. (1985) 'A performance appraisal system for school principals', Paper presented at the Annual Meeting of the Canadian Society for the Study of Education, Montreal, Que.

LANDY F.J. and FARR, J.L. (1983) *The Measurement of Work Performance*, New York, Academic Press.

LANE, B.A. and MURPHY, J. (1988) 'Building effective school cultures through personnel functions: Staff acquisition processes', *Journal of Personnel Evaluation in Education*, **2**, pp. 271–87.

LEITHWOOD, K.A. (1987) 'Using the principal profile to assess performance', *Educational Leadership*, **45**, 1, pp. 63–6.

LEITHWOOD, K.A. and MONTGOMERY, D. (1986) *Improving Principal Effectiveness: The Principal Profile*, Toronto, Ont., OISE Press.

LEITHWOOD, K.A. and STEINBACH, R. (1990) 'Improving the problem solving expertise of school administrators: Theory and practice', Paper presented at the Annual Meeting of the Canadian Association for the Study of Educational Administration, June.

MILESTEIN, M. and FIEDLER, C.K. (1989) 'The status of and potential for administrator assessment centres in education', *Urban Education*, **23**, 4, pp. 361–76.

MORGAN, C., HALL, V. and MACKAY, H. (1983) *The Selection of Secondary School Headteachers*, Milton Keynes, Open University Press.

MURPHY, J. (1988) 'Methodological, measurement and conceptual problems in the study of instructional leadership', *Education Evaluation and Policy Analysis*, **10**, 2, pp. 117–39.

MUSELLA, D. (1983) *Selecting School Administrators*, Toronto, Ont., OISE Press.

MUSELLA, D. and LAWTON, S.B. (1986) *Selection and Promotion Procedures in Ontario School Boards*, Toronto, The Queen's Printer for Ontario.

NAGY, G.P. and ALLISON, P.A. (1988) 'The assessment centre experience', Paper presented at the Annual Meeting of the Canadian Educational Association, Fredericton, N.B., May.

PARKAY, F.W. (1987) 'A behavioural approach to the selection of school administrators', *Planning and Changing*, **18**, 3, pp. 163–69.

PARKAY, F.W. and CURRIE, G. (1989) 'Sources of support for first time high school principals during selection and entry', Paper presented at the Annual Meeting of the American Educational Research Association, San Francisco.

PATTON, M.Q. (1988) in ALKIN, M.C. (Ed) 'Evaluation Reflections', CSE Technical Report, Los Angeles, UCLA Center for the study of evaluation.

PITNER, N.J. and HOCEVAR, D. (1987) 'An empirical comparison of two-factor vs. multifactor theories of principal leadership: Implications for the evaluation of school principals', *Journal of Personnel Evaluation in Education*, **1**, pp. 93–109.

SCHMITT, N., NOE, R., MERITT, R. and FITZGERALD, M. (1984) 'Validity of assessment centre ratings for the prediction of performance ratings and school climate of school administrators', *Journal of Applied Psychology*, **69**, 2, pp. 207–13.

SCHMITT, N., NOE, R., MERITT, R., FITZGERALD, M. and JORGENSEN, C. (n.d.) *Criterion-related and Content Validity of the NASSP Assessment Center*, Reston, VA, NASSP.

SCHMITT, N. and SCHECHTMAN, S. (1990) 'The selection of school administrators', *Journal of Personnel Evaluation in Education*, **3**, 3, pp. 231–8.

SPADY, W.E. and MITCHELL, D.E. (1977) 'Authority, power and expectation as determinants of action and tension in school organization', Paper presented at the Annual Meeting of the American Educational Research Association, Chicago, April.

STIGGINS, R. (1987) 'Design and development of performance assessment', *Educational Measurement: Issues and Practice*, Fall, pp. 33–42.

TRACY, S.J. and SCHUTTENBERG, E. (1989) 'An investigation of participant utilization of assessment centre results for professional development', Paper presented at the Annual Meeting of the American Educational Research Association, San Francisco.

TUCKER, N.A. and BRAY, S.E. (1986) 'Increasing school productivity through the assessment of school leadership', Paper presented at the Annual Meeting of the South-eastern Educational Research Association, Baton Rouge, LA, March.

VALENTINE, J.W. and BOWMAN, M.L. (1986) 'Audit of principal evaluation', Paper presented at the Annual Meeting of the American Association of School Administrators, New Orleans (ED 281 317).

VANDENBERGHE, R. (1988) 'Development of a questionnaire for assessing principal change facilitator style', Paper presented at the Annual Meeting of the American Educational Research Association, New Orleans, April.

Chapter 15

ARGYRIS, C. (1983) 'Productive and counterproductive reasoning processes', in SRIVASTVA, S. (Ed.) *The Executive Mind*, San Francisco, Jossey-Bass.

BERLINER, D.C. (1988) *The Development of Expertise in Pedagogy*, New Orleans, American Association of Colleges for Teacher Education.

COLEMAN, P. and LA ROCQUE, L. (1991) 'Negotiating the master contract: Transformational leadership and school destreat quality', in LEITHWOOD, R. and MUSELLA, D. (eds) *Understanding School System Administration*, London, the Falmer Press.

DONALDSON, G. (1990) 'Principals in transition: Dilemmas in moving from manager to instructional leader', Paper presented at the Annual Meeting of the American Educational Research Association, Boston, April.

GOLDMAN, P., KEMPNER, K., POWELL, W.R. and SCHMUCK, R.A. (1990) 'School administrators' leadership impact', Paper presented at the Annual Meeting of the American Educational Research Association, Boston, April.

GORDON, D. (1988) 'Education as text: The varieties of educational hiddenness', *Curriculum Inquiry*, **18**, 4, pp. 425–49.

HENNESTAD, B.W. (1990) 'The symbolic impact of double-bind leadership', *Journal of Management Studies*, **27**, 3, pp. 265–80.

LEITHWOOD, K.A. and MONTGOMERY, D.J. (1984) 'Obstacles preventing principals from becoming more effective', *Education and Urban Society*, **17**, 1, pp. 73–88.

MARTIN, J. (1976) 'What should we do with a hidden curriculum when we find one?', *Curriculum Inquiry*, **6**, 2, pp. 135–52.

PETERSON, K., HALLINGER, P. and MURPHY, J. (1987) 'Superintendents' perceptions of the control and coordination of the technical core in effective school districts', *Educational Administration Quarterly*, **23**, 1, pp. 73–95.

RICOEUR, P. (1974) *The Conflict of Interpretations*, Evanston, IL, North-Western University Press.

ROGERS, E.M. (1962) *Diffusion of Innovations*, New York, The Free Press.

SCHÖN, D. (1983) *The Reflective Practitioner*, San Francisco, Jossey-Bass.

SIEBER, S. (1981) *Fatal Remedies*, New York, Plenum Press.

TRIDER, D.M. and LEITHWOOD, K.A. (1988) 'Exploring the influences on principal behavior', *Curriculum Inquiry*, **18**, 3, pp. 289–311.

Author Index

Abelson, R., 193
Achilles, C.M., 21
Adduci, L., 6
Adkinson, P.D., 165
Alexander, P.A., 190
Alkin, M.C., 236
Allison, D.J., 222–225, 226, 228
Allison, P.A., 222, 225, 226, 228
Altschud, J.W., 25
Anderson, S.W., 26
Andrews, R.L., 9, 13, 20, 48, 74, 230, 233
Arehart, J.E., 41
Argyris, C., 178, 180, 199, 251
Armstrong, M.D., 233
Austin, N., 73, 74
Avery, C., 164, 166

Bacharach, S.B., 5, 117, 126, 129
Baehr, M.E., 57, 70
Bagentos, N.T., 207, 208
Bagley, M., 165
Baird, L.L., 42, 113, 114
Baker, G.A., 41
Ball, S., 119
Baltzell, D.Z., 221–223, 225–226, 228
Bandura, A., 95, 175
Barnett, B.G., 12, 168
Bass, B.M., 7, 8, 30
Bayles, M.D., 102
Beck, C., 99–102, 106, 107
Becker, H.S., 157
Begley, P.T., 13, 25, 100, 153, 161, 168, 190, 205, 236
Bennet, B., 128
Bennis, W.G., 4, 8
Bereiter, C., 56
Berger, P.L., 144, 194
Berliner, D.C., 55, 56, 252–253

Berry, G.L., 206–212, 229
Blase, J., 13, 14, 18
Bloom, B.S., 55
Blum, R.L., 166, 170, 192
Blumberg, A., 57
Bolam, R., 207, 209–211
Bolman, L.G., 92
Borko, H., 144
Borman, W.C., 239
Bossert, S.T., 125
Boud, D., 200
Bowman, M.L., 232, 233
Boyd, W.L., 48
Bradeson, P.V., 17, 19, 125
Brady, L., 13, 14, 18
Brandon, G.L., 104–108, 109, 111, 112
Brandt, R.S., 117
Bransford, J.D., 196, 200
Bray, S.E., 232, 233
Brill, A.D., 168
Brown, A.L., 191
Brown, B.L., 14, 18
Brown, J.S., 194, 196
Brownlee-Conyers, J., 7
Brownridge, A., 153, 168
Brubaker, D.L., 16, 24
Bryant, B.J., 222, 225, 226, 228
Bryant, M.T., 221, 223
Burns, J.M., 7
Burton, R.R., 194
Butler, J.A., 166, 170, 192

Caffarella, R.S., 176
Caldwell, W.E., 24, 70
Calfee, R., 123, 174
Campbell, G., 190
Campbell-Evans, G., 101, 153, 168
Cantor, N., 92

Subject Index

Affect
  in solving swampy problems, 77, 82–84, 89
Alberta
  principals' values in, 101
Australia
  school reform in, 5

Behavioral description interviewing, 239–240, 242–243
British Columbia
  school reform in, 5
  principals' socialization in, 152, 159, 161–162, 163

Cognitive flexibility, 89–92
  cognitive errors, 92
  definition of, 89, 92
Collaboration
  curriculum deliberation and, 95
  goal setting in, 35, 72–74, 94–97
  motivation and, 96
  predictors of, 130–133
  problem solving and, 83–97
  teacher development and, 122–123
Collaborative school culture, 128–146, 122–123
  Balkanized cultures and, 130
  contrived collaboration and, 130
  description of, 130–132
  goal clarification and, 132
  individualism and, 129, 130, 139, 144–145
  larger context, significance of, 133–137
    initial costs, 136
    leadership, 137
    motivation and, 135–137
    multiple opportunities and, 136

predictors of, 131–133
shared norm of teacher and, 131–132
schemata and, 144–145
strategies used to influence, 137–143
  bureaucracy, use of, 140
  communication, 142
  shared power and responsibility, 142–143
  staff development, 140–141
  strengthening culture, 138–139
  use of symbols, 143
  teacher empowerment and, 128
  variation of form in, 132–133
Communication
  as strategy, 142
  in high ground problems, 74
Constraints in swampy problem solving, 77, 80, 84, 87, 90
Culture
  collaborative, 122–123, 126, 128–146
  considerative qualities of, 7
  of professional work, 9
  of schools, 15, 38–39

Decision-making, 19–21, 57, 67–70, 137, 142–143, 172
  attitude and stance toward, 68–69
  defining decisions in, 69
  definition of, 57
  forms and procedures for, 67–68
  monitoring of, 68–69
  of effective principals, 20–21
  of typical principals, 19–20
  selecting criteria in, 69
  shared, 137, 142–143
Developing expert leadership, see *Leadership development*
District leaders, 47–48, 54, 135, 246–254